D1356374

Forest Recollections

Forest Recollections

Wandering Monks in
Twentieth-Century Thailand

Kamala Tiyavanich

University of Hawai'i Press

Honolulu

Printed in the United States of America

97 98 99 00 01 02   5 4 3 2 1

Library of Congress Cataloging-in-Publication Data
Kamala Tiyavanich, 1948–
Forest recollections : wandering monks in twentieth-century
Thailand / Kamala Tiyavanich.
p. cm.
Includes bibliographical references and index.
ISBN 0–8248–1768–0 (cloth : alk. paper). — ISBN 0–8248–1781–8
(paper : alk. paper)
1. Asceticism—Buddhism. 2. Buddhism—Thailand—History—20th
century. 3. Buddhist monks—Thailand. 4. Ascetics—Thailand.
5. Wayfaring life—Thailand. I. Title.
BQ6240.T53K36   1997
294.3'657'09593—dc20   96–34016
                                         CIP

University of Hawai'i Press books are printed on
acid-free paper and meet the guidelines for permanence
and durability of the Council on Library Resources

Designed by Christine Taylor

To the ajans of all traditions

Contents

List of Figures

Foreword

Some years ago, when the first paper of her first semester's graduate work was due, Kamala Tiyavanich phoned me to ask for an extension. I thought she might be having trouble writing, and so when the paper appeared a week later, I was overwhelmed with a superb paper on provincial Thai Buddhism around the turn of the century that ran to more than one hundred pages.

That incident should have prepared me for her final dissertation, but nothing could have done so. In thirty-plus years of teaching, no other work in Thai history has so completely caused me to think that everything I knew about a subject had to be thrown away and rethought. It is not the case that the book you now hold in your hands is filled with new information, though much of what it contains is new. It surprises and delights because it has taken a great deal of information, processed it through a very exacting and powerful intellectual grinding, and organized it with reference to a new context and new connections to other things we know.

To greater or lesser extent, we all knew there were holy men, or "wandering meditation monks," in the forests of Southeast Asia over the last century and more, but we did not accurately gauge their importance. Kamala persuades us that we have to consider them an integral part of the religious life of their community, and that to probably the majority of believers these monks were more

real than their ecclesiastical chiefs. By implication she is telling us
to think again about the ways in which we conceive civil society in
previous times.

We are grateful to Dr. Kamala for having breathed new life into
an old topic and for stimulating rethinking of what we thought
we knew of the past, not only in Thailand but through large parts
of the world.

DAVID K. WYATT
Cornell University

It may be unusual to find two individuals contributing to a single
foreword. But Kamala Tiyavanich is an unusual scholar whose
book makes multiple contributions. David Wyatt notes that
Kamala has made substantial contributions to the historiography
of Southeast Asian and Thai Studies. This includes not only the
fresh information she has gathered but also the distinctive concep-
tual frame in which it is located. Subsequent scholars must rethink
their terms of engagement in pursuing the trajectory of an earlier
"Siam" becoming a contemporary "Thailand." The comfortable
notion that the historical diversity of Thai Buddhism can be contained in a contrast between two forms of Buddhism, a "reformed"
Thammayut and a "traditional" Mahanikai, can no longer be sustained. Kamala's book is a celebration of religious and social
diversity, of local and regional traditions that transcended and
ignored political boundaries, past and present.

Kamala's contribution is not only historical, it is no less anthropological. This is shown in the meticulous care she uses in re-
constructing the regional and local monastic lineage of Ajan Man
Phurithat. Thereby she "decenters" our understanding of Thai
religiosity and sociality. Her pursuit of these "wandering" monks
led Kamala out of the library and to the remote locales they frequented. There she interviewed elderly monks and laity who knew
these monks and their tradition firsthand. Kamala's perspective is
also substantively anthropological. The religious commitment of
these monks was embedded in the concrete and vivid details of
their everyday life experiences. These are recorded in their own

terms in a variety of biographical materials. Thus, Kamala's anthropological perspective is one that focuses on multifaceted "real life" experience, not a concern either for a generic "human nature" or an abstract "institutional" analysis.

Kamala provides us with much food for thought. *Bon appétit!*

A. THOMAS KIRSCH
Cornell University

Acknowledgments

I would like, first of all, to express my gratitude to my teachers at Cornell University: To David Wyatt, who always encouraged me to explore new paths and who planted the seeds of this project in the fall of 1985 when he suggested that I read the reports submitted by sangha inspectors in Siam at the turn of the century. To A. Thomas Kirsch, who taught me anthropological approaches to the study of Buddhism in Southeast Asia and whose openness to new interpretations I much appreciate. To Richard Polenberg, who immediately recognized the depth and merit of the thudong monks' narratives. This manuscript has also benefited, directly and indirectly, from the comments and insights of Ben Anderson, John Badgley, George McT. Kahin, Stanley O'Connor, and Oliver Wolters. Frank Reynolds offered valuable comments on an early draft and recommended sources that were most relevant to my work. Richard O'Connor generously found time to read a few drafts of the manu-script in its entirety. His constructive comments led to major improvements.

Conversations and interviews with thirty-four administrative, academic, meditation, and village monks in Bangkok, Chiang Mai, Ubon Ratchathani, and Mahasarakham helped me understand the lives of thudong monks. Some of them gave me access to their monasteries' archives and collections. Several asked that their identities not be revealed, and I have respected their wishes. I am indebted to them all for their generous gifts of time, thought, and insight.

I have also learned a great deal by talking to several former monks who are now lay teachers. I would like to single out Khamma Saeng-ngam, Pricha Phinthong, Sobin Namto, Sommai Premchit, and Sawaeng Udomsi for giving me the benefit of their knowledge of local traditions as well as insightful information about the sangha. I am grateful to all of them. My thanks also go to Arkom Vorachinda, who took me to Roi-Et to interview Khamma Saeng-ngam (1891–1990), a master craftsman of the Lao tradition; to Khaneungnit Janthabutra and Artha Nanthachukra, who accompanied me during my interviews with abbots in Ubon and Mahasarakham; and to Chanya Sethaput and Jirawan Amornvej, who sent me relevant news items.

During various stages of writing, many people offered personal as well as intellectual support. Pat Connor sympathetically read a few drafts; she always found something positive in my ideas and helped me improve the clarity of my writing. Susan Nassar read the entire manuscript, made valuable suggestions, and reminded me of the role of a storyteller. Linda Fisher and the students in my seminar "Buddhism Exemplified" at Cornell University gave me their feedback on early drafts of chapters 3 and 4. Dolina Millar read parts of the final draft and alerted me to many errors. Brian Karafin, at short notice, managed to read the main chapters. Micheline Lessard, Elizabeth Milliken, and Titiporn Siriphant shared my interest in new forms of historical narrative. Rhonda Margolis and Toni Shapiro helped to keep me focus on my work. Ngampit Jagacinski urged me not to take too long finishing this book. During their years at Cornell, Supot Chaengrew and Sunait Chutintaranond often engaged me in long, stimulating discussions about history. John LeRoy put in a lot of work at several points during the evolution of the text, reading various versions, checking footnotes, editing the manuscript, and helping me to become competent on the computer. He and David Wyatt skillfully produced the maps and figures according to my specifications. To all the above I give my heartfelt thanks. Many others have helped me in less direct ways; I hope they will realize my gratitude.

I must thank an anonymous reader whose criticism made me clarify important points in my book. I wish to thank my editor,

Pamela Kelley of the University of Hawai'i Press, for her faith in the potential of this manuscript.

I am grateful for financial support of this project to several institutions. The Social Science Research Council funded a year of dissertation research in Thailand (1988–1989). Cornell University's Southeast Asia Program provided funds for a write-up period. The George McT. Kahin Center for Advanced Research on Southeast Asia provided me with facilities for research and writing. The John M. Echols Collection on Southeast Asia contained a large volume of source materials pertinent to my research. Cornell's Society for the Humanities awarded me a Mellon Postdoctoral Fellowship during the academic year 1993–1994. Although my research that year was conducted for a related project on village abbots in regional traditions, much of the material I collected proved valuable for this book.

The long process of working on this manuscript has been a personal as well as a scholarly endeavor. I am fortunate to have the thudong monks as the subject of my study. They have enriched my life. Their exemplary personalities and insightful messages have sustained me at critical moments. I thank the wandering meditation monks for having left such forthright, lively records; their recollections made me realize the diversity of Buddhist traditions in Siam.

Thai Names and Romanization

Generally, in Thailand a monk is known throughout his life by a combination of his given name and a Pali name, for example, "Man Phurithat." Given names are short, usually only one syllable long: Man, Waen, Dun, Fan, Thet, Li, La, Cha, Juan, Wan. Monks receive their Pali names upon entering the sangha. Phurithat, Sujinno, Atulo, Ajaro, Thetrangsi, Thammatharo, Khempatato, Phothiyan, Kulachettho, and Uttamo are all Thai-language versions of Pali names.

Siamese monks with or without titles have the word *phra* ("venerable") preceding their name. Lao people in the Northeast address their monks as *ya khu tham, ya khu,* or *khu ba (khru ba).* To this standard usage I add a few conventions to make monks' names and titles clear to the reader when necessary. When a monk bears a title conferred by the king, the title is followed by the personal name in parentheses, for example, "Phra Ubali (Jan)." If an administrative monk has held several titles during his life, I use the one that pertained at the time under discussion, for example, "Phra Upatcha Uan (Phra Satsanadilok)" for events in 1915, but "Jao Khun Uan (Phra Phrommuni)" for 1925 and "Somdet Uan (Phra Maha Wirawong)" for 1941. In Thailand's Northeast, laypeople address monks by their first names, not their Pali names, even when they have an honorific title. They will say, for example, "Phra Khru Dilot" (and not "Phra Khru Wirot-rattanobon"), or "Somdet Uan" (and not "Somdet Phra Maha Wirawong"). I follow this tradition. Similarly, in the case of forest monks who in their old age have received a title, I follow their disciples' usage by calling them by their personal names: Fan, Li, Thet, Cha. (When writing or speaking in Thai, terms of respect would be attached: Luang Pu Fan, Than Phau Li, Phra Ajan Thet, or Than Ajan Cha.)

The spellings of provinces and districts of Thailand correspond closely to the forms standardized by the U.S. Board of Geographic Names and used, for example, on the maps of the National Geographic Society. Minor changes have been made to keep some spellings consistent with my romanization. For example, Naung ("Pond," commonly found in many village names) is generally used instead of the map spelling Nong. Otherwise, an effort has been made to spell major place names in conformity to the maps, even though my romanization system would suggest a different spelling. For example, Charoen and Kanchanaburi are used instead of Jaroen and Kanjanaburi.

Some of the monks' memoirs and biographies have been translated into English. In these translations, however, many words in local languages are mistranslated, and important details are sometimes omitted. When the English translation is accurate on the whole, I use it, correcting it or adding details from the Thai original when necessary. The accompanying note then cites both the English translation and the Thai original.

The romanization I use resembles that of the American Library Association–Library of Congress system but substitutes roman letters for special characters and diacritical marks. The vowels ư and ư̄ are romanized as *eu* (e.g., *neung,* "one"), the vowel ǭ as *au (phau,* "father"), and the consonant čh as *j (jan,* "dish"). Tones and vowel length are not distinguished. The first appearance of a Thai or Pali word is italicized (e.g., *wat, kamma*); subsequent occurrences are unemphasized and may take English forms for plurals or adjectives (wats, kammic).

The names of several prominent monks have been romanized differently in English-language publications. Bua's name also appears as "Boowa," Man's as "Mun," Cha's as "Chah," Li's as

"Lee," and Thet's as "Thate" or "Tate." When referring to these publications in notes and the bibliography, I retain the original romanization. Finally, as in conventional usage, Thai authors are entered in the bibliography and notes according to their first names.

Introduction

Although the tradition of wandering meditation ascetics has become a victim of Thailand's relentless modernization and rampant deforestation, during the first half of this century the forests of Thailand, or Siam as it used to be called,[1] were home to numerous ascetic monks. The Thai term for such monks is *phra thudong* (ascetic wandering monk) or *phra thudong kammathan* (wandering ascetic meditator monk). A thudong monk is one who observes at least some of the thirteen ascetic practices mentioned in the Buddha's discourses, in particular the practice of eating only one meal per day, sleeping outdoors in a forest or a cemetery, and being content with the very fewest possessions.[2]

My aim in this book is to document the lives of some of these monks in the historical context of local Buddhist traditions as well as modern state Buddhism. I also seek to explain why the thudong tradition, initially little known, has become so popular in Thailand today. I focus on ten monks of the lineage that starts with Ajan Man Phurithat (1871–1949): Man himself, Waen Sujinno (1888–1985), Dun Atulo (1888–1985), Fan Ajaro (1898–1977), Thet Thetrangsi (1902–1994), Li Thammatharo (1907–1961), La Khempatato (1911–1996), Cha Phothiyan (1918–1992), Juan Kulachettho (1920–1980), and Wan Uttamo (1922–1980). Although these monks were born and raised in farming communities and followed a two-millennia-old religious calling, their teachings are relevant to present-day societies.

Much of the local knowledge and wisdom the monks offered can no longer be discovered or recovered. Their teachings came from personal experiences or directly from their teachers. They were Buddhists, of course, but their brand of Buddhism was not a copy of the norms or practices preserved in doctrinal texts. Their Buddhism found expression in the acts of daily life: walking for days in the wilderness; meeting with villagers who were sometimes supportive, sometimes suspicious; spending the nights in an umbrella tent beneath a tree, in a crude shelter, or in a cave; and contending with all sorts of mental and physical challenges. Their lives are worth knowing about and worth hearing as directly as possible, with as much detail as we need to understand them. For it was in their attention to details, no less than in their high purposes, that these monks' lives were exemplary.

This is not the way observers—either Western or Thai—tend to study them, however. Rather than beginning with the details and particularities of these monks' individual lives, scholars more often begin with generalities about institutions and traditions, with sets of assumptions about "Thai" Buddhism or about the Theravada tradition. Having accepted a stereotype of "Thai" Buddhism—as a centralized, bureaucratic, hierarchical religion emphasizing *vinaya* (discipline)[3]—they see wandering monks as anomalous, unconventional, heretical, or (sometimes) saintly.

These scholars maintain that Buddhism in Thailand should be understood in terms of its center—both its geographical and political center, Bangkok, and its doctrinal center, the Pali canon as interpreted by monastic authorities in Bangkok. This Bangkok-Theravada perspective is an urban, literate, middle- and upper-class view of Buddhism. It favors texts, doctrines, and orthodoxy, and it ignores or devalues local Buddhist traditions, even though monks of these traditions have always formed a numerical majority in the *sangha* (monastic community). Indeed, the Bangkok-centered view of Buddhism in Thailand amounts to a form of ethnocentrism, one that many Western scholars, entering Thailand as they do through Bangkok and its institutions and culture, have accepted in some measure.

Outside the influence of the modern state, people lived in a world that presumed plurality. They moved around enough—or knew kinsmen or traders who did—to understand that the land held many people whose languages and customs differed from their own. They expected that the religious practices of monks would also differ. Indeed, before this century there was no standard doctrine or monastic practice. Each temple had its own customs, and each *ajan* (abbot or teacher) followed the disciplinary rules and monastic practices of his *nikai* (sect or lineage), which had its own history.[4]

Naturally the people living in the regions beyond Bangkok did not share the Siamese elite's view that the Buddhism of the Bangkok court was superior to their own. Long after the modern Thai state began to pressure them to accept its official Buddhism —this was at the turn of the century—villagers and local monks continued to follow their own centuries-old Buddhist traditions. Geographical and linguistic isolation shielded them from Bangkok's influence.

BIRTH OF MODERN STATE BUDDHISM

How did the Buddhism of the Bangkok court come to be Thailand's official Buddhism? Historically Buddhism has flourished by accommodating the native beliefs of the cultures with which it came into contact. During the centuries since it spread to Southeast Asia, Theravada Buddhism has displayed an extraordinary ability to adapt to local customs, languages, and cultures. The Buddhism practiced in the area that is now called Thailand was as varied as Buddhism in Tibet and just as much colored and enriched by its interactions with different indigenous cultural traditions.[5]

In the early nineteenth century, Thailand had not yet become a centralized state with the defined borders shown on a modern map (see figure 1).[6] In those days, the region consisted of several kingdoms or petty states, each ruled by a hereditary local lord. Although these kingdoms or *meuang*[7] considered themselves autonomous, they sent tribute to the more powerful kingdom. Bangkok allowed the outlying meuangs to remain more or less indepen-

Figure 1. *Map of Thailand showing provinces. Dotted lines indicate provincial boundaries; solid lines indicate boundaries between regions* (phak).

dent, so long as there was no war between any of the lords of the region. Its control over the meuangs did not extend beyond collecting taxes from the lords. Bangkok had no control over the courts, administrative patterns, currencies, or writing systems established in the meuangs.[8]

Furthermore, Bangkok could not control the meuangs' religious customs and practices. The kingdoms had different histories, literatures, languages, and religious customs. Substantially different forms of Buddhism existed among the Siamese in the Central Plains, the Lao in the Northeast, the Yuan in the North, the Shan along the western border with the Shan states, the Khmer in the southern tier of the northeastern region along the Cambodian border,[9] and the Mon scattered in the Central Plains and the northern region.[10] Even within one principality, religious customs varied from one meuang to the next and from one village to the next. For example, in the Lan Na kingdom[11] there were as many as eighteen nikais or lineages of Buddhist monks in Chiang Mai alone.[12] (The term "nikai" as used in Lan Na in those days referred to a community of monks adhering to common beliefs and disciplinary practices.) In the Lao tradition in the Northeast, Buddhist customs varied among the Phuan, Lawa, Song, Phu Thai, and Yau (or Yo). Or again, in the Mon tradition the religious practices of the Mon in Lamphun differed from the customs followed by the Mon in Ratchaburi, Kanchanaburi, Pak Klet, Pathum Thani, Nonthaburi, or Samut Prakan. Similarly, in the Yuan tradition, the Buddhist customs in Chiang Mai, Chiang Rai, Phayao, Lamphun, Lampang, Nan, and Phrae all differed. Each of these Buddhist traditions was differently influenced by the many different forms of indigenous spirit worship and by the Mahayana and Tantric traditions that flourished prior to the fourteenth century.[13]

In addition to these older traditions, another form of Buddhism emerged in Bangkok in the third decade of the nineteenth century. This late development, creating a new nikai of monks, is generally considered to be a reform movement.[14] The founder of this sect was the thirty-three-year-old Siamese prince named Mongkut, a son of King Rama II. Mongkut had been ordained earlier in a Siamese Buddhist tradition. His ordination coincided with the accession to the throne of a half-brother, later to be known as

Rama III (1824–1851). Mongkut remained in the robes for twenty-seven years until this half-brother died, since leaving the monkhood would have thrust him into the "dangerous maelstrom of dynastic politics."[15] In 1830, after he had been a monk for six years, Mongkut met the abbot of a Mon monastery located across the river from Bangkok. Impressed with the strict discipline observed by the Mon, Mongkut established a new sect in which this discipline was observed. It was called "Thammayut," meaning the order adhering to the *dhamma* (Buddhist teachings and doctrines). In his monastic order Mongkut emphasized Pali studies, especially the mastery of the vinaya. In order to make monastic discipline more strict, Mongkut insisted that laypeople ought to perform such necessary tasks as distributing monks' food, cleaning their living quarters, washing their robes, and caring for their communal property.[16] The majority of the monks in this new nikai were from upper- and middle-class families. To distinguish his nikai from the Siamese tradition observed in Bangkok's monasteries, Mongkut changed some monastic practices. He introduced a new style of wearing robes (covering both shoulders, a Mon practice), new ordination rituals, a new pronunciation of the Pali scriptural language, new routines (including daily chanting), and new religious days to observe. All these changes, Mongkut asserted, made the Thammayut sect more authentic.

As Craig Reynolds points out, the new nikai actually "caused resentment and created dissension rather than unity." Without royal patronage the Thammayut nikai would not have survived, because it arose in opposition to the Siamese traditions of Bangkok monasteries.[17] Mongkut disparagingly referred to monks who followed other traditions as "Mahanikai."[18] He considered the Mahanikai an "order of long-standing habit"—implying that these monks and laypeople blindly followed the Buddhism of their fathers and grandfathers.[19] Since it is misleading to consider all non-Thammayut traditions as belonging to a single sect, I use the term "Mahanikai" only to refer to non-Thammayut administrative monks appointed by Bangkok sangha authorities.

Mongkut also placed greater emphasis on the study of the Pali canon and commentaries than on the practice of meditation, which he considered mystical. He was convinced that true religion was a matter of rational doctrine and belief. Mongkut disdained all traditions in which folk stories and parables were used to teach the dhamma and local culture was integrated with Buddhism. From his perspective, local stories full of demons, gods, miracles, magic, rituals, and exorcism were folklore; they had nothing to do with Buddhism.

This conviction of Mongkut's may have been shaped by Western and Christian influences. Like many Christian missionaries, Mongkut (who left the monastic life and became king in 1851) had an intellectual image of religion.[20] He and the Siamese elite of his generation accepted the Christian missionaries' judgment that traditional Buddhism was too superstitious. They sought to prove to Western missionaries that Buddhism was compatible with science and could support intellectual study and learning. They started their own printing presses, published books on Buddhism, and adopted a rationalist mode of discourse for theological debates with Christians.

During the last half of the nineteenth century, Siam's neighbors fell under the control of Western colonial powers. A few decades before the end of the nineteenth century, the Siamese King Chulalongkorn (1868–1910) began to form a centralized state of Siam with a fixed boundary. To this end, the Siamese court began to restrict the autonomy of the principalities in the northern, northeastern, and the southern regions.[21] The aim was to strip the local ruling families of their powers and transfer their authority to officials appointed by the Siamese court.

One of the major obstacles the court encountered was linguistic diversity among the various Tai peoples.[22] At the time the Siamese authorities began to consolidate these tributary states and principalities, at least eighty languages were spoken within Siam's political boundaries.[23] (The major languages of the four regions are presently Thai Klang in the Central Plains, Tai Yuan or Kham Meuang in the North, Lao in the Northeast, and Pak Tai in the South.) To consolidate these diverse peoples, the Bangkok regime made the Bangkok Thai spoken by the educated elite in Bangkok (and before that in Ayuthaya) the official and national language. This dialect—Bangkok Thai (known today as standard Thai)—became a symbol or focus of identification for the modern Thai state.[24] It was to be taught to local people by teachers, government officials, and monks trained in Bangkok. One result is that both Thai and English speakers now use the word "Thai" to refer to the state religion (as in "Thai Buddhism") as well as to the national language. To prevent confusion, the phrase "modern state Buddhism" will replace the loose and misleading "Thai Buddhism." Similarly, when speaking of languages, "Bangkok Thai" is preferable to the vaguer "Thai."

Although it is impossible to know how many native speakers of Bangkok Thai there were when Siam started to centralize, Bangkok Thai was certainly not the native language for most people. More probably had Lao as their mother tongue. Native speakers of other languages considered Bangkok Thai the language of outsiders. Even in the Central Plains people had to learn Bangkok Thai the way the rest of the country did: primarily through Bangkok's educational system.

In creating a modern Thai state the Bangkok authorities needed not only a common language but a common religion. The Siamese rulers' preoccupation with order, harmony, national unity, and modernization led them to believe that monks as well as laypeople —regardless of their ethnic identities—should have a common religious outlook. They assumed that a rationalized form of Buddhism would provide the most unity and harmony. The architect of modern state Buddhism was a son of Mongkut's, Prince Wachirayan, a half-brother of King Chulalongkorn and the abbot of Wat Bowonniwet in Bangkok. Wachirayan was a Pali scholar eager to strengthen Buddhism, which he considered to be in decline. In his opinion, the scholarly and vinaya-oriented Thammayut nikai was superior to nikais devoted to other Buddhist practices and customs. Like Mongkut, Wachirayan called them Mahanikai. Consequently, the Thammayut nikai, based mainly in the royal monasteries in Bangkok, became closely integrated with the newly centralized bureaucratic government. It became the model for modern state Buddhism.[25]

The 1902 Act created a sangha bureaucracy with a Siamese supreme patriarch (appointed by Bangkok authorities) at the top. With the act's passage, a modern nation-state with a centralized, urban-based bureaucracy began to control local communities distinguished by diverse ethnic traditions. Formerly autonomous Buddhist monks belonging to diverse lineages became part of the Siamese religious hierarchy with its standard texts and practices, whereas previously no single tradition had predominated. This modern ecclesiastical system brought the hitherto unorganized sangha into line with the civilian government hierarchy. Sangha and state now had parallel hierarchies (see figure 2).

Wachirayan also created a monastic education system based on his interpretation of Pali canonical works, commentaries, and vinaya texts. Modern state Buddhism treated Wachirayan's printed texts as authoritative.[26] The system—still in use today—rests on degrees, examinations, and ranks in the sangha hierarchy. It defines the ideal Buddhist monk as one who observes strict monastic rules, has mastered Wachirayan's texts, teaches in Bangkok Thai, carries out administrative duties, observes holy days, and performs religious rituals based on Bangkok customs.

The central government's authority began to be felt in remote parts of Thailand only in the second half of this century when the military regime sought to consolidate the nation-state by imposing martial law on the country. As we shall see, wandering meditation monks were generally uninterested in wider political events. Periods during which broad social changes occurred in Thai society, and which scholars commonly regard as turning points, were not necessarily significant for forest monks. Eventually, however, they were greatly affected by events beyond their horizons: the spread of paved roads and rail links, jungle warfare, and deforestation. The study of forest monks must take into account these economic and political impacts on the environment. One chronology I have found helpful divides the last one hundred years into these three historical periods: (1) the "Forest-Community Period" *(yuk muban pa)* prior to 1957; (2) the "Forest-Invasion Period" *(yuk bukboek)* from 1957 to 1988; and (3) the "Forest-Closure Period" *(yuk pit pa)* from 1989 to the present.[27]

We shall be concerned mainly with the Forest-Community Period. For our purposes, this period spans the late nineteenth century, when Siam became a centralized state, and the first half of the twentieth century. During this period, there were thousands of small frontier communities *(muban pa)* throughout Thailand. These settlements consisted of scattered households living off farmland and forests. For most of this period the population was low and urban areas were undeveloped. Most villages and even many district centers were remote from urban centers. Toward the end of this period, however, urban centers rapidly expanded and forested areas dwindled under increasing deforestation.

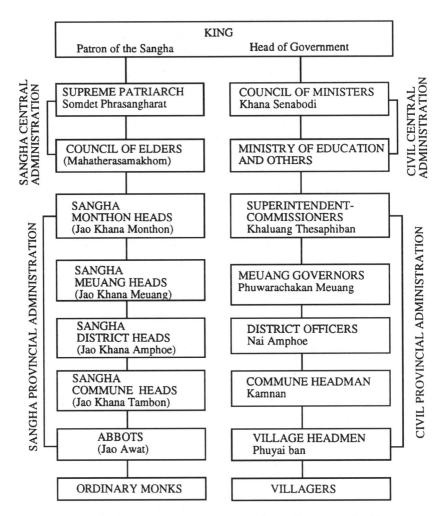

Figure 2. *Sangha bureaucratic structure and its relation to the Siamese government after the Sangha Act of 1902 (Adapted from Somboon 1982, table 6)*

THE MONKS' LIVES AND THEIR RECOLLECTIONS

Two major works about forest monks have been written by social scientists. Stanley Tambiah's *Buddhist Saints of the Forest and the Cult of Amulets* is an important work on amulets and the politics of the two major Buddhist orders in Thailand.[28] It contains several chapters devoted to Ajan Man, a Lao forest monk acknowledged as a highly influential teacher, and Maha Bua, Man's disciple-biographer. For the most part, Tambiah is interested in developing theories about these two monks and their lives. He wants to know whether Man was a paradigmatic *arahat* (liberated person or "saint"), whether Bua's biography is hagiographic, whether Man's teachings or Bua's monastery conform to the canon, and so forth. Though we learn much from his discussion, the forest monks' meditation tradition is not his main focus. Relying mainly on Bua's biography of Ajan Man and on a short article about the life of Luang Pu Waen,[29] he concludes that monastic biographies of "saints" are modeled upon a paradigm—the life of the Buddha.

In my research I have drawn on a large corpus of published memoirs and biographical material that Tambiah left unexamined.[30] In addition to Bua's biography of Man, I have used fourteen other narratives. These texts are diverse; they do not follow the paradigm of the Buddha's life and in fact appear to have no common denominator—which suggests that Bua's version of Ajan Man's life is an exception rather than a typical example.

In *Forest Monks and the Nation-State,* James Taylor offers an analysis of the formation and transformation of the lineage of Ajan Man and his disciples.[31] Casting his discussion in terms of the environment and ecology of the Northeast, Taylor traces the forest monks' gradual "domestication" and accommodation to social conditions in present-day Thailand. His information about connections, networks, and factions among Man's disciples and laypeople are of much interest. But Taylor, like Tambiah, studies the forest monks mainly to examine institutional changes in the relations between "religion" and "polity."

Tambiah's and Taylor's works lack a strong historical grounding in regional traditions, and they do not explore the practices of Ajan Man and his disciples. My particular interest complements Tambiah's and Taylor's. This book does not focus on the forest tradition as an institutional process; it examines the lives of the wandering monks and their styles of practicing and teaching. I am interested in where they came from, what their local traditions were like, what their teachers taught them, how they trained, what they taught, what their religion meant to them and to local people, and why they thought it was worth preserving.

My approach is both historical and anthropological. In my view local histories provide useful and reliable access to an understanding of Thailand's regions.[32] The wandering meditation monks from Thailand's Northeast constitute a distinct type that emerged out of the peculiarities of Lao Buddhist traditions. Hence, they are best understood through the study of their local contexts. Here history merges with anthropology, since the monks' narratives supply textual evidence of their religious beliefs and practices. Moreover, as A. Thomas Kirsch asserts, people's lives are "texts" in their own right, which others can read and comprehend.[33]

The aim of this book is to introduce the reader to the thudong master Man and his disciples through their writings, dictation, and recorded conversations—in short, through their own recollections along with those of others. But the word "recollection" in my title has another intended meaning. It is the English equivalent of a Buddhist term in the Pali language *(anussati)* that refers to the act of remembering, contemplating, or meditating upon an important religious theme: the Buddha, his teachings, the monkhood, the ethical life, and the like. Anussati and the related term *sati* (mindfulness) were integral parts of the forest monks' religious practice and the subject of many of their recorded recollections.[34]

Thousands of monks have wandered through the modern Thai state in this century, and their experiences have been manifold. Surely there is no better way to understand these monks' Buddhism than through their own narratives, especially when these are rich in local color and texture. These texts open a window onto the monks' lives, a window that is absent from the commentaries and analyses of outsiders. Looking through this window, we see monks go about their lives, we hear them speak, we learn their thoughts.

Previously, the few scholars who have had access to these life stories did not quite know what to do with them. Perhaps they did not find anything particularly noteworthy in them. The monks talk about their daily life and its concerns: getting food on the almsround,[35] finding lodging and robes, coping with illness and pain, climbing a mountain, searching for a suitable cave, walking through a dense forest to reach a village, encountering a wild animal, contending with a ghost or spirit. To the modern mind, these accounts may seem like notes from another world. Recently, however, the life stories of forest monks have become very popular among urban people. The reason may be that the world in which these monks lived has disappeared. Today in Thailand one buys packaged food, ready-made clothes, and over-the-counter medicine. Small villages are now towns with roads, cars, and buses, and the forests have yielded to plantations, highways, and hydro-electric dams. Tigers, having lost their forests, are in zoos. Only in the imagination, and with the help of stories such as those related by forest monks, are present-day urbanites able to dwell in an isolated forest hamlet, spend a night or a fortnight in some dark cave, or roam a forest and come face to face with a tiger. If only for that reason, the forest monks' daily concerns hold our attention.

For the historian, too, the details that fill the wandering monks' life stories hold much interest. To ignore them is to risk misunderstanding the monks; life stories hold contextual information that the historian needs. When a certain monk has a vision in which a deity or arahat appears, for example, it helps to know that this monk had spent long months in solitary meditation, often going without food, preparing for this encounter. Otherwise we may conclude he was just dreaming. When a monk travels alone across a forest, wet and cold and hungry, maybe sick or lonely, he tells us. When he feels overwhelmed or uplifted by events and encounters, he reports it. He does so not self-indulgently or sentimentally but in a plain, matter-of-fact, and unforgettable voice—a voice that we do not hear in any administrative or scholar monk's biography.[36]

Although the monks relate their stories in a frank and direct manner, they often avoid specific reference to themselves. They often narrate their stories without using first-person pronouns. It is as if in telling or writing their experiences, a monk's own identity were unessential, as if life were simply a stream of memories and events. Given this reticence, we may wonder why forest monks disclosed their life stories in the first place. As might be guessed, it was often not the monk's idea. One of them wrote his life story as a personal memoir. When his lay devotees asked him to publish his account for distribution on his sixtieth birthday, in 1974, he consented.[37] A second dictated his life story to a lay disciple while in the hospital in 1959, a year before his death. A third was pressured by his disciples into writing his life story on his own; he wrote in an informal style as if talking to a friend, unimpeded by social norms of politeness and free (or so it appears) of either an internal censor or an outside editor.[38] A fourth, also unable to say no to his followers, dictated his stories into a tape recorder, but under the condition that they be published only after his death—which happened not long afterward in an airplane crash.[39] A fifth monk's memoirs were issued—printed in his own handwriting—on the occasion of his cremation,[40] as were the recollections of four other monks. The life stories of another five monks are the work of their disciples, who refer to their teachers as *than ajan* (venerable or respected teacher), *luang phau* (venerable father), or *luang pu* (venerable grandfather).

Most of these life stories take considerable liberty with chronology, as if the temporal order of events did not matter much. Although wandering monks seem to remember events vividly, they often do not record the year when they occurred. Also characteristic of the stories is the absence of reference to the world at large. Either events in the wider world did not affect the monks or they were so isolated in their forests and caves that they really did not know what was going on.

From the historian's point of view, the problem with these life stories is the abundance of information they contain and the number of questions they raise. When we read that a thudong monk journeys on foot to Laos or Burma in search of meditation teachers, his goal is understandable. But what are we to make of the meditative experiences he has along the way? How are we to understand Man's visions of saints, deities, and spirits? The biographies and memoirs tease us with their glimpses of a monk's personal life, resisting our efforts to decode them. Maybe the reason is that no one can tell the whole story about himself. The incidents thudong monks remember and relate are invariably those they consider most important. They give detailed descriptions of their wandering lives and of the various ethnic groups they encountered; they say much less about their lives in Bangkok; and they report hardly anything at all about their last years when, unable to wander, they were confined to life in a monastery—almost as if then there were no more stories left to tell.

On the positive side, the monks' narratives are unaffected by any concern with what a "proper" life story should include. The monks make no attempt to hide their personal failings. Sexual desire, for example, is not too vulgar or embarrassing to reveal. True, they are cautious in voicing criticism of sangha authorities, fearing to offend senior monks who became supporters. Nevertheless, innuendoes here and there provide clues to matters not recorded explicitly or in depth.

Since a memoir is the record of one monk's experiences—how he remembered his own life—the general picture emerges only after comparing several. But how do we know whether the comparative picture is a true one? After all, not all wandering monks have left life stories. The majority of Buddhist monks in Siam/ Thailand have left no written records. Those who did leave accounts either knew sufficient Thai to describe their experiences firsthand or had disciples who could do so. They also had lay devotees able to defray the printing costs. Not surprisingly, many of the monks whose lives have been published are from the royalty-supported Thammayut order, which comprises a minority of monks in Thailand. No historian will ever know how different our picture of the sangha in Thailand would be had village monks and wandering monks of other lineages left as many printed pages as the Thammayut thudong monks have.

The stories of many wandering meditation monks without affluent lay followers are published in cheap popular magazines. Historians of Buddhism have largely ignored these publications, although they contain otherwise unavailable information. These popular magazines began to appear in the early 1980s, several years after the forest monks and their teachings became popular. Today, forest monks' narratives are increasingly reprinted and distributed as gifts at laypeople's funerals. Among the popular monthly magazines about meditation monks are *Lokthip* and *Phra Aphinya*. *Lokthip,* the more useful of the two, aims to satisfy the layperson's desire to know everything about a meditation monk. Between its covers one can find detailed descriptions of monks' family backgrounds, accounts of their wanderings, and their opinions about the local people whom they met in their travels. Articles based on interviews with monks—or, after their deaths, with elderly villagers who knew them—may have much value for a historian.

These magazines have their weaknesses. For example *Lokthip* often takes monks' stories from cremation volumes or from printed memoirs or biographies and fails to credit the original sources. In addition, the magazine tends to portray many meditation monks as arahats or nearly so (as an *anāgāmī,* "nonreturner"), pointing to demonstrations of supernormal power and the appearance of crystalline crematory remains. Nonetheless, these articles contain vital information about wandering meditation monks: where the monks came from, what their occupations were before ordination, where they were ordained, who their preceptors were, why they converted to the Thammayut order if they did, and the like.

I know of no hard and fast rules about how to use these popular magazines. Can a historian or anyone else tell which interviews are verbatim and which are heavily edited? It comes down to experience and judgment. After reading hundreds of issues of such magazines, one acquires a sense of authenticity. Descriptions of events that the monks actually saw are likely to be reliable. One learns to identify passages where the editor or writer has interpolated his own views. When the language waxes didactic, utters sweeping condemnation or praise, and makes stirring appeals to the reader, it is a good bet that this is the voice of the writer or editor, not the monk. Wandering meditation monks usually express themselves in common, ordinary speech, often in the vernacular and using local expressions. When a passage is written in a down-to-earth and straightforward style by an apparently unsophisticated writer, it is almost certainly the monk who is talking or writing. Because so much of the information contained in these sources turns out to be unreliable, I have used them with discretion. I regard them as occasionally useful supplements to the memoirs and biographies in which the monks speak directly.[41]

My final remark is directed to those Buddhologists or philologists who might take exception to some of my translations of Thai or Pali dhamma terms. I have tried to convey the meanings these terms appear to have for the forest monks, even where they depart from doctrinally correct definitions. Monks may depart from doctrinal meanings, in Panyawattho's words, "to preserve the Forest Dhamma quality of this teaching, and though some terms may not correspond to direct scriptural interpretations, they are used as a guide to develop meditation in a most practical sense."[42] It is, of course, beyond the scope of this book to go deeply into the thu-dong monks' dhamma teachings and meditation methods. But I do hope to convey something of their nature and style.

CHAPTER 1

Buddhist Traditions

in Siam/Thailand

During the first half of the twentieth century many regional monastic traditions still existed in Siam. Although these traditions differed from one another as much as they did from modern state Buddhism, they shared common features. Surveying these features will give us an initial understanding of wandering meditation monks and their religious path. We shall begin with a discussion of the geography and culture outside Bangkok during the years when sangha officials—monks from Bangkok or appointed by Bangkok—traveled to inspect *wat* (monasteries) for their superiors. The discussion includes a range of Buddhist customs and practices that the Bangkok authorities clearly considered unworthy of proper monks: participating in local festivals, traveling on horseback, performing heavy labor, delivering sermons in a lively, theatrical manner, practicing meditation in seclusion, and going on pilgrimages.

GEOGRAPHICAL ISOLATION

At the turn of this century, when sangha officials from Bangkok first traveled to other regions as government representatives to inspect wats, about 80 percent of the land surface of Siam was covered with forests.[1] The country was sparsely populated; settlements were far apart and surrounded by forests. The hinterland of the Central Plains, the North, the Northeast, and the South remained remote. Even the countryside close to Bangkok was largely undeveloped and uncultivated; forest monasteries could be found at the edge of the city.

In 1898–1900 Wachirayan, head of the Thammayut order, sent fourteen administrative monks holding the title of education director *(phu amnuaikan kanseuksa)* to inspect monasteries in their respective *monthon.* (A monthon was an administrative unit consisting of a number of meuangs. Each monthon was under the control of a resident commissioner, who had the power to override the semi-hereditary governors. See figure 3.) All but two of the education directors were monks based in Bangkok temples. At the turn of the century most monthons were isolated from Bangkok. Only Bangkok itself and two other monthons in the southeastern region, Chanthaburi and Prachinburi, were sufficiently compact to facilitate travel and communication.[2] In all others, the education directors could inspect only a fraction of the monasteries. Distant meuangs and their remote villages were beyond reach. The officials could not travel to the northernmost region at all. They went only as far as Uttaradit, the northernmost meuang of the Central Plains. Much of the southern region remained inaccessible; large sections of monthon Phuket were still wild and sparsely populated.[3] In the northeastern region, inspectors residing in Nakhon Ratchasima and Ubon Ratchathani could travel only in the vicinity of these two capital towns.[4]

The first road linking Bangkok to the Northeast was initially constructed in 1960 and paved in stages over the next several years. Before road and rail access, the Northeast was like a separate country. Mountain ranges divide it from the central and northern regions: the Phetchabun and Dong Phayayen Ranges to the west and the Phanom Dong Rak Range to the south and east (see figure 4). To the north and east, the Mekong River separates the Northeast from Laos and Cambodia. The Phu Phan Range divides the region into the Sakon Nakhon Basin in the northeast and the Khorat Basin in the southwest.[5] More than half of the Northeast then consisted of extensive tracts of forests abounding with wild animals and birds. The human population, scattered in thousands of villages, belonged to several ethnic groups: Lao Phuan, Lawa, Phu Thai, Yau, Yoi, Khamu, Saek, Kaloeng, Khmer,

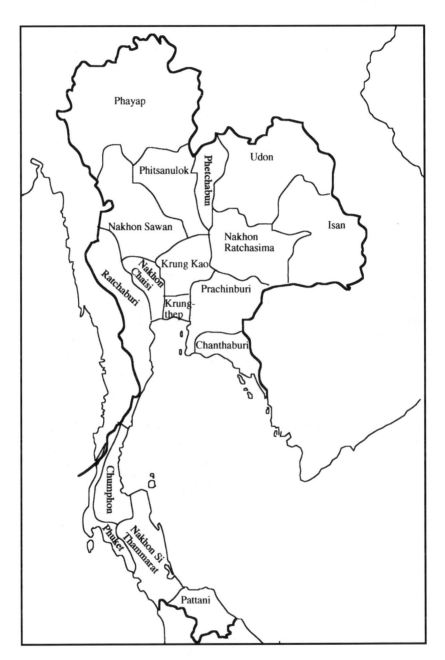

Figure 3. *Map of Siam showing* monthon, *ca. 1910*

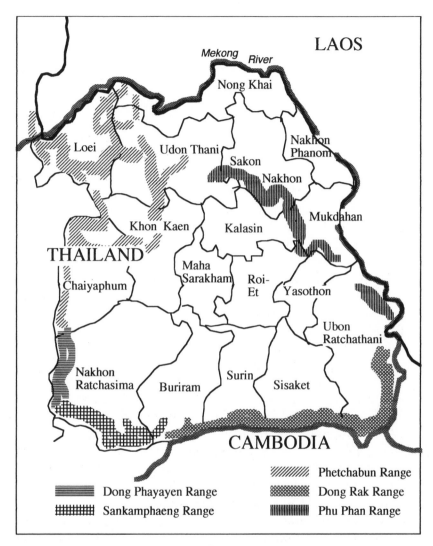

Figure 4. *Mountain ranges in northeastern Thailand*

Suai, and Song. This large region and its people are now called "Isan," but this term came to be applied only after the Northeast was integrated into the centralized Thai state.

Before the construction in 1900 of a railway link between Bangkok and Nakhon Ratchasima (a meuang at the edge of the northeast region known locally as Khorat), the usual way to get to the

Northeast was to cross the mountains in the Phayayen Forest to Khorat and then proceed to other meuangs. Travelers along this route were either cattle traders, bandits, or wandering monks. One Phu Thai monk recalled how his relatives joined a group of cattle traders and walked along with a herd of cattle from Sakon Nakhon to Khorat and then crossed the Phayayen Forest. The round trip took about a year (W, 6–7). The route was risky. Travelers might be attacked by wild animals or waylaid by bandits, and malaria was always a threat.

Another way to get to the Northeast was by boat. This route, longer but safer, was the one Bangkok officials took. It involved taking a steamboat from Bangkok to Prachinburi in the southeast and then going by oxcart through Sisophon (now in Cambodia) to Samet Pass, from there to Surin, Sangkha, and Sisaket, and then on to Ubon Ratchathani.[6] When Uan Tisso, an academic monk, traveled this route with a load of Thai textbooks from Bangkok, it took him fifty days to reach meuang Ubon. On the way a fellow monk caught a fever, probably malaria, and died.[7]

Traveling through all these remote meuangs was slow and arduous, especially in inclement weather. In each meuang the government officials provided the sangha inspectors with the best means of transportation available: a rowboat or a steamboat, a horse-drawn carriage or an oxcart on flat land, and elephants with mahouts over wet and low land. Servants and porters carried the inspectors' supplies. But regardless of the assistance they received, the inspection trips were too long and arduous for many city-bred monks. Despite their relatively young age, some found the physical strain incapacitating.[8] At the end of his second trip one education director was so ill he left the monkhood.

Most laypeople and local monks habitually traveled on foot or on horseback. Local monks in those days customarily kept horses in their wats and traveled on horseback, a most practical means of transportation when towns and villages were widely scattered— especially when a preacher-monk had to get to another wat in a hurry. But the visiting inspectors insisted that Bangkok's disciplinary rules be observed. They told the local monks to get rid of their horses and stop riding them. This ruling proved impractical and could not be enforced. Monks continued to ride horses to villages where they had been invited to preach, and gifted preachers had to travel often. Even the Thammayut head of Ubon, Uan Tisso (titled Ratchamuni), had to yield to the local custom out of practicality. When in 1917–1918 he and local administrative monks went to inspect wats in neighboring districts, all of them went by horseback. Four or five decades after the sangha centralization, local monks in the North and Northeast still traveled on horseback, and many village abbots in the Northeast still kept a few horses in their monasteries.

REGIONAL BUDDHIST TRADITIONS

The inspectors found that local monks and laypeople were observing customs foreign to Bangkok. A common feature of regional traditions was the assumption that monastics would remain engaged in village life. Regional monks organized festivals, worked on construction projects in the wat, tilled the fields, kept cattle or horses, carved boats, played musical instruments during the Bun Phawet festival, taught martial arts—and were still considered to be respectable *bhikkhu* (monks) all the while. Cultural expectations and loyalties of kinship and community made all these activities legitimate ones for monks. Sangha officials, however, considered such activities improper, and they criticized the local monks for being lax. But as these monks saw it, they were neither improper nor lax. They had their own standards, which differed from Bangkok's. Villagers and townspeople knew their monks—knew them well. The local elders knew who were good monks and who were bad, and they did not tolerate bad behavior.

The wat was in fact the center of lay Buddhism. In regional traditions, the monastery served many functions necessary to community life. It was a town hall for meetings, a school, a hospital (monks provided herbal medicine and took care of the sick), a social and recreation center, a playground for children, an inn for visitors and travelers, a warehouse for keeping boats and other communal objects, and a wildlife refuge (if the wat was near a forest). Village or town abbots consequently remained very much in the world, devoting their energies to community work that benefited local people.

Working with Their Hands

The Buddhist tradition that originated in the Bangkok court strongly discouraged manual work. Thammayut monks were to abstain from doing hard labor; they and their temples should instead receive gifts and donations of money and services.[9] The Bangkok elite considered it undignified for a monk to work, sweat, or get dirty like a *phrai* (commoner). He should look clean and neat, like a *jao* (lord). By contrast, in many regional traditions laypeople expected a monk to perform hard labor. They expected him to be self-reliant and self-sufficient. When monks were not gifted in oratorical, artistic, or healing skills (which brought in donations), the wat had to survive any way it could. In many local traditions, monks had to work to support the monasteries by growing vegetables, tending orchards, carving boats, or raising cattle and horses.[10] In all the monthons that they inspected, the sangha officials found that abbots as well as other monks did their own repairs and construction. Here are typical remarks from the reports: "The abbot constantly does repair work in his wat"; "he is much respected by the laity"; "the wat is well maintained, strong and clean."[11] Although sangha authorities wanted temples to be well maintained and to look prosperous, they felt the burden of work should fall on the lay community.

In the countryside, however, monks often were expected to work the land because villagers feared the spirits believed to inhabit the fields. Villagers considered it auspicious to begin the new agricultural cycle by having the monks plow the paddies. Plowing was an acceptable activity for monks because it was done not for personal gain but to benefit the whole community. Villagers respected monks who performed this task. One such village (today in Loei Province) was Monk Field Village (Ban Na Phra), so named because the monks took part in plowing and harvesting as well as in performing religious ceremonies to chase away any bad spirits that might live in the fields.[12]

From Bangkok's perspective, however, monks who performed such work violated monastic rules. In their reports the sangha inspectors criticized local monks for devoting too much time to manual work and not enough to intellectual work (teaching from Bangkok's texts). Some sangha inspectors did understand that laypeople expected monks to keep the monasteries in good repair and that they deemed monks lazy when they did not. Villagers, they knew, were often too busy with their own work in the fields to help the monks, who had all the necessary skills. When one inspector in the Northeast told a local abbot, "From now on, monks are forbidden to cut trees or elephant grass for thatch. Will you agree to this rule?" the abbot replied, "If monks are not allowed to cut grass or trees, who will build our shelters or repair the wats?"[13] Nevertheless, this sangha inspector made everyone present at the meeting agree that manual work was improper for monks and that laypeople ought to do it.

For monks in regional traditions, the physical was inseparably entwined with the spiritual. Mundane activities could be spiritually useful when done with the proper mental attitude.[14] Not only did monks and novices undertake construction work or repairs, they collected whatever raw materials were necessary. The revered monk Buddhadasa recalls the lengths he had to go to in order to get lumber during the 1920s.[15] He and his abbot walked to a forest some distance away accompanied by laymen from a nearby village. After cutting the trees they needed, they floated the trunks downriver to the sea, towed them along the coast, and finally brought them upriver to their wat, where the monks sawed the logs into lumber and built their *kuti* (huts).

Li, a Lao monk, also recalls doing manual work as a village monk in the Northeast back in 1925. He and fellow monks went to the forest to get logs to build a preaching hall. The monks were hungry after their hard work, so they ate a meal late in the day— an offense according to the Pali vinaya.[16] A Phu Thai monk from a village in Sakon Nakhon recalls a similar event:

> When it was time to construct a permanent building in the wat, the monks and novices had to spend the night in the forest felling trees and cutting planks. They usually brought drums along to create a lively atmosphere as a break from work. If the food supplies were inadequate, the abbot would allow some novices to disrobe temporarily and catch fish or crabs or to get other food supplies. Afterward the novices would be reordained.
>
> When it was time to pull the logs to the wat, big rollers would be used for hauling. People of all ages—the young and old, women as well as men—came to help haul the logs. Other people would provide musical entertainment by beating drums, cymbals, and other percussion instruments all the way back to

the wat. The monks, novices, and laywomen often took this opportunity to have fun together. This was all right as long as they [the monks] could keep their celibacy vows. (W, 15–16)

After this violation of disciplinary rules, a monk would seclude himself in a hut in the forest.[17] During his solitary retreat, he would release himself from his offenses. This austere practice, called *khao pariwatkam* (entering confinement), is part of the twelve festivals *(hit sipsong)* of the Lao tradition in the Northeast and the twelve traditions of the Yuan tradition in the North (as well as in the Lan Sang kingdom in Laos).[18]

The hard labor in which monks as well as villagers participated was usually done during the slack period or at the beginning of the agricultural cycle. Village monks and abbots either helped villagers cut down trees and work the land or did all this themselves. Since villagers were often afraid of being punished by spirits that guarded the land, having monks working alongside gave them a sense of security.[19] In the Lao tradition, it was the monks and novices who repaired and did clean-up work at sacred stupas such as Phra That Phanom. Local people refused; they believed that anyone who touched, scrubbed, or climbed the stupa would sicken.[20] In the Yuan tradition, similarly, it was the duty of the monks to clear or clean up the forest cemetery.[21] If monks refused, nobody else would do it.

Participating in Local Festivals

Before Bangkok established control over regional Buddhist traditions, the wat and community were close. A community's cultural life centered on the wat.[22] When there was a festival in a town or a village, everyone including the monks participated. In the northern and northeastern regions there were as many as twelve yearly festivals.[23] In his travels through Siam at the turn of the century, James McCarthy, a surveyor, came across monks participating in boat races in one northern community: "The river had overflowed its banks, and a number of people, the majority being women, had assembled in their boats for races. A special feature of these races is that the boats' crews are either all men or all women—never mixed. The women are young and marriageable, and, in fact, have only come for a grand flirtation. They challenge a boat of men to race. In the boats there are more priests than laymen, in some cases priests only."[24]

This religious ritual was similar to those in the upland Lao kingdoms of Luang Prabang and Vientiane. Each Lao polity (meuang) had its own rituals, but as O'Connor observes, all Lao rituals were motivated by a search for "fertility": the source of protection, renewal, and rain.[25] In key royal rituals, "the king or his men were one pole; the other was, variously, autochthonous peoples, commoners, or 'rebels'; and their opposition crystallized in boat racing and polo playing [*ti khli*] contests."[26] Competition was a way of incorporating contrary principles, especially that of male and female. From the union of the two would come fruitfulness and fertility. In the regional Buddhist traditions in Siam these same concerns are apparent. Every local festival was connected to some kind of religious ritual to ensure the well-being of the whole community. Boat-racing contests with monks in one boat and women in the other symbolized the same ritual male-female opposition and expression of fertility. Boat racing was specifically linked to the growth of rice.[27] Good harvests depended on the rain and having the right amount of water in the fields. If the paddies were in danger of flooding, it was commonly believed that boat racing and singing would drive the water level down. The inspector monks saw similar practices throughout the Central Plains. Their reports offer evidence of the popularity of this custom. "A widespread practice in every meuang is monks engaging in boat racing and throwing water at women."[28]

The custom of throwing water occurred typically during Songkran, the New Year festival celebrated in April. Although Songkran was celebrated in all regions, regional customs differed significantly from those of the Siamese court. At court, where the dominant concern was order, people would respectfully sprinkle water on the Buddha images, monks, and elders.[29] Regional peoples were not interested in such restrained and dignified rituals. In Lao traditions (in the Northeast) monks and elders were splashed with water until they were soaked. Bangkok authorities were appalled that monks were treated with such disrespect. But for the Lao, Songkran was a day when people could break the rules. Everyday moral and social restraints fell aside as the young and old indulged themselves to their hearts' content. The festival was a time of joy and permissiveness. Not only would women throw water at the young men of the village, they would come with water to the huts of young monks and throw it on them too.[30] A Phu Thai monk recalled how they used to celebrate Songkran in his village in the Northeast:

> [It did not matter] whether the monks (and novices) threw water at the laywomen first or the women initiated it. Once it started, there were no holds barred. The monks' robes along with their requisites in the kutis were all soaked. The women would chase the monk if he retreated. Sometimes they caught only his robes. If they caught a monk he could be tied to a post in the hut. In the midst of this chasing, sometimes the women's clothes fell off. The monks always lost [the games] or gave in because they were outnumbered by the women. The laywomen really played to win.
>
> After the game was over, a lay leader would escort the women, bearing gifts of flowers and incense sticks, to ask the monks' forgiveness. This has always been the rule. (W, 16)

From the sangha authorities' perspective, any deliberate physical contact between a monk and a woman was an infraction of the Pali vinaya. Most Thai people today would regard such behavior as scandalous, but villagers thought differently. During the festivals, women were allowed to tease monks and vice versa, and children were allowed to tease their elders—behavior normally forbidden. These events were, in short, ritual occasions during which people could rebel against the normal order with impunity.[31]

To understand the regional Buddhist traditions, we must look at Songkran not from the Bangkok elite's perspective but in the context of local histories. In the Lan Na kingdom, Songkran—called *paweni pi mai* (New Year festival)—comes in mid-April (the 12th, 13th, or 14th).[32] "Songkran" is derived from the Sanskrit *sankranti*, meaning the shift of the sun from one sign of the zodiac to another.[33] According to popular legend, this day is called *wan sangkran laung* (or *wan sangkhan pai* in Lao), meaning the day on which the goddess Sangkhan passes by. That day is the last of the old year. Among the early Tai, the Songkran festival was intended to "reenact the early high female status and to help the renewal of . . . nature through ritual sexual intercourse."[34] In the early decades of this century, the regional Buddhist traditions still retained this spirit.

Before the advent of radio, television, and films, these monthly festivals provided whole communities with much-needed relaxation and fun after weeks of hard work in the fields. A Phu Thai monk explained how it was in the local tradition: "During the yearly or monthly festivals, people of all ages played hard. Old people, in order to take part in the amusements, stopped being respectable for the day. In some groups, the play turned into a fist fight, at times bloody. But whether they won or lost, their victory or defeat did not last beyond the festival day" (W, 13).

Besides boat racing, monks and novices participated along with laypeople in drum beating *(seng klaung)*, polo playing *(ti khli)*, kickball *(takrau)*, and chess *(mak kruk)*.[35] During a wake *(ngan heuan di)*, Lao village monks in meuang Ubon might be seen playing chess or playing match games with women.[36] In the Central Plains the Siamese had a similar custom. During a wake laypeople wanted the monks to stay around long after the funeral rites were performed. Monks who went to a wake usually did not get back to their wat until after midnight.[37]

People in villages and towns saw nothing wrong with monks participating in boat races, throwing water at women, or playing chess because they knew the monks and were in fact often their relatives. Many of the monks were sons of villagers who had been ordained at least temporarily, and their lay providers were their parents, aunts and uncles, or acquaintances. But for outsiders— sangha inspectors, Christian missionaries, and Western travelers —the regional monks' behavior was, to say the least, questionable. "In many wats the monks do not behave properly," is a typical remark of a sangha inspector. McCarthy puts it more strongly: "in view of the celibacy of the priesthood the circumstances tend to scandal."[38] Although sangha authorities forbade monks to follow these customs, in remote areas these practices persisted for several decades after the imposition of modern state Buddhism.[39]

Another distinctive tradition followed by Lao Buddhists during Songkran was *kin khao pa* (eating food in the forest). Villagers in northeast Siam as well as in Laos organized a communal lunch in the forest near a pond or swamp where fish were abundant. They usually went in the morning in a large group, and monks were invited to go along. The kin khao pa picnics varied among different groups of Lao people. According to one custom, monks stayed away from food gathering. "Upon arriving at the destination, the gathering of food is started: a group of the women go into the forest to collect forest products, while the men go fishing with the fishnet [or] shovel water out of a pond to catch . . . fish. All these people who join the picnic try to engage in a variety of activities, except for the elderly and monks who usually spend their time in talking and relaxing."[40] In the hinterland of the Northeast, such local customs persisted into the middle of this century. A thudong monk who wandered to Ox Mountain (Phu Wua), Lion Mountain (Phu Sing), and Thauk Mountain in the 1950s found the Moei and Yau still practicing the kin khao pa custom. Monks and novices were even participating in the food gathering along with villagers.[41]

For sangha authorities, unlike regional Buddhists, hierarchy was important. Bangkok insisted that laypeople treat monks with the greatest respect; much emphasis was placed on the formalities of monasticism. Local traditions, however, promoted horizontal relationships. During Songkran, all people—monks and laypeople, men and women, old and young—were equals and friends, despite their different statuses.

Preaching the Dhamma with Drama

Prior to the imposition of modern state Buddhism, monks of regional traditions used *jātakas* ("birth" stories) along with myths, legends, and folk tales to convey dhamma.[42] Jātakas recount events in about five hundred of the Buddha's previous existences as a *bodhisatta* (future Buddha), in which he assumed a variety of human and nonhuman forms: king, rich man, minister, brahmin (holy man), robber, hare, lion, parrot, naga (mythological serpent), garuda (mythological bird-human). In sixty-four previous births the Buddha had been a hermit who had renounced all worldly things.[43]

The sangha inspectors' reports provide evidence of the widespread popularity of jātakas in all regions of Siam. This report is typical: "Most monks preach about alms giving, generosity, precepts, and moral conduct. Basically, the monks' sermons consist of jātakas, especially the Great Birth story." In the Central Plains monks sought to master the Great Birth story "because it is very popular among local people."[44] In the South as well, "Monks rely mostly on jātakas and the *Questions of King Milinda* to propagate dhamma."[45] In the northeastern region, where the Lao Buddhist tradition prevails, "Laypeople share similar values; they prefer to listen to folk tales and jātakas, not dhamma sermons that expound doctrine. It is the villagers who choose the sermon they want to hear. They invariably choose folk stories such as Sang Sinchai, Phra Rot Meri, Phra Jao Liaplok, as well as the Wetsandon Chadok."[46]

In the Lao tradition, the festival of reading the Wetsandon Chadok (Vessantara Jātaka in Pali) is called Bun Phawet; in the Siamese tradition it is called Mahachat (Great Birth), and in the Yuan it is Tang Tham Luang (Setting the Great Text).[47] Reading this jātaka was one of the most popular of regional customs. The story tells of the Buddha's life as the bodhisatta Wetsandon (Vessantara) and of his last rebirth before becoming the Buddha. Local people were willing to sit all day and long into the night listening to the story when it was told dramatically. The themes of the Wetsandon Chadok are similar in different traditions, although the cultural identities of the characters vary according to local customs and languages. Prince Wetsandon, known for his generosity and selflessness, fulfills his vow to practice *dāna* (generosity) by giving whatever he is asked. He surrenders not only the sacred regalia of his father's kingdom but even his own wife and children.

The sangha inspectors observed that many monks wanted to learn from their elders how to recite the story. Not everyone could be a preacher, of course: it took a lot of discipline and long training to master even a section of the Wetsandon Chadok, which consists of thirteen "chapters" *(kan),* each chapter divided into thirty to forty sections. During the festival these chapters were assigned to particular monks and novices at the host monastery as well as to monks in neighboring monasteries who had been invited to take part.[48] In training, however, a monk would try to recite all thirteen chapters by himself. A former preacher recalled: "I started reciting at 7 A.M. [and] gradually I began to lose my voice. Yet I kept it up until I reached the final chapter. By then it was 6 P.M. and my voice was completely gone. For seven or eight days I had no voice."[49] There were good reasons for this intensive training. In the days before microphones, a preacher had to project his voice and enunciate clearly, so that an audience of hundreds could hear him. He also had to know how to conserve his voice. Preaching improved his memory and mindfulness, which in turn helped him in his dhamma studies. Finally, he gained much merit if he succeeded in mastering the entire jātaka.[50]

Only a master storyteller could do it well, altering his voice as he portrayed the tale's many characters—demons, animals, old men, hermits, kings, princesses, children—evoking all the while a strong sense of involvement from his audience. In many traditions, special enclosed seats or booths helped preachers deliver their readings dramatically. In the Lan Na tradition, for example, the dhamma booth was a small enclosure in the shrine hall *(wihan)* raised about a meter and a half above the floor. It had walls of carved wood on three sides, while the fourth was left wide open for entry by means of a ladder. As a former preacher explained, "In this dhamma booth the monk could sit comfortably, since he could look out but the audience could not see him. He did not have to be dignified. He might remove his robes, put his hands over his ears, open his mouth widely, or tap his hands on the floor to aid his rhythm. [Instead of sitting on the floor] most preachers preferred to squat. My teacher told me that squatting lets the testicles hang naturally, so the preacher has no constraint in projecting his voice loudly."[51] Bangkok authorities forbade monks to use these dhamma box seats. By doing so, they hoped to put an end to this kind of dramatic preaching.

Another integral part of a Great Birth story performance was music, especially the *phin phat* ensemble. Inspector monks reported that in several monthons monks played various kinds of musical instruments.[52] In every town and village large crowds of people would listen with rapt attention for hours while local monks took turns reciting stories about the Buddha's former lives as bodhisattas. Such stories figured more prominently in sermons than episodes from the life of the Buddha himself.

Because preaching the Wetsandon Chadok was an art requiring arduous discipline, few preachers achieved great oratorical skills. Those who did were much respected and in high demand. Their popularity was not without a price, however, as a former preacher explained: "Often, monks with lesser skill are jealous and seek to ruin the preacher by using black magic *[khun sai]*. So a good preacher must possess magical knowledge for self-protection. (1) He must learn to recite sacred mantra for self-defense as well as to attract people with goodwill. (2) He must tattoo protective amulets on his body for the same reason. (3) He must always keep certain kinds of amulets or magic cloth *[pha yan]* to make him invulnerable."[53]

Why did jātakas exert such a strong influence upon the religious life of rural people? Sangharakshita points out that jātakas (and the sermons based on them) have a pragmatic value. They embody an ideal of human conduct, the bodhisatta ideal. This ideal is not exclusively monastic, for it can be followed by laypeople as well as monks.[54]

Another reason why jātakas were popular among regional Buddhists is that they teach about the interconnectedness of humans and animals, of nature and spirit. In them, animals interact with people as equals; animals change to human forms and vice versa.[55] According to these folk stories, all of us are capable of extraordinary transformations—from animal to human, from human to animal, from animal to animal. The stories are filled as well with poetic descriptions in appreciation of nature, celebrating the forests, waters, and wild creatures.[56] They must have seemed especially vivid to monks and villagers who, living close to nature, would have encountered many wild animals—deer, bantengs (a species of small wild ox), bears, tigers. Some wats were themselves wildlife refuges, providing a safe haven for animals hunted in the countryside. In Phichit Province in northern Siam, for example, abbot Khian made his Wat Wangtaku a shelter for monkeys, gibbons, barking deer, bantengs, and crocodiles.[57] Under the abbotcy of Noi, Wat Thammasala in Nakhon Pathom Province, central Siam, became home to at least a hundred monkeys and a variety of birds.[58] The jātaka tales taught villagers "cross-species compassion," an immediate empathy toward creatures not of their own biological species.[59]

But sangha authorities in Bangkok failed to be moved by the ancient kinship of man and nature. Bangkok academic monks dismissed jātakas and folktales as "false," "nonsense," and useless. From the sangha officials' perspective "regional Buddhist sermons are ineffective for teaching dhamma. The sermons play upon myths, jātakas, or folktales solely to entertain. In effect, the doctrine is not explained at all."[60] State Buddhism decided that a different sort of message should be spread. Sermons should bear on the Buddha's own life, not his previous lives, and they should draw on the Buddha's *sutta* (discourses) rather than on tales or parables.

One of the fundamental differences between Bangkok ecclesiastics and regional Buddhists lay in the figures that the two groups revered. The Bangkok elite attributed great importance to events in the Buddha's life; hence they insisted that regional Buddhists observe Makha Bucha[61] as well as Wisakha Bucha[62]—days that commemorate important events in the Buddha's life. Regional Buddhists, however, attached more significance to the stories of bodhisattas, particularly Vessantara.

An incident in the southern region illustrates what happened when a sangha official introduced a Bangkok holy day with its recommended sermon. During his inspection trip in 1900 to meuang Ranong in the South, the sangha inspector wanted to demonstrate how Wisakha Bucha should be observed. The ceremony, attended by some seventy local people, was supposed to last from 8 P.M. until dawn. Soon after the official monk started preaching the Mahā Bhinikkhamāna Sutta, however, the laypeople started to leave. By the time the monk got to the Mahāparinibbāna Sutta, only one person—the lay leader—remained in the audience.[63] The abandoned sangha official commented in his report, "People in this town have no appreciation or respect for dhamma sermons."[64]

What exactly drove people away from the temple that day is unclear. Maybe people left because they had no allegiance to Bangkok's holy days; maybe they did not understand the Bangkok Thai dialect; or maybe the sermon was too abstract or too dry. Probably they were expecting a bodhisatta story or a folktale. Unless a sermon was entertaining as well as instructive, it would not capture the villagers' attention. After a day's work in the fields, villagers did not want to sit through a boring discourse. But they were willing to sit through the day and long into the night listening to a jātaka. Not just listening, participating as well: "Luang Pu La was gifted in storytelling. His detailed and descriptive sermons about nature and wildlife drew a large crowd of adults as well as children. When he preached, the whole hall vibrated with his dramatic voice and the audience's laughter and cheers."[65] Villagers listened to stories word by word, and to the music note by note. A tragic moment brought tears. A well-turned phrase brought an exclamation of satisfaction or a gale of laughter, enough to encourage the preacher yet not interrupt him.

Sangha officials, however, were very critical of the audience's enthusiasm as well as of the monks' performance, lamenting that "It was disorderly [*mai riap roi*], crude, and noisy."[66] They refused to recognize that the spoken word often called for different treatment than the written word. The following incident illustrates the contemptuous attitude of administrative monks' toward the local style of preaching.

In 1934 a Thammayut administrator from Bangkok traveled to Nakhon Ratchasima to supervise monastic exams. He arrived at a Lao village during the Bun Phawet festival. He noticed that nearly all of the local people spoke Lao. One afternoon he walked into the village wat and heard a Lao monk reciting the Vessantara story. Although the audience enjoyed the preaching, the administrator was full of criticism: "I had no idea what section of the Great Birth story the old monk was preaching. I have a hard time understanding the Lao language in conversation, let alone in dhamma verses spoken in rhythm, the way this sermon was delivered. It was like listening to pigeons cooing. Seeing that there was little point in listening to something that I didn't understand, I was prepared to leave." But before he could do so, the Phra Khru (the monk in charge) ordered the same Lao preacher to do a section of the story in Thai "for my sake, so I could compare it with the Mahachat story in the central Thai version and determine if the authentic Thai version was better than the phony Thai [Lao] version."[67] The sangha official's next comment provides good evidence of what could happen when a local monk was forced to preach in Bangkok Thai:

> The Phra Khru's order was loud enough to be heard throughout the hall. As many as three hundred pairs of eyes turned to stare at me, and I heard people whisper, "He came from the south [their term for Bangkok]." I had difficulty keeping a

straight face. In any case, I got to listen to the Mahachat chanting in Thai, as I wished. This section of the Great Birth story is called Matsi [Vessantara's wife]. The monk who recited this section came from another village. He was quite old. Hearing him reciting the story, I completely lost faith. Not only was his accent horrible—like a Chinese speaking Thai—his rhythm was no better than that of the one-armed beggar who sings for money on the Rama I Bridge in Bangkok.

I sat through the recitation and felt relieved when it was over. Perhaps the preacher was relieved, too. I excused myself on the pretext that I had to supervise some students. That was only half of the truth. In fact I regretted having to sit through such a disastrous sermon.[68]

Clearly, preachers prevented from reciting in their native tongues would fail to move their audiences.

In contemporary times it is rare to hear an indigenous recitation of the Wetsandon Chadok.[69] This ancient art in its original form has become virtually extinct. Modern state Buddhism insisted that sermons be sober and didactic. But since local people found the standardized, official sermons abstract, dry, alien, and irrelevant to their everyday lives, they ceased to pay attention. Attending sermons dwindled to a ritual of merit making.

Evidently the Siamese elites and local people approached Buddhism from different starting points. Modern state Buddhism, influenced by nineteenth-century Western scientific views, aimed to reform regional Buddhists and convert them to a kind of rational Buddhism. Beyond Bangkok, communities sought to preserve their own local customs and their ethnic identities. Folktales and sermons drawing on local lore contained matters of crucial importance. Sermons reinforced bonds of ethnicity, religion, occupation, age, and kinship. Myths, legends, and folktales were important vehicles for the transmission of distinctive heritages. The narratives were not esoteric; they were familiar to the adult population, and they were the domain of entire communities. They were inspiring stories containing insight and wit. And as Thanissaro Bhikkhu observes (with regard to origin stories in the vinaya), "the element of wit . . . is especially important, for without it there is no true understanding of human nature."[70]

Combining Meditation and Study

Before the state monastic education system became dominant, monks of regional traditions usually taught *samatha* (tranquillity) meditation in addition to teaching dhamma from their palm-leaf texts.[71] Depending on the time of the year, regional monks might either be settled in a monastery or living in a forest. In many meuangs monks stayed put in their wats only during the three-month-long rains retreat.[72] After the retreat they would go their separate ways. Some would withdraw to the forests or to charnel grounds; others would visit their teachers or go on pilgrimages.

During the cool season (from December to February), particularly in the North and the Northeast, monks of the Yuan and the Lao traditions would leave their monasteries and stay in forests to meditate. Originally developed from the thirteen thudong practices, the practice was called *khao kam, khao sosanakam,* or *khao rukkhamun* (retreating for serious practice, to a charnel ground, or to the base of a tree).[73] In those days cemeteries were located in a forest some distance away from the village or monastery. Many monks would be away from their monasteries for the entire period of the cool season. Laypeople—women as well as men—who wanted to practice meditation could join the monks and novices during these meditation retreats. Laypeople helped build small bamboo huts with thatched roofs and walls to accommodate the monks, and children were assigned the daily task of filling water jars in the latrines. Monks who practiced this temporary confinement were called *luk tup* (sons of the huts).[74] For the monks, this practice had a number of purposes: it lessened their attachment to the monastery; it gave them an opportunity to perform community work such as clearing the forest cemetery; it trained the monks to endure hardship by sleeping in the cold, damp outdoors; it provided an opportunity to live an ascetic life; it served to eliminate mental defilements; and finally, it helped liberate the souls of the dead.[75]

In addition to khao kam, monks of regional traditions spent the months between rains retreats going on pilgrimages. This custom was part of their religious training. While traveling they practiced asceticism, paid homage to sacred sites, or visited their teachers to seek advice, learn further meditation practices, or hear new teachings. Novices would accompany their preceptors, since traveling was part of their training. For example, it was a Yuan custom that after the rains retreat abbots would lead a group of novices to Laos or the Shan states on a pilgrimage. By the time they got back it was time for the next rains retreat. Since the novices experienced considerable excitement from their travels, they were willing to remain in monastic life for at least another year. Had they stayed in the village wat all year round, they might have disrobed out of boredom.[76] Traveling on foot, they learned both practical skills as well as lessons of nature. In an era when traveling was mostly done on foot, a well-trained mind was a useful asset. It could help the traveler deal with the threat of attack from wild animals, bandits, or bad spirits.

Regional Buddhists seem to have valued meditation practice as much as book learning.[77] They judged the monks by their basic characters, their deeds, and their asceticism. Just the opposite was (and is still) true of administrative Buddhists in Bangkok, who saw spiritual development as primarily a scholastic achievement and judged monks by their proficiency in Bangkok's Pali texts. As Zack observed in 1977, "an educated monk in Thailand would probably understand the Dhamma-Vinaya primarily on the basis of Wachirayan's . . . texts."[78]

Lay Buddhist Practices

Modern state Buddhism changed the concept of religiosity from a community orientation (lay asceticism benefiting individuals as well as society as whole) to a temple orientation (gift-giving benefiting individual monks—and the higher a monk's rank, the more he and the wat benefited). Regional traditions emphasized the needs of householders and the community rather than those of monks and the monastery. Bangkok elites viewed the laity's kind of Buddhism as inferior to that of the monks. It may be significant that the Siamese call the lunar holy days *wan phra* (lord's or monks' days), which invokes a hierarchical and categorical distinction (Buddha and monks versus laity),[79] whereas in regional traditions like that of the Shan and Yuan the holy days are called precept days (*wan sin*—from the Pali *sīla*, "discipline")—a designation that stresses renunciation.[80]

Whereas for regional Buddhists lay asceticism was of paramount importance, for the Bangkok elites it was wealth that mattered. Wealth was indispensable in merit making.[81] A person's *bun* (merit) was largely knowable through his wealth and especially his merit-making gifts.[82] Kathin, a gift-giving ceremony, was state Buddhism's preeminent festival. In Bangkok the royal kathin displayed wealth as well as rank and royal favor.[83] Although the Lao and the Lan Na courts also made kathin gift-giving displays, common people offered robes anonymously by leaving cloth near the monks' huts or walking routes.[84]

Another difference between Bangkok custom and regional tradition can be seen in the observance of Bun Phawet. In the Bangkok Siamese custom, individual persons made gifts to monks; in the Lao tradition the whole village made a collective gift. As O'Connor observes, collective gifts leave no room for status competition.[85]

In the Bun Phawet ceremony, moreover, local people did not choose the monks who would receive their gifts. As a Phu Thai monk recalled, while the monks were delivering sermons at the wat, "groups of villagers carrying honorary gifts walked in a procession from the village. As they entered the wat they would offer the gifts to whoever (a monk or a novice) was preaching [the Vessantara story] at that moment. This ritual is called *kan laun*. Every group followed this custom."[86] During this festival, laypeople from other villages would stay at the host wat to observe the precepts.

Whereas Bangkok sangha authorities required all regional monks to observe Makha Bucha and Wisakha Bucha days according to Bangkok's customary forms of reverence—worship of Buddha images and circumambulation of the *ubosot* (ordination hall) —regional Buddhists had their own festivals called *paweni wai phra that* (festival of paying homage to sacred relics). There was a strong belief among the Buddhists of the Yuan and Lao traditions that they should make a pilgrimage to a stupa holding the Buddha's relics at least once in a lifetime.[87] The abbot of a local wat usually led the pilgrimage. In earlier days making a pilgrimage required considerable commitment and effort from laypeople. It involved traveling on foot, clearing the trail to the pagoda, bringing food to offer to monks, undertaking the eight precepts, listening to sermons, and alternating worship with meditation practice often until late at night. These religious ceremonies might last for a few days.[88]

By de-emphasizing meditation and discouraging pilgrimages, modern state Buddhism eventually contributed to the decline not only of these practices but of asceticism and renunciation generally. The concept of merit making was changed from participating to supporting. One result is a lay population that seeks physical well-being but does not exert itself spiritually. Lay supporters offer gifts to high-status monks, not necessarily out of faith or devotion but in order to make merit. They are not to be blamed, of course, for this is what their religious environment expects of them. "When displaying status carried such high stakes," O'Connor asks, "how can Buddhism's other status-denying options—asceticism, meditation, and ethical deeds—have stood a chance?"[89]

CENTRALIZING STRATEGIES

The king passed the Sangha Act of 1902 in order to integrate monks of all traditions into a national sangha hierarchy. Under this law a standard Buddhist practice, based on Bangkok court custom, was enforced throughout Siam. Until then no ruling center had attempted to control the diverse traditions found within Siam's borders. In the Central Plains, the Siamese of the kingdoms of Ayuthaya (1350–1767), Thonburi (1767–1782), and Bangkok (1782 to the founding of the modern Thai state) followed a Buddhist tradition closely linked to that of the Khmer.[90] In the North, the local Buddhist traditions had greater affinities to those in the Shan states and neighboring parts of Laos. In the Northeast the Lao followed Buddhist traditions related to both the Lan Sang kingdom (Luang Prabang and Vientiane in Laos) and the Lan Na kingdom.[91]

One centralization strategy was to offer rewards to those who agreed to come within the center's control. As O'Connor observes, the bestowal of titles, honors, positions, gifts, and invitations gave rulers control over monks and wats. "Such rewards were old but Bangkok's reach was new."[92] Prior to 1902, honors and positions were decided by local elites or villagers. The Lao of the Northeast, for example, had a ceremony called *song nam pha,* which took place around the Songkran days. This ceremony was performed to confer promotions on local monks. At his first song nam pha a monk would get the title of Somdet; at his second, Aya Sa; at his third, Aya Khu; and at his fourth, Aya Than. The title preceded the monk's first name (e.g., Aya Khu La). Note that Somdet, the lowest title in the Lao tradition, was the highest in the Bangkok scale.[93]

To restrict the autonomy of these locally titled monks, Bangkok established a higher authority intended to outrank the local one, as this report by the sangha inspector of monthon Isan makes plain:

> In this monthon there is a local tradition called *samoson sommut* [authority based on popular consent]. Laypeople as well as monks in each village vote and confer their own titles of Phra Khru and Sangharat. In order to reflect his greater importance, the sangha head appointed by the king should bear a higher honorific title. We should title each Phra Khru according to the name of the district where he has authority. This way there should be no question of who has the higher authority, the locally appointed or the Bangkok-appointed monk. The Phra Khru title without the district name attached will have no meaning here, for there are already many Phra Khrus appointed by local people all over the northeast region.[94]

To prevent the local monks from perpetuating regional Buddhist traditions, the Sangha Act stripped locally appointed abbots of their power to ordain monks. Before the imposition of this rule, local custom permitted monks who had been ordained for ten years to perform ordinations. Ordination was the concern of a spiritual master and his local lay followers, and of a local community of monks as well. Since 1902, only those abbots appointed as preceptors by Bangkok authorities have been allowed to perform ordinations. The act also restricted which monasteries qualified as ordination sites. "No longer were the local abbot and the village wat at the heart of every ceremony. Now ordainers had to meet educational standards and ordination sites needed royal approval."[95]

Thus Bangkok ecclesiastic authorities gained legal control over who became a monk. They therefore had the power to prevent regional Buddhist traditions from growing. Now the power to confer full ordination was vested not in a spiritual master but in a Bangkok-appointed preceptor and his subordinates. This meant that an abbot lacking Bangkok's cachet was debarred from ordaining monks, no matter how senior or highly realized he might be. He could no longer induct a disciple into his own lineage without contravening the Sangha Act of 1902. The shift of authority away from the abbots of regional traditions became complete.

In the same way that the modern Thai state undermined the old elite and created a new one,[96] state Buddhism demoted the old ajans and elevated new ones. Bangkok provided new status symbols to construct the new sangha elite—honorific fans and ecclesiastical titles—and new measures of mastery. An abbot was now judged by his wat: how big and how clean it was, how many resident monks had passed the *naktham* (dhamma curriculum) and Pali exams,[97] and how regularly monks performed religious rituals based on Bangkok customs (reciting the 227 disciplinary rules fortnightly, chanting every morning and evening, and observing Wisakha Bucha and Makha Bucha yearly). Yoneo Ishii aptly sums up the implications of this standardization of Buddhism: "The adoption of this system to give the monks an official status by State examinations helped to strengthen the State control of the monks. This system, which aimed at deepening the monks' knowledge of Buddhism, enforced a sort of orthodoxy by banning free interpretations of the Buddhist doctrines which are liable to bring about schism within the Buddhist Order. Thus the Thai monks' understanding of Buddhism became stereotyped and the monks' subjugation to the state was strengthened."[98]

The modern education system destroyed regional monastic traditions. Knowledge came to be transmitted in the form of textbooks written in Bangkok Thai by individuals who had little direct contact with those for whom the books were intended.[99] Gradually, Bangkok's textbooks became surrogates for regional traditions. The knowledge that local monks traditionally acquired through palm-leaf texts, medicinal works, astrology, music, rituals, chants, and meditation was considered inferior to the Bangkok curriculum. These authorities repeatedly told monks and laypeople of various ethnic groups that Bangkok court culture is superior to theirs. Thus regional Buddhism gradually dwindled as a locus of social control and power.[100]

REACTING TO CENTRALIZATION

Bangkok's attempts to impose its form of Buddhism generated a conflict between two different concepts of spiritual authority. In the past, spiritual authorities always shared the local community's religious customs and language and embodied its values. Monks of different ethnic identities and lineages accepted and coexisted with one another in the same polity (meuang); no one group imposed its religious customs and practices on any other, and there was no concept of a centralized state power.

Modern state Buddhism (modeled after the Thammayut sect) bore little resemblance to the religious traditions of rural communities. It had a different set of texts and a new language and culture; it celebrated different religious days and ceremonies; it promoted unfamiliar forms of behavior, symbols, and ways of seeing. The demands it placed on the regional monks were foreign: stay put in the wat all year round, cease pilgrimaging and celebrating local festivals, learn bureaucratic skills, behave according to the customs of the Bangkok elites, and study books written in an alien language. In monthon Prachinburi, east of Bangkok, for example, monks living inland on the plains had never seen printed texts before (the local manuscripts were written on palm leaves). Unable to read Thai, they thought these books came from Christian missionaries. They took no interest in textbooks sent to their wats by Bangkok authorities in 1899.[101]

How did local people react to Bangkok's assertion of authority? Many abbots outside Bangkok's influence could not accept that after centuries of autonomy their power to ordain monks had suddenly become illegal. Many monks rejected modern state Buddhism and continued to follow their local nikais.[102] The most well known case is that of a Yuan monk, Siwichai (1878–1937), a village abbot in Lamphun who ran afoul of sangha authorities from 1908 to the 1930s.[103] After the passage of the 1902 Sangha Act, Siwichai and his disciples were classified as monks of the Mahanikai order. Siwichai was arrested after he continued to ordain monks and novices into his nikai. To members of his nikai, Siwichai was not just their teacher, he was their upatcha. But from the sangha officials' perspective, Siwichai was not a qualified preceptor because he had not studied Bangkok's religious texts and had not taken Bangkok's exams. The exams and texts were, of course, in Thai, and Siwichai did not know this language (nor did many of his disciples and lay followers). This illustrates just how much the Bangkok elite acted like a colonial power, imposing its own rules and language over local customs and languages in the name of "modern education."[104]

Siwichai's followers—over 2,000 monks and novices from ninety wats in the North (Chiang Mai, Lamphun, and Chiang Rai)—refused to be part of the Bangkok sangha hierarchy.[105] Government officials were dismayed to see that the locals, whom they thought docile, were openly protesting modern state Buddhism. The following official report of 1935 illustrates how local people felt about the imposition of Bangkok's culture and language on their religion.

> In general, people in Li District [Siwichai's natal district] are submissive. The local government officials report that compared to other districts, there is hardly any violence in this area. (The people here are dumb.) But when it comes to religion, they are very stubborn. They only listen to the one person whom they respect. About 80 percent of the people in this area who follow Siwichai's lineage refuse to take up modern education. Only less than 10 percent of the people here know Thai. The anti-Thai language feeling is widespread. In some government schools, desks, chairs, and benches were either burned or thrown into the forest. The district education officers are constantly worried. The village headman did not dare to take action. He is more concerned about his own safety.[106]

The crisis reached a head when Siwichai was summoned to Bangkok and detained for over six months (from 1 November 1935 to 18 May 1936) at Wat Benjamabophit.[107] His supporters believed that the sangha provincial heads of Lamphun and Chiang Mai (Mahanikai administrators) had accused him of violating the 1902 regulations because they were jealous of his popularity. Indeed, Siwichai was able to mobilize large numbers of local monks and laypeople to repair wats or stupas—something that the sangha administrators could not accomplish.[108] In local traditions, it was not unusual for capable monks with grassroots support to inspire people to donate their labor or skills. Local people saw Siwichai as a natural leader and sangha administrators (appointed by Bangkok) as outsiders. Eventually, the sangha authorities had to compromise by allowing local wats to continue practicing some Yuan customs, and in turn Siwichai "accepted the authority of the Thai sangha to determine who would be allowed to perform ordinations."[109]

Another example indicates that religious autonomy persisted in remote areas three decades after the 1902 Act. In Mae Hong Son, a meuang in the northwest of Siam, monks as well as local people still maintained their cultural, linguistic, and kinship links with people in the Shan states. This became clear when sangha officials from Bangkok went to Mae Hong Son in 1934 to inspect monasteries there and to distribute religious texts written in Bangkok Thai. In his report to the regional sangha head, the inspector complained that local people refused to send their children to government schools and that the local monks preferred to study the Shan language: "Most monks and novices in this province do not want to learn Thai," the inspector wrote. "They prefer the Burmese [actually Shan] education and tradition. This is because the majority of local people are Burmese [Shan]. They have more contact with the Burmese than with Thai. It is more convenient to travel to Burma [Shan states]. All their trading is with the Burmese. Goods in Mae Hong Son come from Burma; Thai products have not been able to reach here. When I suggested that they take up Thai, they [the Shan monks] argued that the language is useless here. It is very difficult to convince people to learn Thai."[110] Note that this sangha official, who came from Bangkok, called the Shan people "Burmese" *(Phama)*. A wandering monk who went to Rangoon as well as to the Shan states, however, correctly identified the monks in Mae Hong Son as Shan (Thai Yai).

Local resistance to Bangkok's religious control came in various forms, sometimes open and violent. In addition to Siwichai's resistance in the North, a number of other uprisings occurred in the Northeast. In 1901 and 1902 various uprisings led by *phu mi bun* (men with merit, "holy men") occurred independently and spread over the vast area of the Lao- and Khmer-speaking regions.[111] Other revolts included the Naung Bakkaew rebellion of 1924 and the Mau Lam Noi Chada rebellion of 1936.[112] Although all were suppressed or crushed by Bangkok's standing army, their occurrence is significant. The revolts suggest that even after forty years of centralization, Bangkok's control over the whole region was still far from secure. They also indicate that the Lao in the Northeast were brought under Siamese control by military power.[113]

Elsewhere resistance was more subtle or passive. Among ethnic monks and villagers living in outlying areas, religious customs persisted several decades after Bangkok attempted to change them. In those meuangs or villages where the sangha law unrealistically contradicted local customs, it took much longer to enforce. Elder monks of regional Buddhist traditions (Siamese, Shan, Yuan, Lao, Khmer, Mon, etc.) continued to follow their local religious practices as before. They did not take up the Bangkok curriculum but generally were experts in their indigenous customs. They were jacks-of-all-trades: teachers, construction workers, artists, painters, sculptors, craftsmen, storytellers, community leaders, astrologers, animal tamers, and healers. For them, as for local people, there was no dichotomy between being a monk and being a craftsman, a healer, or a community leader; these roles were all part of the same life. These local monks had extensive day-to-day contact with local people.

Other regional monks accepted the Bangkok monastic system, taking the naktham or Pali exams while pursuing their involvement in local matters (studying palm-leaf texts, engaging in painting or sculpture, working at construction or repairs, practicing herbal medicine, or preaching folk stories in the indigenous language). But gradually young monks turned their backs on traditional knowledge to pursue Bangkok's path.

These village monks and particularly abbots were bound by commitments, obligations, and responsibilities toward their local communities. Another category of monk, comprising those who wanted to devote more time to meditation practice, would withdraw into the wilderness and wander alone or in the company of other like-minded ascetics. The dense forest and the isolation of villages shielded these wandering ascetics from political intrusion throughout the Forest-Community Period—that is, until 1957.

The following chapters examine the lives of the wandering meditation monks who refused to follow Bangkok's path, including their experiences of life in the forest, their encounters with monks in other Buddhist traditions, and their relations with various ethnic groups who likewise lived on the margin.

CHAPTER 2

The Path

to the Forest

During the late nineteenth century and early decades of this century, it was customary for young men to ordain in their local traditions to learn the dhamma and acquire practical knowledge relevant to rural communities. Those who were committed remained in the robes and eventually became village abbots. Most young men, however, left monastic life after a number of years to become householders. The ten monks who concern us became lifelong monastics and lived a wandering life for several decades. These monks chose a route that most others (lifelong monks included) found too distasteful or difficult: an austere life in the wilds, in which hardship and suffering lead to self-knowledge. To understand why they chose this path, we have to follow their tracks, noting where their individual ways crossed, converged, or parted. This chapter examines the thudong monks' family backgrounds, their education, their reasons for becoming monks, and their search for the right meditation master.

FAMILY BACKGROUND AND EDUCATION

Ajan Man and his disciples comprise a lineage spanning three generations of teachers and pupils. Although in the early 1900s the new centralized government was beginning to extend its control into the Northeast, the villages in which these monks lived during their childhood years—from the 1870s to the 1920s—remained largely unaffected by Bangkok's culture and values. The Northeast's rich and diverse regional traditions set these monks on a strikingly different path from monks in the city. An examination of their early years shows how different the Northeast of Siam was back then.

When Man was born in 1871, the land along the Mekong River consisted of small tributary states (meuangs) where people of multiple ethnic identities commingled. These principalities maintained a high degree of autonomy in their internal affairs, including their religious practices. They remitted taxes in currency or in kind to Bangkok. By the time Fan was born in 1898 the centralized state of Siam had been created, and Bangkok had begun to impose central administrative control over these semi-autonomous principalities. Meuangs in the borderland of Siam had been organized into administrative units (monthons), each named after the local population's ethnic identity: monthon Lao Klang (Nakhon Ratchasima), monthon Lao Kao[1] (Ubon Ratchathani), and monthon Lao Phuan (Udon Thani). By the time Thet was born in 1902, these monthons had been renamed to indicate their directional location from Bangkok. Thus, monthon Lao Klang became monthon Nakhon Ratchasima, monthon Lao Kao became monthon Isan ("Northeastern monthon"), and monthon Lao Phuan became monthon Udon ("Northern monthon").[2] A year after La was born, monthon Isan was divided into two monthons, Roi-Et and Ubon Ratchathani. By 1912 the term "Isan" was being used to indicate a wide geographic designation instead of a narrow administrative one. When Wan was born in 1922, the territories under the four monthons—Roi-Et, Ubon Ratchathani, Udon, and Nakhon Ratchasima (Khorat)—became known collectively as *phak isan* (Isan region). Nowadays the region's Lao and Khmer inhabitants call themselves *khon isan* (northeastern people).[3]

The Northeast in the 1920s comprised a variety of ethnic groups. Much of the local population was ethnically related to the Lao people of Luang Prabang in the north of Laos, Vientiane in the center, and Champasak in the south.[4] The thudong monks were conscious of the many different ethnic affiliations in their region. Five of our ten monks came from southern Isan. Man, Li, Cha, and Juan were born in Lao villages in Ubon Ratchathani, while Dun came from a village in Surin. The other five were born in northern Isan. Thet and La were Lao Phuan and Lao Lawa from Udon Thani. Fan and Wan were Phu Thai from Sakon Nakhon. Waen's ancestors migrated from Luang Prabang. None of the monks' parents spoke Thai; the monks learned it later either in monastic schools, from monks trained in Bangkok, or in government elementary schools.

All ten monks grew up in large families of five to ten children. In those days villagers wanted to have many children so they would have help in the fields. Birth order seems to have had little to do with their later decisions to take up the thudong life. Only Man, the teacher of the others, was an oldest child. Dun was the second child but the oldest son. Fan and Cha were middle children. Juan, Li, and Thet were all next-to-youngest children. La was the youngest. Waen and Wan were only sons; both were raised by grandparents after their mothers died. Being raised by grandparents was not uncommon during the Forest-Community Period.

We should not impose modern Thai or Western standards of well-being on the monks or their villages. Like most villagers before Bangkok culture and values reached them, they did not see themselves as economically impoverished.[5] Their parents owned farmland and were self-sufficient. Fan's and Juan's fathers were village headmen. Thet's parents had little money, but this concerned them little: "Food and rice were abundant and money wasn't so necessary in those days."[6] La's grandfather had several hundred *rai* of land and over a hundred cattle.[7] Wan's grandfather also owned paddy fields, orchards, and cattle. Cha describes his parents as prosperous.

Their childhood experiences might have helped account for their later ability to live in the forest and suffer hardship. All of them were sons of farmers and lived in villages surrounded by or at the edge of forests. Unlike upper-class children in cities, they started working in their early years. In their early teens they were assigned responsibilities such as fetching water, pounding rice, tending water buffaloes, taking care of younger siblings, or helping in the fields. By the time they became adults they were accustomed to hardship. Although Fan was descended from the local nobility, his childhood was not much different from that of other village children. He worked and got around on foot like the others.

In all regional traditions the monastery had always been a center of learning, for secular as well as religious knowledge. The older generation of monks—Man, Waen, Fan, and Thet—began their education at the village wat. In the Northeast in those days, spirit worship was a significant part of the local religion. Thudong monks' parents were practitioners of spirit worship as well as Buddhists. Man and his first-generation disciples Waen, Fan, and Dun were ordained as Buddhist monks before Bangkok's monastic education system spread to their village wats. They were fluent in their indigenous languages and able to read palm-leaf texts (printed books had not yet appeared). In addition to writing in their native languages they learned the Khmer, Thai Noi, and Tham scripts.[8]

After the passage of the Sangha Act of 1902, however, revered teachers of regional traditions were subordinated to a national hierarchy whose senior monks were Siamese.[9] They were required to adopt Prince Wachirayan's religious curriculum for teaching local monks. Many old monks continued to follow the Lao traditions, however. Novices *(samanera)* and young monks who were born after 1902 were more likely to study religious books written in Bangkok Thai, learn Pali written in Thai script, and take nak-tham exams. Dun and Thet, for example, started out in their local traditions and then went on to study Bangkok's textbooks in the town of Ubon.

The other monks in our study came of age at a time when all children were required to attend government schools.[10] The purpose of education at the time was to teach the children to read and write in Bangkok Thai and to read books advocating the views of the central government.[11] Like many village children of their time, Li, Juan, and Wan completed elementary school. At school their texts were in Thai; at home they spoke Lao. Most village teachers still could not speak much Thai or felt they could not communicate with students in Thai. Village folk generally were not happy to send their children to state schools. They saw no advantage in learning Thai, and besides, the children were needed at home to take care of younger siblings and tend water buffaloes.[12] This might have been the case with La's and Cha's parents. La never attended a state school and Cha went for only one year. After they became monks, however, La and Cha took up naktham studies and read religious books in Thai. The five youngest of our ten monks—Li, La, Cha, Juan, and Wan—all passed their naktham exams with little difficulty.

We shall now consider the monks' backgrounds individually, beginning with Man, the oldest monk and the teacher of the rest.

Man Phurithat (1871–1949)

Little is known of Man's early years. He was born in Khambong Village, Khong Jiam, on the western bank of the Mekong. (Today the village is part of Si Meuang Mai District, Ubon Ratchathani Province.) Like most inhabitants of the Northeast, Man's parents were Lao. The eldest of nine siblings (eight boys and one girl), Man was of small stature, of fair complexion, agile, full of vigor, intelligent, and resourceful. He also had an excellent memory. As a youth he was an amateur singer in his village. His biographer recounts an event that tells us something about his character. During a festival, Man dared to compete on stage in a singing contest with a considerably older woman, even though he was no match for her.[13] Such fearlessness would prove to be useful later in his life.

Man took up the monastic vocation in 1886 at the age of fifteen. Like monks in regional traditions, Man was multilingual. He studied the Khom, Thai Noi, and Tham scripts and became well versed in local history and folklore. After two years of training as a novice, he disrobed because his parents needed his help in the fields. In 1893, when he was twenty-two, Man became a monk in the Lao tradition.

Waen Sujinno (1888–1985)

Waen's natal Pong Field Village (Ban Na Pong) was a Lao settlement in meuang Loei. Waen's ancestors had migrated from Luang Prabang in the mid-nineteenth century. In 1892 the Siamese state incorporated the population of Loei, but Waen's village was too remote for Bangkok to exercise effective political authority over it. Loei eventually became a province of Siam.

Waen's parents were both farmers; his father was also a black-smith. Waen had only one sibling, a sister. His childhood was beset with adversity. He lost his mother at the age of five, and soon afterward his father took a second wife. Waen moved in with his maternal grandparents, who lived in the same village. Waen's mother's last request was that her only son make merit for her by being ordained for life. When Waen was eight, his grand-mother had a dream that she considered auspicious: after playing in a turmeric bush Waen came out orange, the color of monks' robes. She took him and another boy his age to the village wat to be ordained as novices in the local Lao tradition. A few months later Waen's companion fell ill and died, which caused him much grief.

In 1908 Waen traveled on foot with his uncle, a monk, from Loei to Ubon, a distance of over 480 kilometers.[14] At the time several village wats in Ubon were well known for Pali grammar studies.[15] Waen studied at Sangthau Village Wat in Kasemsima District. In those days there were no formal classrooms. Students had to carry palm-leaf books to the teacher's wat. Waen recalls spending a lot of time making these books and carrying them to the wats where his teachers resided: "When students had free time from studying, they would go to the forest to collect palm leaves for making books to practice writing. One had to be careful to pick leaves that were neither too old nor too young. The best leaves were one year old. Older leaves were not supple and broke easily. One stripped the palm leaves from their mid-ribs and left them out for three nights until moist, then tied them into a book using a string or thread. When we went to study with an ajan we used these palm leaves to write on or to copy manuscripts from the teachers"(W, 25).

At twenty Waen took higher ordination as a monk at the village wat where he was studying.

Dun Atulo (1888–1985)

Waen's exact contemporary, Dun was born in Ban Prasat (today in Surin Province), a village first settled by his grandfather.[16] As the oldest son of five children (two boys and three girls), Dun took care of his brother and younger sisters in addition to doing house-hold chores such as fetching water, pounding rice, cooking, and tending water buffaloes. Dun was a healthy boy with good manners and fine features. When he was eighteen, he was selected for a female role in a play (public theater was very popular before the advent of motion pictures).[17] It was while he was with the theater group that Dun learned the Thai language.

Working in the theater also provided Dun with the opportunity to travel. In 1905, when he was seventeen, he was assigned a leading female role in a play to be performed at the Surin ruler's court. The play required a costume that Dun had to procure from Bangkok. At the time the railroad from Bangkok to the Northeast reached only as far as Khorat, a four-day journey from Surin. The young Dun made the 198-kilometer trip to Khorat by elephant and then took a train to Bangkok. Dun had a good impression of the big city. In those days Bangkok was not yet crowded with buildings and people: "It's very easy to get around in Bangkok. When nature called [we] just went into the woods to relieve ourselves. The water in the canal is clean enough to bathe in and drink."[18]

At the age of twenty-two Dun thought of becoming a monk. His parents did not want to lose his labor, so they discouraged him. Eventually his father acquiesced, on the condition that Dun remain a monk until he became an abbot (like his grandfather). In 1910 Dun was ordained at Wat Jumphon Sutthawat in Surin. The ceremony was sponsored by the governor's relatives, who were Dun's theater patrons.

That year Dun went to practice meditation with the abbot of Wat Khaukho on the outskirts of Surin. Abbot Aek was a monk of a local tradition who taught a *kasina* method of meditation.[19] In this method Dun learned to focus his mind by staring at five candles and chanting a mantra: "May the five *piti* [raptures] come to me." Abbot Aek also encouraged the practice of austerity: eating fewer spoonfuls of food every day. But Dun became so thin that he gave this up. Like many village abbots of local traditions, Aek stressed meditation practice and chanting (of *suadmon jet tamnan* or *sipsong tamnan* texts). Reciting the 227 precepts was not so important. While residing in the wat, Dun was assigned the task of building bullock carts and looking after oxen. The manual labor bored young Dun—he was not yet able to understand that doing manual work was Buddhist training just as much as devoting oneself to meditation—but he stayed on for six years.[20] When he heard about the new monastic school in the town of Ubon, he asked permission from his *upatcha* (preceptor)[21] to study there under the monks trained in Bangkok. Dun's upatcha disapproved, but then he relented and allowed Dun to go in the company of two older monks.

At first Dun had difficulty finding a wat close enough to the monastic school to allow him to commute. (The school was in a Thammayut wat and its abbot would not allow non-Thammayut monks to reside there.) Then he met a fellow monk from Surin who took him to Wat Suthat, another Thammayut monastery.[22] The abbot of this wat got around the rules by classifying Dun as a visitor rather than a resident. While staying at this temple Dun passed the lowest level of the naktham exam. After four years of "visiting" this Thammayut temple, Dun wished to affiliate with the Thammayut Order, but the monthon sangha head, Uan Tisso (titled Phra Thampamok), had other plans for him. He wanted to send Dun back home to establish a monastic school and to teach religious texts in Thai. He chose Dun because a Thammayut monk would have had a hard time in Surin, since the Thammayut order had not yet taken root there. But Dun had made up his mind. With the help of Sing,[23] a resident monk, Dun converted to the Thammayut order at Wat Suthat. He was then thirty-one years old.

Fan Ajaro (1898–1977)

Fan's background differs from that of other wandering monks. His grandfather was the ruler of meuang Phanna Nikhom, a Phu Thai polity nominally attached to the Bangkok kingdom. When the Bangkok king began the process of changing Siam into a modern nation-state, all the outer territories including Phanna Nikhom were incorporated into the new centralized government of Siam. Hereditary lords like Fan's relatives were put on fixed salaries and lost their power, prestige, and economic independence. They felt that the imposition of Bangkok's system of provincial administration was undermining the local nobility.[24] When Fan was born in 1898 his father had been demoted to a mere headman in Egg Mango Village (Ban Muang Khai, today in Phanna Nikhom District, Sakon Nakhon Province).[25] Under the central government's new administrative system, his father's position was at the bottom of the national hierarchy.

Fan's experience of working with his relatives convinced him of the fragility of a livelihood in the new civil service system. Fan's brother-in-law was a deputy district officer in the town of Khon Kaen. When he was still a boy, Fan left his village to study with this relative, hoping to enter the civil service once he grew up. But contact with some senior officials made Fan change his mind. In Khon Kaen, Fan had the duty of carrying food to convicts. One of the prisoners was a meuang governor who had been convicted of murder. At the time quite a few civil servants, descendants of local nobility, had been charged with similar crimes. Later, when Fan's brother-in-law was transferred to meuang Loei and Fan traveled there to visit him, he found that his brother-in-law, too, had been charged with murder. Fan decided that he did not want to get into the civil service. He left Loei immediately and returned to his home village, walking barefoot for ten days. The sight of his relatives in prison had made such a strong impact on him that he took to the robes. Fan became a novice that same year, and at the age of twenty (1918) he took higher ordination as a monk at a monastery in Hai Village.

Fan entered the monastic life at a time of great social turbulence. Perhaps these unsettled conditions induced the young Fan to despair at the thought of the world's instability. He had seen how low many local nobles had fallen. Men who should have been leaders of their communities were sitting in prison. (This suggests, perhaps, that the new centralized government of Siam had successfully disempowered the local political hierarchy.)

Thet Thetrangsi (1902–1994)

Thet was born in Sida Field Village (Ban Na Sida) in meuang Udon Thani. Ten years before his birth, the village of Udon had been upgraded to a meuang (today it is a province). The years 1901 and 1902 were a period of social unrest: a series of rebellions led by white-robed phu mi bun with large followings broke out in the Northeast. In the Lao tradition, these wandering white-robed monastics were highly respected; local people believed that they possessed magical power. The uprisings against Bangkok's political, economic, and sociocultural domination shocked the

Siamese leaders for several months.[26] During the same year the Sangha Act of 1902 was passed, putting monks of local traditions under the control of the Bangkok sangha administration, but Thet's village was too remote to be affected by either the rebellion or Bangkok's new law.

Thet was the youngest son in a family of ten children (four boys and six girls). His parents were Lao Phuan—the main ethnic group of Chiang Khwang principality (Sieng Khouang, Plains of Jars, in Laos). Phuan people, including Thet's grandmother, were among the captives of war who were forced to settle in underpopulated areas of Siam.[27] Thet's father was devout; after marrying and producing six children, he became a monk for two years. Thet was born after his father resumed a householder's life. As a child Thet enjoyed hanging around the village wat, playing with friends or serving the monks and novices. During this time he saw a novice in the local tradition whose behavior inspired him.

> I still remembered an occasion from my early days in the monastery, when I went with my elder brother [a monk] to visit another monastery. There was a novice there whose demeanour and behaviour was exemplary. He made such a strong impression on me, he was so inspiring and admirable, that I felt a special sympathy towards him. I found myself following his every movement, whether he was walking or sitting or going about his various duties. The more I gazed after him the stronger my faith and feeling grew. On returning to our monastery, I couldn't get his image out of my mind. I could think of only one thing: "Oh, when will I be able to ordain and become a novice like him." This was my continual preoccupation. (T1, 25–26)

In those days, bandits and cattle rustlers were common in remote areas, indicative of Bangkok's lack of control over the region. The young Thet wanted to learn occult powers of invulnerability to help protect his family. He saw an opportunity when a Phu Thai monk claiming to possess such knowledge wandered to Thet's village. Thet, then ten years old, believed him. After the rains retreat ended, he and three older village youths, one of them his brother, ran away from home and accompanied this monk to his home in Egg Mango Village. The trip took them three days. On reaching their destination the youths found that the monk possessed none of the magical knowledge he had claimed and that he had duped them into escorting him back home. Feeling humiliated and ashamed of themselves, they returned to their village. Perhaps because of this experience, Thet became disillusioned with charms and magical powers.

Thet started his schooling at the age of nine at the Phuan village wat whose abbot was his eldest brother. At the time government elementary schools had not reached this village. The abbot had picked up a bit of Thai from his travels, and he taught it to Thet along with the Khmer script. Three years later Thet's brother, the abbot, left the monastic life. Since the other monks did not want to teach, Thet and several other boys returned home. But Thet continued to go to the wat regularly for six years, serving as an intermediary between the monks and villagers. He became closely acquainted with the monks and novices.

Li Thammatharo (1907–1961)

Li was born in Double Marsh Village (Ban Naung Saunghaung, today in Muang Samsip District, Ubon Province), a community of eighty houses spread around three ponds, surrounded by scores of giant *yang* trees. A wat of a Lao Buddhist tradition was located in one of the hamlets that made up the village.

Li's original name was Chali. He had five brothers and four sisters. His mother died when he was eleven, and since his older siblings had by then left home, it was up to Li to look after himself and his younger sister. He and his sister helped their father in the rice fields. Li started attending the government school when he was twelve. He learned enough to read and write Bangkok Thai, but he failed the elementary exams. At seventeen he left school.

Li, it appears, did not get along with his father. "My father and I seemed always to be at odds with each other," he writes. "He wanted me to start trading in things which seemed wrong to me, like pigs and cattle. Sometimes, when it came time to make merit at the wat, he'd stand in my way and send me out to work in the fields instead. There were days I'd get so upset that I'd end up sitting out alone in the middle of the rice fields, crying. There was one thought in my mind: I swore to myself that I wasn't going to stay on in this village—so I would only have to put up with things just a little bit longer."[28] At the age of eighteen Li left his village to visit his older siblings in the Central Plains. His brother was employed by the Irrigation Department building a watergate in Saraburi Province. At the time Li felt that making money was the most important thing in life. After working for a few years in central Siam, he returned to his village when his stepmother died. He had saved about 160 baht—a lot of money in 1925. By then he had reached the age of twenty, so he asked his father to sponsor his ordination. Li was ordained as a monk in the local tradition at his village wat.[29]

La Khempatato (1911–1996)

La was born in Ban Kudsa, a village about ten kilometers north of the present provincial capital of Udon Thani. He was the youngest child in a family of eight (five girls and three boys). And like Thet, La gives a detailed account of his grandparents, Lao Lawa farmers who settled in Udon Thani (La, 5–11). La's mother and maternal grandparents came from a village that is now in Pak Thong Chai District, Nakhon Ratchasima Province.

In those days there was plenty of unsettled land. Villagers were able to relocate freely. After La's grandmother died, his grandfather sold their land and house and left Khorat (Nakhon Ratchasima) for good. He had heard there was land suitable for cultivation in the area north of Mak Khaeng Village, in Udon Thani. The family walked there, a two-week journey, and settled in what became Kudsa Village. Other people from Khorat followed. Later, when the village numbered some two hundred households, it was integrated into Bangkok's administrative system as a commune *(tambon)*.

La attended the state elementary school up to the second level. He quit at the age of twelve to help his parents in the fields. At eighteen he was ordained as a novice in the local tradition at his village wat. By then Bangkok's religious books had already arrived, but the village abbot, much respected by local people, continued to preach from palm-leaf texts. La took the naktham exam during the third year of his novitiate and passed the lowest level (naktham 3). But when he reached draft age, he had to disrobe. The military lottery did not select him, however, so he went back to his village wat and, now that he had reached twenty, was ordained as a monk. He took the naktham 3 exam again and passed for the second time. Then he disrobed and got married. After his wife died in 1943, he became a monk again.[30] La's father, who wished all his sons would become monks for life, was very happy about his decision. La continued to reside in the village wat, about two kilometers from his village, until his mother died. During this period he studied the naktham textbooks and passed the highest level (naktham 1). All the while he observed the vinaya strictly: "I ate only once a day. . . . I refrained from digging the ground and cutting greenery. I also did not keep money." The other monks were following the Lao tradition (La called them "Mahanikai"). The abbot was flexible; he approved of the way La observed the vinaya.[31]

Cha Phothiyan (1918–1992)

Cha was born in Jikkau Village, today in Warin Chamrap District, Ubon Province. He came from a family of ten (six boys and four girls). By local standards his family was prosperous. By the time Cha reached school age, a law had been passed requiring all children, regardless of their native language, to attend government schools and learn Thai. But since the law was not strictly enforced in this area, Cha spent only one year in elementary school. He left the state school at thirteen and asked his parents' permission to be ordained as a novice. Three years later he disrobed to help his family in the fields. He preferred the monastic life, however, and upon reaching the age of twenty he was ordained as a monk at a village wat.

Cha studied Wachirayan's texts at monastic schools in Ubon Province. He passed naktham 3 during his first year. He was intending to take the next higher exam, but his father fell ill and Cha went back home to look after him. He ended up losing both an opportunity to take the exam (given only once a year) and his father. Cha eventually passed the highest level of naktham in 1945, after six years of study.

Juan Kulachettho (1920–1980)

Juan was born in Lao Mankaew Village in Modyang Forest Commune (today within Amnat Charoen District, Ubon Province). He was the next youngest of seven children (six boys and a girl). His parents' ancestors were Lao war captives from Vientiane when the kingdom was ransacked in the early nineteenth century. His father was a farmer who became a respected village doctor through his knowledge of herbal medicine. Indeed, villagers so respected Juan's father that they elected him headman. Like many village children of his time, Juan started attending the government school at the age of nine or ten.[32] Of the ten thudong monks, Juan had the most formal education. He finished the sixth year of elementary school (the highest level in the village school at the time) at the age of sixteen. Unlike Li, Juan had taken well to the Bangkok educational system. He ranked first every year. When not in school, Juan could have learned herbal medicine from his father, but instead he helped him keep his official village records. His father died after being a headman for eight years, when Juan was sixteen.

Juan was ordained as a monk at his village wat in 1941. Studying Wachirayan's texts had by then become a common route that many young monks pursued. Like Thet, La, and Cha, Juan sat for the naktham exam and passed it in the first year.

Wan Uttamo (1922–1980)

Wan was born in Hollow Palms Village (Ban Tan Kon), seven kilometers from the Yam River. Today the area is part of Leaning Palms Commune (Tambon Tan Noeng), Sawang Daen Din District, Sakon Nakhon Province. In those days each household in the village had its own gardens and orchard as well as rice paddies. The land beyond was forested. The forest at Ya Khu Hill, west of the village, was particularly dense. Nobody dared enter it alone for fear of guardian spirits.

Like Li, Wan was not an easy child to raise. "I was the most difficult child," he writes. "No other relatives had the patience to take care of me. . . . I cried all the time and . . . kept my parents up almost every night. . . . During the day my mother would carry me to look at things here and there, just to keep me quiet. But I didn't stop crying for long. When I started to cry again, my mother would pick me up and walk around the village. Sometimes this would go on all day. Once I learned to talk I would ask my mother to take an umbrella to keep the sun off and to take me for a walk to the neighbors' huts. After that I wanted to go to the forest. I would make my mother comply with my every wish" (W, 17). Wan lost his mother when she died giving birth to his brother.

At the age of three, Wan and his father moved in with his paternal grandfather, a widower, while his younger brother stayed with his maternal grandmother. Later on his father remarried, set up a new household and had three more sons. Wan remained under the care of his grandfather and helped him in the fields. His father died when Wan was thirteen. Unlike Waen, whose childhood was unhappy, Wan was surrounded by kind relatives.

The first government school in his village was established in 1932. Wan was ten when he started going. Like Juan, he did well in class. His overall grade was always near the top, and he excelled in mathematics. Since Wan was the oldest child, his father wanted him to continue his education and study law, "to keep other people from exploiting us" (W, 18). He started Wan on this path by sending him to stay with the village headman, where Wan was to make a copy of the Bangkok law book by hand.

Wan completed the elementary schooling in 1935. His father died earlier that year after expressing his hope that Wan would be ordained as a monk. By then Man's disciples had begun to establish forest wats in the Thammayut order, and in one of these, Wat Aranyikawat in Egg Mango Village (Fan's natal village), Wan's grandmother was staying as a *mae chi* (white-robed renunciate).[33] She wanted him to become a novice there. So Wan's uncle took him to this forest wat, where he was ordained by Wang Thitisaro —a disciple of Ajan Man's. In those days, local people still identified themselves with their native villages. Young Wan describes his feelings about being away from home and living with people from other villages:

> These first few days [at the wat] I feel very lonely especially in the evenings. It is so quiet here. Not that I miss anybody in particular, I just feel homesick. I probably won't get to go home for a visit until after three years. The fact that one of the monks in the wat, Venerable Father Aun, is an old relative of mine does not always make me feel secure. I'm not really close to him because his house was at the opposite end of the village from ours. Some young men came and put on white robes waiting to be ordained, but they chickened out and ran away. They did not care about their honor or losing face. I, for one, am determined to overcome my loneliness until I accomplish my goal. (W, 20)

Gradually Wan's attachment to his village lessened. He concluded that regardless of which villages monks come from, as human beings they are more or less the same.

As a novice, Wan went to spend the rains retreat at Wat Suttha-wat in the capital town of Sakon Nakhon. Jao Khun Ariyakhu-nathan (Seng Pusso) was abbot of this Thammayut wat at the time (1940). Wan studied naktham texts under Khamphaung, a disciple of Ajan Man's.[34] He passed the first exam with a good score. The following year Wan went to study the second naktham level at Splendid Jewel Pond Monastery (Wat Sakaew Rangsi) in Phibun District, Ubon Province. He ranked second in the exam. During the 1941 rains retreat, Wan's teacher suggested that he take higher ordination, now that he had reached twenty. Although Wan wished to leave the monastic life to spend four or five years in lay life before being ordained as a monk, he could not go against his teacher's wish. Now a monk, Wan studied the highest naktham texts on his own and passed the exam with a top score.[35]

BECOMING A THUDONG MONK

As more young monks in the Northeast pursued the study of dhamma from texts written and printed in Thai, Man and a small number of monks turned elsewhere. Despite the pressure from the sangha authorities in Bangkok urging them to abandon their regional traditions and settle in official wats, many local monks remained committed to the thudong tradition. What motivated these monks to take up this difficult life?

Man, Waen, Dun, and Fan

Man came to the town of Ubon in 1893 to study at Wat Liap. At the time monks in Ubon followed one of three Buddhist tradi-tions.[36] The Lao tradition, brought from the kingdom of Vientiane, was the local one. The Siamese tradition had been introduced to Ubon in the early nineteenth century by Ariyawong (Sui), a Lao monk who had gone to Bangkok to study at Wat Saket, which was a center of meditation practice in Bangkok in those days.[37] The Mon tradition had been introduced in the mid-nineteenth century by another Lao monk, Phanthulo (Di), who had adopted it from King Mongkut.

The majority of monks in Ubon followed the Lao tradition, which varied from one wat or *samnak* (hermitage, unofficial wat) to another. These diverse practices arose as a result of pupillages —that is, teacher-disciple relationships continuing from one generation to the next.

When the Mon tradition spread to Ubon it blended with the local culture and attracted monks who found its strict adherence to the vinaya conducive to their meditative inclination. After Bangkok began to centralize the sangha, the Mon tradition became known as the Thammayut order, while the Lao and the Siamese traditions were lumped together into another order, the Mahanikai. The separation occurred because the Thammayut saw themselves as superior to the Lao, the Siamese, or any other tradition. They would not allow non-Thammayut monks to take part in religious rituals with them. By contrast, monks in the Lao and Siamese traditions did not mind participating in religious rituals with one another or with Thammayut monks, should they be willing.

Man was trained in a Lao tradition but was reordained in the Thammayut order. After the ordination ceremony at Wat Sithaung,[38] he returned to his residence at Wat Liap to study with his teacher, Sao Kantasilo.[39] Man's biographers do not say how many years Man stayed at this wat. Sao taught Man a mantra meditation method to calm the mind: the mental repetition of "buddho." Sao, although a Thammayut, still followed the Lao tradition of combining a settled monastic lifestyle and thudong practices. Between the rains retreats Man went wandering with Sao, searching out forest sanctuaries suitable for meditation.

As for Waen, he found that living at the village wat of Sangthau, right next door to a lay community, made it hard to resist temptation. His decision to become a thudong monk came when all of his teachers, including his uncle, left the monastic life to get married. This incident brought his studies to an end. He realized that the only way he could remain a monk for life was to stay away from towns and villages.

Dun decided to try out the thudong practice after meeting Ajan Man. This was in 1919, when Man came to spend the rains retreat at Wat Burapha in the outskirts of Ubon not far from Wat Suthat, where Dun was staying. Having heard about Man's reputation, Dun went with Sing to listen to his sermons. Both were impressed by the clarity of Man's sermons and his serene manner. At the end of the rains retreat both Dun and Sing left their studies and went wandering with Man. But Dun was not yet ready to give up Bangkok's religious texts entirely. After a few years of wandering and meditation practice, he went to Khorat to drop off a novice at a monastic school. While there, he decided to give himself another chance. So he traveled to Bangkok and stayed at Wat Samphanthawong (Wat Kau) for a rains retreat. Here he discovered he was no longer interested in academic study. He found it difficult to concentrate on textbooks; his mind now tended more exclusively toward meditation. At the end of the rains retreat he returned to the thudong life.

Like Man, Fan was ordained in a tradition that combined a settled monastic lifestyle with a nomadic, forest-dwelling existence. In those days, when village wats were never too far from wild areas, village abbots could easily fit periods of meditation into their daily schedules by retreating to a grove or forest nearby. Those with a desire for more intensive practice would leave the wat to meditate in a cave after the rains retreat ended. This was the case with Fan's Phu Thai preceptor, who taught Fan to meditate the day he was ordained. When his first rains retreat was over, Fan returned to the wat in his natal village. He continued meditation practice under the guidance of the village abbot, Aya Khu Tham.[40] This abbot also taught young monks to meditate. At the end of the rains retreat the abbot took Fan and other young monks on a thudong.[41] For several months they wandered in the forests and mountains of the Northeast and practiced meditation in caves and forest cemeteries.

Thet

Thet spent practically all his formative years in a wat. From the age of nine to fourteen Thet served as a connecting link between the monks and laypeople in his village. Wandering monks frequently came to stay at his Lao Phuan village wat. Thet looked after the monks' food, filtered water for them, and collected flowers for the monks to offer to the Buddha. If the monks lacked food, Thet would ask the village folk to bring more. His parents and the villagers encouraged him to do this work and treated him with love and kindness. Thet's father, in particular, was deeply religious.

In 1916 when Thet was fourteen, two wandering meditation monks, Sing and Kham, wandered into Sida Field Village.[42] They were the first Thammayut monks to reach this area (a three-day walk from meuang Udon Thani). Thet was impressed with their religious practices and found that their meditation method suited him: "Their way of practice was different from other groups of meditation monks. . . . The visiting monks taught me about their various obligations and duties. For example, I learnt the do's and don't's of offering things to a monk and about meditation using the mantra-word 'Buddho' as an object of preliminary recitation. My mind was able to converge in *samadhi* to the stage where I lost all desire to speak to anyone. This was where I first experienced the flavour of meditation's peace and stillness. It's something I've never forgotten."[43]

After the rains retreat was over Thet left home to accompany Sing on a thudong—the first boy of his age to venture away from the village on such a long journey.[44] Although his relatives were glad that Thet had found a teacher, they could not help weeping when he left.

Sing then took Thet to Wat Suthat in the town of Ubon, settled Thet there to continue his Thai language studies, and then left. Thet spent six years learning to chant, reciting the *patimok* (rules of conduct), studying the naktham texts, and learning to read Pali in Bangkok Thai script.[45] He took higher ordination in the Thammayut order in 1922 at the age of twenty and then passed the basic naktham exam on his first try. That year Maha Pin[46] (Sing's brother and a parian five monk—that is, a monk who had passed the fifth level of Pali studies) returned from Bangkok and started teaching level-two naktham material for the first time in Ubon or, for that matter, in all of the Northeast.

Sing, accompanied by four other monks and two novices, came back to Ubon. This occasion marked the first time that a group of forest meditation monks spent a rains retreat in that Thammayut wat. Sing convinced Pin to try the thudong life. After the rains retreat, Sing led a group of twelve monks and novices on a thudong. Among the newcomers were Pin, Thet, two other monks, and two novices, all of whom had studied under the Bangkok monastic system. Thet did not finish his naktham studies.

Those who adhered to modern state Buddhism considered it shameful to live a thudong life, and some even saw it as undisciplined vagrancy. Pin in fact was the first scholastic monk of *maha* grade—that is, a monk who had passed the third-level Pali exam —to follow the thudong path. Thet observes that "most of the academic monks considered the going off on thudong a disgraceful thing to do. It was due to Ajan Sing being our leader that I was able to go along on thudong because without my presence my preceptor was obliged to recite the Patimok Rules himself."[47]

Although Thet had always wanted to lead a thudong life, when the opportunity came he found it painful to leave the wat. During the years away from his village, Thet had had no relative or close friend nearby. Long absences from home while studying in a major town became the norm after the centralization of the sangha. Young monks like Thet coped with the absence of family and friends by forming bonds with monks or novices from other villages. During this period in Ubon, two novices and two temple boys became Thet's pupils and a surrogate family. The strong bond that he formed with them may have characterized many teacher-disciple monastic relationships.

> When it came time to separate they all began to weep, thinking how much they were going to miss me. I too was almost unable to hold back my tears. But being their teacher it would have looked bad if I cried in front of them, so I gritted my teeth and suppressed my sorrow, not letting my true feelings show. Even so, I found my voice hoarse with emotion.
>
> At the time those feelings hadn't seemed too overpowering, but later, after we had left, they seeped in and made me feel dull and listless for a remarkably long time. Whether I was walking, standing, sitting or lying down, even while talking or eating, my heart was preoccupied in gloom and sadness, longing for my "disciples." How will they manage? What will they eat? Will they have enough to eat or have to go without? Who will teach them? Or perhaps someone would come along to bully and boss them about. This was the first time in my life that I had ever experienced such depression. (T1, 64)

Thet was amazed at the strength of his attachment to the boys, considering that they were not his relatives. He began to see how attachment causes suffering. "I now perceived the drawback and danger in such longing and yearning, and this realization permeated right through my heart. This understanding has never been lost" (T1, 65).

Li

Li became a wanderer after finding life in his village wat unsatisfactory. In 1925, when he was ordained as a monk at his village wat in Ubon, village monks were required to memorize chants and study the dhamma and vinaya texts sent from Bangkok. But in practice they still followed the Lao Buddhist tradition. It bothered Li to see that adhering to the vinaya came second to following local customs. Monks were "playing chess, boxing, playing match games with girls whenever there was a wake, raising birds, holding cock fights, sometimes even eating food in the evening."[48] Perhaps because local monks often had to walk considerable distances to preach and also do physical work around the wat, when hungry they had no qualms about eating after noontime.[49]

Another thing Li disliked about the life of a village monk was performing funeral rites. Before becoming a monk, he had managed to avoid approaching cremation pyres. In fact he never set foot in a cemetery until he was nineteen. Even when his mother or another relative died, Li refused to go to the cremation. As a newly ordained village monk, he still tried his hardest to avoid going. "One day," he writes, "I heard people crying and moaning in the village: someone had died. Before long I caught sight of a man carrying a bowl of flowers, incense and candles, coming to the wat to invite monks to chant at the dead person's place. As soon as he entered the abbot's quarters, I ran off in the opposite direction, followed by some of the newly ordained monks. When we reached the mango grove, we split up and climbed the trees— and there we sat, perched one to a tree, absolutely still. It wasn't long before the abbot went looking for us, but he couldn't find us" (Li1, 5–6).

A chance encounter gave Li's monastic life a new direction. During his second rains retreat in 1928, he was invited to give a Mahachat sermon at another village during a Bun Phawet festival. When he arrived, a meditation monk happened to be on the sermon seat. Li was taken by the way he spoke. He asked laypeople there about the monk and found out that he was Bot, a disciple of Ajan Man's. At the end of the festival Li went to see him. The thudong monk's way of life and the manner in which he conducted himself pleased Li. Bot told Li that Ajan Man had come down from Sakon Nakhon and was staying at Wat Burapha in the out-skirts of Ubon. Li returned to his wat to tell his father and his pre-ceptor that he had decided to leave the village wat.

La

Like Thet, La encountered a thudong monk when he was a boy. This was in 1923 when La was twelve. The thudong monk, Khampha, belonged to a Lao tradition and was an old friend of La's father. La's father built Khampha a small raised platform out-side the village for him to camp on and sent La to attend the monk during his meals. His father spent every night learning the dhamma from the thudong monk. Young La was much impressed by the monk's conduct, and he was intrigued by the adventures that the monk related. He heard, for example, a story about a cave called Aewmaung, across the Mekong in Laos.[50] "There was a stone pathway about eighty-eight yards long bordering a cliff. At the bottom [Khampha] could see scattered corpses and alms bowls. Those were thudong monks who had fallen to their deaths. He himself slipped while crossing the bridge, and although he managed to save himself, his bowl got dented. The other four monks traveling with him died, either from falling off the cliff or from stomach illness" (La, 15). The fact that many wandering monks died from accidents or illness en route did not deter La from wanting to be a thudong monk.

La became a monk and resided near his village wat until 1945, when his mother died. Her death freed him from remaining in the village wat.

Juan, Wan, and Cha

Juan's first encounter with the thudong way of life came the way La's did, through a visiting monk. In 1935, when he was fifteen, Juan saw a wandering monk at the edge of the forest near the vil-lage.[51] Having heard that thudong monks often handed out amu-lets, Juan fetched water for the monk, hoping to get an amulet or learn a mantra. Instead the monk asked Juan if he wanted to be ordained and gave him a copy of the booklet *Trisaranakhom*, written by Ajan Sing.[52] He told Juan to follow the book's instruc-tions on how to practice meditation.

Juan was ordained as a monk in a village wat in 1941. By then Man's disciples had established many forest wats in the upper Isan region. Juan found that the life of a settled monastic did not suit him. He thought of converting to the Thammayut order and becoming a thudong monk.[53] When he asked his preceptor's permission to convert, the village abbot refused. So Juan left the monastic life.

As a layman Juan earned a living by sewing cloth. This was during the Thai war with the French (1940–1941), when cloth was expensive and hard to find. Juan had to travel from village to village to find handwoven silk. On one occasion he came down with malaria and became gravely ill. Taking medicine did not help. He made a vow, "If I have enough merit to be ordained, let me recover soon. Once recovered, I will ordain right away" (J, 29). After asking around he located Samranniwat Forest Monastery (in Amnat Charoen District) and ordained as a monk in the Thammayut order.

Young Wan's monastic life differed from Thet's and Juan's in that he was familiar with sangha administrative work. By the time Wan took higher ordination as a monk in 1942, he had already spent six years as a novice studying under Bangkok's monastic education system. In those days Thammayut monks who passed the naktham exams would be assigned administrative posts. Since Wan ranked first in the highest-level naktham exam, the sangha head of Bunthrik District (Ubon Province) intended to make Wan his assistant and also a sangha commune head. Unlike most of his fellow monks, Wan had no ambition for titles or status:

> I had thought about it and decided that it was not a path leading
> to self-knowledge. If anything, honorific titles and prestige
> would lead to self-delusion. Why did I dare to say this? Because
> I had been a *pariyat* [academic] monk and had many such
> friends. Some of them had gone to Bangkok, others remained in
> rural areas in various provinces. I know what pariyat monks
> think. I had also assisted the sangha head in his administrative
> work for several years. I socialized with other administrative
> monks and understood quite well what they were talking about.
> Nobody could really fool me about this. Therefore I did not
> want to be a teacher or a sangha head. I have always tried to rid
> myself of these burdens.[54]

In 1943 during the Japanese occupation of Thailand, the Thai military was aggressively drafting young men from rural Sakon Nakhon. Wan had to return to his natal village to report to the government. As a holder of a naktham certificate, however, he was exempt from conscription. While he was in the village, he suffered another attack of malaria. Constant relapses prompted him to contemplate whether he wanted to be an academic monk or a practicing monk. Although a few years earlier he had stayed with the meditation teacher Ajan Sao (Man's teacher) and had attended him, Wan did not pay much attention to samatha or *vipassanā* (insight) meditation practice. But as his body became infirm, he concentrated his mind on the breathing. Then something unusual happened. Regardless of his posture, his mind remained focused.

> When my mind attained a meditative state despite my lack of interest [in meditative practice], I was dumbfounded. I could not help laughing at myself, since with all my academic knowledge I was unable to figure this out. I don't know if other monks had such an experience, because everyone differs. Later on, I met skilled meditation teachers who clarified my confusion. One teacher told me that what I had experienced was an early state of *samādhi* [concentration] resulting from *ānāpānasati* [mindfulness of breathing] meditation. Had I directed my mind to stay one-pointed for a long period of time, I would have attained *appanā samādhi* [attainment concentration]. It is a pity that I didn't know then that I was only a step away. What a missed opportunity! It is not so easy to direct the mind to reach [this state]. To put it bluntly, I could have killed myself for being so ignorant despite my schooling. (W, 27–28)

Wan thought about the life stories of those noble monks *(phra ariya jao)* of the past, so much different from his contemporaries. He believed that during the Buddha's time, people were ordained in order to practice meditation and free themselves from samsara (W, 32). Finally, Wan made up his mind to take up the meditative path.

During this same year (1943) Cha was studying at the monastic school in Muang Samsip District (Ubon Province). After passing the lowest naktham exam, he returned home to look after his dying father. When his father died, he went back to his naktham

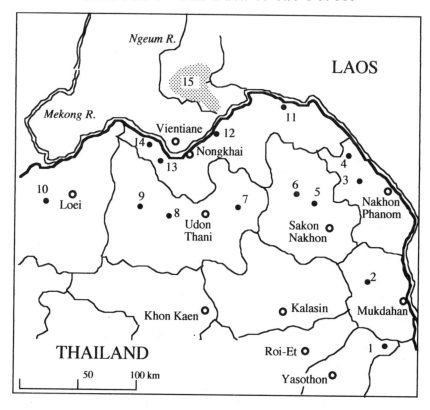

Figure 5. *Vicinities most suitable for thudong kammathan practice. Solid circles are district centers: 1. Loeng Noktha; 2. Khamcha-i; 3. Si Songkhram; 4. Ban Phaeng; 5. Phanna Nikhom; 6. Sawang Daendin; 7. Naung Han; 8. Naung Bua Lamphu; 9. Na Klang; 10. Wang Saphung; 11. Beung Kan; 12. Phon Phisai; 13. Tha Bau; 14. Si Chiangmai; 15. Phu Khao Khwai.*

Village Wat in his natal village, he became ill. Seeing that his relatives did not really care about him, he wondered what to do. He did not want to return to his studies in Ubon, since his friends and preceptor had left the monastic life, nor did he want to stay in this village wat any longer. Once he recovered from his illness, therefore, he gathered his *klot* (umbrella-tent), alms bowl, kettle, and bag and walked to where Man was staying in Mafai Tree Forest outside Kau Village.

Fan, Dun, Thet, and Li

Fan did not meet Ajan Man until 1920, when Man was about fifty years old. During that year Man and several other thudong monks and novices stayed near Egg Mango Village, Fan's natal village (in Phanna Nikhom District, Sakon Nakhon). At the time villagers there were following the Phu Thai tradition, directing their faith and ritual efforts toward guardian spirits of trees and mountains. In his dhamma talks Man explained how inadequate such beliefs and rituals were. He urged villagers to take refuge in the Triple Gem: the Buddha, the dhamma, and the sangha. Man's clear articulation of the dhamma impressed Fan and two other Phu Thai monks in the audience, Di and Ku.[57] The three of them decided to become disciples,[58] but Man went off without them. Lacking proper thudong gear, they could not follow him right away.[59]

At the same time Dun, who had been wandering along the Mekong River looking for Man, arrived at Egg Mango Village and stayed at Wat Phochai. So Di, Ku, and Fan studied the dhamma with Dun. Once the three monks acquired their thudong equipment, they set out with Dun to look for Man (F, 18). They walked to Khambok Village in High Pond District (now in Khamcha-i District, Nakhon Phanom Province). There they found that Man was at Sai Pond Village (Ban Huai Sai) and that he was on his way to Sawang Daendin District, Sakon Nakhon. The four village monks quickened their pace and caught up with him. Four years later, in 1925, Fan converted from his Phu Thai tradition to the Thammayut order. Fan was thirty-seven years old then and had been a wandering monk for seven or eight years.

Li met Ajan Man a couple of years later. In 1927 he left his Lao-tradition village wat—displeasing both his father and his preceptor, but they could not stop him—and walked to Muang Samsip. Upon arriving, he was told that Ajan Man was staying at Kuttat Village, a little over ten kilometers outside the town. Again Li set out on foot to find him (Li1, 7). He reached the forest hermitage at Kuttat Village only to find that Ajan Man had just returned to Wat Burapha in Ubon. So the next morning Li walked back to Ubon. At Wat Burapha, Li paid respects to Ajan Man and told him his purpose in seeking him out. Man taught him to meditate on the single word "buddho." It so happened that Man was ill at the time (he was then fifty-seven years old). So he sent Li to his senior disciple, Sing, who was staying at Stone Whirlpool Landing (Tha Wang Hin)—a very quiet and secluded area. With Sing were Maha Pin and forty other monks and novices. Young Thet was probably part of the group, although Li does not mention him in his memoirs.

Wan, La, Juan, and Cha

Although Wan may have heard about him much earlier (maybe from his grandmother, a mae chi), he came across Ajan Man quite by chance. This was in 1945, when Man was looking for a place to settle. By then he was seventy-six, too old for wandering. During that year Wan and a fellow Thammayut monk left their academic studies to wander without a fixed destination. They thought of going north toward Udon Thani and Nongkhai. But since traveling in these border provinces was not safe during the war, they wandered to the east of Sakon Nakhon. They stopped to rest at Lomkhao Mountain. The next day they reached Pheu Pond Village (Ban Naung Pheu), an isolated community in the heart of the Phuphan Mountains. The inhabitants of this community were Lao Yau. There they met Lui Janthasaro (1901–1989), a disciple of Man's, who was supervising the restoration of a deserted wat and turning it into a forest hermitage. Because Lui was planning to invite Ajan Man there, he would not let Wan stay at the hermitage; he explained that Man refused to stay where there were too many resident monks. So Wan and his companion stayed at a nearby village wat.

After Ajan Man took up residence at the Pheu Pond forest hermitage Wan came regularly to listen to his sermons. Later, Man heard from his lay supporters that the sangha head (Mahanikai) of Phanna Nikhom District did not want a large number of thudong monks to stay at the village wat. So Man took Wan into his forest hermitage for the 1945 rains retreat. Although Wan's companion changed his mind and returned to his naktham studies, Wan stayed with Man until the latter's death.

La met Ajan Man later that same year. Seeing no reason to remain as a village monk after his mother died, he went to see his nephew, who was secretary to Jum Phanthulo (then titled Phra

Thepkawi), abbot of Wat Phothisomphon in Udon Thani.[60] La heard about Ajan Man from this abbot, who converted him to the Thammayut order and then sent him to the Bodhi Victory Hermitage in Salt Water Pond Village (Ban Naung Namkhem), Udon Thani. The abbot of this hermitage, the seventy-two-year-old Bunmi, had practiced meditation under Man. At the end of the rains retreat La left to wander and train himself for meeting Man.[61] Like Wan, La served Man until the latter's death.

Juan, too, met Man in 1945. He was staying at Jik Field Village (Ban Na Jik), a new Thammayut wat in Pling Pond Commune (Amnat Charoen District, Ubon) when a high-level Thammayut monk, Ariyakhunathan (Seng Pusso), came to visit.[62] This senior monk took Juan with him by car as far as Sakon Nakhon, and from there they traveled by oxcart or on foot to Man's isolated samnak at Pheu Pond Village.[63] When Man and his disciples first met Juan, they looked at his light complexion and assumed he was Chinese, not Lao like them. Juan had to explain that he was a full-blooded Lao from Ubon (J, 28–29).

When Cha arrived at Man's hermitage, Wan and La were already there. It had taken him a while to find Man, perhaps because in Ubon he did not know anyone connected to the ajan. In his search, he came across a number of meditation teachers, none of whom was Thammayut. At first Cha started looking in his home province and found a monk named Man (not Ajan Man Phurithat) at Wat Philo in Det Udom District. Finding that this monk's method did not suit him, however, Cha left after ten days. In 1946, Cha's eighth year in the monkhood, he and a fellow monk wandered to Saraburi Province in central Thailand. He found the area there unsuitable for meditation practice, and he also failed to find meditation teachers there. From Saraburi he headed toward Wongkot Hill (in Lopburi Province), an area with a large population of Lao Phuan.[64] But here Cha found that the meditation teacher he was looking for had passed away.[65] In his place was a disciple named Wan, a thudong monk from Cambodia on his way to study in Burma. This Wan (not Wan Uttamo) was good at both theory and practice. Cha was particularly impressed that Wan took the vinaya seriously. Although Cha admired the sincerity and earnestness of the Khmer monk, he found that the meditation method did not suit him, so he experimented on his own while staying at Wongkot Hill.[66]

It was while he was at Wongkot Hill that Cha learned about Ajan Man from a layman. After spending two rains retreats there, Cha returned to the Northeast to look for Ajan Man. Three other monks, two novices, and two laymen went with him. They practiced thudong according to the Lao tradition: studying with various meditation teachers and paying respects to stupas along the way. It was a very long, hard trip on foot. They went to Ubon first, stayed for a while, and then walked to Nakhon Phanom. It took them ten days' walking under a hot sun to reach the Phanom Stupa. Cha was not in a hurry to meet Ajan Man. He stopped along the way to study meditation with other teachers. For instance, he stayed briefly at Khau Mountain in Na Kae District to practice under Ajan Saun. He was not impressed with Saun's method, however. At this point the novice and the two laymen were too exhausted to walk to Sakon Nakhon, so they dropped out and returned to their home village. Cha and two monks walked on to Sakon Nakhon, where they finally arrived at Pheu Pond Village. Man asked Cha about his previous teachers. It turned out that Man knew of Ajan Phao. Although Cha stayed with Man for only two days, he took up the ajan's method.[67] By then Man was seventy-nine years old. A year later, in 1949, he died, after which his disciples dispersed and went wandering on their own. Today Pheu Pond hermitage is in Nanai Subdistrict, Phanna Nikhom District, Sakon Nakhon. It did not become an official Thammayut monastery until 1982. It is now named Wat Pa Phurithat after Man's Pali name.[68]

Having surveyed the ten monks' backgrounds, it would be appropriate to put forward some general conclusions. But no clear pattern emerges. The few generalities we can discover are only mildly informative and tell us little about why these ten young men became thudong monks: they were natives of the Northeast, their parents were Lao, they grew up in large families, they were sons of farmers, and they were accustomed to working hard, to living near the wilderness, and to traveling through forests. These characteristics they shared with the vast majority of their contemporaries in the Northeast, who of course did not follow their calling. No sociological pattern or personality structure stands out: not birth order within the family, not poverty, not childhood experience of loss or crisis (perhaps with the exception of Waen, who had no close relations with his kinsmen). One character trait that separates these ten monks from other people is that they were all deeply attracted to discipline and the ascetic life. They were conscious of the thudong tradition as the right path and were not tempted by prestige or status conferred through ranks and titles, which drew many regional monks into Bangkok's ecclesiastical hierarchy.

These thudong monks differed from monks who followed Bangkok's path in their character and religious outlook. They believed that the practice of wandering mendicants went back to the Buddha's time. They knew that if they studied the dhamma without practicing it, they would remain unaware of its deeper meaning. They realized that the value of the dhamma was not to be found in reading and studying but in training the mind through the thudong life.[69] Finally, they understood that the best place to study the Buddha's teaching was not in a comfortable monastery but in their own school, their own "university" (as Bua calls it): the heart of the forest, a grove, the shade of a single tree, the cemetery, the open air, the slope of a mountain, the foot of a mountain, a valley. They believed that such places were recommended by the Buddha as the supreme university.[70] The next chapters will explore these aspects of the thudong monks' training.

CHAPTER 3

Facing Fear

During the Forest-Community Period, the North and Northeast were sparsely populated. Paved roads were few. Vast tracts of the land were covered by forests that were home to elephants, tigers, clouded leopards, black panthers, bears, wild buffaloes, gaurs,[1] bantengs, boars, and snakes. These animals ruled not only the wilderness but also the fears and fantasies dwelling in every monk's and villager's imagination. As Ajan Man told his disciples, until a monk actually faces these animals, he will never know how much or how little he fears them. In the North and Northeast, too, spirit worship was a major part of the indigenous culture. Fear of ghosts was so ingrained that it remained intact even after young men entered the monkhood. If one wanted to live a thudong kamma-than life and work toward spiritual liberation, the fear of ghosts and of wandering alone in the forest needed to be rooted out.

One of the thirteen thudong practices requires that practitioners stay in the forest for prolonged periods of time, and this practice was observed by all ten thudong monks discussed here. For all of them, advancing along the path of dhamma meant developing the mind. Since fear discourages the aspirant and dissuades him from seeking seclusion, staying in the wild was a proven method for reducing and eventually eliminating this *kilesa* (defilement).[2] The deep forest and the forest cemetery were thus training grounds for the thudong monk, who saw himself as a "warrior battling the

unwholesome forces inside" for the sake of spiritual liberation.³
To survive, the monk had to rely on his individual skill, experience,
and knowledge, although *kamma* (karma) had its part to play.

TIGERS

The tiger occupies a conspicuous place in the monks' accounts of
their life in the forest. The monks regarded this animal with a
mixture of fear and respect. Fear of tigers and the vivid imagining
of oneself being devoured by tigers often drove the mind to one-
pointed *samādhi* (concentration).

Samādhi, a thudong master explains, "is a gathering of the
mind's energies so that they have great strength, able to uproot
attachments ... and to cleanse the mind so that it is, for the
moment, bright and clear."⁴ Any of the forty meditation methods
that the Buddha taught could, if practiced seriously, bring the
mind to samādhi. The chosen meditation practice varied according to the temperaments of teachers and disciples.⁵ The concentration method that Ajan Man taught his disciples was the recitation
of the mantra "buddho."

In the early stage of his training, a monk or novice stayed with
his teacher; he participated in daily rituals, received instruction,
and learned by observing. During this stage the disciples depended
on the teacher for inner guidance. If a monk was afraid of tigers,
Ajan Man sometimes put him deep into the forest, at some distance from the other monks. At night, when fear attacked his
mind, a monk would force himself to do walking meditation in
the open.⁶ Each monk slept on a platform built by villagers, high
enough off the ground to discourage tigers from leaping on them.⁷

Thudong masters believed that this method of learning the
dhamma was far more difficult than studying scriptures.⁸ In the
wilds a student had to be ever cautious of lurking dangers, which
forced him to be constantly alert. He was defenseless except for
his mind, which could fix itself on a theme of meditation or a recitation of "buddho" until, as Ajan Man said, the mind became
"absorbed in dhamma." Man's theory was that at such a critical
moment, strong concentration would develop or deepen, and further wisdom or insight would occur. In the battle between fear
and dhamma, as Man's biographer observes, "If the fear is de-

feated the mind will be overwhelmed by courage and enjoy profound inner peace. If fear is the victor, it will multiply itself rapidly and prodigiously. The whole body will be enveloped by both a perspiring heat and a chilling cold, by the desire to pass urine and to defecate. The monk will be suffocated by fear and will look more like a dying than a living man."[9]

In their second stage of training, a monk wandered with other monks or novices and practiced the meditation method learned from the master. Living in the forest, monks developed finely tuned senses and became experts in using their eyes, ears, and nose. Some of Fan's and Cha's experiences illustrate how the monks dealt with their fear when they heard, glimpsed, or encountered tigers, and how each situation served as an exercise in mindfulness and concentration.

During his fourth year of wandering, Fan took his nephew (a novice) along with him. One day, as they were walking along a forest trail parallel to the Mekong River, Fan spotted tiger tracks and droppings, some of them recent. As dusk was falling, they heard the snarling and growling of tigers ahead of and behind them.[10] To keep calm Fan and the novice meditated while walking, but they were disturbed and had difficulty concentrating. They were afraid that the tiger would attack at any moment.

To boost his courage, Fan recited an old saying: "Should a tiger kill cattle, it's no big news, but should it devour a villager or a thudong monk, the news spreads far and wide" (F, 22). The recitation made him feel brave; he was ready to face any kind of danger. He thought, "A monk who is afraid of wild animals is not an authentic thudong monk." He reassured his nephew, "When we have mindfulness, the mind is at peace. It's not afraid of danger. Even if we're devoured by a tiger, we will not suffer" (F, 24). As it turned out, Fan and the novice saw no tigers on this trip.

Some monks deliberately put themselves into risky situations to learn about the mind. While wandering with a fellow monk and young boys on a forested mountain, Cha remembered an old saying, "When in a forest, do not sleep on a trail" (C3, 39). He thought about this and decided to test it out. That night he set up his klot on a forest track. The other monk set up his klot away from the trail, while the two young disciples agreed to stay halfway between them. They all sat in meditation for a while before they retired to their klots for the night. Cha, concerned that the boys might be scared, raised his mosquito net over the top of his klot so they could see him from where they lay. Then he lay down on the track with the mosquito net suspended above him. Off the path behind him was the wilderness, ahead of him was the village. Such a dangerous situation provides the monk with an opportunity to contemplate whatever takes place in his own mind. While Cha was concentrating on his breath before falling asleep, he heard leaves rustling.

> Slowly the animal stalked closer . . . and closer until I could hear its breathing. In that moment the *citta* [mind] told me, "A tiger is coming." It couldn't possibly be another animal. The way it walked and the breathing gave it away. Knowing that it was indeed a tiger . . . I couldn't help thinking about death. In that instant the *citta* told me not to worry: even if the tiger doesn't kill you, you're going to die anyway. It's more meaningful to die for the dhamma. I'm ready . . . to become a tiger's meal. If we are bound to one another through kamma [*khu wen khu kam*], let it kill me. But if we aren't kammically connected, it won't harm me. With this in mind, I took refuge in the Triple Gem. Having done so, the mind was free from worrying. As it turned out, the tiger stopped pacing. I heard only its breath . . . about six meters away. While lying there, I listened carefully. Who knows, it might be thinking, "Who is . . . sleeping on my track?" After a while it moved off. Its footfalls became fainter and fainter until the forest fell silent.[11]

This account reflects Cha's firm belief in kamma, which kept him calm and possibly saved his life. From this incident Cha learned that once he let go of attachment to life, he was no longer afraid of death and was able to remain calm. He also learned that it sometimes makes sense to heed old sayings.

If a monk continued to lean on the teacher, on a friend, or on a group, he would never become wise. In his third stage of training, the monk wandered by himself, living alone on a mountain, in a cave, or under a tree in a forest. At times the thudong monk might end up being alone not by his own choice but by force of circumstance. This is what happened to Fan.

In 1925 Fan traveled to Phrabat Buabok, the "Buddha's foot-print" at Buabok (a hill in Udon Thani), to meet two other thu-dong monks. But when he reached Phak Bung Village at the foot of the hill, the two had already left, so Fan spent the next five days meditating alone on the mountain. One day, while walking uphill, he was startled by an unusual noise. It sounded like a big animal digging in the ground. As the thought of a tiger entered his mind, he froze. Although the encounter was sudden, Fan's quick reac-tion indicates his strong mindfulness:

> Within seconds he concentrated his mind so it wouldn't react to the situation. The animal raised its head out of the thick brush. "It's a tiger all right," he thought, "and judging from the size of its head it must be huge."
>
> Seeing the tiger he felt a chill run up his spine. Sweat broke out on his face. Intuitively he knew that if he turned his back and started running he would be killed. The tiger would cer-tainly attack him. So he focused his mind to face the critical sit-uation calmly, even though his breathing was not as relaxed as usual. The tiger took one glance at him, gave a loud growl, and leaped into the forest. (F, 39)

In the early decades of this century, villagers who lived in or near the forests accepted the presence of tigers as natural and inevitable. Accounts left by Thet, Li, and Chaup illustrate the extent to which the tiger once dominated the hearts and minds of thudong monks as well as villagers.

In late 1936 Thet spent a meditation retreat by himself near a Lahu village on a mountain in northern Siam. He was about thirty-four years old then and had been wandering in the wilds for many years. Hearing a tiger's growl was nothing new, but this time, alone in a hut outside the village, he was stricken with fear. He could neither sleep nor focus his mind in meditation. He heard villagers fire a shot into the air, and he saw them throw firebrands at the tiger. But the animal was undeterred. It showed no fear of humans. After retreating for a while, it came back at the crack of dawn and sat on the trail used by the villagers. When the villagers spotted the tiger, they all fled. The tiger did not pursue them, however. Thet, who admitted that he had had a nervous disorder since childhood, remembers how frightened he was:

I sat down to meditate, but my mind wouldn't focus. At the time I did not know that the mind was terrified of the tiger. My body sweated so much that perspiration streamed down. . . . Why all the sweating when it was so cold? Spread the robe and kept covered but the body kept trembling. The mind was too exhausted to meditate. Thought of lying down for a while before trying to meditate again. When I was about to recline, the tiger roared again. I was shaking as if I had a jungle fever. Only then did I realize that the mind refused to focus out of sheer fright. Immediately I sat up and cajoled my mind to have courage to face death if it came. Then the mind became calm . . . no longer heard the sound of the tiger. At times when hearing the tiger again my mind simply ignored its roar. Like the wind making contact with an object, it's just noise. (T2, 72)

Thet's experience confirmed Ajan Man's belief that living among tigers and hearing them roar nearby was the best thing that could happen to a thudong monk. Man meant that monks who were frightened of tigers or other wild animals had not yet realized the truth of the dhamma. Fright was the response of the ordinary, untrained mind, while the mind with knowledge and insight into the Four Noble Truths knows the tiger's growl as simply sound. As Cha explains, "The sound arises and we simply note it. This is called truly knowing the arising of sense objects. If we develop 'buddho,' clearly realising the sound as sound, then it does not [frighten] us. . . . It's just sound. The mind lets go" (C2, 70). For the thudong monks, the clear and penetrative knowing of buddho indicated an awakened knowledge.

Ajan Man often sent young disciples out alone so they could "realize buddho." In 1932, at the age of twenty-six, Li was sent to meditate alone on Thumb Mountain (Doi Khau Mau), in Lamphun Province. Local people believed that a fierce spirit inhabited the summit. Though afraid, Li forced himself to climb the mountain. On his way to the top, he stopped at an abandoned temple and stayed there for two nights. Like Thet, Li recalls how fear could drive the mind into deep samādhi:

People had told me that whenever the lunar sabbath came around a bright light would often appear there. It was deep in the forest, though—and the forest was full of elephants and tigers. I walked in alone, feeling both brave and scared, but confident in the power of the Dhamma and of my teacher.

. . . The first night, nothing happened. The second night, at about one or two in the morning, a tiger came—which meant that I didn't get any sleep the whole night. I sat in meditation, scared stiff, while the tiger walked around and around my klot. My body felt all frozen and numb. I started chanting, and the words came out like running water. All the old chants I had forgotten now came back to me, thanks both to my fear and to my ability to keep my mind under control. I sat like this from 2 until 5 A.M., when the tiger finally left.[12]

In the morning Li went for alms in a settlement consisting of two houses. A man working in his garden told him that a tiger had killed one of his oxen the night before.

Having lived in the wilds for so long, Thet also knew that a tiger could attack massive animals like a gaur or a large deer. In 1937, when he was spending a meditation retreat near a Lahu village, his strong mindfulness enabled him to see how unyielding a tiger could be: "One night a tiger came to attack a buffalo near my kuti. I banged a piece of wood and shouted loudly to chase the tiger away. But the tiger wouldn't let go, and it managed to drag the buffalo away. This time I wasn't frightened, but I dared not step out to rescue the buffalo for fear of being eaten too."[13]

Sometimes a wandering monk deliberately put himself in a risky position by traveling at night. One such monk was Chaup,[14] considered by his fellow monks to be most adventurous. Walking alone through a forest forced him to be constantly alert and aware. He often ran into nocturnal tigers on the prowl. Once while wandering in northern Siam, Chaup set out in the direction of Lom Sak in Phetchabun Province. Approaching the Great Forest (Dong Yai) one afternoon, he met some villagers who invited him to spend the night in their village and continue his journey the following morning. Concerned for his safety, they warned him that the forest was large and that ferocious tigers inhabited it. If he entered it that afternoon, night would catch him there. Tigers had killed travelers who had spent the night in the forest, they said. But despite their advice and concern, Chaup insisted on going. Like Cha, Chaup believed that if he became a tiger's meal, then that was his kamma. And he told the village folk so.

Traveling alone, Chaup was able to take acute notice of his environment. He had not gone far when he came across tiger tracks and saw both fresh and old droppings everywhere. Noticing the spoor, he fixed his mind on his recitation while walking. At nightfall, when he was still in the middle of the forest, he heard two tigers growl. As they moved nearer their roars became deafening. Suddenly a tiger emerged on the trail walking toward him. Chaup stopped, turned, and saw another tiger approaching from behind. Each moved to within two meters of him. They were the biggest tigers he had ever seen. Each of them looked as big as a horse, its head about forty centimeters wide. Seeing no way out, Chaup stood motionless, his feet frozen, thinking this was to be the end of him.

> At that critical moment, mindfulness came to his rescue. Determined not to abandon sati even though he might be killed by the tigers, his mind withdrew from the tigers, dwelt within, and became one-pointed. Intuitively Chaup knew then that the tigers could never kill him. In an instant he was oblivious to the tigers, to his body, to his standing position, and to everything around him. His mind withdrew completely into a deep concentration and remained there for several hours. When he came out of his concentration, he found himself standing at the same spot, with the klot on one shoulder and the alms-bowl in its sling across another shoulder, the lantern still in one hand but the candle long since out. He lit another candle, but no tigers were to be seen. The forest was quiet.[15]

After emerging from his samādhi, Chaup was surprised that he was still in one piece, untouched by the tigers. His mind was filled with courage and compassion. "He felt that he would be able to face hundreds of tigers, now that he knew the power of the mind. He felt great love for those two tigers, who were really friends in disguise, for having 'lifted' him to the dhamma and for helping him to realize its wonders" (M1, 296). Chaup's life may have been saved by his ability to concentrate deeply, which allowed him to stand still for several hours.[16]

Chaup continued on his journey. Overjoyed by his discovery, he continued to meditate while walking. At about 9 A.M. he reached the edge of the forest. Approaching a small village, he put on his outer robe, set down his thudong gear, and began his almsround. The sight of a thudong monk coming out of the forest in the morning surprised the villagers. They knew that he must have spent the night there. Many came outside to offer him food and to inquire how he had managed to come through the Great Forest unharmed. The biographer concludes that it was the power of the dhamma that enabled Chaup not only to survive his encounter with the tigers but also to find his way through the forest.

The following recollection illustrates how thudong monks accepted tigers as a natural and inescapable part of their lives. Juan, his fellow monks Khaw, Saun, Bunthan, and some lay practitioners stayed in the vicinity of tigers when they were practicing in Golden Pot Forest.[17] They lived in stark simplicity. Juan and Saun built huts on rock outcrops, shelves of stone about five meters wide, over twenty meters long, and fifteen meters high. Below their platforms, which stood parallel to each other like two stone walls, was a pond where wild animals came to find food and water. From his thatched hut on the rock platform, Juan could see wild boars, elephants, tigers, barking deer, and bears. One afternoon he saw at least ten wild elephants by the pond and heard the rest of the herd breaking bamboo and *yang* trees in the grove. It was not unusual to hear tigers howling or see them prowling about the huts.

> One night the monks got together in a kuti to recite the patimok. Heard tigers play-fighting with each other by the rock near the hut. Judging from the noise there must have been several of them. From the time the monks began to recite the patimok until they finished, the tigers remained at the same spot and the growling did not let up. Ven. Grandfather Khaw was so annoyed that he told them to shut up, though in an affectionate way: "Hey, you guys, stop being so loud. The monks are listening to the dhamma. This is not a place to play. Listen to me, or you'll all go to hell." They quieted down a bit but still growled for a while longer.[18]

This incident confirms Man's teaching that "If you are terrified of tigers, be where the tigers are, and make friends with them."

It appears that Khaw had succeeded in putting this advice into practice.

The younger thudong monks, however, were still learning from their experiences. In the forest, no hut was completely safe from animals. The monks had to live according to the laws of nature, and nature is unpredictable. They learned that the rule of survival was to always be mindful and alert for any surprise visit. Juan remembers an occasion when "Bunthan, a fellow monk, was about to step out of his kuti [and] saw a big tiger sitting on the steps. He had to wait for quite a while until the tiger went away before he could get out of his hut." He also recalls the time when "the monk Saun and a novice had diarrhea. They ran to the latrine, but the novice got there first. The monk couldn't restrain his urge so he went in the bush. As he was squatting a tiger leaped over his head—which set every nerve in his body tingling. The tiger ran toward the latrine. Hearing the sound, the novice quickly fled. Luckily, the tiger ran off into the forest, and the boy didn't have to face it."[19]

WILD ELEPHANTS

Wild elephants also occupy a conspicuous place in the monks' recollections. The inexperienced monk learned from his thudong teacher how to handle encounters with these formidable animals. Aware of the elephant's intelligence, a thudong monk would first try to reason with it. During the 1930s, for example, Ajan Man and two disciples—Khaw and Maha Thaungsuk—were wandering in the North.[20] One day, while approaching a narrow pass in the mountains, they came upon a bull elephant, its tusks about two meters long. The elephant was eating bamboo; it was facing away from the monks and completely blocking the path. There was no way to get around it. The monks stopped five meters from the animal and consulted with one another. Man asked Khaw, who had some affinity with elephants, to handle the situation. Realizing that it was they who were trespassing in the elephant's territory, Khaw addressed the animal with respect and humility: "Big brother! I'd like to talk to you." The elephant immediately stopped eating and turned around to face the three monks. Though standing still, its ears were spread in full alert for any danger. Khaw spoke again. "Great, powerful brother! I'd like to talk to you. We monks are powerless and so are afraid of you. We'd be grateful if you'd let us pass. As long as you stand there like this, we can't possibly go forward."[21] As Thaungsuk tells it, upon hearing Khaw's voice the elephant moved into the bamboo clump and buried its long tusks in the thicket. Then the monks mindfully walked past it in single file, Khaw ahead, Man in the middle, and Thaungsuk in the rear. Only half a meter separated them from the huge animal. Thaungsuk's fear may have distracted him. As he approached the elephant, the hook on his klot got caught in the tangled twigs of bamboo branches. Man and Khaw turned back and watched. Thaungsuk, untangling the hook, was in a sweat. Uneasy and apprehensive he kept glancing at the animal. As soon as he freed his klot, they continued on. Khaw turned around to thank the elephant. "My big brother, we have already passed. Now you are free to go on with your eating." The elephant, breathing heavily, withdrew its huge tusks from the bamboo clump.

Later, at their shelter, the monks talked about the incident. Thaungsuk admitted that while walking past the elephant, he was preoccupied with the thought that it might change its mind and charge them for amusement. Man reproached him, "There you are, distracted by your own wild thoughts. If your mind were equally industrious and tireless in thinking about the truth it would be far better for you, but such is the habit of most people. They like to cherish thoughts that only cause them trouble and then neglect to think about the truth" (M1, 162).

Juan, too, had a close encounter with an elephant when he stayed at the edge of Pot Village Forest (Dong Ban Mau) in Wanon Niwat District, Sakon Nakhon Province. This was in 1951, when elephants, tigers, and bears still roamed the forest. Juan spent a meditation retreat with a fellow monk, staying in a couple of huts that villagers had built for them in the forest. One night Juan was awakened by the sound of wild elephants crashing through the forest. Through the darkness he could see a herd of elephants coming toward him. A big bull elephant stopped about six or seven meters from his hut. "It must be the leader of the herd," Juan thought. "It's gigantic, like a huge wall in front of my kuti" (J, 51). The elephant let out a loud, shrill trumpeting sound and began to thrash the brush and to paw the ground. It was a terrifying sight to see in the middle of the night. Juan was scared and almost lost his mindfulness:

> [I] felt goose bumps all over. My heart almost stopped. Felt dizzy, and frightened. Broke out in sweat. The body was shaking as if possessed by a spirit. Got up and lit a torch with shaky hands. Took a while to strike the match. Stepped outside, carried the torch with trembling hands. It is said that elephants are afraid of light. Wonder if it's true? What if, having seen the light, it charges?
>
> One thought said, "If the elephant approaches I'll jump up into a tree." Another thought argued, "You are a meditation monk. Why be afraid of an elephant? The elephant is not afraid of you. You have devoted your life to the thudong kammathan tradition. You are a human being and superior, and you're also a monk. The elephant is an animal and it's not afraid of you. If you're afraid you're worse than an elephant."[22]

Having thus encouraged himself, Juan regained his mindfulness. Taking refuge in the Triple Gem, he went back inside his hut and started to meditate on death. As his mind became calmer, fear gradually decreased until it disappeared completely. With his concentrated mind Juan was able to see things in a new light, the light of wisdom: "I was no longer afraid of elephants or death. The mind was cool, calm, full of courage, and cheerful. Felt grateful to the elephant, who taught me to face death, to contemplate dying. It was probably still lingering outside. I thought about the elephant with compassion and pity. The focused mind must have a very strong power. Within seconds the elephant trumpeted as if it had been hit by something, an explosive sound that vibrated throughout the whole forest. It then walked away into the forest, ripping up trees as it went. In the morning one could see the traces of broken branches. From then on no other elephants approached us" (J, 52).

Juan's experiential wisdom attests to Man's belief that the mind that dwells on the dhamma is "equipped with self-protection." It can hold its ground despite attacks of fear, and then will come courage (M1, 66).

Another incident illustrates how a lay ascetic, without the

monk's depth of practice, reacted to a sudden encounter with an elephant. A *pha khaw* (white-robed renunciate)[23] was on a thudong with Khaw, Saun, and Juan—the same trip during which the monks had their run-ins with tigers. Khaw's hut was built on a rocky area thick with vegetation, and the pha khaw had built his hut deep in this bush. "One day a wild elephant got into the area and walked to the pha khaw's hut. Using its trunk, it picked up the man's slippers [left outside] and threw them into the forest. It also tossed the ladder away. Then it reached its trunk into the hut but couldn't find anything to grab. Just before it walked away it pushed the wall with its trunk, which set the hut shaking. The pha khaw was hard of hearing so he didn't hear the elephant's activities until the hut started swaying. As soon as he saw the wild elephant, he jumped out of his hut and ran to Luang Pu Khaw, so terrified and shaken he couldn't talk. It took [Khaw] quite a while to calm him down and find out what had happened" (J, 58).

In a life-threatening situation such as this, a layperson might flee, but not the wandering monk. Juan, together with four other monks and novices, returned to the area to spend the rains retreats in 1957 and 1958. The liveliness and spontaneity of living in the wilderness domain appealed to them. They found it conducive to their meditation practice because the wild kept them alert. They also felt at home there. As Juan tells us, "The monks, novices, and wild animals shared the same area. Each did his own duty and we all coexisted peacefully" (J, 62–63).

THE POWER OF THE DHAMMA

What gave thudong monks confidence when wandering alone through dense forests or high mountains? In addition to strong mindfulness, four convictions were instrumental in protecting them.

First, they believed in the merit of the thudong practice: if they strictly adhered to sīla and its precepts, the dhamma would protect them. With the thudong robe draped over their bodies, they felt they could face any danger. After their sudden encounter with the elephant Man told his disciples, "Seeing the color of our robes, the elephant knew that we were harmless to him."[24]

Second, the thudong monks had trust in their ajan. They

believed that he would not send them off to a wholly unfamiliar place. Previous thudong teachers had survived sojourns in the caves or the mountains where they stayed. When Ajan Man sent young Li to meditate alone on a mountain in Lamphun, he told Li that although the mountain was guarded by a fierce spirit, it would not harm dhamma practitioners.

Third, the monks had faith in the law of kamma and in the good they had done by not harming any creatures, no matter how small. La's account is an example of the monk's belief in the protective power of *metta* (loving-kindness). In his wandering La often came across big snakes. When he told Ajan Man about his instinctive fear of snakes, the teacher responded, "Why be afraid? If you're devoured by a snake, simply brace your feet against its stomach wall" (La, 127). Man probably meant that then the snake would not be able to swallow La all the way down. He was surely joking, but his reply suggests that his meditation training had enabled Man to overcome much fear. He wanted La to understand that encountering a snake need not be a horrible experience. After Ajan Man's death, La went to southern Thailand, and here he put Man's advice to the test. In 1953, while wandering in Phangnga Province, the local villagers guided La to a rock shelter at Turtle Mountain Cave (Tham Khao Tao). The shelter had a platform for sitting or sleeping, raised half a meter off the ground. Here La spent a week meditating. "Arrived in the afternoon and lay down for a rest under an overhanging rock," he recalls. "A big snake came crawling from the north along the cliff to the edge of my platform. Slowly it crept forward and raised its body half a meter off the ground. Its eyes were as big as my thumb. I sat up with my legs folded on the platform. By now its head was less than an arm's length away. Its body was over four meters long and about ten centimeters in diameter. It looked at me quietly." La was afraid, yet he observed the snake carefully. Then he waved his hands at the snake and said, "Go away. Go over there. Why suspect me? I send metta to you every day... Not only to you, but to all sentient beings, which I consider as fellow beings... May all beings be happy. Go. .... Go." The snake then crawled toward the spirit shrine nearby and eventually went into a deep hole underneath the rock shelter. "About ten minutes later it came right back, approaching the edge of the platform. More mindful this time, [I] spoke while waving my arm at the snake, 'Go, go, go, go away. Don't you hear me? I'm not here to dig any treasure from the earth or the water. Go away.' The snake moved backward one handbreadth, its tail pointed forward, and then went back into the hole" (La, 238–239).

La seems to have thought that the snake might be a guardian spirit of a treasure in the area. But after he pondered the incident, La decided that the snake was neither a spirit nor a *devata* (deity) in disguise. He thought that the snake might be connected to him through past kamma *(khu sang barami)* and wanted to test the extent of his fear by seeing if he would grab a stick to hit it. La believed that he was saved by the power of the Triple Gem and also the purity of his heart, which held no harmful intentions toward the animals.

A fourth source of the thudong monks' confidence was their belief that tigers, wild elephants, and snakes were devatas or guardian spirits that had disguised themselves as animals and had come to test the depth of a monk's understanding and faith. Another of Chaup's encounters illustrates this belief. In the late 1930s Chaup wandered into the Shan states. On one occasion he went to meditate alone in a mountain cave. After a period of sitting meditation one evening, he opened his eyes and saw a big tiger sitting at the entrance of the cave. Perhaps because of his frequent encounters with tigers in the past, Chaup was not afraid this time. Both man and beast looked at each other silently. After a few moments, the tiger casually leaped to a flat rock near the mouth of the cave about two meters away. Chaup observed the tiger mindfully. Oblivious to the monk, it started cleaning itself and licking its paws. Having cleaned itself, it rested on the rock, sitting like a dog. Although Chaup had no conscious fear of the tiger, according to his biographer, "he admitted that he was unable to do his usual walking meditation at the cave entrance: this would bring him too close to the rock where the tiger was reclining. He could not help feeling uneasy, so he continued his sitting meditation on the small platform inside the cave. He thought that the tiger would not stay there very long, but to his disappointment it appeared that the tiger was taking up permanent residence there" (M2, 394).

When dusk fell, Chaup lit a candle and noticed that the tiger paid no attention to the light. He hung his mosquito net over his klot, went inside the klot, and sat in meditation until it was time to rest. He woke up around 3 A.M., put the mosquito net away, and lit a candle. The tiger was still lying there. Now it was time to go for alms. To get out of the cave he would have to pass within a meter of the tiger. Putting his robe on, Chaup kept glancing at the tiger and saw that it was watching him. "Its eyes are as soft as a dog watching its master," Chaup thought. Preparing to leave the cave, the monk spoke to the tiger calmly, "It's time for me to go on my almsround. I need food to sustain my body, as all animals and people do. Please allow me to leave. You may stay here or go out for your own food, as you wish." He then walked out of the cave, passing the rock where the tiger lay.

Chaup went to a nearby hamlet for alms food, but he did not mention the tiger for fear that it would upset the householders. By the time he returned to the cave the tiger was gone. Reflecting on the situation, Chaup thought that this particular tiger must have been a devata who had taken the form of a tiger to test him. In the nights that followed he often heard tigers growling, but the animal did not return while he was staying there.[25] In this case Chaup was probably saved by his sati, specifically his mindful movements around the tiger.

The experiences of these thudong monks who survived in the wilderness confirmed their beliefs in the power of the dhamma. As Man told his disciples, "From such a mind an attacker will draw back, be it a tiger, a snake, or an elephant. The aspirant may even be able to walk right up to it. His attitude toward animals is based on metta, which has a mysterious but real and profound influence. It is true that animals do not know this, but they can feel and sense it. This is the power of dhamma which gives protection to the aspirant, meanwhile softening or neutralizing the ferocity of the animals. This is the mysterious power of mind which is self-evident but which is still difficult for others to realize who have not yet developed to the same level."[26]

Dangerous animals seem to have an inexplicable forbearance toward forest monks. The monks themselves were often surprised that the wild beasts, supposedly fearsome, did not harm them. In Phuang's view, "Tigers never attack thudong monks. Often a tiger will just stalk past a klot or quietly lie down beside it, so close that the monk can hear its heavy breathing. The tiger simply ignores the monk."[27]

Occasionally wandering monks were attacked, of course. Dun had a near miss with a wild water buffalo[28] near the border between Cambodia and Siam. In 1934, when he was forty-six years old, Dun took two disciples with him on a trip to Cambodia. They walked along the Dong Rak Range toward Phra Wihan Hill and Krasan District in Cambodia. On one occasion when they were traveling through dense forest, Dun walking ahead and the novices following, a wild buffalo appeared from nowhere and charged them from behind. The two novices quickly climbed a tree, but the buffalo knocked Dun down. Luckily he was not seriously injured, but his robes were torn. The young novices were badly frightened.[29] But, as a result of the event, they learned from their teacher a practical as well as a spiritual skill: how to fall down while maintaining mindfulness. The thudong monk teaches by example, and the students that travel with him see him in all aspects and in many different situations. This increases their respect for him, since often their lives depend on his survival skills.

Not all attacks ended with a scrape and a fall. Some monks—we have no way of knowing how many—were killed by wild animals while traveling alone. Occasionally a thudong monk would find some scattered robes and a bowl in a forest or in a cave. The monk might have died from disease or from an unlucky encounter with a tiger or python. The following incident was told by Khaung, a thudong monk who lost his way while wandering in the mountains in Loei Province.[30] In those days this terrain was wild and rugged; locals believed that anyone who lost his way was surely in trouble, since he would have to stay overnight surrounded by wild animals. Khaung ended up spending the night halfway up a mountain. Continuing his travels in the morning, he came upon a heap of bones, an alms bowl, and some thudong gear. The robe and klot were badly torn but the bowl was intact. Khaung had no idea how the thudong monk had died. But he vowed that if he found his way out of the forest, he would ask lay devotees to make merit for the deceased monk. After walking for a while he eventually found a trail that led to a hamlet. To fulfill his vow, he went back with some villagers and made merit for three days and three nights on the spot where the thudong monk died.

To ordinary people, the practices adopted by the thudong kammathan monks might seem unnecessarily risky, but from the thudong teacher's perspective living in the forest was indispensable to
spiritual liberation. The monks' belief in the merit of their thudong practice set them apart from monks who followed Bangkok's path. It led them to accept risks willingly, even the risk of
death. As Man told his disciples, "The Dhamma is on the other
side of death. Without crossing that threshold there can be no
hope of realizing that Dhamma."[31]

CHARNEL GROUNDS

All ten wandering monks observed another important thudong
practice, that of staying in a charnel ground. In the past, cemeteries were not like they are today. As one thudong monk describes
them, "Unburied bodies were scattered all over the place—old
bodies and new, scattered around like logs. When you saw them,
you'd see clear evidence with your own eyes."[32] Of our ten monks,
only Cha and Li have described their experiences at a forest cemetery in detail. All thudong monks, however, mention their encounter with ghosts or local spirits. Such experiences were not unusual,
since the monks grew up in villages where belief in ghosts and
spirits came naturally.

When a wandering monk arrived in a village at dusk, the inhabitants would often lead him to a cemetery or to a tract of forest
that they believed was inhabited by malevolent spirits.[33] The villagers did not always tell the monk where they were taking him;
they decided this among themselves without consulting the monk.
Although not all thudong monks would choose to stay in a cemetery, they usually complied with the villagers' wishes. In fact, the
experienced monks often sought such a place, generally avoided
by others, so they could practice meditation undisturbed. For those
monks who were afraid of ghosts, the experience was often trans-
formative—as the following example illustrates.

Man told about an unnamed disciple who, during his wanderings, came upon a village at dusk.[34] Unfamiliar with the area, he
asked the inhabitants for a suitable place to stay. The village folk
guided him to a forest but did not tell him that it contained a cemetery. The first night he rested peacefully. On the following day he

saw the villagers pass by carrying a corpse, which was later cremated on a pyre a few meters from the spot where he had set up his klot. The burning of the remains took place right before his eyes. After the villagers left at nightfall, he was tormented by fear. Neither recitation nor meditation on death would help. When he closed his eyes to meditate, all he saw was a long line of ghosts coming toward him. After several hours of this, he reminded himself that as a thudong monk, he should be fearless, able to face death, ghosts, and any other danger, and that if he succumbed to this haunting fear, he would be a disgrace to the thudong tradition. So, confronting his fear, he approached the burning corpse.

> Putting on his robes, he started toward the funeral pyre, but after a few steps he couldn't move. It was as if his feet had been nailed to the ground. His heart pounded, and his body perspired as if it were exposed to the noonday sun. Through sheer strength of will he managed to drag himself to the pyre. "Whatever is going to happen, let it happen," he said to himself.
>
> He forced himself to look at the partly burnt corpse. He almost fainted when he saw the skull burned white through long exposure to the fire. But, fighting his fear, he sat down facing the corpse a few feet away and made it the theme of his meditation. He forced the mind to recite: "I'm destined to die like this corpse. Why should I be afraid? I'm going to die sooner or later. What's the point of being afraid?" (M1, 46; M2, 59–60)

While focusing on the recitation, still struggling with his fear of ghosts, the monk heard a strange sound behind him, as if somebody were approaching. The footsteps were silent for a while, then started again. Someone was preparing to attack him from behind, or so it seemed. Fear overcame him, and his breathing became violent. He was about to jump up and run away crying, "Ghost! Help!" when he heard a sound like someone chewing something crunchy. He managed to restrain his panic and opened his eyes. In the darkness he saw a village dog. It was sniffing the food that the villagers had left as offerings to the spirits. "So, it's you who have frightened me all this time," he thought, pitying himself and thinking what a coward he had been, despite his resolution to face whatever came his way. Had this monk not been able to use "the dhamma of self-control" to check his fear, Man's biographer writes, his fear might have driven him mad (M1, 46–47; M2, 60). This experience enabled the disciple of Man's to take his teacher's training to heart. From then on he made a resolution to confront whatever he feared the most.

A monk might wander for several years without spending a night in a cemetery. An account of Cha's shows how devastating the first experience can be, no matter how well prepared the monk is. In late 1947 Cha was in Na Kae District in Nakhon Phanom. When he arrived at Khrong Forest Monastery, he found that the meditation teacher there was following the traditional thudong practice of dwelling in a cemetery. If Cha wanted to stay at this wat, he had to do likewise. He had never stayed overnight in a cremation ground. Now, at the age of twenty-nine, he forced himself to try it. He persuaded a pha khaw to stay with him.

> If I tried to reason with myself I'd never go, so I grabbed a pha-khaw and just went. . . . When I got there, words can't describe the way I felt. The pha-khaw wanted to camp right next to me but I wouldn't have it. . . . I made him move away, otherwise I'd have counted on him for support. . . . Well, just as it was getting dark I had my chance. In they came carrying a corpse. Just my luck! I couldn't even feel my feet touch the ground, I wanted to get out of there so badly. They wanted me to do some funeral chants but I wouldn't get involved, I just walked away. In a few minutes, after they'd gone, I just walked back and found that they had buried the corpse right next to my spot, making the bamboo used for carrying it into a bed for me to stay on.[35]

Though afraid, Cha told the pha khaw to set up his klot about forty meters away. A distance closer than that, he figured, would make him feel too secure. "When it was dark," Cha says, "I got into my mosquito net. It felt as if I had a seven-tiered wall all around me. Seeing my trusty alms bowl there beside me was like seeing an old friend. Even a bowl can be a friend sometimes! Its presence beside me was comforting. I had a bowl for a friend at last" (C1, 72).

Cha survived the first night there, having gotten his initial fear under control. Then, later in the afternoon villagers brought another corpse (this time an adult) and cremated it about twenty meters from Cha's spot, right in front of his klot. Again Cha did not go and do any rites for them. He waited until they left before he forced himself to take a look. "The fire from the burning corpse flickered red and green and the flames pattered softly. I wanted to do walking meditation in front of the body but could hardly bring myself to do it. Eventually I got into my [mosquito] net. The stench from the burning flesh lingered all through the night. . . . As the flame flickered softly, I turned my back on the fire. . . . I forgot about sleep, I couldn't even think of it, my eyes were fixed rigid with fear. And there was nobody to turn to, there was only me. I had to rely on myself. I could think of nowhere to go, there was nowhere to run to in that pitch black night" (C1, 73).

Because of the cultural context in which they were reared, thu-dong monks believed that the world they inhabited consisted of spirits as well as people. Even in the most isolated places, a monk knew that sooner or later some being would pay him a visit. This happened to Cha. As he sat with his back to the fire, he heard someone or something approach his klot.

> I don't know what it was, but there came a sound of shuffling from the fire behind me. Had the coffin just collapsed? Or maybe a dog was getting the corpse? But no, it sounded more like a buffalo walking steadily around. . . . then it started walking towards me, just like a person!
>
> It walked up behind me, the footsteps heavy, like a buffalo's and yet not. . . . The leaves crunched under the footsteps as it made its way round to the front. . . . But it didn't really come up to me, it just circled around in front and then went off in the direction of the pha-khaw. Then all was quiet. . . .
>
> It must have been about half an hour later . . . when the footsteps started coming back from the direction of the pha-khaw. Just like a person! It came right up to me, this time, heading for me as if to run me over! I closed my eyes and refused to open them.[36]

Cha did not know what it was, but his fear and his belief in the existence of local spirits made him think of many possibilities. He had never experienced such fear in his life. "It got closer and closer until it stopped dead in front of me and just stood still. I felt as if it were waving burnt hands back and forth in front of my closed eyes. Oh! This was really it! I threw out everything, forgot all about Buddho, Dhammo and Sangho. I forgot everything else, there was only the fear in me, stacked in full to the brim. My thoughts couldn't go anywhere else, there was only fear. From the day I was born I had never experienced such fear. Buddho and Dhammo had disappeared. I don't know where. There was only fear welling up inside my chest until it felt like a tightly-stretched drumskin" (C1, 74).

Cha managed to regain his mindfulness, and then he began to look inward to see where his fear lay.

> I sat as if I wasn't touching the ground and simply noted what was going on. The fear was so great that it filled me, like a jar completely filled with water. If you pour water until the jar is completely full, and then pour in some more, the jar will overflow. Likewise, the fear built up so much within me that it reached its peak and began to overflow.
> "What am I so afraid of anyway?" a voice inside me asked.
> "I'm afraid of death," another voice answered.
> "Well, then, where is this thing 'death'? Why all the panic? Look where death abides. Where is death?"
> "Why, death is within me!"
> "If death is within you, then where are you going to run to escape it? If you run away you die, if you stay here you die. Wherever you go it goes with you because death lies within you, there's nowhere you can run to. Whether you are afraid or not you die just the same, there's nowhere to escape death." (C1, 74–75)

By investigating his fear, Cha was able to deal with it effectively, and this led to insight: "As soon as I had thought this, my perception seemed to change right around. All the fear completely disappeared as easily as turning over one's own hand. It was truly amazing. So much fear and yet it could disappear just like that! Non-fear arose in its place. Now my mind rose higher and higher until I felt as if I was in the clouds."[37]

Later that night rain began to fall. The wind was strong and the rain thundered down in a heavy torrent: "But I wasn't afraid of dying now. I wasn't afraid that the branches of the trees might come crashing down on me. I paid it no mind. . . . I sat unmoving" (C1, 75). By the time the rain had stopped Cha, his robes, and his klot were soaking wet. It was like being out in an open field.

Cha now experienced a wave of self-pity, a feeling of being forsaken. Such feelings were common among young thudong monks when facing similar situations. He felt sorry for himself. "I cried! The tears flowed down my cheeks. I cried as I thought to myself, 'Why am I sitting here like some sort of orphan or abandoned child, sitting, soaking in the rain like a man who owns nothing, like an exile?' . . . Then I thought further, 'All those people sitting comfortably in their homes right now probably don't even suspect that there is a monk sitting, soaking in the rain all night like this. What's the point of it all?' Thinking like this, I began to feel so thoroughly sorry for myself that the tears came gushing out." Cha must have caught himself brooding, since his next thought was "They're not good things anyway, these tears, let them flow right on out until they're all gone." He continued to sit with this thought. "I sat . . . sat and listened. After conquering my feelings I just sat and watched all manner of things arise in me, so many things that were possible to know but impossible to describe. And I thought of the Buddha's words . . . *Paccattaṁ veditabbo viññuhi* —'the wise will know for themselves.' . . . That I had endured such suffering and sat through the rain like this . . . who was there to experience it with me? Only I could know what it was like. There was so much fear and yet the fear disappeared."[38]

At dawn Cha got up from the sitting meditation and realized the price he paid for feeling so terrified. When he woke up in the morning and looked around, everything for some reason looked yellow; when he went to urinate, there was blood in his urine.

When it was time to go on an almsround, the pha khaw came to Cha. "Ajan, Ajan," he said, "did you see anything last night? It came from where you were. Its behavior scared me. I had to take out the knife and threaten it. Then it went away."[39] Cha, however, refused to discuss it and told the pha khaw to stop talking. Actually, he did not want to say any more for fear that the pha khaw might run away. Unlike the monk in the preceding case, who found that the "ghost" was just a dog, Cha and his companion never figured out the mystery.

Cha might seem a bit cowardly for not having stepped outside his klot to find out who or what the visitor was. But maybe he was doing the right thing. One of the survival rules that many wandering monks adhered to was not to respond to strange noises heard in the forest at night. It was safer to stay put, meditating in the klot and keeping silent. Some thudong monks believed that whoever (monk, novice, or pha khaw) stepped outside his klot to investigate a strange noise was doomed.[40]

Li is the only other thudong monk to have given a detailed account of his ordeal at a forest cemetery. Li admits to having an instinctive fear of charnel grounds. Throughout his lay life he never stepped into one. Even when his relatives died, he managed to avoid approaching cremation pyres. One of the reasons he left the life of a village monk was because he had to perform funeral rites. But now he was a wandering monk, and villagers expected him to stay right next to the cremation pyres in the cemetery.

It was while he was wandering in the northern region in 1932 that Li had to face his fear of the dead. Li was then twenty-six years old. He had met another thudong monk, Choei, and they became travel companions. One day they came upon a village in Saket Mountain (Chiang Mai Province) and were invited to stay. Some villagers built a hut for them in the midst of a large charnel ground full of graves and heaps of white, weathered bones. The two monks had been staying in the hut for several days when some villagers invited Choei to stay in another spot. Now Li was left alone—the remains of an old cremation only about six meters away.

> A few days later, well before dawn, a villager came with a little cone of flowers and incense, saying that he was going to bring someone to stay with me as my disciple. I thought to myself, "At least now I'll be a little less lonely." I had been feeling scared for quite a few days running, to the point that every time I sat in meditation I'd start feeling numb all over.
>
> Later on that morning, after my meal, a large group of villagers came, bringing a corpse with them. The corpse hadn't been placed in a coffin, but was simply wrapped in a cloth. As soon as I saw it, I told myself, "You're in for it now." If I were to leave, I'd lose face with the villagers, but the idea of staying on didn't appeal to me either. The realization hit me: the corpse was probably my "disciple."[41]

Around 4 P.M. the villagers cremated the corpse near Li's hut. From where he lay he could see the corpse being burnt, and the same fear again arose in Li. "When it caught fire, its arms and legs started sticking up into the air, as yellow as if they had been smeared with turmeric. By evening the body had fallen apart at the waist—it was still black in the flames" (Li1, 44). Just before nightfall, the villagers returned home, leaving Li alone. Unlike Cha, who chose to investigate his fear, Li prevented the feeling from overwhelming him by withdrawing into samādhi: "I hurried back to my banana-leaf hut and sat in meditation, ordering my mind not to leave the hut—to the point where my ears went blank. I didn't hear any sound at all. My mind still had a certain amount of self-awareness, but no perception of where I was, of courage, or fear, or of anything at all. I stayed this way until day-break."[42]

At the crack of dawn, Choei got back. Li felt a bit more secure, now that he had a companion. Li was curious if his fellow monk was as brave as he appeared to be.

> Phra Choei had a habit of sitting in the hut with me and having Dhamma talks—he'd do the talking, I'd do the listening—but I could tell from the tone of his voice that he wasn't all he made himself out to be. Once a villager came and asked him, "Are you afraid of the dead?" Phra Choei didn't say yes or no. All he said was, "What's there to be afraid of? When a person dies, there isn't anything left at all. Why, you yourself can eat dead chickens, dead ducks, dead cows and dead water buffaloes without a second thought." That was the sort of thing he'd always be saying. I thought to myself, "What a show-off. He doesn't want other people to know he's afraid. Well, tomorrow we'll have to see just how brave he really is." (Li1, 45)

The next day a villager invited one of the thudong monks to accept donations at his home. Li accepted and went to the village, leaving Choei in the hut by himself. When he returned the following day, Choei was gone. Li learned that late the night before, some villagers had brought the body of a dead girl to bury in the cemetery. Choei immediately gathered his klot, bowl, and robes and fled in the middle of the night. This was the last Li ever saw of Choei.

This experience in the cemetery must have cured Li of his fear, because a few years later we find him spending three months in a cemetery. In 1935 Li passed through the town of Chanthaburi in eastern Thailand. Upon arriving at the provincial capital he stayed in an open field to the south of the town.[43] Then he went to visit a lay supporter who found a quiet place for him to stay—in an active forest cemetery *(pacha phi dip)* about eight hundred meters from town. This was an area of bamboo and *taew* trees, thickly overgrown with grass, with only one clearing where cremations were held. In this clearing Li stayed with an old monk (who had followed him from Prachinburi) and one boy. As the rainy season was near, a number of local people asked Li to spend the retreat in the cemetery. Li accepted.[44] He had quite overcome his fear—a big transformation for someone who for nineteen years of his lay life refused to go near a cremation ground.

Unlike Li, Juan does not seem to have been afraid of corpses. He came across a dead body during his first year as a thudong monk. He was twenty-three then. This was in 1943, when he was on his way to Ubon. Walking through Ma-i Forest around noon-time he smelled a strong stench. Knowing that it was not the smell of a dead animal, he looked around. In a ditch he found a corpse: "It stank so badly. Near the corpse was a tin pail, a machete, and a *pha khawma* cloth with a small bag." Juan thought, "I have come across a treasure which is hard to find. I should use it as a subject of meditation" (J, 22). So he put his thudong gear under the shade of a tree and came back to meditate standing near the corpse. "The corpse must have been left here at least five or six days ago. The body was disintegrating. The intestines were infested with maggots. Vultures and crows must have scrambled for it. Both eyes were full of maggots, and the mouth full of worms. Chest and both legs were also infested with worms. The urinary organ and the anus were full of maggots. The stench was strong" (J, 22–23).

He had been meditating on the corpse for a few hours when two villagers came by. He asked them if he could spend the night by the corpse to meditate on it all night. The villagers thought it was not a good idea. "If you stay here and the police come by, they may suspect that you killed him," they told him. "You'd better leave."

So Juan continued on his journey. At dusk he reached another village, Phon Namthang (in Amnat Charoen District, Ubon Province). He set up his klot under a tree at the edge of a cemetery and then bathed. At nightfall he went inside his klot, prayed to the Buddha, chanted, meditated, and visualized the corpse that he had seen during the day. When his mind was calmed, there appeared a vision of "a dozen corpses all over me. Can't even move my body or legs. Every time I move, my body touches the corpses. I then meditate on my body and realize that it will disintegrate like these corpses. . . . This process is inevitable. This night the mind is calm, cool, and rested. The happiness is beyond expression" (J, 23).

What do the monks' accounts tell us about confronting fear? When a monk receives the visit of a tiger or a ghost, he may react in one of three ways.[45] First, if he cannot handle the fear, his meditation goes to pieces (*kammathan taek)*; that is, he may lose his mind and flee in horror. Second, if he is able to calm his mind, he gains wisdom and learns to face his fears with mindfulness. Third, he may be so transformed that he no longer has any fear at all. This happened to many monks who, during their many years of observing thudong practices, gradually purified their minds, steadily replacing fear with indomitable courage until, as Ajan Man said, they were fit to live anywhere, go anywhere, and rest anywhere, no longer troubled by fear.[46]

At this point a monk would no longer need to stay in a charnel ground. Once a monk had contemplated death externally and had formed a clear picture of it, he then turned inward to contemplate his own body and his own death until he became thoroughly familiar with the idea. Then, as Bua says, "the external cemetery gradually becomes unnecessary, because we've caught onto the principle within ourselves, and don't need to rely on anything outside. We contemplate our body to see it as a cemetery just like the external cemetery, both while it's alive and after it dies. We can compare each aspect with the outside, and the mind gradually runs out of problems of its own accord."[47]

CHAPTER 4

Overcoming

Bodily Suffering

Although fear forced many an inexperienced monk off the thudong path, the ten monks under study here all passed this obstacle, some easily and others after much difficulty. But even more
daunting than fear was the risk of catching jungle fever and other
diseases. It was not uncommon for monks or novices to die from
illness during their early years of wandering. Whether the ailment
was serious or minor, we see the same pattern of response. Sometimes monks sought cures through traditional remedies and native
healers. When these failed, they sought to heal themselves through
meditation or relied on their great powers of endurance to carry
them through.

NATIVE HEALERS AND TRADITIONAL REMEDIES

In their early years of thudong practice, many monks had not yet
learned how to heal themselves. Sometimes young thudong monks
received treatment from local healers (*mau phi,* literally "spirit
doctors"). Two wandering monks, Li and Juan, recalled how they
were saved by native healers when they fell ill in remote areas. In
1932 the twenty-six-year-old Li was spending the rains retreat
with Ajan Man at Wat Jediluang in Chiang Mai. A few days after
the retreat ended, Man sent him to meditate alone on top of
Thumb Hill in Lamphun, where Man had once stayed. When Li

reached the foot of the hill, he camped there for ten days. One afternoon, while sitting in meditation, he heard a whispering voice telling him he had to go to the top of the mountain. After climbing the mountain the next day, Li scouted the area and found a deep spring with crystal-clear water surrounded by the heads from old Buddha images. Li recalls that the spring was protected by a local belief: "They say that a person who falls into the spring won't sink, and that you can't go diving down under the water. Women are absolutely forbidden to go into the spring, for if a woman does happen to enter the water she'll go into convulsion. People in the area consider the whole mountain to be sacred" (Li1, 40). Ajan Man had told Li that a powerful spirit dwelled in the mountain, but it would not harm him or disturb him because it was acquainted with the dhamma.

The next day Li had nothing to eat. "That night I felt faint—the whole mountain seemed to be swaying like a boat in the middle of a choppy sea—but my mind was in good shape and not the least bit afraid." The next day he did walking and sitting meditation in the area around an old abandoned sanctuary. Although there was a village about four kilometers away where he could have gone for alms, he vowed not to eat until someone brought him food. That night he suffered from severe stomach pains and a fainting fit. Just before dawn, he heard something or someone moving up the steep slope toward him. He could not tell whether it was human or animal. "I heard huffing and panting sounds outside the sanctuary. At first I thought it was a tiger, but as I listened carefully, it sounded more like a human being. That side of the mountain, though, was very steep—not too steep to climb up, but I can guarantee that it was too steep to go down. So who would be coming up here? I was curious, but didn't dare leave the sanctuary or my klot until it was light outside" (Li1, 40).

Li waited until dawn to step outside. He found a laywoman about seventy years old sitting with her hands raised in respect. She had some red sticky rice wrapped in a banana leaf, which she put in his bowl. She also gave him some roots and pieces of bark. She told Li, "Take this medicine, grind it down and eat it, while making a wish for your health, and your stomachache will go away." After he finished eating the glutinous rice and the roots and bark, he chanted some blessings for her. Then she left, disappearing down the west side of the mountain. Li's life may have been saved by this native doctor. The following day he was well enough to travel back to Chiang Mai to be with Man (Li1, 41).

Juan, too, was cured by a local healer while he was staying in Crystal Cave (Tham Kaew) at Ox Mountain, Nongkhai. He was then thirty-six years old. Although Juan's father was a folk doctor, Juan followed the Bangkok education system and did not learn herbal medicine from his father. During the 1956 rains retreat Juan suffered from an infection on his thumb. At one point the infection brought on a fever, and he could not sleep because of the pain. One day, while his fellow monks were seeking alms in a hamlet nearby, a spirit doctor brought food to Juan at the cave. "She quietly looked at my thumb. Then she went into the forest to find some medicine. She returned with some root, scraped it, and put it on the infection. It was a root from the *lamduan* plant" (J, 61). The root was effective in healing Juan's infection.

If herbal medicines failed or were unavailable, many thudong monks turned to a remedy they dated back to the Buddha's time: drinking their own urine.[1] Fan and his nephew used this medicine when they spent fifteen days meditating in Phrabot Cave in Ban Pheu District, Udon Thani. This was in the early 1920s, when the area was isolated. The nearest inhabitants—an old farmer couple —lived in a hut four kilometers away. These farmers cultivated rice, chilies, and cotton. On their almsround Fan and the novice each got a handful of rice, chilies, and salt. In the evening Fan swallowed the medicine that he had prepared for himself—olives pickled in his urine and heated in a bamboo container (F, 21).

Thet also believed that drinking urine was an effective cure. In 1933 he went wandering in the North with a fellow monk and a pha khaw. While staying in an orchard near Phrabat Thakpa (a Buddha's footprint shrine), the pha khaw fell ill. As Thet recalls, "He had no fever but felt exhausted and weak, and his urine was thick and reddish like water that has been used to rinse meat. We were far from any doctors and so had to resort to the Lord Buddha's medicine and depend on ourselves. So we told him to drink his own urine, even though it appeared so clearly reddish. He drank it straight after urination, while it was still warm. It worked wonders! Within less than ten days he was back to normal" (T1, 128).

La, too, resorted to such natural remedies in 1947 when he lived as a recluse in Daen Cliff Cave (Tham Pha Daen) in Sakon Nakhon Province. "[I have] no medicines of any kind—not for fever, colds, or insect bites. Didn't bother to get them. For a long time [I] have lived without a candle or a match. In case of snakebite the only things [I have] are urine, feces, or soil. Don't even think about wood ashes. Taking urine and feces mixed with soil would do. If not, then meditate till death comes. . . . Don't even worry about the corpse. At least [I] can always leave it to my 'lay supporters'—the flies, maggots, crows, vultures, foxes, or wild dogs" (La, 115).

Cha—unlike Fan, Thet, and La—did not think that it was such a good idea to rely on urine, whether one was sick or well. While wandering alone in Nakhon Phanom, Cha came upon a forest hermitage near a cemetery. Since the 1948 rains retreat was approaching, Cha asked for permission to stay. After a while, however, he considered staying alone on a hilltop and coming down for alms every week or so. The main obstacle, however, was the lack of drinking water at the summit. He then thought about how frogs survive by drinking their own urine during the dry season, so he decided to experiment. "One day after having the meal, [I] drank fresh water until full. Three hours later, having the urge to urinate, did it in a glass and drank it. It's a little salty. Two hours later felt like urinating again, did the same thing and drank the urine. This time the urge was an hour later. Urinated into the glass and drank it again. Thirty minutes later repeated the same process. This time the urge was fifteen minutes later, urinated and drank it. After five minutes, urinated and drank it again. This time the urge to urinate was immediate. The color of urine came out white. Then [I] realized that the last urine is not drinkable" (C3, 51). Having given up the idea of drinking urine when water was unavailable, Cha had to abandon the idea of going to meditate on the hilltop.

FACING PAIN

If traditional herbal remedies and local healers failed, the monks would try to heal themselves through meditation or what they called *thamma osot* (spiritual medicine).[2] Unlike textual study, meditation practice was an oral tradition, passed down through the centuries from teacher to student. No formal course of study, no classroom or textbook prepared the thudong monk. Although their initial attempts to deal with pain and illness through meditation proved exceedingly difficult, monks eventually became proficient.

While living in the forest, Ajan Man trained monks in his own way.[3] This was not the way of scholars; he taught by personal example. He drew upon his experiences, and his teachings reflect his vitality. Man told his disciples that if they wanted to understand suffering (the First Noble Truth), they must look into the situation at hand: "Wherever a problem arises it must be settled right there. Where suffering lies is right where non-suffering will arise, it ceases at the place where it arises."[4]

In the ajan's opinion, the most difficult monks to teach were the maha monks—monks with third-level Pali studies or more—who came to challenge his teachings.[5] A typical example is Maha Pin. When Pin began to practice meditation under Man's guidance in 1917, he had doubts: "Unlike me, Ajan Man has never studied the Pali texts. He couldn't possibly have superior knowledge. I have passed the fifth-level Pali exam and probably know the dhamma better than he does. I wonder if what he is teaching me is correct" (M3, 52). But in Man's opinion, the Pali scholars had a lot to unlearn before they could proceed along the spiritual path to liberation. As he saw it, the purpose of thudong practice is to train the mind, not to follow a text. To instruct these disciples in handling pain, Man often used forceful and "hard" methods to shock them out of their habitual attitudes. His favorite techniques were insults, humiliation, and shouting at his disciples. If a monk avoided facing painful sensations, for example, Man would scold him:

> Keep moaning. Anyone can moan. Even children can moan—if it serves a purpose. But here it doesn't serve any purpose at all other than to annoy those good people who are unflinching in the practice. So you shouldn't moan out of weakness. You're a meditation (kammathan) monk. When you act like this, who can bear to see it? If you were a child or an ordinary person, there wouldn't be anything wrong with it, because they haven't

received any training. They don't have any knowledge or under-standing of the various ways to contend with the pain, such as contemplating it.

But you, you think you already know everything. Yet when trouble comes along, such as this illness, you can't find any methods or tactics that will help you care for yourself. You just go to pieces. This won't do at all. You're a shame to yourself and your fellow meditators."[6]

Man's approach was to cajole a monk into having sati and then using it to control and supervise the mind. Once the mind was unified in deep concentration a new kind of awareness would emerge. The monk would be able to accept his pain and suffering with equanimity.

Compared to his teacher, Sao, Man was fierce and strict.[7] Dur-ing the late 1930s while Man and three disciples were staying in a forest in northern Thailand, one of the monks, a maha, contracted malaria, a disease against which no existing medicine was effec-tive. The monk suffered intensely from its attacks. Man believed that instead of trying to relieve physical symptoms, monks should go to the root of distress and cure their minds. He instructed ill disciples to observe the pain without reacting, for thereby they would realize the truth of suffering. But he found this maha's will too weak to follow his instructions. He proceeded to scold him sternly.

> You are called a maha . . . but where is the knowledge you
> studied from the scriptures, right now? . . . What a waste of time
> and effort, your maha title! The purpose of learning is to make
> knowledge available in time of an emergency. But what kind of
> knowledge is yours? It's practically useless. You are going to die
> and all that knowledge which you took so much time to gain
> cannot be called on to help you. What was the purpose of your
> studying? I am not a maha, I don't even have the lowest grade.
> But what I do have with me are the five basic meditation themes
> taught to me by my preceptor on ordination day. It seems the
> more you learn, the weaker you become, weaker even than an
> uneducated woman. You are a man and also a maha. How
> could you be such a weakling? During this illness you have done
> nothing to justify your manhood and monkhood.[8]

Man was teaching the maha monk to develop mindfulness and concentration, to use the mind to contemplate the body and its illness, and to meditate on discomfort until painful sensations left the mind. If the monk had sufficient mindfulness, his mind could withdraw from the body. The dhamma, Man was also saying, cannot be found on bookshelves. To really see it, a monk has to look within his own body and mind, because both happiness and suffering arise right there.[9]

Man's harsh criticism reflects his low opinion of monks who have engaged exclusively in book learning. He seems to have believed that a strong intellect often conceals emotional weakness, and he showed little compassion for a monk's suffering if he thought it came from self-pity or self-indulgence. This particular maha monk wept when he was scolded. But then Man, still striving to bring his disciple to realization, changed his technique to the opposite extreme of gentleness and encouragement. For the next few days he softened his tone and assured the monk he would recover soon. His gentle, cheerful, and even motherly consolation produced a soothing effect on the sick monk, who recovered steadily during the next few months.

PERSEVERING

Like many novices who started out by accompanying a teacher, Thet learned about the importance of perseverance by observing experienced wandering monks. Others, such as La and Wan, already possessed this quality. Still others, like Waen, developed it through long meditation practice.

In 1916 Thet was practicing under Sing, Man's oldest disciple, at a deserted wat in Tha Bau in Udon Thani. Sing was suffering from malaria, and although he was feverish throughout the rains retreat, he continued to teach and train Thet. When the retreat was over, Thet and his teacher departed. There were no roads then, and they had to walk through mud and wade across streams and paddies. When the fever attacked, Sing took shelter in a hut in the fields or lay in the shade of a tree. In the morning he would go on an almsround, despite the fever, to feed his young pupil. Thet learned that regardless of his condition, a thudong monk rises in the morning, follows the path to the village, and makes an almsround.

Meditation monks were known for their ability to bear disease and illness bravely. La has left a detailed account of his marathon encounter with jungle fever.[10] For example, he kept his meditation practice going during intermittent attacks of jungle fever while wandering with Maha Bua in November 1946.[11] From Pheu Pond Hermitage, Sakon Nakhon, where Man was residing, the two monks walked along trails or oxcart tracks through the forest and paddy fields until they reached an abandoned wat in Phra Kamphu Village. They stayed there to meditate. Although La had an attack of malaria every three or four days, this did not stop him from serving Bua, his senior. To train La, Bua gave him many tasks to perform: "You must fetch water and fill up the water containers for washing alms bowls and for my bath. Fill the kettle and the jar with drinking water. A layperson will wash the bowls. Leave them outside to dry and then take them inside. No need to assist me bathing, sweeping the kuti, or preparing the bedding. I'll do these things myself since our kutis are quite far apart. . . . Meditate rigorously. Except when necessary, don't speak to me, but don't assume that I dislike you" (La, 87).

Despite his fever, La performed the rigorous daily duties that Bua assigned him. "For almost a month, water for washing and drinking was brought in from the stream about 120 meters from the hermitage. I started carrying the water at four o'clock in the morning, stumbling through the dark since there was no torchlight. He [Bua] meditates day and night. But I'm usually seized by fever around midday. Although the fever dies down in an hour, the headache persists. Can eat a little. Every three or four days I'm overtaken by fever, but at night it's a little better" (La, 87).

Bua eventually got hold of some quinine tablets and brought them to La.[12] Not familiar with modern medicine, La says he "swallowed the six tablets all at once. All day the ears felt out of whack. So [I] skipped the meal, just let the drug take over. The fever disappeared for fifteen days; then it came back. But [I] continued to fetch the water, sweep the grounds, and do walking meditation regardless of the recurrence. If it were typhoid and I kept on like this, I probably would be dead" (La, 88).

La had not quite recovered from malaria when Bua moved them half a kilometer deeper into the forest. But they still went to Phra Kamphu Village for alms, and La continued to fetch water from the same stream. "The villagers built me a platform big enough to spread a mosquito net, about eighty meters [two *sen*] away from that of the Phra Ajan Maha [Bua]. It must be my kamma that some of the small and smooth round sticks they used for the platform were cut from *nam kliang* trees. My skin is allergic to them. After three or four days my face became so swollen it almost concealed the eyes. When he saw my face, the ajan said with a laugh, 'A stinky fart on top of smelly shit!' "[13] When Bua went to inspect La's platform and found the *nam kliang* sticks, he asked a villager to remove them and replace them with safe ones. La was equanimous; he did not blame the villagers. "All things considered, they had no bad intentions. During this time [the dry season] the leaves had fallen off so they couldn't tell by looking at those sticks which were right. They just gathered any smooth, round sticks. They built the platform in a hurry and didn't have time to make the roof and sides. In the morning, both the mosquito net and the klot were wet. Just let them hang there to dry out" (La, 88).

Under such conditions, it is little wonder that La suffered from chronic fever during the two months that he stayed with Bua. La, however, felt that he was a burden to his teacher and decided to find solitude elsewhere. Hearing La's reason for leaving, Bua suggested with a laugh, "Go to the prairie area of Sakon Nakhon. Pitch your klot and mosquito net in the middle of a pasture. Do the walking meditation in the blazing sun. The open air might be more suitable to your body" (La, 90). He wrote a letter to Phan, a fellow Thammayut monk at Phon-ngam Village, asking him to accommodate La. So La departed, a villager accompanying him for a short distance to be sure he was going in the right direction.

La says that he did not know whether to take Bua's advice seriously or not. Bua, however, was not joking. He had known a number of monks from the towns of Ubon, Roi-Et, and Mahasarakham who could not adapt to living in the forest or withstand the diseases (M1, 84). He knew that those who were born in town or who lived surrounded by fields and open places had a hard time adjusting to the forest environment.

It took La half a day to walk to Phon-ngam village. There he gave Bua's letter to Phan.[14] Phon-ngam was Phan's home village, and he was back for a visit, staying at a deserted wat. Phan asked his father to assemble the villagers. Thirty people showed up.

They decided to build a shelter for La at Tum Nokkatha Hill. They believed that the hill was inhabited by fierce *bangbot* spirits, and they may have asked La to stay in there to test the depth of his practice. "They built me a hut with a roof and walls made of straw. They also made a latrine with a ditch for urination, and they cleared a path for walking meditation. There was a well for water in the area. The forest was full of tall *sal* trees. The village was about one kilometer away—a good distance to go for alms" (La, 92).

Although the villagers in Sakon Nakhon were generally attentive to thudong monks, La preferred to be self-reliant: "The fever attacks every two or three days and then goes away for a few days. Can eat all right but the headache persists. When I'm overtaken by the fever, [the villagers] want to come and look after me, but I won't let them. They want to visit daily to grind the [herbal] medicine. But I say no. I want to be alone when ill. Only ask them to provide medicinal roots and a rock so I can grind them" (La, 92–93).

La stayed for a month. Then, although the fever persisted, he decided to proceed to Phawet Cave. It appears that La treated his illness with what Cha calls "right view": "If it heals, it heals; if it doesn't, it doesn't." That, says Cha, is how thudong monks saw things (C1, 100). La departed early one morning in the company of some villagers, who showed him a path along the foothills toward the east. "Actually, on the day of my departure I still had a fever, but I didn't tell them for fear that they would be worried. After the villagers returned, I practiced mindfulness while walking. Barbet birds were singing. All the leaves had fallen off, leaving the treetops bare. Free from worry, I walked mindfully. Despite the raging fever, I kept up the walking meditation. Koel birds were calling far away" (La, 101).

In the evening La arrived in the vicinity of Owl Field Village (Ban Na Nok Khao). Here he ran into Fan, who was leaving the wat of Weng Field Stupa with four other thudong monks on their journey to Daen Cliff Cave. In addition to the other thudong monks, Fan was accompanied by two local soldiers. Kneeling on the ground to pay his respects, La briefly told Fan his story. "So, you've been walking all day with a fever," said Fan. "I sympathize. Go and stay at Weng Field Stupa Monastery. It's deserted now. I'll have these two soldiers go with you."[15] Then Fan addressed the soldiers: "From here to Daen Cliff Cave, I'll be all right with these monks. Soldiers, make sure that tomorrow morning Sergeant Amphon gives this monk an injection." Turning to La, he said, "Don't leave until you have recovered."[16] La bowed gratefully to Fan and the two parted.

Fan headed south with his monks, and La went north with the soldiers, who carried his thudong gear for him. By then it was getting dark. "Fever was still raging. It was a ten-kilometer walk. Took a shortcut along a trail only wide enough for a mouse. It was pitch dark and we had no torchlight. Couldn't even see where I was stepping. That was up to kamma [*siang bun siang kam*]. Was meditating on loving-kindness for fear that I might step on a snake" (La, 102).

They arrived at the village of Weng Field Stupa around 9 P.M. The soldiers took La to the deserted wat and returned to their quarters. Late at night the fever diminished, but the headache remained. All night long La meditated lying down. In the morning he found that water for drinking and washing had been provided for him. He swept the floor and went on almsround. A layman followed him back and gave him eleven quinine tablets with instructions from the sergeant. This time La did not take them all at once.

After staying there for eleven days, La felt strong enough to move on. When he told a villager that he was leaving for the cave, the latter objected, "Now that you're cured, you want to run away from us!" This comment made La laugh, and he reminded the laypeople that both of them would gain merit from his seclusion:

> I'm one of Venerable Grandfather Man's guilty ones. He warned those who sought solitude that if they made no progress in meditation they wouldn't be allowed to spend the retreat with him. [He thinks that we] simply wander for the fun of it. And Phra Ajan Fan also told me to continue wandering when I recovered. Lay supporters, I'll gain merit in complete seclusion in a cave, in a forest, or on a hill. And you too will gain merit. We both lose nothing. If Ajan Man heard that I went wandering and then stayed in a wat, he'd think that I simply wanted to

get away from the teacher to hide, and that I lacked courage.
He'd condemn me and refuse to teach. It would be my loss.
(La, 102–103)

Upon hearing La's plea, the villager said, "We'll let you go then. Please extend some loving-kindness to us."

The local belief that lay supporters would gain merit from monks' meditation was common in the Lao and Yuan traditions. Monks accordingly felt they had a responsibility to practice diligently. Thet alludes to this duty in a comment he makes about his meditation (the year was 1924): "Increasing my exertion also raised my appreciation for the villagers' goodwill—it seemed to follow like the shadow its subject. I was very aware that . . . my existence rested in the hands of the villagers and I therefore continued my meditation practice to repay my debt to them. I became certain that my meditation efforts during this time completely fulfilled the obligations of my indebtedness" (T1, 74).

Waen also provides a good illustration of a thudong monk's dedication to his practice, even in sickness. In this case it was jungle fever, which Waen caught in 1918 when he was meditating in the wilderness under Man's guidance. Wandering alone in the North Waen would meditate until the fever died down, but it kept coming back every three to five days. The fever reached its worst one day while he was walking from Phayao to Lampang in the rain. "It was a difficult journey," he recalls. "[I] had to cross streams and walk through narrow canyons in dense forests. Leeches everywhere" (Wn, 51). Coming upon a village in the evening, he saw a spirit shrine on the outskirts of the hamlet that was big enough for a person to lie down inside. Waen took shelter in it for a night. "Used the bathing cloth to sweep the floor clean and then spread the cloth over the floor. Put the klot up. Stepped outside and bathed in a nearby stream, filled by the rain. Solitude at night. Folded the outer robes into a pillow and lay down. Having rested, chanted some prayers and radiated loving-kindness to all sentient beings. Alternated walking meditation with sitting meditation. Heard tigers calling nearby—*pep pep*—and could tell that they were big ones, big enough to kill cattle. They kept howling nonstop: when one paused another started up and so on. It was like a group of people shouting at each other back and

forth. Late at night it was so cold that [I] could hardly sleep"
(Wn, 51–52).

When Waen resumed his journey in the morning, he felt weak;
his head felt heavy, the way it does when a fever comes on. Finding no hamlet in the dense forest, he pushed ahead. After a few
more hours of walking, he felt utterly exhausted and realized that
he was indeed feverish. The walk had been too much for his sick
body. He stopped in the shade of a tree beside the path. "Put
down the klot and bowl, and sank to the ground out of sheer
exhaustion and illness. Don't know how long [I] slept. The *zu zu*
sound of a strong wind swaying the tree branches woke me.
Lightning and thunderstorms everywhere, and the sky was now
full of dark clouds. The wind and storm became more violent.
And the fever hadn't gotten any better. Then it began to rain.
Couldn't set up the klot since it would have been blown away.
Didn't know where to find a shelter to get out of the wind and
rain" (Wn, 52).

Seeing there was no way out, Waen got up. With meditative
concentration he prayed to the Triple Gem and made a vow: "I
have devoted my life to the Triple Gem. If I have sufficient *barami*
[perfections], let me remain in the monkhood until I am released
from suffering. Please keep the rain away from where I am."[17]
Then, after radiating loving-kindness to the deities, the nagas, and
the garudas, he prayed, "I'm on my way to Lampang. Now sick
and tired in the middle of the forest. No strength to move forward. Please have mercy. It may not be proper to stop the rain,
but please change the direction of the wind so that it won't rain
where I am."[18]

After this prayer, Waen concentrated his mind and again radiated loving-kindness to all sentient beings in the cosmos. Then:
"What a miracle! In the midst of the downpour, the wind started
blowing the branches above me in a new direction. The wind
shifted, and the rain moved a *sen* [forty meters] from my spot.
The rain continued for a long time. After it let up I still hadn't
recovered from the fever. Lay down again with nothing for shelter.
Woke up late at night and found the whole body wet. Didn't
know whether it was because of mosquito bites or sweating. The
fever went down, and I felt lighter and thirsty. Took the kettle to
the stream to get some water" (Wn, 52–53). Before he continued

the journey, Waen calmed his mind and once more meditated on loving-kindness.

HEALING THROUGH VISIONS

Man was known for his ability to conquer serious ailments through concentrated meditation. He once told a disciple, "Last night I healed my illness. During my meditation a dhamma phrase appeared in my *nimit* [vision], 'yayi tapati athi jajo.' Just as I did once before when I was ill, I continued to meditate. After the pain went away, some kind of dhamma would appear in my nimit. I therefore seek no medicine when I feel ill. To count on medicines or doctors alone would go against my taking refuge in dhamma."[19]

Visions and signs do not occur to all meditation monks, however. This depends on an individual's temperament. As a thudong monk explains, "Visions and signs arise from mundane *jhāna* [concentration states]. . . . With some people, no matter how refined a level their minds attain, visions and signs won't appear. With others, the mind may gather in a flash for a brief moment, and all sorts of visions and signs will appear."[20] Among Man's disciples, Fan, Li, and Juan were predisposed to having signs and visions appear in their meditation.

Fan cured himself by means of a vision during a recurrence of malaria in 1932. At the time he was wandering with a fellow monk, Aun, in the environs of Bamboo Canal Village (Ban Khlaung Phai) in Sikhiw District, Khorat. Fan tried all kinds of medicine including quinine, but nothing worked, so he turned to dhamma practice. He sat in meditation until his mind became one-pointed. "In his vision he saw something leap out of his body and stand in front of him. Concentrating his mind, he looked at this thing and it turned into a deer jumping into the stream. It then leaped out and turned into a big elephant and forced its way through the forest, noisily breaking tree branches before it went out of sight" (F, 89–90). In the morning Fan's fits of fever had all disappeared.

Ajan Man taught his disciples to analyze their visions and dreams for clues about the workings of kamma. Many thudong monks accepted their illnesses and other things that befell them as the fruits of previous kamma, which had to be patiently examined and endured in order to break the chain of causality. Li, for example, made several references to a caged dove that appeared to him in dreams and visions. During the 1937 rains retreat, when he was staying at Prawn Canal Hermitage (Samnak Khlaung Kung) in Chanthaburi Province, Li suffered from stomach pains that no medicine could cure. He sat in meditation through the night. Around 4 A.M. a nimit appeared in his meditation. In it he saw "a bird-cage containing a thin, famished dove. The meaning was this. I had once kept a pet dove and had forgotten to feed it for several days running. This kamma was now bearing fruit, causing me to have gastritis. Therefore, there was only one way to cure it—to do good by way of the mind" (Li, 74). Because this vision appeared when he was ill, Li took it as a message that he should accept his disease as brought on by kamma.

Like Fan, Juan was healed after a vision he had during a malaria attack. In 1959, when he was thirty-nine years old, Juan spent the rains retreat alone in Jan Tree Cave (Tham Jan) in the Pink Forest of Phon Phisai District, Nongkhai. The nearest hamlet, whose inhabitants were Khamu, was about four kilometers away. Juan found the secluded cave and the cool climate conducive to his meditation, so he stayed on in the cave after the rains retreat was over. During the dry season jungle fever attacked him again. Having no medicine, he let the body heal itself. For a month fits of fever and shaking attacked him in the afternoons and went away in the evenings. Living alone, Juan had to do everything himself. When the fever lessened he would descend to the foothills to get some drinking water. By the time he got back to the cave it would be dark.

One day while stricken with fever, Juan meditated lying down. As he was about to fall asleep, his father, a highly respected specialist in herbal medicine who had died when Juan was sixteen, appeared before him. Juan recalls that in the vision his father came with a bag of medicine and asked him, "Son, what ails you?" "I came down with a jungle fever a month ago. I haven't recovered. There are no medicines," Juan replied. "Well, I'll mix some medicine. You'll recover soon," his father said. Then he untied his bag, scraped the medicine, and mixed it with water. The aroma of the medicine was so inviting that Juan felt himself gaining strength just by inhaling. He drank it all. At this point Juan woke up. At first he thought that he had indeed taken his father's medicine, but then "I realized that it was either a nimit or a dream. The next day the fever diminished. Then it was gone completely. The body regained its strength, and the appetite became normal. Never had a similar recurrence of the fever from then on. I don't know why. It can't be because I drank my father's medicine. I didn't really take it, I only drank it in the vision" (J, 66). In any case Juan felt grateful to his father for having looked after him. So he prayed and transferred all the merit that he had accumulated to his parents.

FACING DEATH

Progress in meditation necessitates intensive and sustained practice, which requires seclusion and freedom from distractions. During their periods of seclusion, thudong monks went through an arduous training that sometimes brought them close to death. Indeed, watching a fellow monk die of jungle fever was not an uncommon experience among the thudong monks. Dun did so in 1918, when he and four Lao monks—Sing, Bun, Sitha, and Nu—were staying in a forest in what is now Tha Khantho District, Kalasin Province.[21] At the time the area was remote and wild. The monks set up their own hermitage for the rains retreat. Soon all but Nu came down with jungle fever. Although they took care of one another as best they could, by the middle of the retreat one of them had already died. Seeing a fellow monk die, Dun was moved to put more energy into his meditation practice, and he contemplated his own death. Dun credited his survival to this meditation. He recalled that while in samādhi he had a vision in which his body appeared to merge with a Buddha image. He continued to meditate all day and all night until he was able to remove defilements from his mind.[22]

Dun had a similar experience the following year. In 1919, he and a young novice spent the rains retreat at the edge of a forest near Kudkom Village in Sakon Nakhon. When the novice came down with malaria, Dun tried his best to nurse him, but the fever was beyond cure. Watching the boy die Dun, remarked sadly, "It's a pity that there was no medicine. Were medicine available, he might not have died. He was still young."[23] The experiences of nursing and facing his companions' untimely death taught the monk many things, especially about the truth of impermanence, suffering, patience, and compassion.

Waen's biography illustrates how this skilled meditator with tremendous patience dealt with pain. During 1946 Waen was spending the rains retreat alone at the hermitage of Pong Village in Mae Taeng District, Chiang Mai. A painfully infected wound on his leg prevented him from going for alms. There were no other monks or novices in the hermitage, and the villagers in the area did not pay much attention to him. A fellow monk, Nu,[24] was staying at Mae Pang Mountain in Phrao, another district. Many thudong monks believed that the mental currents of different individuals can impinge on one another,[25] and this seems to have happened between Waen and Nu. One day while Nu was meditating, an image appeared; he saw Waen lying on the ground. When he came out of his samādhi, he reflected on this image and concluded that it was a sign that something had happened to his friend. So the following morning he walked to Pong Village, where he found Waen in serious condition. Nu asked the villagers to fetch a doctor, and they brought Ji, a man who had been in the army and had sufficient nerve to perform surgical operations. Ji removed the infected tissue from Waen's wound in an hour-long operation without anesthetic. Waen kept his mind concentrated in samādhi. According to the biographer, "Waen calmly lay down and remained motionless as if in deep sleep. When the surgery was over, Ji dressed the wound. About five minutes later, Waen came out of samādhi and opened his eyes. Nu asked, 'Were you in pain?' Waen replied, 'It was bearable.' . . . Ji had no pain reliever to give him. The next day when Ji returned to clean the wound, Waen told him, 'Be more gentle today. Yesterday your hand was quite heavy.' This is all he said" (Wn, 82).

Nu nursed Waen for a week before he returned to Mae Pang Mountain. This was in the middle of the rains retreat, when monks were not supposed to travel. He asked some villagers to look after Waen and admonished them for neglecting the monk. It took Waen several months, until April of the following year, to recover from the raw surgery. Even then, he was unable to walk very far.

Endurance or perseverance *(othon)* were qualities highly praised not only by thudong teachers but also by laypeople of the Northeast, who were proud of their ability to endure difficulties and respectful of those who faced hardship with courage.

Take, for example, Man's experience in 1913 at Great Mountain (Khao Yai) in Nakhon Nayok. At the time there were many isolated caves in the Central Plains, and Man had been wandering from one cave to another when he heard about the sinister Sarika Cave. The local people warned him about a great demon who guarded the cave and tolerated no intruders. They also told him that six wandering monks had died of serious diseases while staying there. Man, however, was not discouraged by the villagers' story. He saw it as a challenge and made up his mind to go to the cave and face whatever might happen.

At the ajan's insistence, the villagers led him up to this quiet, secluded cave. His first two nights were uneventful. The body and mind both rested satisfactorily. The only noises he occasionally heard were from wild animals roaming the area. On the third night, however, he was stricken with stomach pain. Man had been afflicted with hemorrhoids and gastric pain since his younger days, but this time his condition was more serious. He developed diarrhea, felt weak, and lost his appetite. He remembered the villagers' accounts of thudong monks who had died in that cave. If this illness continued, he thought, he might meet with a similar fate. In the morning some villagers stopped by, and Man took them to gather medicinal roots in the forest.[26] After several days of taking this medicine, his stomach condition worsened: he became more enfeebled and his willpower waned. The bowel trouble brought on a fever. Man refused to give in to self-indulgent patterns of response to illness and pain. "Why should I become disheartened and enfeebled by this pain and suffering?" he asked himself (M1, 19).

Seeing that the medicines were proving useless, Man stopped taking them. He also did not go for almsround for three days, since his stomach pain had grown worse. Meanwhile he sought to balance his energy through sitting meditation, relying on the therapeutic effect of the dhamma alone.

Attachment to life was then abandoned, whereupon the body was allowed to undergo its natural curing process. . . . No attention was paid to the disease as to whether or not it could be cured or whether it would destroy the body. . . . The pitched battle raged from dusk to midnight and ended with the mind being considerably empowered and able to realize the nature of the aggregates, including the gripping pain which had been fully manifesting itself. The illness totally disappeared and the mind withdrew into absolute, unshakable one-pointedness. . . . When the mind later emerged to a less profound and more responsive level called *upacāra,* there seemed to be a light radiating from his body which revealed a tall black man about ten meters high. He was carrying a club about four meters long and as big around as his leg.[27]

In Man's vision, the demon threatened to kill him if he did not leave the cave. Man refused to get up. A disciple of his, Wiriyang, records Man's description of his experience: "Suddenly the demon hit him with the gigantic stick. Ajan Man felt as if his body had been buried ten *wa* [fifty meters] deep into the ground. Then it floated up above the ground. Having no fear, he remained focused in his meditation. The demon then uprooted a nearby ironwood tree with both hands. The trunk was so gigantic that it would have taken ten men to encircle it. The demon hit the ajan with the tree until his body was flattened out on the rock where he sat. At this point he almost lost his mindfulness and opened his eyes. But he did not give in."[28]

Man's battle with the demon lasted into the early morning hours. Finally, he defeated the demon and admonished him to accept the dhamma.[29] When Man emerged from his samādhi, "the disease which had raged during the early stage of his practice had totally disappeared" (M1, 22).

Man's acceptance of his illness was the result of the steady energy he put into his meditation. He directed his mind onto the feeling of suffering itself—focusing on the pain without trying to escape or resist—until his mind withdrew into one-pointedness.[30] After this experience in the cave the chronic illness which had troubled Man for so long was completely cured, for "his mind had attained to a level where many doubts were cleared away . . . and many kinds of knowledge occurred to him which he had never dreamed of before, both of the eradication of defilements and of how to apply such methods of eradication to various individuals with different dispositions" (M1, 23; M2, 29).

On the fourth day Man went to the village for alms. That day he contemplated why the other wandering monks had died in this cave. The first monk had lasted for two months, the second for three, the third for four, and the fourth, fifth, and sixth for five to seven months. Man noted that each monk had broken a rule in the vinaya that he had been following. "The first thudong monk . . . stored food in the cave. . . . The second monk . . . had cut a tree to build two raised platforms, one to serve as a bed inside the cave, another for sitting outside the cave. The third monk . . . dug wild roots in the forest and boiled them for food. The fourth, fifth, and sixth monks . . . each had stored food that he received on almsround and had also picked fruit in the forest" (M3, 28). Of course, these other monks were not necessarily following the same disciplinary code as Man's. They may not have been breaking any rules in their local traditions. But Man did not look at things that way. As he saw it, these monks all died because they had violated the vinaya in some way, whereas he had strictly adhered to his ascetic practices. Indeed, adhering to the disciplinary rules was an essential element in the teaching of this thudong master. He and other wandering monks drew confidence from their conviction that purity and asceticism were shields protecting them from danger.

Man lived alone in Sarika Cave for a whole year. Through intensive practice and solitary confinement, he learned a great deal about himself and about pain. Once he accepted pain, observed it, and did not run from it, he found that he could work with it. The experience transformed him. He told a disciple that "from then on, whenever I felt ill I have not counted on medicine alone. Most of the time I meditated until the pain disappeared. I used meditation to overcome my illness, just as the Buddha taught in the Bojjhanga Sutta. Thus have I heard, once when the Buddha was ill he exerted himself in meditation on the seven *bojjhanga* (factors of enlightenment). His illness went away. Although I had strong faith in the dhamma that I heard, my faith was not confirmed until I put the dhamma into practice. Then it became true faith" (W, 45).

It was in Sarika Cave that Man was said to have attained the stage of nonreturner (anāgāmī).[31] He was about forty years old then and in his twenty-first year of the wandering life.

As these accounts suggest, one of the most distinctive aspects of the thudong tradition is its insistence on self-reliance. Among people in the Northeast, it was considered a virtue to be able to face hardship and endure pain. No matter how ill he was, the thought of leaving the monkhood never crossed the mind of a serious thudong monk. He would sooner die in his robes.

This attitude stands in stark contrast to that of clerical monks, the followers of Bangkok directives, many of whom had little tolerance for physical hardship and were inclined to disrobe in time of illness. Indeed, among the letters written by administrative monks to the supreme patriarch asking for permission to disrobe, most of them give "too ill to remain in the monastic life" as their reason.[32] Wandering meditation monks often intimated that book-learning monks generally do not want to experience suffering or difficulty. "They want everything to be cozy." Cha sums up the thudong experience thus: "The monks suffered many deprivations living like this. If someone caught malaria and went to ask for medicine, the teacher would say, 'You don't need medicine. Keep practicing.' Besides, there simply weren't all the drugs that are available now. All one had were herbs and roots that grew in the forest. The environment was such that monks had to have a great deal of patience and endurance; they didn't bother over minor ailments. Nowadays you get a bit of an ache and you're off to the hospital!"[33]

Having learned to observe the mind and contemplate feelings in times of illness, the wandering monks learned that pain is not a static experience but is constantly changing. They came to see that bodily sensations are just what they are and that thoughts and feelings are something apart from sensations.[34] The thudong monks realized that since the mind plays a large part in creating suffering, it could free one from suffering as well. By exerting themselves in meditation and being mindful of it, they learned that pain was just another experience. In return, pain taught them how to cultivate calmness, concentration, and equanimity. But it was never an easy lesson to learn.

CHAPTER 5

Battling

Sexual Desire

Judging from the thudong monks' accounts, sexual desire may have been an even bigger obstacle than illness or fear of death. Many monks found such temptation more difficult to resist than hunger, loneliness, and illness. All feared the female power to undermine the rule of celibacy, a fear that was reinforced by seeing many fellow meditation monks, young and old, meet defeat in their battle against sexual desire. A monk's ability to keep his mind under control was the true test of the strength and depth of his meditation practice.

Of the ten monks discussed here, only Man, Dun, and La do not recount a struggle to overcome sexual desire. Each of these three monks had spent at least a few years as a young man in the secular world before they took full ordination. La, however, was the only one who had experienced married life before becoming a thudong monk. Having been married twice, he had probably grown tired of being a householder when he took to the robes. But Waen, Juan, Wan, Cha, and Thet all had to battle sexual desire while wandering or living upcountry, and Fan and Li while staying in the city. In the recollections of these monks, temptation awaits everywhere and will likely snare a monk when he is off guard.

The thudong practice of living in the forests was not the best test of a monk's ability to resist women. Ajan Man knew it was bad for wandering monks to live in extreme solitude for too long, and he encouraged them to come to town occasionally to test themselves against temptation. "Living in the forest, monks do not have to talk to anyone. Forest dwellers usually don't bother monks. The senses are not stimulated to any great extent, so sensory deprivation sets in and monks find themselves becoming tranquil. There are both advantages and disadvantages to living in the forest. The monk can get attached to the isolated life. . . . Many monks are deluded into thinking that living in a forest is superior to living in town" (M3, 105). The solitude of the forest, Ajan Man believed, should be used to develop mindfulness; it was not a place for isolation and escape. Villages, town, and cities supplied monks with a constant stream of annoying challenges they could use to measure their accomplishment.

GLIMPSES OF WOMEN

A thudong monk's best measure of his mental development was his sense faculties. If sensory contact struck the mind with great impact, then mindfulness was weak, its foundation still shaky.[1] This was the case with Waen and Fan in their younger days.

During one of his trips to Laos, Waen went wandering on his own, looking for suitable places to meditate.[2] After crossing the Mekong and walking through Vientiane, he came to the Ngeum River. While bathing in the river late one evening he saw two village women rowing a boat. As the boat passed, the younger of the two women glanced at the young monk. "When [our] eyes met," he recalls, "the power was so strong and mysterious that it was stunning. Walking back, I could not keep the mind off the pretty woman" (Wn, 39). Later on the two women, who were mother and daughter, came to offer him food and homemade cigarettes.

Having entered the monastic life at the age of eight, Waen had few worldly experiences. This was the first time he felt a strong attraction to a woman. He wondered why his mind was so sensitive to the sight of this village woman. Then he remembered that when he was studying at a village wat in Ubon, an astrologer had told him that his soul mate would be living in a certain place, that she would be of medium height, and that she would have "a light-yellow complexion and a face shaped like a bodhi leaf" (Wn,

39). Now Waen reasoned that since the young woman on the river matched this description, she must be the one the astrologer had in mind. So he decided to leave immediately and head back to northeast Siam. He crossed the Mekong to Si Chiang Mai (today a district in Nongkhai Province). Here he came upon Man, who had just left his disciples and was practicing meditation alone. Waen was elated to see his teacher again, and he stayed with Man to practice. Although his mind grew quiet, occasionally the picture of the beautiful woman arose. During the rains retreat Waen attempted to get the young woman out of his mind by meditating. From this experience he realized the nature of the mind: thoughts arise on their own, without our intention and beyond our control.

> The defilement was strong. The mind refused to be controlled. It kept darting to the beautiful woman on the bank of Ngeum River in Song Field Village [Ban Na Song]. [I] tried various tricks but was unsuccessful. Exerting harder was like adding fuel to a fire. If [I was] off guard for one moment, that was enough for the mind to run to that woman. Sometimes, while trying some new trick to control the mind, it immediately leaped right back to the woman. Tried all kinds of tricks to punish the mind. Refused to lie down. Meditated alternately in sitting, standing, and walking positions for days and nights in a row, observing whether the mind had fallen out of love. Yet this [method] did not work. Then [I] stopped sitting or lying down and only stood or walked. In spite of this effort, the mind would not give up. (Wn, 39)

Waen then changed tactics. He began to fast, eating nothing and drinking only water. Then, to reverse his sexual desire, he started to meditate on revulsion, using the woman's body as a meditation object. By visualizing the disintegration of her body and comparing it to the decomposition of his own body, as he imagined it in meditation, he was able to pacify the distracting, lustful thoughts and finally get the woman out of his mind.[3]

Fan, too, was caught off guard by the sight of attractive women. This happened during his first trip to Bangkok. Fan was then thirty-three years old and had been a monk for thirteen years. During that year, 1931, Fan accompanied two older meditation monks, Sing and Pin, on a train trip from Khorat to

Bangkok to visit Jao Khun Ubali (Jan), abbot of Wat Boromniwat, who was very ill.[4] They stayed with this senior Thammayut monk for three months. One day Sing took Fan to pay respects to Panyaphisan (Nu), abbot of Wat Pathum Wanaram.[5] On the way back, Fan caught sight of a woman, and fell in love. (She may have been Lao. At the time this monastery was on the outskirts of Bangkok, and the area around the wat had been settled by Lao people.) From then on he knew he was in deep trouble. The strong attraction must have perplexed Fan, who had entered monastic life when he was in his early teens. Like Waen, Fan lacked any prior experience with young women.

Back at Wat Boromniwat, Fan had difficulty directing his mind to meditation. His meditation on buddho was weak; as soon as desire arose, his concentration immediately deteriorated. For three days he could not get the woman out of his mind. Realizing that his mind was beyond his control, he confided in his teacher, Sing. Had this happened in the countryside, Sing probably would have told Fan to undertake a solitary retreat in a cave. But in an urban temple the quietest place is the ordination hall, so Sing locked Fan up in the hall and insisted that he meditate on *asubha* (loathsomeness or impurity of the body) until he overcame his sexual desire.[6] After a week of intensive meditation practice, Fan came to the conclusion that the woman must have been his mate in a former existence. "This explained the strong feeling he had for her. Once he realized this, he could detach himself and got her off his mind."[7] This account also tells us about Fan's belief in rebirth, which he shared with his fellow wandering monks. Like Waen, Fan attributed his strong attraction to an unknown woman to his past kamma.

Unlike Waen and Fan, who were caught off guard, Wan believed that it was his meditation on buddho that saved him from falling for women. He recalled an incident that took place at the edge of a forest near Lotus Village (Ban Bua) in Sakon Nakhon Province. This was in the 1940s, when he was in his twenties. "Around noon, I went a hundred yards [from my kuti] further into the forest to do walking meditation. I saw a young woman walking to my kuti. I recognized her because she gave me food every day in the village. I hid myself by a tree near the meditation path so she would not see me. She sat down at the spot where I had my meal, then quietly sang to herself. Observing her behavior, I became convinced that her presence would be harmful to my purity. An hour or so later, she quietly walked away. What a relief! I did not have to face her in such a risky situation. I thought about my teachers with gratitude for their teachings. My faith in the meditation practice must have saved me" (W, 63). Here, visual contact with an attractive woman had only a minor impact. Wan remained mindful, so sensual desire could not move him. Although he entered monastic life when he was a boy, Wan was clearly aware of the power women had. "A woman, more than any force in the world, can easily put a man under her power," he says. "She can make a man attach to her or destroy him with five weapons: her body, her voice, her smell, her taste, and her touch" (W, 64).

THOUGHTS ABOUT WOMEN

Even when a monk did not encounter any women, he sometimes created a problem for himself by imagining them. The most graphic recollection of a struggle with sexual thoughts comes from Cha. In 1947, the ninth year of his monkhood, Cha spent the rains retreat at Ki Pond Forest Hermitage in Nakhon Phanom, living the ascetic life with Kinnari, a meditation teacher in the local tradition. Cha recalled that at one point during his meditation practice, sexual desire arose so intensely that he could not concentrate his mind.

> Regardless of the position, walking or sitting, that [I] took in meditation an image of the female genitals kept appearing. Lust was so strong that it almost overwhelmed me. Had to struggle hard to fight off the intense feelings and the nimits. Struggling over lustful feelings was as difficult as battling the fear of ghosts in the forest cemetery. [The lust was so intense that] it was impossible to do the walking meditation, as the penis became sensitive when it came in contact with the robe. Requested a walking meditation track be made deep in the forest where I could not be seen. In the dark forest, I rolled up my lower robe all the way to my waist, tied it, and kept up with my walking meditation. I battled the defilement for ten days before the lust and those nimits died down and disappeared.[8]

Although Cha won this battle, he found it hard to give up sexual desire. From his sixth or seventh rains retreat up until the twentieth he had to put up a fight. His method was to use skillful means: "Consider sexual pleasures as like eating meat which gets stuck in your teeth. Before you finish the meal you have to find a toothpick to pry it out. When the meat comes out you feel some relief for a while, maybe you even think that you won't eat any more meat. But when you see it again you can't resist it. You eat some more and then it gets stuck again. When it gets stuck you have to pick it out again, which gives some relief once more, until you eat some more meat. . . . That's all there is to it. Sexual pleasures are just like this, no better than this. . . . I don't know what all the fuss is about."[9]

Li's experiences during his stay in Bangkok illustrate the great impact mental constructs have on a monk with weak mindfulness, and they confirm Man's teaching that practice in the city and practice in the country are complimentary. Unlike Fan, who went to Bangkok for only a short visit, Li got stuck there. He was forced to stay in the city indefinitely to attend to his preceptor, the abbot of Wat Sapathum.[10] It seems that Li arrived in Bangkok with a generalized fear of living the householder's life, an attitude that may have arisen from boyhood experiences in the village.

> During my childhood, at the age when I was just beginning to know what was what, if I saw a woman who was pregnant to the point where she was close to giving birth, it would fill me with feelings of fear and disgust. Back then the custom in my village was to tie one end of a rope to a rafter. The pregnant woman, kneeling down, would hang on to the other end of the rope and give birth. Some women would scream and moan, their faces and bodies all twisted in pain. Whenever I happened to see this, I'd run away with my hands over my ears and eyes. I wouldn't be able to sleep, out of both fear and disgust. This made a deep impression on me, which lasted for a long time. (Li1, 3; Li2, 2–3)

It was in Bangkok that Li first contemplated leaving the monastic life. He had been spending three years in a row (1929–1931) doing administrative work at the urban Thammayut temple. Feeling upset, bored, and restless, his mind slid into sexual fantasies. He constructed an elaborate story in which he imagined himself leading a householder's life. He saw himself working as a clerk in a drugstore in Bangkok, dating a sophisticated urban woman—she was beautiful and had "a good figure"—eloping and living with her, and raising children (Li2, 18–21). He gave his fantasy a realistic ending, however: he and his wife had a hard time making ends meet, and the marriage turned sour.

During this period his thoughts about worldly matters started flaring up anywhere and at any time. Although Li foresaw the disasters that potentially awaited him should he disrobe, the persisting fantasies involving women not only disturbed his practice of mindfulness, they made him ill:

> One day I started feeling constipated, so that afternoon I took a laxative, figuring that if the medicine acted as it had before, I'd have to go to the toilet at about 9 P.M. For some reason, it didn't work. The next morning I went for my almsround down the lane to Sapathum Palace. Just as I was coming to a house where they had prepared food to give to the monks, all of a sudden I had to go to the toilet so badly I could hardly stand it. I couldn't even walk to the house to accept their food. All I could do was hold myself in and walk in little pigeon steps until I came to an acacia grove by the side of the road. I plunked down my bowl and hurried through the fence into the grove. Felt so embarrassed I could have sunk my head down into the ground and died right there. When I had finished, I left the grove, picked up my almsbowl and finished my round. That day I didn't get enough to eat.[11]

Li daydreamed about finding the woman of his fantasy, sneaking off with her, making love, and living with her (Li2, 19). When the meditator's mind is utterly distracted by thoughts of pursuing and possessing a woman, the consequences can be devastating, as a second incident illustrates:

> It was a holiday. I had started out on my almsround before dawn, going down to the Sapathum market, and then up the lane behind the temple. This was a dirt lane where horses were stabled. Rain was falling and the road surface was slippery. I was walking in a very composed manner past the house of a layperson I knew who frequented the temple. My bowl was full of food and my mind drifted toward worldly matters. [I was] so

absent-minded that I slipped and fell sideways into a mud hole by the side of the road. Both of my knees were sunk about a foot into the muck, my food was spilled all over the place, my body was covered with mud. I had to hurry back to the temple, and when I arrived I warned myself: "See what happens when you even just *think* of such things?"[12]

A third incident, an event that Li witnessed, made him realize the *dukkha* (suffering) of living a householder's life and confirmed his decision not to disrobe.

One day I went out early on my almsround . . . as I was passing a row of shops, I saw an old Chinese man and woman yelling and screaming at each other in front of their shop. The woman was about fifty and wore her hair in a bun. The old man wore his hair in a pigtail. As I came to their shop, I stopped to watch. Within about two seconds, the old woman grabbed a broom and hit the man over the head with the handle. The old man grabbed the woman by the hair and kicked her in the backside. [Seeing this] I asked myself, "If that were you, what would you do?" and then I smiled: "You'd probably end the marriage for good." I felt more pleased seeing this incident than if I had received a whole bowlful of food.[13]

Li's heart was slowly becoming more and more disenchanted with worldly matters. His old opinions had reversed to the point where he now saw marriage "as something for kids, not for grown-ups." But Li could not get out of Bangkok. He knew he was standing at the crossroads between the worldly life and the way of dhamma: "If I continue to stay in Bangkok, I'll probably end up disrobing. If I want to remain in the monkhood, I must leave the city and go to the forest" (Li2, 17). He finally was saved from his misery when Man came to visit the abbot of Wat Sapathum at the end of the 1931 rains retreat and requested that Li accompany him to Chiang Mai, up north.

ENCOUNTERS WITH WOMEN

According to Wan, "The worst fear that any ascetic has is to encounter women," for this is "worse than a tiger, a bear, or an

many opportunities to get out, his stupefaction kept him t|
But gradually his disquiet and irritation grew, and he told he
was leaving for the monastery. She pleaded with him to spen(
night at her house and return to the monastery in the mor|
This increased Thet's bewilderment and brought on an atta(
bashfulness (T1, 134–135), but finally he managed to get ;
and walk back to the monastery. He felt ashamed of himsel|
feared that his fellow monks and his teachers would find ou
then it was midnight, but he lay sleepless till dawn, reflecti|
what had happened and why. "I had somehow escaped
risky circumstances in a miraculous way," he concluded.[16]

Thet was of the opinion that being naive was not neces
bad. He believed that he escaped because of his merit and
kamma. "If . . . I hadn't been so innocent, and if my mer|
good kamma hadn't been so protective, and if I had been rel|
to offer my life for Buddhism, I would probably have b
crows' bait long ago. . . . Recollecting my escape from such
ening situations brought up immense feelings of exhilaratin|
and satisfaction in my heart, so much so that my body was (
ing for days afterwards. Later, whenever I was to mentio|
episodes, those same feelings would arise and such a reacti(
sisted for almost twenty years" (T1, 135).

Unlike the thudong monks who spent their entire youtl
robes, Juan had a whole series of encounters with temptati
recollections go back to the age of eighteen. During 193£
he was working for the Royal Highways Department on th(
Nakhon Phanom road, he fell in love with a sixteen-year-
whom he saw each morning but never spoke to. "Every r
on her way to the grove to defecate, she would pass my h
those days villagers in the countryside used the edges of tl
or pastures to relieve themselves. In the morning when I \
to wash my face, I usually saw this girl walking pass my
breasts bare and wearing only a sarong. At first I felt noth
looking at her every day, I soon began to like her—she ha(
ful breasts."[17]

Thudong monks found it too tempting to stay near villz
the young Juan was no exception. In 1947 and 1948 he ;
rains retreats at Wat Jediluang in Chiang Mai. Between
rains retreats he went wandering outside the city. H

---

them make a living." This time th
Juan's mind wavered. He made a
to see the dhamma, something
dilemma" (J, 36).

The next morning he went f(
waited at the same location to off|
at her face," Juan recalls. "As I r(
menstrual pad fell to the ground
piece of cloth]. She was shocked
foot, she pressed the cloth into tl
already seen the blood-soiled clc
caught this glimpse of her blood,
holder's life and gone forth. Escal
life. Why should I walk backwar(
bowl, returned to his residence, s|
dong gear, and left the area imme(
and a layman, he wandered furtl|

In Chiang Tung, Juan observe(
faith in Buddhism. He also noti|
assertive, and he had to be caref|
one occasion he overheard them
appearance: "They talked aloud
at this monk. How handsome!
Prettier than a woman!' They
about the monk's feelings. It's a
piece of wood." An older Shar
marrying their daughter. They to
would be his if he lived with the|
ing machine will be yours. The |
fields will be yours. We will giv(
monastic life to live with us, so |
in Chiang Mai, Juan found lif|
Juan's typical solution was to le;
to the Northeast region for goo(

MONKS WHO L(

Although all the thudong mon|
their battles with sexual desire,
not. The story of one of them

evil spirit" (W, 65). Thet's and Juan's recollections suggest why. Thet—like Wan, Fan, and Waen—started monastic life when he was still a boy and spent his entire adult life in the monkhood. But Thet's naiveté led to what he called "risky encounters." One of them occurred when, as a young monk, he was paying a visit to a married woman's house. "Sometimes, if I had spare time, I would go with a boy, usually at night, to visit my lay supporters," Thet explains. "On one such evening, I went up into a house to call on one of the lay supporters. She came out and closed the door behind us. That gave me quite a fright. At that time, she was alone with her young child. Anyway, we began conversing about various things in the way that people who have regard for each other do. One thing she always seemed to ask me about was whether I wished to disrobe. Being both a straightforward sort of person and naturally shy, I would always just say 'No' and quickly go on to talk about spiritual matters."[14] But the woman instead told him about her personal life. Before her marriage, a monk had fallen in love with her. She had married her present husband because her parents and his had arranged it. She hinted that she was not happy and that this marriage might not last. It appears that Thet was well acquainted with her. "I let her talk while I listened indifferently, believing that she just wanted to talk. This time was no different. . . . I just sat listening, assuming that she was confiding in me like this because we were close friends and that she had no ulterior motive."[15]

A more experienced monk or one who had been a householder would have sensed what was coming. But Thet's innocence led to what he describes as the closest call of his life. "Her behavior did seem strange in the way she was gradually drawing herself closer to me, always edging in closer and closer. Light from the torch began to flicker and was about to go out. I told her to poke the torch to make it brighter. She smiled and did nothing. My heart quivered. I began to feel the inner heat from arising desire, mixed with a strong fear of wrongdoing and of being discovered. Even to this day, I find that moment difficult to explain. It was as if I was totally stupefied. As far as I could make out, she must have been feeling it as strongly if not more so—her facial expression seemed bereft of all mindfulness" (T1, 134; T2, 53).

Thet was frightened by the woman's boldness. Although he had many opportunities to get out, his stupefaction kept him there. But gradually his disquiet and irritation grew, and he told her he was leaving for the monastery. She pleaded with him to spend the night at her house and return to the monastery in the morning. This increased Thet's bewilderment and brought on an attack of bashfulness (T1, 134–135), but finally he managed to get away and walk back to the monastery. He felt ashamed of himself and feared that his fellow monks and his teachers would find out. By then it was midnight, but he lay sleepless till dawn, reflecting on what had happened and why. "I had somehow escaped those risky circumstances in a miraculous way," he concluded.[16]

Thet was of the opinion that being naive was not necessarily bad. He believed that he escaped because of his merit and good kamma. "If . . . I hadn't been so innocent, and if my merit and good kamma hadn't been so protective, and if I had been reluctant to offer my life for Buddhism, I would probably have become crows' bait long ago. . . . Recollecting my escape from such frightening situations brought up immense feelings of exhilarating relief and satisfaction in my heart, so much so that my body was quivering for days afterwards. Later, whenever I was to mention these episodes, those same feelings would arise and such a reaction persisted for almost twenty years" (T1, 135).

Unlike the thudong monks who spent their entire youth in the robes, Juan had a whole series of encounters with temptation. His recollections go back to the age of eighteen. During 1938, when he was working for the Royal Highways Department on the Ubon-Nakhon Phanom road, he fell in love with a sixteen-year-old girl whom he saw each morning but never spoke to. "Every morning on her way to the grove to defecate, she would pass my house. In those days villagers in the countryside used the edges of the forest or pastures to relieve themselves. In the morning when I woke up to wash my face, I usually saw this girl walking pass my hut, her breasts bare and wearing only a sarong. At first I felt nothing; but, looking at her every day, I soon began to like her—she had beautiful breasts."[17]

Thudong monks found it too tempting to stay near villages, and the young Juan was no exception. In 1947 and 1948 he spent the rains retreats at Wat Jediluang in Chiang Mai. Between the two rains retreats he went wandering outside the city. Here Juan learned that coming in contact with women during the almsround could be risky if he was not mindful. On one occasion, he was walking along a trail to a village. A woman standing alone at some distance from the others called him to stop for alms. "I went to her spot. As I removed the lid from the bowl to receive the food, she came to a sudden stop. Putting the tray and rice container down, she began to adjust her sarong. Unfolded it in a wide circle right in front of me. It was obvious that she wore nothing underneath. It was evident that she was revealing the lower part of the body before a monk. I'm only human and couldn't help feeling lustful. But I had enough sati. Quickly [I] covered the bowl and walked away."[18] To avoid running into the woman again, Juan immediately left the village.

On another occasion, Juan and his fellow monks were looking for a quiet place to meditate and went to the foot of Suthep Mountain in the outskirts of Chiang Mai. They came upon an old pagoda with several caves nearby, and here they pitched their klots. After the morning meal the others went into town, leaving Juan alone in his cave. He heard a group of women approaching and talking among themselves: "There are thudong monks in this area; let's go find them" (J, 34). One woman came upon Juan sitting and meditating in his klot. "She raised the net of the klot and yelled, 'Here's a monk! Here's a monk!' She opened the klot, stared at me disrespectfully, and smiled sensually. I looked at her. At my eye level were her full breasts. Lowering my eyes, I looked at her thin sarong and felt lust arise. Then I remembered Jao Khun Ubali's teaching, 'Keep your mind equanimous,' and tried to stay calm."[19]

The woman went to get her friends. Some of them gave Juan gifts. One exclaimed, "Tu jao suai!" (The monk is handsome). After receiving Juan's blessings, they left (J, 35). Juan left soon afterward when he saw that more women were coming to look at the monks. Hoping to avoid similar encounters, he headed for the forests and mountains of San Kamphaeng and Mae Taeng Districts.

In another incident that Juan recalls, a lay supporter, a pretty woman with a pleasing manner who was a sister of the district officer, offered him alms regularly: "She often looked at me in a sensual way. Her guardians also urged me to disrobe and help them make a living." This time the temptation was so strong that Juan's mind wavered. He made a vow: "If I have enough barami to see the dhamma, something must happen to solve this dilemma" (J, 36).

The next morning he went for alms as usual. The woman waited at the same location to offer him food. "I tried not to look at her face," Juan recalls. "As I removed the lid off the bowl, her menstrual pad fell to the ground [in those days this was simply a piece of cloth]. She was shocked and tried to cover it. Using her foot, she pressed the cloth into the mud to hide it. By then I had already seen the blood-soiled cloth. I felt sorry for her. Having caught this glimpse of her blood, I knew that I had left the house-holder's life and gone forth. Escaped from the lower to the higher life. Why should I walk backward?" (J, 36). He covered his alms bowl, returned to his residence, skipped the meal, packed his thu-dong gear, and left the area immediately. Accompanied by a novice and a layman, he wandered further north into the Shan states.

In Chiang Tung, Juan observed that the laypeople had strong faith in Buddhism. He also noticed that the Shan women were assertive, and he had to be careful around the younger ones. On one occasion he overheard them commenting about his physical appearance: "They talked aloud among themselves, saying, 'Look at this monk. How handsome! Nice complexion and nice face! Prettier than a woman!' They were neither shy nor concerned about the monk's feelings. It's as if the monk were a statue or a piece of wood." An older Shan couple tried to talk Juan into marrying their daughter. They told him of their wealth, of all that would be his if he lived with them: "We really like you. The sew-ing machine will be yours. The house will be yours. These paddy fields will be yours. We will give you everything. Please leave the monastic life to live with us, so we can depend on you" (J, 36). As in Chiang Mai, Juan found life in Chiang Tung too tempting. Juan's typical solution was to leave the area. This time he returned to the Northeast region for good.

MONKS WHO LOST THE BATTLE

Although all the thudong monks we have been discussing won their battles with sexual desire, a number of Man's disciples did not. The story of one of them was told by another disciple of

Man's staying in the hills outside Chiang Mai. It occurred during the 1930s, when Man was wandering in northern Siam. The events resemble Waen's and Fan's experiences, except that this particular thudong monk was unable to resist his desires.

One day Monk X (no name was given) went with other thudong monks to bathe at a water hole near a path leading to the village farms. The path was quite some distance from the village and was deserted most of the time. While the monks were preparing for their bath, a number of young Lahu hill-tribe women happened to pass by. Monk X caught sight of one of them and immediately fell in love with her. From that moment on he could not sleep. He was overcome by worry and fear of this strange feeling, the strength of which he never imagined existed. He was also frightened that Ajan Man would find out. Meditating all night, he tried to control his desire, hoping that it would drop away during meditation. But Man learned of this monk's struggle, supposedly through his mind-reading ability, and tried to help him. He allowed Monk X to skip going on almsround so he could intensify his efforts in meditation alone in his hut. This did not help, however. Frustrated and embarrassed, Monk X decided to seek another location for solitude. Having received permission from the ajan, he went to stay near a hamlet farther away. But as fate would have it, he ran into the young Lahu woman again. Eventually he disrobed and married her. His fellow thudong monks saw him as a "poor victim of circumstances," unable to get away from his kamma (M2, 168).

Even thudong monks with a strong meditation practice were not immune to temptation. In 1937 Thet spent the rains retreat at a forest hermitage near Pong Village in Mae Taeng District, Chiang Mai. He was heading a group that consisted of Buntham, Kheuang, Chaup, and an unnamed monk from Loei. Of these four others, Thet recalls, Chaup and Kheuang were the most experienced.

> In this group it was Ajan Chaup who was the most strict in his thudong practices. . . . Venerable Kheuang was particularly gifted in the faculty of knowing another person's mind. If something was preoccupying anyone's mind or if someone had committed any breach of the monastic rule, it would be detected by one of these two monks. . . .

Ven. Kheuang was adept at training his mind to enter tranquillity, and he could remain in a state of calm all day and night.
While walking around in seemingly quite an ordinary way, in
his mind he would feel as if he was walking on air. While at
other times he might feel as if he had penetrated into the interior
of earth.[20]

Shortly after the rains retreat Thet and Kheuang went off in
search of solitude, following the Mae Taeng River upstream. They
stayed in a secluded place in a mountainous area where tea shrubs
were growing. One day, Thet left his thudong gear with Kheuang
in an abandoned wat while he climbed a ridge to find a suitable
place to stay. When Thet returned he noticed that Kheuang was
moody. The following morning Kheuang lost his temper with
Thet over some small matter, but at the end of the day he admitted he was at fault. Then he explained what happened the previous day while Thet was away. A young woman had strolled by in
the company of some local young men. Kheuang had watched her
flirting with them, and this had excited him. As a result, his meditation was now going badly. He wanted to take leave of Thet and
go off wandering alone. Thet tried to counsel him and recommended various ways of stilling the emotions—but without success.
So Thet let him go. Three months later they met again. It appears that Kheuang had stopped meditating. Thet encouraged him
to make a fresh start with his meditation, but again he had no success: "Afterwards I learnt with great regret that he had disrobed.
He was a strong-willed individual and did nothing in half measures, but he was also very opinionated and even Ajan Man's
dhamma talks didn't always convince him. He had once been a
'tough guy' [*nakleng*] back in his home village before being
ordained as a monk. He left the village wat without any real goal
in mind."[21]
Like his fellow thudong monks, Thet believed that a nimit
could portend the future. Before ever meeting Thet, Kheuang had
a vision about him that foretold his later act of disrobing. "A road
appeared leading straight from [Kheuang] to where I was. He
made a trouble-free journey along the road that ended right at the
foot of the stairs leading to my hut. He then seemed to catch hold
of the stairs and started climbing—they seemed extremely long

and steep—up to me. He bowed to me three times; I offered him a complete set of robes but he refused to accept them" (T1, 179; T2, 77). Thet concluded that Kheuang was one of those monks in whom samādhi did not develop into *pañña* (wisdom): "Even though Ven. Kheuang's mind didn't withdraw from concentration, he lacked the wisdom to investigate *tilakkhana* [the three characteristics—impermanence, unsatisfactoriness, and nonself]" (T1, 180).

Young monks were not the only ones whose minds were troubled by sexual thoughts; older ones were, too. One such monk was Samret, a revered teacher. Samret was ordained as a novice in early youth, became a meditation monk, and eventually started teaching. He was known as a strict, serious meditator and was much respected. When he was nearly sixty years old, he fell in love with a lay supporter's daughter. His decision to quit the monastic life shocked his disciples and lay followers, who had expected that he would remain in the robes for the rest of his life. To the senior monks, the disrobing of a teacher was a disgrace to all practicing monks. They tried in vain to stop Samret from leaving the monkhood. Dun in particular reminded him to exert himself harder in meditation, so as to understand his mind better. But practicing meditation did not help. "I can't remain in the monkhood. Every time I meditate, all I see is her face," Samret told Dun. Dun, realizing that Samret's case was hopeless, responded loudly, "[This is] because when you meditate, instead of looking at your mind, you focus on her ass. No wonder only her buttocks appeared. Go, go follow your desires. Go away."[22]

Samret's case indicated that older monks may have had harder battles with sexual desire. As one teacher warned his pupil, "The real trouble begins well after 45—between then and 60 you will have a hard time. For then your body revolts, your mind panics—they want to enter into their rights ere the gates close."[23] Decades of meditation practice did not necessarily mean that the monk was beyond temptation.

Clearly, thudong monks were not immune to sexual desire. What about Isan administrative monks? A thudong monk's account tells of one such monk, Ariyakhunathan (Seng).[24] Maha Seng was a sangha provincial head who took up meditation and practiced it seriously for decades. It was believed that Seng had attained the higher jhānas. Yet later on, in the 1950s, he left the monkhood. Lui, who spent the 1952 rains retreat with him at Deer Garden Hill in Khon Kaen, recalls: "Ven. Ariyakhunathan had a pleasant disposition. He could discuss many mystical matters. It's a pity that he did not go directly to the Four Noble Truths. Since his practice was not supported by the three characteristics, all the supernormal knowledge he attained in his meditation practice, such as different levels of jhāna, eventually deteriorated. So he had to disrobe."[25]

Lui implies that Seng disrobed because he could not resist sexual desire.[26] So in two cases, Seng and Kheuang, monks highly skilled in mental concentration lacked clear insight into this aspect of reality.

Thet and Cha are better representatives of their fellow thudong monks' wisdom. Thet learned from experience that when clear insight occurs together with strong concentration, the mind will become disenchanted and dispassionate with regard to all conditioned things. The mind will dwell entirely in a state of mature and chastened dispassion, no matter what it sees or hears, and no matter where.[27] Once knowledge and insight into impermanence, unsatisfactoriness, and emptiness arise, Cha confirms, it is "the beginning of true wisdom, the heart of meditation, which leads to liberation."[28]

CHAPTER 6

Wandering

and Hardship

Thudong monks valued wandering as an ascetic practice, as a means of training the mind to face hardship and the unpredictable. Whenever they wandered far from the relative comfort and security of the monastic life, they had to contend with fear, pain, fatigue, hunger, frustration, and distress; and sometimes they risked death. The areas in which they wandered were not confined by the political boundaries of Siam/Thailand. They often walked across national borders to the Shan states, Burma, Laos, and Cambodia. In Man's time a monk could wander freely into neighboring countries, and thudong monks willingly did so. Unlike academic and bureaucratic monks in the sangha hierarchy, they had a keen interest in faraway places and thought nothing of walking great distances to reach them.

The wandering monks' journeys were uncharted. They had no maps, no guides, and often no specific idea of where they were going. It did not matter how long it took to get from one place to another. It was the going, the wandering, that counted. Wandering into unfamiliar terrain forced a monk to be constantly alert and aware. He never knew where he would spend the night, where the next meal would come from, or what difficulties he would encounter. He learned to live with insecurities and discomforts—life's inevitable dukkha.

Although, during their wanderings, thudong monks would stop to pay homage to a local stupa containing important relics, visiting famous shrines or sacred sites was not their main goal. They were more interested in visiting meditation teachers or in exploring unfamiliar environments, both natural and cultural. Sometimes monks found themselves in the company of villagers who had never seen a Buddhist monk before and had little idea how to treat him. Sometimes they encountered monks belonging to other Buddhist traditions. Studying these meetings will enrich our understanding of the thudong monks' training and the diversity of religious practices in Siam/Thailand.

SEARCHING FOR SUITABLE CAVES

To understand the thudong monks' training, we must take into consideration the forests, mountains, and caves that were their schools. Wandering from place to place was an exercise in ascetic living, training the mind not to be attached to places or to comforts. During the dry seasons a monk would practice under a tree, on a rocky promontory, or in a cave. Thudong monks were continually on the lookout for suitable caves, ones with good air circulation, for example. They believed that many monks in the past had attained enlightenment while meditating in such places. Man told his disciples that "caves or rock shelters provide suitable conditions under which the mind can attain one-pointedness without much difficulty. Once the mind is focused, it can see many mysterious things that an ordinary mind cannot."[1] Isolated caves were good testing grounds. A steadfast monk, one with a strong practice, was the monk who could seclude himself in a remote cave in the dense forest and survive whatever came his way without abandoning his meditation.

During the first half of this century thudong monks from the Northeast went wandering in the North as far as Chiang Tung (Keng Tung) and Chiang Rung (Jeng Hung). No roads as yet linked the Northeast to the northern hinterland. Traveling, particularly on foot, was extremely difficult. The three rules that Thet laid down for his companions before setting out on their first cross-region trip indicate that the thudong practice was not for the faint-hearted.

1. There should be no grumbling about hardships encountered along the way, for example, difficulties with the journey, food, or shelter. If either of us should fall ill, then we will assist each other to the best of our ability—"together to the end."

2. If one of us should become homesick for family or friends—for example, for one's parents—there should be no aiding the other to go back.

3. We must be resolved to face death, wherever and however it comes.[2]

Unless a fellow monk agreed to abide by these rules, Thet would not take him along on a thudong.

Today there are hardly any isolated caves left in Thailand, but in Man's time there were many, particularly in the northern region. Man, Waen, Thet, and Li left records of their search for suitable caves in the North. Man himself had his near-death experience in Sarika Cave, in which, we know already, he supposedly became an anāgāmī.

Li left a detailed account of the importance of an isolated cave for mental training. While searching for Ajan Man in Chiang Mai, Li investigated a number of caves that Man had said were good for solitary meditation.[3] When Li did not find Man at Wat Jediluang in Chiang Mai, he started his search on a mountain about three kilometers from Meuang Aun Village in Doi Saket District. Here he entered Dark Cave (Tham Meut), where, Man had said, nagas came to worship—a stalagmite inside the cave was their pagoda. Although he was traveling alone, Li was not afraid to investigate the cave. Like other wandering monks, Li remembered the interior of the caves in considerable detail, and he clearly felt that his memories were worth recording—a testimony to the importance of caves in the thudong monks' lives.

"This was a strange and remarkable cave. On top of the mountain was a Buddha image—from what period I couldn't say. In the middle of the mountain the ground opened down into a deep chasm. Going down into the chasm, I came to a piece of teakwood placed as a bridge across a crevice. Edging my way across to the other side, I found myself on a wide shelf of rock. As I walked on farther, it became pitch dark, so I lit a lantern and continued. I came to another bridge—this time a whole log of teak—reaching to another rock. This is where the air began to feel chilly" (Li1, 42). Exploring further, Li reached an enormous cavern. "I'd say it could have held at least 3,000 people. The floor of the cavern was flat with little waves, like ripples on water. Shooting straight up from the middle of the floor was a spectacular stalagmite, as white as a cumulus cloud, eight meters tall and so wide it would have taken two people to put their arms around it. Around the stalagmite was a circle of small round bumps—like the bumps in the middle of gongs—each about half a meter tall. Inside the circle was a deep flat basin. The whole area was dazzling white and very beautiful" (Li1, 42).

Local people believed that the mountain was sacred. They told Li that at the beginning of each rains retreat the mountain would give out a roar: "Any year the roar was especially loud there would be good rain and abundant harvests" (Li1, 43).

Leaving Dark Cave, Li walked on to Pong Village, where he ran into a monk named Khian. Having once stayed with Man and understanding the importance of caves, Khian agreed to join Li in exploring Golden Gourd Cave (Tham Buap Thaung), ten kilometers away in the middle of dense forest, far from human habitations. The cave was so named because at one place fool's gold seeped through a crack and lay at the bottom of a pool of water. "It was a deep cave. . . . The people of the area claimed that there was a fierce spirit living in the cave. Whoever tried to spend the night there, they said, would be kept awake all night by the feeling that someone was stepping on his legs, his stomach, his back, etc.—which had everyone afraid of the place" (Li1, 43).

Ajan Man had told Li that a monk named Chai had once come to this cave to spend the night, but Chai couldn't get any sleep because he kept hearing the sound of someone walking in and out of the cave all night long. Man had recommended that Li meditate here—perhaps so that Li might test the truth of the rumors about the cave and test his resistance to fear. That night Li and his companion stayed in the cave, but they saw no ghosts and heard no footsteps.

After leaving the cave Li and Khian wandered separately for a while. They then rejoined to spend a week in the Chiang Dao

Mountains, three days of which they spent in Chiang Dao Cave.[4] They made an all-out effort both day and night to practice centering the mind. Li recalls the night of the full moon of Makha Bucha, when he decided to sit in meditation as an offering to the Buddha: "A little after 9 P.M. my mind became absolutely still. It seemed as if breath and light were radiating from my body in all directions. . . . my breath . . . was so subtle that I scarcely seemed to be breathing at all. My heart was quiet, my mind still. The breath in my body didn't seem to be moving at all. It was simply quiet and still. My mind had completely stopped formulating thoughts. How all my thoughts had stopped, I had no idea. But I was aware—feeling bright, expansive, and at ease—with a sense of freedom that wiped out all feeling of pain" (Li1, 49).

His mind was quiet until it attained the stage of fixed penetration when insights arise. After an hour of stillness, Li recalls, the Buddha's teachings began to appear in his heart. "This, in short, is what they said: 'Focus down and examine becoming, birth, death and unawareness to see how they come about.' A vision came to me as plain as if it were right before my eyes: 'Birth is like a lightning flash. Death is like a lightning flash.' So I focused on the causes leading to birth and death, until I came to the word *avijja* —unawareness. . . . I considered things in this manner, back and forth, over and over until dawn. When it all finally became clear, I left concentration. My heart and body both seemed light, open and free: my heart, extremely satisfied and full" (Li1, 49).

Li was pleased with his meditation progress. He had now stayed in the two caves that Man had recommended and had passed the test. From Chiang Dao he and Khian went north to Fang District, where they spent some time meditating in another cave, and from there they wandered on to Chiang Saen, Chiang Rai, Phayao, Lampang, and Uttaradit Provinces.

Thudong monks also believed that no matter how isolated the caves were, monks meditating in them were never really alone. As Man told his disciples, "In those caves on the mountains the meditator should guard his behavior. He should not think that no one is around to see what he is doing. He should always be mindful and conduct himself so that the sight of him would be pleasant to the eyes of deities from various realms who lived in the area."[5] This belief, embedded in local Buddhist traditions, kept the thudong monk on his guard. Even in a solitary cave high on a mountain, monks felt that their behavior was being watched.

As a rule, thudong monks did not stay in one cave for too long. As soon as they felt comfortable and got used to a cave, it was time to pick up their thudong gear and leave. This practice of moving from cave to cave prevented the monk from getting attached to a particular cave. From 1943 to 1945, for example, Chaup spent the rains retreats among the Karen hill tribes in the Chiang Tung and Chiang Kham Mountains.[6] Between the rains he wandered from mountain to mountain, staying in various caves to meditate. The length of his stay was anywhere between six days to a month in each cave.

ADAPTING TO LOCAL CULTURE

During the first half of this century, many thudong monks wandered extensively in the northern region or crossed the border into the Shan states and lower Burma (see figure 6). In their wandering, the monks had to face various kinds and degrees of deprivation and inconvenience. Of the thirteen ascetic practices, the hardest ones to observe were the rules requiring going out for alms, having only one meal a day, eating out of their bowls, and not accepting food presented afterward. But as Bua says, thudong monks were not afraid of places where food was scarce and comfort could not be expected.[7]

Most villages were isolated, and their religious customs were diverse. In many places where thudong monks traveled, the local people knew something about who they were and what their needs were. But many customs that people today regard as traditionally Buddhist were unknown to villagers in remote areas. In northern Siam, Laos, the Shan states, or Cambodia, thudong monks often came across individuals or even whole communities that were unfamiliar with them. These encounters were good tests of a monk's resourcefulness.

In northern Siam, for example, the hill tribes were not at all sure how to treat monks. Once Waen and Teu, exhausted and hungry after walking through the forest in meuang Phrae, entered a Yao settlement hoping to find alms. But the houses were empty, the inhabitants having left for the fields. As they approached the very last hut, a man stuck his head out. "Friend, we have nothing to eat," Waen said. "Please give us some rice." "I have only a small supply of rice," said the man. "I have cooked rice, but it's for us to eat. The uncooked rice is for sale." Then he looked straight at Waen's empty alms bowl and offered to buy it; he wanted to use it as a pot for cooking rice. "Almost laughed at this," Waen recalls, "and for a moment forgot how starved we were."[8] Waen, like many thudong monks, was accepting of local diversity and did not pass judgment. "The Yao man was straightforward and honest. He had no pretension; he spoke what was on his mind. He wasn't intending to hurt anyone's feelings or displease anyone. He was sincere" (Wn, 36).

Figure 6. *Map of northern Thailand and neighboring countries*

But, seeing that it was hopeless to get alms, Waen and Teu pushed on. Along the way they encountered a Yao woman. Determined to get some food this time, Waen was more direct: "Friend, we are starving. We have no rice to eat. Please give us some."[9] The woman asked the monks to wait, then she went into the hut and came back with a container full of rice, which she then emptied into the monks' bowls. Having found a good place to sit and eat, the monks poured some water into their bowls, mixed it with the rice, and ate.

In Lampang, another northern province, Li too found that villagers were unfamiliar with the custom of the almsround. Li and Khian had been staying in the isolated Great Rapids Cave. It was a fine place to meditate, peaceful and quiet, but they could not find enough food. Li complains, "We went for alms in a nearby village, but no one paid much attention to us. For two days we had nothing to eat but rice—not even a grain of salt. The third day . . . I got nothing but a ball of glutinous rice."[10]

Khian decided to leave. "I've had nothing but rice for two days now," he said, "and I'm starting to feel weak." Li was determined to stick it out. Unlike Waen, Li did not want to ask for food directly, but he was willing to compromise his thudong practice of getting food only from the almsround. He made a resolution: "Today, I'm not going to ask anyone for food, either by going for alms or by out-and-out asking. Only if someone invites me to have food will I be willing to eat" (Li1, 55). He gathered his thudong gear and continued his journey. After walking for an hour, Li passed a village of three households. A woman came running out of a house, her hands raised in respect, and invited Li into her home to have some food. "My husband shot a barking deer yesterday and I'm afraid of the bad kamma," she said. "So I'd like to make merit with a monk. You have only to come to my house and have something to eat."[11]

Although Li had never eaten deer meat before, he was hungry enough to try it. The meal was substantial and Li was grateful. He was spared from hunger by this woman's fear of the kammic consequences of violating the first precept (not to kill). As for the villager, she was obviously glad to see the wandering monk because she lived so far from a wat. It gave her an opportunity to make merit.

In Mae Hong Son, the most isolated province in northern Siam, local people did not know about the custom of the almsround either. Waen reports that the local custom was to bring food to the monk. Waen had found a cave near a stream and was staying there alone for a rains retreat. The people in this area, mostly Shan, were glad to see a wandering monk. What struck Waen was the importance they placed on receiving a blessing *(pan phon)* from him. "They started coming here early in the morning. At sunrise they were already at the cave entrance. Besides food, they brought candles. They waited until everybody got here before they presented the food and candles to me. They wouldn't leave unless I gave them a blessing. . . . They would fuss or hang around if I didn't give them a blessing. No matter how small the gifts, they wanted the receipt of blessings. They believed it was important, and that otherwise they would get no merit. I told them that the next day I would go on an almsround in their village. But they preferred to bring the food here. Since it was their custom, I complied."[12]

Thet also encountered local people unused to monks. In early 1933 he and Aunsi, a fellow monk, went north to search for Ajan Man, who had left Wat Jediluang in Chiang Mai without a trace. After staying for a few nights at this Thammayut wat, they continued their journey. They went to various hermitages where Ajan Man had once stayed. When they could not find him, they decided to go beyond Siam's border into the Shan states. They would treat the journey as an opportunity for mind training while living under trees or in caves.

This journey into unfamiliar terrain was, according to Thet's recollection, a training of the mind beyond his anticipation. He and Aunsi had to cope with a series of mishaps and all kinds of mental states: hunger, pain, fatigue, fear, frustration, irritation, and anxiety. Thet recalls an occasion when "there was no longer any path forward [and] we had to turn back. Almost straight away I mis-stepped on a rock and fell so that the sole of my foot was deeply gashed. Night was approaching so I used my shoulder-cloth to bind the wound. We decided to scale the steep side slopes that were mostly scree. Well, it was quite a scramble, for wherever one placed a foot it would slip and slide" (T1, 145). They reached the summit around 7 P.M. and saw an indistinct footpath winding its way along a ridge. They were glad because it meant they were near a village. But when they examined the trail closely, they realized that they were still a long way from human habitation. As it was very late, they decided to rest where they were for the night: "We each arranged a place to our liking amongst the thick grassy undergrowth. Yet all night long we were unable to get any sleep. The wind was too strong to hang the mosquito nets from our *klots*, while on the ground it wasn't just termites attacking us, for swarms of ants also came, attracted by the blood from my wound and the sweat of our bodies. We had to wrap cloths around our eyes to prevent the ants from getting in to drink from our tears" (T1, 146).

At dawn they rose and looked back down on the way they had come. Far below they saw paddy fields as tiny squares. They walked back, cutting across jungle and more open forest, hoping to pick up the trail they missed the day before. Around nine o'clock they reached a village. When a village woman came out to see them, the monks told her about their mishaps: "We thought to ask straight out for something to eat but were afraid that this was something blameworthy." They inquired indirectly if some food might be brought to them. The woman seemed to indicate that they would get something to eat. The two wayfarers went to bathe in a stream.

"When I had finished washing, the pain in my foot grew so excruciating that I couldn't walk on it at all," Thet recalls. "Ven. Aunsi, my companion through all this suffering, felt faint and dizzy and couldn't stand up himself. All we could do was to wait for her to bring us something to eat—but there was no sign of that." Now their hunger and fatigue overcame them. "Fortunately I had some smelling salts for dizziness with me in my shoulder bag and so was able to attend to Ven. Aunsi, but it was well after ten o'clock in the morning before he was able to get up" (T1, 147).

Aunsi went into the hamlet, which consisted of only two houses, and found it inhabited only by two boys; all the adults had gone to work in the jungle. As it turned out, the inhabitants of this village did not know the custom of offering food to the monks, so the monks traded the only possession they had—two boxes of matches—for some cooked food. "In exchange we got two small baskets of sticky rice, two dishes of chili and fermented soya bean paste with two small bunches of steamed vegetables. We had our meal and how good it tasted!" After the meal was over, the pain in Thet's foot increased, so much so that "my whole leg was inflamed and throbbing. I endured this until just after three o'clock in the afternoon, when we moved on. I hobbled along for about three kilometers before we reached another village, where we stayed for eleven nights. We rested and recovered our strength and I was able to attend to my wound."[13]

Thet and Aunsi's trip to the Shan states had demanded considerable physical and mental strength, as well as remarkable resilience in the face of hardship. Waen encountered a different sort of problem when he went wandering alone in 1921. From Mae Sot District (today in Tak Province) he crossed a river into Burma. Waen and the customs officers in Burma could not understand each other, but he was allowed in. After walking through some hilly forests, he spent the night in Kawkareik and then traveled by boat all night to Moulmein and to Mataban. In that town Waen saw many monks, but when he went on the almsround nobody came outside to give him food. He was puzzled.

> The next day a Shan monk saw me. He asked if I got any food. I told him that nobody had given food. The Shan monk then told me to follow him on the almsround. When he went up into the house I realized that [in their custom] food was offered inside the house. Each householder gave a tiny bit of food: one spoonful of rice and one spoonful of peanut curry. With this small portion, even if I received alms from ten households it still would not fill me. Some days I had to walk for such a long distance that I got very hungry. So when I reached an isolated area I stopped to eat whatever I had in my bowl, then continued the almsround. . . . To practice dhamma in Burma would be futile. Not enough food to survive. (Wn, 45)

While in Burma, Waen ran into a Khmer monk who had been living there for several years. The Khmer monk shared Waen's opinion. He told Waen it was tiring to go for alms in Burma. He usually got only a small amount of food, some days barely enough. "It's better in Siam. [I] often got plenty of food during almsround—enough to feed myself and several animals. Here I can barely feed myself" (Wn, 45). Waen did not say to which part of Siam the Khmer monk was referring.

The difficulties that these monks experienced while wandering in the northern region were compounded when they wandered even further afield. In northern Laos, it was apparently customary to offer food to monks in the evening (although Theravada vinaya forbids eating after noon). In the early years of his thudong life, Waen wandered extensively in Laos with his fellow monk, Teu, and they came across this custom in many areas. One evening they stopped just before dusk not far from a village. They had just sat down to rest when they saw a group of ten village women walking toward them. The women were carrying containers of glutinous rice, which they put down in front of the monks. Unable to understand the language that the women spoke, Waen tried to tell them to bring the men. Apparently understanding this, they left. After a while a group of village men came and said, "*Jao bun* [monks], please eat the rice. You have been walking very far. You must be exhausted and hungry."[14] Waen declined the offer, asking them to bring rice in the morning and requesting some hot water to drink.

In their wandering, adhering to the monastic rules set by Bangkok authorities was not always possible. When it was a matter of survival, the thudong monks adapted to the circumstances. Waen recalls how difficult it sometimes was to receive alms. "To get food from forest villagers [*chao ban pa*], we have to do it the old way: we stand in front of their huts and make noise by coughing or clearing our throats. Once they hear the noise, they come out. Sometimes we have to tell them to bring rice and put it in our bowls" (Wn, 35).

Years later, during Waen's second trip to Buffalo Mountain (Phu Khao Khwai) in Laos, he discovered that monks in this area followed a different practice—they were vegetarian. "There is a strange practice among these villagers. When they see a monk going for almsround they call each other out, saying, "Come, let us give alms. *Ya tham* [respected teacher] is here. Bring sugar-cane juice to the monk. *Ya tham* likes sweet stuff." When the neighbors hear this announcement, they all come out and fill up [my] bowl with molasses" (Wn, 39). Waen explains that these villagers, like the Shan, give monks rice with sugar-cane juice or molasses. They were under the impression that monks did not eat meat,[15] only sweet things. Waen comments, "It was all right to eat rice with sugar-cane juice for a few days. After that [I] got tired of it" (Wn, 39).

Wiriyang and Kongma (both were Man's disciples) encountered a similar custom on the Thai border.[16] Coming back from Cambodia, they stopped at Thaton Village, whose inhabitants were all Khmer. The thudong monks were given only rice and sugar-cane juice. Here, too, the villagers apparently believed that thudong monks did not eat meat. "So we ate only rice and sugar-cane juice. . . . I thought they might bring more rice for us. [We] drank a lot of water to make it easier to swallow it. Felt contented nevertheless."[17]

Thet does not disguise the fact that he found it hard to be a stranger among people on whom he had to depend. He says that he felt "at home" with the various hardships he always had to put up with, but as soon as he crossed over the frontier, his "frustrations and hardships increased a thousandfold." He had to contend with different cultural traditions and customs as well as the language barrier. Referring to Shan Buddhists, for example, he comments, "Although we were all supposed to be Buddhists, the customs were sometimes very different from what we were familiar with and sometimes they didn't seem even in line with the *Dhamma-Vinaya* that the Lord Buddha had set down. It was very trying and bothersome for us as we were their visitors and guests."[18]

But for Kongma and Wiriyang, differences in custom and language proved only minor inconveniences. Wiriyang recalls an experience at a village on the outskirts of Battambang in Cambodia: "In the morning we went for alms. The Khmer people who gave us food noticed the size of our bowls. They kept staring at them. They had never seen such big ones and commented, 'La au, la au,' meaning 'how pretty.' We got acquainted with the Khmer monks and novices in the wat. Although we didn't understand each other's language, as fellow monks we felt connected to one another."[19]

RESPECTING DIFFERENT CULTURES

Sangha authorities have always taken Bangkok's centrality for granted. Bangkok is the center of their world, and all customs differing from Bangkok's are "other."[20] They have believed that their rationalized form of Buddhism was superior to local "superstitions," and they have insisted that state Buddhism was applicable to everyone. One of the main goals of the sangha centralization was to change the religious and cultural values of indigenous peoples and make them follow Bangkok's form of religious orthodoxy. The thudong monks, whose religion was grounded in local traditions, were too open-minded for that. Because they had wandered widely and had been exposed to many kinds of people, they recognized that other religious practices were also effective and therefore were true dhamma.

In the Shan states, for example, the monks noticed that people took their local religious practices to heart. They observed that local people had high moral values; there was no need for the thudong monks to teach them precepts. Man, in particular, was impressed by the Shan people he met in 1911. He considered Shan villagers to be highly ethical. "Owners of shops, for example, did not have to be around all the time. If they had to leave the shop unattended, they wrote the prices on the products. The customers took the goods and left money as required. There were no thefts. People here were good-looking and well behaved. [Ajan Man] wondered what aspect of the dhamma they were observing."[21]

Thet too had seen that many local Buddhist traditions were highly effective. Although the rigors of his journey into the Shan states in 1933 had changed Thet's feelings about a second trip to Burma, it did not cloud his judgment of the Shan people. "We had seen many admirable features. The people there liked peace and quiet, and they were generous and open-hearted. There were no thieves or crooks, and no domestic animals—no poultry or pigs—because they wouldn't kill animals. Their diet was basically vegetables, seasoned with chilli, salt, beans and sesame. . . . I really appreciated their sincere goodwill and religious faith, and their peaceful and orderly way of life. No disturbing noise would be heard at night even though village houses might adjoin the monastery's fence. It was just as if there was no village at all" (T1, 142–143).

Unlike Thet and Aunsi, Chaup had little difficulty in the Shan states. This might be because he stayed there longer than his fellow thudong monks, learned the language, and was able to preach in Shan fluently.[22] Chaup wandered into Burma twice during the late 1930s and mid 1940s and spent nearly six years in the Shan states. Chaup particularly singled out the beauty and the moral conduct of the Shan women. "They have a light complexion. [They're] beautiful physically as well as fine mentally. This must be the result of their strict adherence to discipline. It reflects in their behavior. While staying in this area there's no need to teach them precepts."[23]

Thudong monks who wandered into Cambodia also had an ability to relate to unfamiliar cultures and languages. Li, Kongma, and Wiriyang have described their trips in detail.

In 1933–1934 Li went to Cambodia with two monk disciples and two boys. As was customary, they stayed in the forest, in cemeteries, or in caves. Li did not know anyone in northern Cambodia, but his thudong practices helped him gain many Khmer followers along the way. In Sisophon a number of Khmer people came to discuss dhamma with Li: "They became very impressed and began to follow me in throngs. When the time came to leave, some of them—both men and women—began to cry" (Li1, 61; Li2, 46). From Sisophon, Li and his disciples went on foot to Battambang and stayed in the cemetery of Wat Ta-aek, about a kilometer from town. On their way to Phnom Penh they walked across Wild Lychee Mountain (Phom Kilen), which had about twenty small villages at its foot. They stayed a few days in a Vietnamese temple with a statue of the Buddha carved out of a high, overhanging cliff. Li went to explore the caves, and afterward the thudong monks divided their time between the Vietnamese temple and a nearby cave.[24] They stayed there for about a week before continuing their walk to the south of the mountains.

In one village in the forest they heard a strange story, one that would arouse fear in an inexperienced thudong monk. About three kilometers from the village there were three mountains covered by open forest. "The strange thing about the mountains," Li relates, "was that if anyone went to cut any of the trees, they would either die a violent death, become seriously ill, or suffer misfortune of one sort or another. Sometimes on the lunar sabbath, in the middle of the night, a bright light would come shooting out of the summit of the third mountain. It seemed that a number of times monks had gone to spend the rains retreat on top of the third mountain, but had to leave in the middle of the retreat, either because of strong winds, rains or lightning strikes."[25]

The villagers wanted Li to climb to the mountain top to see what was there. So the next morning the thudong monks set out for the third mountain. Li looked over the area and found it to be a nice place to stay. But his four disciples were afraid, probably of the spirits on the mountain, and refused to stay there. (Belief in the guardian spirits of mountains and forests was also a strong component of the Lao and Yuan traditions in Siam.) So they descended and spent the night in a quiet forest nearby. The following day they went into the village for alms. The villagers had spread the word among themselves about the thudong monks. That night a large number of them came to listen to Li's sermon. By then Li had been in Cambodia for over a month and was able to preach in Khmer well enough.

Almost a decade after Li wandered into Cambodia, Kongma and his pupil Wiriyang traveled on a similar route. This time the thudong monks did not need passports because that part of Cambodia now belonged to Thailand (Siam's new official name).[26] At the time, Kongma was residing in a wat in Chanthaburi, in eastern Thailand. In April 1941 he heard that his teacher, Man, whom he had not seen for twelve years, had finally returned to Isan from the North. So Kongma and Wiriyang set out on the long walk to the Northeast. The purpose of their wandering was to meet Man in Sakon Nakhon and, along the way, to meditate in solitude.

After crossing the border of Thailand into Cambodia, they walked to Phaya Kamput Commune. They spent the night under the trees and went for alms in the morning. They soon found that the people here had their own Buddhist customs: "The inhabitants were mostly Khmer. When they saw us, they called out to each other, 'Luk song mok hoei.' I don't know what that means. Moments later many people came out to give alms—but rice only, nothing to accompany it. After [we] returned to our place, a layperson brought us a small bowl of soup. Their rice, though not glutinous, was delicious and had a nice fragrance. [We] mixed the rice with water so it would be easier to swallow" (Wi, 20). After the meal, the thudong monks continued their walk.

They reached Olamjiak Village at the end of the day. The village abbot, having heard of Kongma's reputation, asked them to spend the night at the wat. At first Kongma turned down the invitation, for he preferred to stay in the forest, but then he acquiesced. When they were alone in their sleeping quarters, Kongma mentioned this dilemma to Wiriyang. "Look at me. Try as I might to stay out of a wat, I end up in one." "But he offered his hospitality," Wiriyang replied, "so one should accommodate him." "Such compromising destroys the thudong tradition," said Kongma (Wi, 20). Clearly there were differences of opinion among Man's disciples: some thought there was nothing wrong with accommodating town monks' or laypeople's wishes; others held that they must be firm in their ascetic practice.

Like his fellow thudong monks, Wiriyang made an effort to learn about the local people wherever he went. The Kula people, for example, hoped that he and Kongma would stay permanently in their village wat. Every day they sent the village chief to beg Kongma to stay. Wiriyang was in favor of at least delaying their departure; he believed that thudong monks have a duty to teach lay folk. But Kongma wanted to leave immediately; in his opinion this sort of involvement was a trap. Wiriyang recalled that while giving him a massage one night, Ajan Kongma said, "Wiriyang, I managed to leave Beautiful Banyan Monastery in Lotus Pond Commune, Chanthaburi. I shouldn't get involved in another wat. Being an abbot is a burden—an obstacle to practicing meditation. We should leave tomorrow." Wiriyang tried to convince him to stay. "I've observed that these people are devout," he said. "They've accepted whatever you have taught. Please stay a little longer." Kongma refused. "Wiriyang, you're young and naive, and easily swayed by their goodness. It's a trap. I insist we leave tomorrow." Wiriyang urged Kongma to teach the villagers to meditate: "We're already here and may never pass this way again" (Wi, 24).

Finally Kongma agreed to stay for two more weeks. During this period he trained the Kula laymen and laywomen to meditate. Wiriyang spoke highly of the Kula: "It was amazing how quickly they could develop their minds. Within two weeks of practicing they reached one-pointedness of mind. They were very sad to see us go. Many of them cried. It was a memorable scene. It has been a few decades, but I still remember the purity of these devout Buddhists."[27]

TEACHING NON-BUDDHISTS

For these monks, training the mind was not simply a matter of perfecting a meditation technique; it involved, as Cha says, the cultivation of metta in one's heart (C2, 52). The thudong monks' interactions with the hill tribes are indicative of the compassion and loving-kindness that they cultivated.

The hill tribes of Siam were undoubtedly the people least familiar with wandering monks' customs. Thudong monks who went to the North had wandered into secluded mountains and interacted with highland peoples such as the Akha, Hmong, Lahu, Karen, and Khamu. Chaup and Thet as well as Man lived in the vicinity of highland tribes in Chiang Mai and Chiang Rai for long periods.[28] Each encounter was an educational experience for the monks as well as for the highlanders, challenging their perceptions and making them look at things differently. Thet and Man have left the most detailed accounts of their experiences.

In 1935 Thet ventured alone into the mountainous wilderness of Chiang Rai. He was then thirty-five years old. He passed one or two isolated houses but kept on going, knowing that the inhabitants might not be able to give him food.[29] He stopped when he came upon a Lahu village in Mae Suai District (the monks called these people the Muser).[30] The community, consisting of twelve households, was called Puphaya Village. Thet found an abandoned hut and decided to stay for a while. He thought the location would be a good one. The language barrier would mean that the Lahu would leave him alone, and he would have plenty of solitude for his meditation.

Thet was in for a surprise. As it turned out, the Lahu in this village had never seen a thudong monk before and were most curious. The whole village, from the youngest to the oldest, came to stare at him. The way the Lahu reacted to his presence convinced Thet that he was the first thudong monk to spend a rains retreat near their settlement. The people found his meditation practice bizarre. As Thet started pacing back and forth, they all thronged around him, so he was unable to concentrate. Afterward, Thet was able to discuss the matter with the village leader. Although this man did not understand Thet's religious practice, he respected the monk's behavior: "We agreed that it wasn't suitable for them to trail behind me and that if they wanted to make merit, then whenever they saw me out doing walking meditation they should *pi* [join their hands in the gesture of respect]. That would certainly be meritorious. From then on, whenever they saw me going out to do walking meditation they would all approach, stand together in a line, and *pi*. Anyone missing would be called out to come and join the group" (T1, 157; T2, 64).

Although Thet's first impression of the Lahu was that they were dirty and smelly, after he got to know them well his perception changed. "One couldn't help feeling sympathetic toward these forest people, who, though living far from material civilization, were so honest and upright. . . . They were self-governing and strictly trusted and relied on their 'Chief.' Bad characters, trouble-makers who refused stubbornly to heed their Chief's admonitions, were expelled from the village by the Chief. If the perpetrator refused to go, the villagers would all move away from him. You can be assured that nothing like stealing and thievery existed" (T1, 156).

Thet and other wandering monks from the Northeast came in contact with the hill tribes at a time when they were self-govern-ing as well as self-sufficient.[31] But the year before Thet arrived, the rice crop had been poor—only three households in the hamlet had enough to eat. Only these three households gave Thet alms, yet each gave him so much that he had plenty. Sometime later the vil-lage chief came to see Thet and explained that although everyone wished to offer food on his almsround, many were embarrassed because they had no rice to give. Thet learned that most Lahu in the hamlet ate boiled yams and tubers instead of rice. Touched by their generosity, he told the chief that he, too, liked steamed yams: "I said that was why I was able to come up to live with them—if I hadn't liked [yams], I wouldn't have come. Once they all knew about this, they dug up wild yams to steam and offer into my bowl, which was consequently filled every day. They also were delighted with the idea, laughing and smiling, their faces lit up in an endearing way. They did, though, remain apprehensive that I wouldn't be able to eat their yams, and so they followed me back to my hut to see for themselves. Having received their gifts, I was determined to show my appreciation by letting them see me eat them."[32]

The Lahu considered Thet's stay auspicious. It had not been raining much. Ten days before the rains retreat began, the Lahu started building a hut for Thet. When it was completed, rain began to pour. It rained so frequently that they had a splendid rice crop, more than they could use, and some of them sold their surplus. The Lahu were overjoyed, thinking that the beautiful harvest was the result of the merit they had made in building a "wat" for the monk.

When the rains retreat ended and Thet prepared to leave, the Lahu chief offered him a length of white cloth for robe material. The people were in tears over his departure and pleaded with him to return. Thet found their genuine faith and sincerity an inspiring and memorable part of his training. He went back to Ajan Man at Makhao Field Village (in Mae Pang District) and told him about the Lahu. The following year (1936) Man went with Thet to spend the rains retreat near Puphaya Village.

Man's encounters with the hill tribes changed both his attitudes about them and theirs of him. On one occasion Man and another disciple spent the night in a forest about two kilometers away from a Lahu settlement. The village chief, who had never seen a thudong monk before, thought that the monks were tigers in disguise.[33] He forbade women and children to go near the grove where the monks were staying. Men were allowed to visit the monks, but only in groups and always carrying a tool or weapon. After watching Man and his disciple for some time and seeing that the monks did no harm, the Lahu approached Man and asked him why he sat still and what he was searching for while walking back and forth.

> "My *buddho* is lost. I sit and walk in order to find buddho," said Ajan Man.
> "What is *buddho?* Can we help you find it?" they asked.
> "*Buddho* is the only priceless gem in all the three worlds. *Buddho* is all knowing. We would be able to find it sooner if you help us. . . . Whoever finds *buddho* is supreme in the world, and he can see everything," replied Man. (M1, 144–145)

The Lahu then asked whether children and women might help him find buddho and whether, once they found it, they would be able to see heaven and hell, and see dead relatives—their dead children, their husbands and wives. To all these questions Ajan Man replied yes. He then showed them how to look for buddho—that is, how to concentrate their minds:

"If you really want to find *buddho,* you must sit or walk repeating to yourselves *buddho, buddho, buddho.* During this time you must not think of anything else. Let your thought dwell in *buddho* inside you. If you can do this, then you might be able to find *buddho.*"

"But how long shall we sit or walk to find *buddho?*"

"At the outset, fifteen to twenty minutes is enough. *Buddho* does not want us to hurry, for then we shall be tired and cannot find *buddho.* This is enough for today." (M1, 145)

Many villagers including the headman and women and children took great interest in his instructions, and before long they were all earnestly reciting buddho. Man's instructions soon produced wonderful results. One man told Man that he was rewarded with a blissful peace soon after he faithfully followed the method. Several villagers eventually made considerable progress in their meditation practice. From that time on, the Lahu accepted the thudong custom. They took good care of the monks, offering them alms, building them comfortable shelters (the monks had been sleeping on leaves spread beneath trees), and clearing the ground for walking meditation.

Man and his disciple spent over a year outside this Lahu village. Their eventual departure was a dramatic, tearful scene.

On another occasion Man was staying near another group of hill peoples (not identified). The villagers asked for a *gāthā* (mantra) that would protect them from ghosts and demons. Man told them that if they recited "buddho, dhammo, sangho" mentally, no ghosts would be able to withstand the power of these words. Here again Man was teaching them mental concentration, knowing that fear cannot disturb a mind that is in samādhi.

Man thought so highly of the hill tribes that he encouraged his disciples to locate themselves near their settlements. In Bua's estimate, hill tribes people were honest and pliable, and that was why they were able to follow Man's instructions faithfully. Some of them even developed psychic powers like the ability to read other people's minds.[34] Bua echoes Man's opinion: "The hill tribes people are very honest, unsophisticated and unspoiled. Once they know the ajan [Man], they are devoted to him and would be willing to sacrifice everything they have for his sake. In general people think of forest people such as the Akha, Khamu, Muser [Lahu], Meo, and Yang [Karen] as being dark, ugly, dirty, and unkempt. In fact, they are fine looking and clean. They have good manners and fine customs. They have high respect for their elders and their leaders. They seldom quarrel or fight. They obey their leaders. They are not stubborn. It's easy to teach them [to meditate]."[35] The thudong monks came to appreciate the highlanders' culture and religious beliefs. Man, for example, thought that the hill tribes were morally superior to city people. "A jungle is not an uncivilized place full of wild beasts. It holds honest people with morals—not thieves or bandits like the jungles made of cement. It is safer to be in a forest than in a city full of people. In a city one is more likely to be taken advantage of" (M2, 164).

It is not surprising that Man had such a high opinion of the hill tribes. He felt grateful for their regular provision of alms. The remote area in which they lived shielded him from high-ranking Thammayut monks. And according to Bua, it was here, while living in solitude near a hill-tribe village, that Man attained enlightenment.[36]

Some of the Lahu villages where the thudong monks stayed were so isolated that Lahu cultivators shared the forest with hunter-gatherers, the Mlabri. While staying near one such village in 1936, Thet came upon a group of Mlabri whom the Lahu called *phi taung leuang* (spirits of the yellow leaves). In Thet's opinion, no other monk or traveler knew these foragers as well as he did. Certainly no one before him has left quite so rich a description. But we shall pass over Thet's interesting account.[37]

Staying among people very different from themselves taught the thudong monks to appreciate the goodness in other cultures. They also knew that meditation practice is not for monks only; it is good for everybody regardless of their religious beliefs. Note that the thudong monk made no attempt to change other people's convictions or convert them to their kind of Buddhism. It is not surprising that forest peoples and the hill tribes trusted these wandering monks. Their live-and-let-live attitude is evident in a remark of Man's: "One of the amazing things is that many missionaries have gone to the [Lahu] villages and tried to convert them into Christians. They gave away many gifts. Yet the Lahu would not convert. When the thudong monks came, the hill tribes gave alms to them. This doesn't mean they became Buddhists, because they had their own belief—spirit worship."38

ENCOUNTERING MONKS WITH DIFFERENT CUSTOMS

We have seen that the thudong monk was open-minded about the beliefs and customs of forest dwellers, whether or not they were lay Buddhists. But was he equally tolerant of *monks* who followed rules or rituals that were by his standards incorrect? As we shall see, here too the wandering monk was not judgmental.

The wandering monks' encounters with monks of other traditions occurred within the borders of Siam as well as in neighboring countries. As the monks' accounts demonstrate, although political boundaries (imposed by Western colonial powers or by Siamese elites) may divide a people into different nation-states, that could not stop them from following their indigenous customs.

Waen and Teu wandered one evening into a village wat in northern Laos. No monks were around, but a novice came out to meet them.

> The novice was glad to see us. He brought water for us to drink and wash with, and provided us with sleeping materials. He asked us to stay. Seeing the novice's good disposition, [we] decided to spend the night there. Once he made us comfortable, he disappeared. Then we heard the *jok jok* sound of a chicken. After a while we smelled grilled chicken. Still, we were not suspicious. The novice was gone for about an hour. He came back with steamy hot glutinous rice and a big barbecued chicken.
>
> Putting the food in front of us he said, "*Khuba* [respected teachers], please eat this meal. You are exhausted from traveling. I grilled this big chicken especially for you. Eat as much as you want."
>
> We told the novice "Don't worry about us. Take the food back. We will have a meal in the morning. In the evening some hot water to drink is adequate for us."

We did not know what the novice did with the chicken. Perhaps he offered it to the spirits of the dead. We did not pay attention. (Wn, 35)

Notice that in telling this story Waen did not pass judgment on the novice's ignorance of the vinaya (monks and novices may neither kill an animal nor eat the flesh of an animal killed for them). Instead Waen mentioned the novice's hospitality. Waen probably knew that in northern Laos, as well as in northern Siam, it is customary to offer food to monks in the evening.

Wandering in northern Siam, Waen came across a somewhat different rule about food. In Mae Hong Son he met up with some Shan monks who considered themselves to be more strict than the Yuan monks in Chiang Mai. "In those days," Waen remembers, "the Shan monks often accused the Chiang Mai monks of eating supper. True, the Mae Hong Son monks did not eat in the evening, but they ate cooked rice in the middle of the night. They started cooking by candlelight at 1 A.M." (Wn, 57).

This comment of Waen's suggests that monastic rules in the Shan and Yuan traditions differed from those of the Siamese. Obviously eating after midday was not regarded as an offense. "*Tu jao* [monks] in Chiang Mai eat in the evening at 5, 6, or 7 P.M., whereas *jao bun* [monks] in Mae Hong Son eat in the first hour of the day before the sunrise. In both cases it is not a new day yet. So what difference does it make? Both practices deviate from the vinaya" (Wn, 57).

There were other differences. Like many monks adhering to local Buddhist traditions before modern state Buddhism became dominant, the monks in Mae Hong Son did not recite the patimok on "ubosot days." Waen recalls, "The Shan monks simply got together in the ordination hall to confess their offenses and confirm their purity."[39]

Another aspect of Shan Buddhism that Waen found peculiar was the Shan custom of holding frequent debates about *abhidhamma* (Buddhist higher psychology). Monks who followed Bangkok's official Buddhism would instead debate matters of vinaya. "Like the Burmese [monks], they often discuss [abhidhamma]. They have learned about the dhamma from their 'map' [books]. They take the debate seriously, often differing sharply in their interpretations."[40]

In a northern district of Chiang Mai, thudong monks encountered a very different form of Buddhist custom. Li and Khian had been traveling together in search of Ajan Man. After meditating in the caves that Man had told them about, they continued north in the direction of Fang District. In an isolated area they came across two large caves, which they explored. In one of them they saw several rows of ancient Buddha images, and in the other an enormous statue of the Buddha. Reaching the base of the hill, they found a grove of banana and papaya trees beside a clear-flowing stream. They thought this odd, for there were no villages nearby. When they stopped at a hut to inquire about monks, they were told that a Venerable Father Pha was out in the fields. As Li recalls,

> We went east, following the stream up the mountain. We came across an old man wearing maroon shorts and a maroon short-sleeved shirt—like the color of a newly dyed fishing net. He had a large knife in his hand, with which he was cutting back the forest. His movements were vigorous and strong, like those of a young man. We walked towards him and called out, "Do you know where Father Pha is?" When he caught sight of us, he came quickly towards us—with the knife still in his hand. But when he sat down with us, his manner changed into that of a monk. "I'm Father Pha," he said. So we paid him our respects.
>
> He led us back to his quarters, where he changed from his shorts and shirt into a dark set of robes with a sash tied around his chest and a string of rosary beads in his hand. He told us the stories behind each of the caves. (Li1, 50; Li2, 37)

The old monk invited Li and Khian to stay for the rains retreat. Learning that the thudong monks were disciples of Ajan Man's and were therefore strict, he said, "But you can't take me as your ajan, because at the moment I'm growing bananas and papayas to sell in order to raise enough money to finish my Buddha image." In the evening he showed them around the banana and papaya grove, which he had planted himself. He told the thudong monks, "You have my permission to take and eat as much as you like. Ordinarily, I don't allow other monks to touch them."[41]

It was not so unusual for a monk like Pha to wear short pants and a shirt. It appears to have been a northern custom for local monks to switch into laymen's garments when engaging in worldly matters. For example, Phra Phau Pan (born in 1932 at Bankat Commune, San Pa Tong District, Chiang Mai) would wear a black peasant shirt *(mau haum)* when he went to help farmers in their fight for water rights. When not engaged in this activist work, Pan would wear the usual orange robes and practice meditation in his forest hut. This tradition, Pan believed, originated with the Buddha, who is said to have appeared in a princely garment on the battlefield when trying to settle a dispute between King Koliyawong and King Sakhayawong, rulers of two kingdoms who were fighting over the ownership of a river.[42]

Not only did Li not judge this northern monk's custom by his own disciplinary rules, he was impressed by the monk's kindness, his asceticism, and his intimacy with the wildlife.

> It hadn't occurred to me that I'd want any of his fruit, but I appreciated his kindness. Every morning before dawn, he'd send one of his disciples to where we were staying with bananas and papayas for us to eat.
>
> I noticed a lot of strange things about the area. The peacocks in the forest weren't at all afraid of Ven. Father Pha. Every morning doves would come to where he'd be eating, and he'd scatter rice for them to eat. Sometimes they'd allow him to touch them. Every evening monkeys would descend in hordes to eat the papayas he had spread out for them. If any villagers happened by on their way to worship the Buddha image, though, the animals would all run away.[43]

In Cambodia, Wiriyang encountered a similar custom. One morning, when he and his teacher Kongma were staying in a monastery in Olamjiak Village, Wiriyang saw what he describes as an unforgettable sight. "I could hardly believe my eyes when I saw the abbot up a coconut tree breaking off coconuts and carefully dropping them onto a pile. After climbing down, he cracked open a couple of green coconuts and handed them to me. I presented them to my teacher, Kongma, and I noticed his discomfort. I, too, had to suppress some uneasy feelings. We drank a lot of coconut juice that day. The abbot was glad. He wanted us to stay several days, but the ajan [Kongma] told him that this was not our plan. We left after the meal. The abbot seemed sad to see us go" (Wi, 20–21). Kongma was probably touched by the local abbot's hospitality. He voiced his criticism only when he and his disciple had resumed their journey: "These local monks may have strong faith, but they are ignorant of the vinaya. Climbing a coconut tree and pulling off the nuts violates the vinaya. [I] didn't know how to tell them that. As a visitor, I decided to let it go" (Wi, 21).

This example illustrates a pattern that the thudong monks found among village abbots who observed local traditions. Although these abbots followed different rules, they were hospitable both to thudong monks and Bangkok monks. Perhaps local religious practices placed more emphasis on compassion and generosity than on strict adherence to the letter of the vinaya.

After a few days, Kongma and Wiriyang went to Battambang, where they visited a Thammayut monastery. Here they found the Khmer monks (who followed the Thammayut sect) critical of *their* vinaya.

> We rode trishaws to the wat. The monks in the wat kept staring at us. They thought that we were not Thammayuts, since Thammayut monks in Cambodia would not ride trishaws. Since they didn't welcome us, we stayed at a *sala* [open hall]. They tested us by asking a layman to give us money. The ajan refused to take it. Yet they were still skeptical. They did not become friendly until days later. The abbot, who was paralyzed, came to talk to us in a wheelchair. It's a good thing a Thai merchant and a government official who knew the ajan came and gave us food. People in the wat did not take good care of us. We ate only rice for several days. (Wi, 25)

In his wanderings outside Thailand, Juan also met monks who followed monastic rules different from his own. Although he acknowledges that these differences bothered him, his criticism is muted: "It is all right to practice meditation by myself. But I would find it difficult to have to stay with a Shan monk because of the different rules. Some of them are in violation of the vinaya. In some wats monks cook and eat in the evening. In other wats the abbot as well as junior monks lie down casually to smoke opium, and they even ask me, a visiting monk, to join them. According to the Thai, this behavior goes against the vinaya rules, it is a violation of precepts; but here it is not the same" (J, 35).

Li seems to have been more interested in other monks' knowledge of the dhamma than in arguing over minor points in the vinaya. For example, he talked about being impressed with some Khmer monks' understanding of the Buddha's teachings. After Li had been in Cambodia for over a month, he was able to pick up the language and preach the dhamma to the Khmer people. At night large numbers of villagers came to listen to his sermons. One day one of the laypeople told Li that a certain Khmer monk wanted to quiz the thudong monk on the dhamma. This monk had studied the Tipitaka (the Buddhist scriptures) and was expert in translating Pali. Li welcomed the challenge. The dhamma discussion went well. As Li recalls, "We discussed and debated the dhamma until we were able to reach a good understanding of each other's practices and ways of conduct. The whole affair went by smoothly and peacefully without incident."[44]

Li and his disciples stayed for two nights in Sisophon. Then they went to explore a nearby mountain and met a Chinese monk living alone in a secluded cave. Li's ability to connect with a Mahayana monk is a measure of his open-mindedness. He recalls, "We sat and discussed the Dhamma. We hit it off so well that he invited me to stay and spend the rains retreat there. None of my followers, though, wanted to stay on."[45] Li liked the area, but he felt he could not go against his disciples' wishes.[46]

Li's attitude toward the Chinese monk contrasts with that of the sangha administrators in Thailand, many of whom felt superior to Mahayana monks or monks of other Buddhist traditions. (Today many Thai monks share this sense of superiority, although they may never have met a Mahayana monk.) For example, in 1933 when Li was wandering in Cambodia, Pan (a Mahanikai monk from southern Siam) and Maha Loet (a Thammayut pariyat monk from Thepsirin Monastery in Bangkok) were traveling together in Burma.[47] They had difficulty communicating with the local people since neither of them knew the local languages. On their trip back to Siam, however, they found hospitality in a Mahayana monastery in Burma. The language barrier did not prevent the old Chinese abbot from providing them with food and shelter for four days. In addition to giving them free room and board, the abbot took the Thai monks to the train station. He bought them train tickets to Moulmein and gave them a letter to a Chinese layman in that town asking him to buy the Thai monks boat tickets to the nearest village in Siam. Feeling a debt of gratitude to the Chinese monk, Pan made a *wai* (respectful salutation) before getting on the train. His companion, the Thammayut Bangkok monk, immediately scolded him, "Why do you wai the Chinese monk?" Although Pan was not himself a thudong monk, his reply typifies the thudong monk's thinking. "I paid respects to the Chinese monk's goodness, to his generosity, and to the quality of his mind. It is irrelevant what kind of garment he wears. I did not pay respect to his trousers. That's all external. My wai was to the essence of the monk. I feel right making a wai to him."[48]

As thudong monks' recollections have shown, during the Forest-Community Period the North and Northeast still contained ethnic groups whose religious practices differed significantly from the norms established in Bangkok under modern state Buddhism. The wandering monks' experiences served as tools or aids to their meditation practice, teaching them the importance of loving-kindness, compassion, and tolerance for people with different religious customs. These qualities, Cha asserts, "should be maintained as the foundation for mental purity" (C1, 52).

Government and sangha authorities in Bangkok, however, did not share the wandering monks' tolerance, open-mindedness, and high regard for local customs. Decades later, in the mid-1960s, the Thai government, with the cooperation of the Sangha Council of Elders, set out to assimilate peoples of different traditions into the dominant Thai culture. The Thammajarik (Pali: *dhammacarika,* "wandering dhamma") program, a missionary effort, was instituted specifically to convert the tribal peoples of Thailand to modern state Buddhism.[49]

CHAPTER 7

Relations with

Sangha Officials

During the Forest-Community Period, the same wandering monks who had little difficulty communicating with villagers or coping with wild animals frequently had problems relating to certain administrative Thammayut monks, who viewed them either as outlaws or just lazy. The relationship between the wandering monks of Man's lineage and the urban-based Thammayut administrators was complex and ambiguous. After the passage of the 1902 Sangha Act, wandering monks were under the control of sangha officials in the major towns of the Northeast or in Bangkok where their preceptors resided. Three senior Isan monks are most often mentioned in thudong monks' accounts: Jan Sirijantho (Ubali Khunupamajan), abbot of Wat Boromniwat; Nu Thitapanyo (Panyaphisan), abbot of Wat Sapathum; and Uan Tisso (Somdet Maha Wirawong), sangha leader of monthon Nakhon Ratchasima. Although all three were born and raised in the Northeast—they were natives of Ubon Ratchathani—these senior Thammayut monks were wedded to modern state Buddhism, and their overall attitudes rep-resented those of Bangkok.[1]

Due to the isolation of the region and the small number of local monks with academic training who could teach Thai, the sangha authorities had difficulty spreading Bangkok's curriculum to the remote towns. It took them over two decades, until 1925, to finally establish state monastic schools in all four major towns in the Northeast (the capital towns of monthon Ubon Ratchathani, monthon Nakhon Ratchasima, monthon Roi-Et, and monthon Udon).[2] Although initially the central sangha did not approve of the thudong practices, it tried to recruit Man's disciples during the early 1930s. It got them to help convert villagers to its form of Buddhism and establish new Thammayut wats—activities which helped the state consolidate its influence over the countryside. During this period the monastic order to which the wandering monks and their superiors belonged had been weakened by the decline in power of the Thai monarchy. A series of events that took place in Bangkok reveals why the Thammayut elders began to accept Man and his disciples. One Thammayut leader in Bangkok, who was nearing the end of his life, underwent a complete change of attitude with regard to wandering monks and abandoned his suspicions about them.

THE VIEW FROM BANGKOK

Whereas villagers who followed the Lao and Khmer traditions respected wandering ascetics, sangha authorities saw them as undisciplined vagrants. This suspicion created considerable tension within the small Thammayut order. Like many other high-level monks of his time, Uan Tisso, an academic monk and a monthon sangha head known for his administrative skills, paid no attention to meditation practice.[3] Having become a sangha head at a relatively young age, Uan got a strong dose of Bangkok values and looked down on thudong monks. Although he performed ordinations for Thammayut monks in the Northeast, many of them had later turned their backs on academic studies and embraced the thudong practice. Until late in life, Uan was known for his contempt for wandering meditation monks. He believed that a monk's main duty was to teach and serve in a monastery.

Thet recalls how Uan tried to get monks who had passed the naktham or Pali exams to teach and do administrative work. Such monks, he hoped, would teach local Lao or Khmer monks and novices to read Thai textbooks. In 1923 the first Thammayut monastery, Wat Phothisomphon, had just been established in the

capital of meuang Udon Thani.[4] Maha Jum was brought from a
Thammayut wat in Bangkok to be its abbot, but Uan wanted
more Bangkok-trained Thammayut monks to stay there.[5]

In November of that year Sing, Maha Pin, and Thet were summoned from Ubon to Udon Thani.[6] They traveled on foot, accompanied by eight other monks and novices. To avoid going into
town they stayed at Chiang Phin Village, west of Udon, and
waited there for Uan to arrive from Bangkok. After arriving, Uan
summoned the thudong monks in order to assign them administrative posts. Pin was to go to the capital of meuang Sakon
Nakhon; Thet was to stay with Abbot Jum in Udon. The sangha
head reasoned that since Thet was a local and had some academic
training, he should stay to help with the administrative duties.
(Lao-speaking monks in Udon did not yet know about the new
religious texts from Bangkok.) Thet, however, did not want to be
confined to a temple. In the Thammayut order, he felt, "meditation monks were few and far between, whereas scholastic and
administrative monks were numerous and wouldn't be difficult to
find" (T1, 69). So he requested that he be allowed to go off to
practice meditation "to honor the sangha head's authority and
dignity." Uan gave his permission, provided that Thet stay with
Maha Pin to assist him at the Thammayut wat in Sakon Nakhon.

After the thudong monks had settled their business with their
superior, Uan, they went with Sing to Khau Village in Pheu Pond
District (today in Nongkhai Province) to meet the thudong masters Sao and Man. Later all of them walked back to Udon Thani
and from there went to Sakon Nakhon, in compliance with their
agreement with the regional sangha head. Maha Pin fell ill, however, and could not take up the administrative duties entrusted to
him. So all of them—Maha Pin and Thet along with Sing and
other thudong monks—spent the rains retreat at the forest wat of
Lat Pond Village (Ban Naung Lat). This caused the monthon
sangha head to be highly displeased with Sing and his group, so
the thudong monks sent in their place a monk who had obtained
the highest naktham diploma and was willing to teach at the
Thammayut wat in Sakon Nakhon.

Uan saw the wandering monks as lazy and unwilling to study
and thus as an obstacle to the integration of the Isan sangha into
modern state Buddhism.[7] Since he could not integrate them into

Bangkok's monastic education system, he tried to force them out of his monthon by forbidding villagers to give them alms. This ruling resulted in government officials temporarily detaining Ajan Man's disciples.

These events occurred in 1926 when Fan and twenty thudong monks of local traditions were reordained in the Thammayut order. The ordination ceremony was performed on a raft on a pond outside Samphong Village in Nakhon Phanom.[8] Afterwards the new Thammayut thudong monks walked to Daeng Kokchang Village (Tha Uthen District) to spend the rains retreat. After the rains Man arrived at the village with seventy monks and novices to see Fan. They held a meeting and discussed which meuangs they should go to next. Until then they had been wandering in the northern meuangs of what is now the upper Isan region: Sakon Nakhon, Udon Thani, Nongkhai, and Loei (previously remote meuangs that are now provinces). The majority of the thudong monks wanted to go south toward meuang Ubon to spread the dhamma. After reaching a collective decision, they dispersed and, traveling along separate routes, eventually regrouped in Hua Taphan Village, which lies today in Amnat Charoen District, Ubon Province.

When Uan, the monthon sangha head, heard that Man's disciples had come to stay at a village in Ubon, he ordered the religious and civil district officers of Muang Samsip and Amnat Charoen to chase the thudong monks away. Villagers were warned that if they did not cease to give food to the thudong monks, they would face arrest. Villagers ignored this order and continued to give alms, however. They did so probably because the thudong monks' conduct had impressed them—so much so, in fact, that many villagers, women as well as men, would later become pha khaws or allow their sons to follow Man's disciples on their wanderings.[9]

When a district officer arrived, Sing, the senior thudong monk, argued in vain that he had the right to stay in his natal village.[10] Fan also negotiated in vain with the district officer, who refused to compromise. The officer detained all the thudong monks (including Sing, Pin, Tiang, Aun, Fan, Koeng, and Sila)[11] and recorded information about their backgrounds: "their parents' names, their birthplaces, and their wats [where they were ordained]. It took [him] from late morning until midnight to finish writing down the information about the fifty monks and novices and over one hundred pha khaws. He did not even take a break for lunch."[12]

It was after midnight when the district officer left. The thudong monks then got together and tried to figure out what to do next. Fan immediately went to see Ajan Man at Log Pond Village, about two and a half kilometers away. According to his biographer, Man told Fan to put his mind in samādhi.[13] It took Fan until dawn to coax his mind to withdraw into jhāna, and then a nimit appeared. In his vision he saw the land *(phaen din)* where he sat split wide open into two territories with no bridge between them, such that people on either side could not meet. Fan's biographer does not explain what the vision implied (F, 52). Nevertheless, it can be interpreted that the image represented the chasm between the thudong and the official Buddhist traditions—a chasm too broad to cross.

In the morning, two of the thudong monks in the group, Maha Pin and Aun, went to the town of Ubon and met with the meuang sangha head, who denied that he had given any orders to detain the monks. He then gave the thudong monks a letter to take to the district officer to effect a compromise. The situation was thus settled, and Fan continued his wanderings.

In Man's biography, there is no mention of this incident. Thet, however, gives a brief account of it even though he was not in the group detained by the district officer:

It was necessary for me to accompany my mother on her journey back home [to her village in Udon Thani] and so I was not able to go with Ajan Man. It was on this trip that Ajan Man and his party encountered major upheavals. There were both good and bad results from this.

The good side was an increase in the number of [Thammayut] forest monasteries for meditation monks, which up to then had not existed at all. This was the occasion when Ubon Province was permanently settled by forest monks for the first time. From that time forward it [Ajan Man's lineage] has continued to spread out until today there are monasteries with Thammayut monks in virtually every district.

The negative side was the deterioration in the quality of the monks' practice. In fact, the decline this time . . . was unprecedented, until Ajan Man was finally obliged to turn away from the community there and leave for Chiang Mai Province.[14]

Thet ends the account abruptly, and neither he nor Fan says what really happened among Man's disciples after the trip to Ubon. Fan's vision of the land splitting and Thet's allusion to a deterioration of practice suggest that there might have been a schism among Man's disciples that disturbed him so much that he fled.

At any rate, many thudong monks certainly felt ambivalent about going to Ubon to teach dhamma. Ubon had always been known as a *meuang nakprat* (town of scholars) and the center of pariyat tham, that is, doctrinal studies.[15] They probably felt more at ease teaching in the remote areas in Sakon Nakhon, Udon Thani, Nongkhai, and Loei, where villagers respected wandering monks. One thudong monk, Aun, expressed his apprehension during the group's journey to Ubon. "We are going with Ven. Ajan Man to Ubon, where many people have studied pariyat tham and are well versed in it. If they ask questions about the dhamma, Phra Ajan Man can probably answer them without difficulty. But what if, after asking our ajan, they turn to us, his disciples, to see if we are as good? What if we can't answer their questions?" (F, 49). Fan, who did not seem to share Aun's fear, reassured his fellow monks. "Why worry about being questioned? All dhamma originates in our heart [*jai*]. It is this, the basis of a person, which is central. We have firsthand experience and we know the dhamma. We'll manage and won't get stuck."[16] Aun's concern about not being able to measure up to the learned monks and lay devotees in Ubon implies that many forest-dwelling monks, in their early years, had little confidence in the knowledge of dhamma that they derived from meditation practice. Man's extensive firsthand experience gave him firm self-confidence, but his disciples lacked his self-confidence and depended a great deal on their teacher.

RECRUITING WANDERING MEDITATION MONKS

A few years after this incident, high-level monks in the Northeast attempted to co-opt Ajan Man's disciples in order to promote Thammayut policy. According to Thet, in 1929 the government issued a proclamation prohibiting spirit worship and urging people to take refuge in the Triple Gem (T1, 112). The sangha head of meuang Khon Kaen, Jan Khemiyo (titled Phra Khru Phisan), accordingly mobilized Sing and his group of thudong monks (about seventy monks and novices) to help tame the demons and spirits. He asked them to come to Khon Kaen to teach dhamma and instruct people how to take refuge in the Triple Gem. Those who answered the call include Maha Pin, Fan, Chaup, Kongma, and Lui. They went to Khon Kaen in 1929 and stayed at Lao-nga Forest Hermitage (now called Wat Wiwektham) for a rains retreat, after which they visited villages in the meuang to propagate dhamma. Li had decided not to go to Khon Kaen. Thet arrived the following year, and he too became involved in the government's mission.

While his disciples were helping sangha authorities in the Northeast, Man was in the North serving as an acting abbot—for the first time in his life—at Wat Jediluang in Chiang Mai.[17] He found himself in Chiang Mai after a series of unplanned events. During the 1927 rains retreat, Man was in Ubon teaching monks and laypeople at Wat Suthat, Wat Liap, and Wat Burapha.[18] While he was there, Abbot Nu (Panyaphisan Thera) of Wat Sapathum in Bangkok arrived to perform an ordination.[19] Abbot Nu asked Man to accompany him on his return trip to Bangkok, which Man did. Before leaving Ubon, Man assigned Sing and Maha Pin the task of teaching his disciples according to his guidelines while he was gone (M3, 85). Man spent the next rains retreat (1928) in Bangkok and then—at the request of Ubali (Jan)—he went to Chiang Mai to stay at Wat Jediluang. He did not return to the Northeast for a decade. Sing was left with the task of supervising the thudong monks while Man was away.

During their first year in Khon Kaen, Sing and his fellow thudong monks established eight forest samnaks, where they spent the next couple of rains retreats. From 1929 to 1931 these hermitages served as centers for the teaching of meditation and the advancement of the government's directive to eliminate local spirit worship. This was the first time the thudong monks are known to have cooperated with government officials.[20]

The next year Uan, now sangha head of monthon Nakhon Ratchasima (Khorat), decided to put a large number of wandering monks to work for him.[21] On 6 May 1932, less than a month before a military coup seized power from the king in Bangkok, Uan summoned the thudong monks from Khon Kaen to the town of Khorat.[22] In those days there was no road or railroad linking Khorat to Khon Kaen. Man's disciples had hitherto never ventured near Khorat, believing that the area was unsafe.[23] Upon arrival, the thudong monks stayed in an orchard near the Khorat train station on land belonging to the police chief of Khorat (he later donated it to establish a Thammayut forest wat). Thet organized the monks in erecting temporary shelters there. Then he went to help Maha Pin construct another place for monks to stay outside a nearby village, this time on the charnel ground where people who had died from cholera and bubonic plague were cremated. These sites became the first two Thammayut forest wats in Khorat. Sing was appointed the abbot of Salawan Forest Monastery and Pin the abbot of Sattharuam Forest Monastery. These administrative duties ended their wandering life.

From then on, thudong monks were busy establishing forest samnaks in several districts. These samnaks were bases from which to spread the dhamma to local people. For example, in 1933 the district officer of Sikhiw District invited Fan and Aun to set up a hermitage at New Samrong Village in Lat Bua Khao Commune. Then Fan left Kongma to teach dhamma and instruct villagers in religious rituals, after which he went to Non Sung District to set up another hermitage.[24] Fan spent two rains retreats at this hermitage.

To the government authorities, the wandering monks' presence and the building of a wat were means of integrating various ethnic groups into modern state Buddhism. Until then the Lao and Khmer people of the Khorat Plateau had followed their own local Buddhist traditions and lineages. Among the customs that differed from Bangkok's were the style of chanting (in indigenous languages), the manner of dress (local monks wore *muak tumpi*, a headgear showing local monastic rank), and ordination rituals.[25] Bangkok elites regarded these local religious customs as distortions *(fanfeuan)* of the monks' proper discipline.[26] To convert these Lao and Khmer people, the sangha authorities recruited Isan monks who knew Bangkok's monastic rules and could also connect with the local people.

Wiriyang's account provides an example of how thudong monks won local support in Khorat and eventually turned a temporary hermitage into a Thammayut wat.

> In those days the area that became the New Samrong Village was a forest settlement far from civilization. The area was surrounded by uncultivated forests. Various groups of people had settled and built hamlets. Conflict arose among these groups, one fighting another. . . .
>
> When the hermitage was first established in the forest, there were only huts and a pavilion with thatched roofs. Ajan Kongma patiently and diligently taught dhamma to monks, novices, and lay folk, most of whom were illiterate. He taught them the morning and evening recitations. He paid little attention to building the hermitage. I was attracted to his teaching and his asceticism, so I was ordained as a novice. The hermitage had quiet spots for meditation practice. People came to practice, experienced peace in their hearts, and became devoted followers. Gradually the hermitage became a center for various groups of people to meet for religious rites and rituals. During his three rains retreats here [1933–1935] the ajan succeeded in unifying people. The area became more peaceful. The inhabitants agreed to construct permanent buildings for the wat.[27]

Thudong monks gained the support of the government officials in Khorat because of their ability to mobilize local people to build Thammayut samnaks. Once the thudong monks entered into a working relationship with the local officials, many of them began to stay in monthon Nakhon Ratchasima for the rains retreats. Between the rains, they would wander on their own and then return to the forest wats in Khorat. Fan, for example, spent twelve rains retreats in a row at Sattharuam Forest Monastery in the capital town of Khorat. During this period (1932–1943) Fan became acquainted with Captain-Major Phin Chunahawan, deputy commander of the army in the Northeast.[28]

How did Ajan Man feel about his disciples who strayed from his example? Neither of Man's biographers says, but the following brief account may give us a glimpse into Man's feeling.

After spending two rains retreats at Sattharuam Forest Monastery, Fan and his fellow monk Aun went by train to visit Ajan

Man in Chiang Mai in January 1937. At the time Man was sixty-seven years old and Fan was thirty-nine. Man was glad to see his disciples and showed them to their kutis. Later on they gave him a massage. After a while Man got up and lectured Fan and Aun, addressing them as "you two dandy Venerables!" *(phra jao chu).*[29] Fan and Aun were puzzled, not knowing what the teacher meant. Then they concluded that Man must have been referring to their bright new yellow robes and the lid of Fan's new alms bowl, which was inlaid with mother-of-pearl. Man was probably criticizing the way Fan and Aun, although belonging to the thudong tradition, were living like town monks—spending the rains retreat at the same monastery yearly, receiving expensive gifts from lay supporters, and so forth.

That night Fan and Aun sat in meditation with Ajan Man all night. The next day Aun and Fan decided to travel to Phrao, a district in Chiang Mai. Man gave Aun permission to go but asked Fan to stay with him. It is curious that the two disciples wanted to leave so soon. Perhaps Man scolded them too harshly. Later Fan again sought to go off by himself, but again Man urged him to stay at Wat Jediluang. Eventually he allowed the two to go off alone for a period of time before returning to Wat Jediluang. Fan and Aun stayed in Chiang Mai for five months before taking the train back to Khorat (using money sent by the police chief there) to spend the 1937 rains retreat at Sattharuam Forest Monastery.

Not all thudong monks were content with their lives in monthon Nakhon Ratchasima. Thet, for example, found that organizing the construction of shelters and meditation huts (at Salawan Forest Monastery) in the hot weather was unbearable. He also realized that being in a group was not conducive to meditation practice.[30] On top of that he had difficulties with his teacher, Sing, who was not sympathetic to a problem Thet had with his meditation.

My heart certainly felt as if it had totally lost everything that it could depend on. It was as if all ties and attachment to the group were gone. One of Ajan Sing's wishes had been that the group of monks not split up. He wanted us all to assist each other in spreading Buddhism in that province. But I had long desired—ever since I had joined up with the others while staying

in Khon Kaen—to separate myself and go off to seek some solitude. This was because I was well aware that my meditation
efforts and the necessary skillful techniques were still weak and
ineffective. I had continually tried to detach myself but always
in ways that would not give the impression to my teacher or
companions that I didn't like them.[31]

So Thet decided to get away from the monks in Khorat and search
for Ajan Man in the North. He left at the end of the 1932 rains
retreat accompanied by a fellow monk, Aunsi. Thet wandered and
practiced meditation in Chiang Mai and Chiang Rai with Man
and other thudong monks for five years.[32] But although Thet got
away from Khorat, he could not escape missionary work in the
North. In 1938 Yandilok (Phim Thammaro), acting abbot of Wat
Jediluang in Chiang Mai, appointed Thet as abbot of Du Pond
Village Monastery (in Pak Chong District, Lamphun), a wat originally of the Mon tradition.[33]

The following year Thet went back to the Northeast and spent
the next rains retreat at Wat Aranyawasi in Tha Bau District,
Nongkhai. In fact he spent all of the rains retreats from 1939 to
1947 at this monastery, which was unusual given his thudong life.
Before 1939 Thet had never stayed in the same place longer than
three years. Being in charge of the wat, Thet had to shoulder
responsibilities that as a thudong monk he could avoid.[34] Previously Thet had never taken an interest in any building projects,
since he did not consider them duties for a recluse. But after he
arrived at this wat he began to change his attitude. "This was when
I began to guide lay supporters in building projects," he writes.
"However, at no point have I gone out and solicited donations for
this work. I have always been extremely sensitive about this—if
the resources were available the work went forward, if they weren't
then the work was simply stopped. I never allowed myself to become bound to any project, so that if it couldn't be finished or
was underfunded I could easily abandon it without any feeling of
attachment" (T1, 18). After Thet arrived, he added two new huts,
a large study hall, and many other smaller buildings.

In 1946 Thet had a recurrence of a neurological disorder, which
handicapped his preaching: "After I took the Dhamma seat to
give a sermon, I had no idea what I was talking about."[35] Thet

thought that his problem may have been brought on by his excessively long stay at the monastery. Then, just before the local festival of Khao Salakphat, he fell ill—so ill that he was unable to take part in the festival. "I felt so bad that I couldn't stand up without vomiting. I lay down with closed eyes and when I opened them again I found myself gazing at the sky with clouds passing across the sun. It hurt my eyes and I vomited."[36] Thet recovered the following day, but it is likely that the illness kept him away from his duties for a while. After staying nine years at this wat, Thet finally got away. This time he went as far as Chanthaburi, about 860 kilometers from Nongkhai, and spent the 1948–1949 rains retreats there.

Unlike Thet and Fan, Dun never got back to his thudong life again after this period. In 1934, while his fellow thudong monks were in Khorat, Dun was staying at Wat Suthat in Ubon helping his Thammayut preceptor construct an ordination hall. He was intending to resume the life of a wanderer after he finished this project, but then he received a letter from Uan instructing him to go to Surin and help an academic monk there restore Wat Burapharam.[37] Dun designed the wat's ordination hall and supervised the monks, novices, and villagers during construction. The fact that sangha administrators chose Dun to oversee the construction suggests that they knew that Dun would get along with the local Khmer people and mobilize their labor successfully. Dun's appointment as abbot of Wat Burapharam—the first Thammayut wat in Surin—ended his nineteen years of thudong life. Like Sing, who became abbot of Salawan Forest Wat in Khorat for the rest of his life (he died in 1961),[38] Dun remained at Wat Burapharam until he died in 1985 at the age of ninety-seven.

SERVING THE ISAN ABBOTS IN BANGKOK

Whereas thudong monks were concerned with protecting their independence and maintaining some distance from the laity, the Thammayut authorities wanted to turn Thammayut thudong monks into settled monastics. Beside serving the high-level monks in the Northeast, Man, Waen, Sing, Pin, Fan, and Li also spent some time in Bangkok during the 1920s and the early 1930s attending two Thammayut administrators: Ubali (Jan), abbot of Wat

Boromniwat, and Panyaphisan (Nu), abbot of Wat Sapathum.[39] With the exception of Li's, their accounts are brief, however.

Man went to Bangkok a few times. The earliest date was probably before 1911, when he met Bunman, a fellow Thammayut monk who resided at Wat Sapathum. The two went together on a thudong to Burma, but after eight months of wandering, Bunman decided he wanted to return to his studies. Man accompanied him on the trip to Bangkok in 1912 and stayed briefly at that wat.[40] Then he went wandering on his own until 1915, when Abbot Jan asked him to spend the rains retreat in Bangkok. At the time Jan, demoted by King Rama VI for criticizing his policy on World War I, was confined to Wat Boromniwat. Man, however, chose to stay at Wat Sapathum, walking occasionally to Wat Boromniwat to listen to Jan's sermons.[41]

Waen went to Bangkok for the first time in 1921 to meet Jan. He was about thirty-three then and had not yet converted to the Thammayut order. It is curious that Waen, a monk of a local tradition, would go to stay with the abbot of a Thammayut wat of his own accord. It was a long way to go to visit someone he had never met. Waen walked over three hundred kilometers from Udon Thani, passing through several villages along the way before arriving at Khorat to catch the train to Bangkok. It is more likely that Jan had asked Man to come and that Man had sent his disciple instead. In any case, it appears that Jan was pleased to have Waen stay and attend him at his temple.

When, ten years later (1931), Jan became ill, Waen made his second trip to Bangkok. This was after Waen had been converted to the Thammayut order.[42] He found it difficult to practice meditation in the city, and he received hardly enough food on his almsround. Some days he got no food at all.[43] Clearly, during the first half of the century, urban monks as well as laypeople in Bangkok paid little attention to wandering meditation monks. Waen left after a month in Bangkok to go up north and spend the rains retreat in Chiang Mai. About a year later the thirty-three-year-old Fan made his first trip to Bangkok with two other thudong monks, Sing and Pin, to attend Ubali. They stayed for a few months.

Li's account of his life in a Bangkok wat is somewhat fuller. Li was only twenty-three when he took his first trip to Bangkok alone. It was 1928, the year after he converted to the Thammayut order. He thought Ajan Man was staying at Wat Sapathum and he wanted to visit his teacher as well as seek a cure for his earache. Although he had no idea where Wat Sapathum was located, he took a train from Khorat to Bangkok. There he found that Ubali had taken Man up north to Chiang Mai. Li ended up spending the rains retreat at Wat Sapathum. He made a resolution to practice meditation as he always did and at the same time to perform duties for his preceptor, Nu. That year Li kept to himself most of the time to maintain stillness of the mind. However, when Li asked permission to leave for a forest the abbot assigned him more duties. Li realized that his good intentions had backfired. "I observed my duties towards my preceptor as best I could . . . looking after his bed, cleaning his spittoons, arranging his betel nut, keeping his mats and sitting cloths in order. . . . After a while I felt that I was serving him to his satisfaction and had found a place in his affections. At the end of the rains he asked me to take on the responsibility of living in and watching over the temple storehouse, the Green Hall, where he took his meals. Although I had set my mind on treating him as a father, I had never dreamed that being loyal and good could have dangers like this" (Li1, 17–18). Not until the beginning of the hot season was Li allowed to go out for a few months of solitude in the forest. He went wandering in the Central Plains: Ayuthaya, Saraburi, Lopburi, and to Nakhon Sawan near Boraphet Lake, where his brother lived.

Li returned to Bangkok in May 1929. During his second rains retreat there he had difficulty keeping up with his meditation. In addition to attending his preceptor, Li was assigned to keep the temple accounts and inventories. At the same time, his fellow monks talked him into studying for naktham exams. With all these added responsibilities, his state of mind began to grow slack. Li describes how living in Bangkok had changed him: "This can be gauged by the fact that the first year, when . . . young monks came to talk to me about worldly matters—women and wealth, I really hated it, but the second year I began to like it. My third year at Wat Sapathum I began to study Pali grammar, after having passed the Third Level Dhamma exam in 1929. My responsibilities had become heavier—and I was getting pretty active at discussing worldly matters."[44]

As bookkeeper of the monastery, Li encountered a problem that he never faced as a wandering monk. During the second rains retreat he found that a large amount of money—nine hundred baht—was missing from the wat's accounts. Li was apprehensive and decided to investigate the matter before reporting it to the abbot. A temple boy eventually confessed to the theft, but the abbot was angry because the money had already been spent. Before the affair was settled, Li lost sleep. "All I could think of was that I would have to disrobe and get a job to make up for the missing funds. At the same time I did not want to disrobe. These two thoughts fought back and forth in my mind until dawn."[45] This incident seems to confirm a discrepancy between the public image and the private life of many urban Thammayut monks. In principle, Thammayut monks are known to be more strict than the non-Thammayut in that they do not handle money. But in reality Thammayut monks commonly handle money.[46]

After this affair had been taken care of, Li asked to resign so he could go off to the forest to meditate. His preceptor refused to let him go. "I'm an old man now," said the abbot, "and aside from you there's no one I can trust to look after things for me. You'll have to stay here for the time being."[47] This Thammayut abbot was more concerned about his administrative work than his disciples' meditation progress. So Li had to stick it out for another year.

When he had first arrived in Bangkok, Li had already seen himself as stricter than the Bangkok Thammayut monks. Now, after spending three rains retreats in a row in a Bangkok wat, he was even more convinced that Thammayut monks in the city were lacking in discipline. Furthermore, after being around the urban Thammayuts for a while, Li noticed that his thoughts about worldly matters would start flaring up at any time. One night he fell asleep while reading a book "lying down and meditating at the same time." He dreamt that Ajan Man came to scold him. "What are you doing in Bangkok?" Man asked in the dream. "Go out into the forest!" "I can't," Li answered, "My preceptor won't let me." Man replied with a single word, "Go!" Li made a resolution: "At the end of the rains, let Ajan Man come and take me with him out of this predicament" (Li1, 32).

Several days later, when Li was accompanying his preceptor to a funeral service at Wat Thepsirin, he saw Ajan Man at the crematorium.[48] It had been four years since he had last seen his meditation teacher. Li was overjoyed, although he had no chance to talk with him.

Abbot Nu finally allowed Li to leave after Man came to visit at Wat Sapathum and requested that Li accompany him to Chiang Mai. Li did not have enough money to pay for the train ticket. Such was his luck, however, that the day before Lady Noi's cremation, Man was invited to deliver a sermon at the home of Phraya Mukkhamontri (the superintendent commissioner of monthon Udon Thani). Afterward Man received donations: a set of robes, a container of kerosene, and eighty baht.[49] Man used some of the money to buy two train tickets and gave the rest away (along with the robes and kerosene). At the end of that year (1931) the two took the train to Uttaradit, where they stayed at a Thammayut wat before traveling to Chiang Mai.

Man and Li were staying at Wat Jediluang in Chiang Mai when they heard that Ubali had passed away on 19 July 1932. This came a month after a military coup in Bangkok toppled the absolute monarchy (a fact not mentioned in either Li's or Man's accounts).[50]

A CHANGED ATTITUDE TOWARD WANDERING MONKS

What prompted the changes in the (Thammayut) monthon sangha head's attitude toward Thammayut thudong monks? Why did he attempt to co-opt them? For clues, we might look at the political climate during this period.

On 24 June 1932 a revolution ended the absolute monarchy. The king became a figurehead, stripped of actual power to rule. A year later, in October 1933, a rebellion led by the Siamese prince Boworadet broke out. Although the rebellion was suppressed, it increased the new government's distrust of the king.[51] During this year the new government abolished the monthon system, along with the powerful monthon officials appointed by the king, and replaced it with the provincial system and provincial governors (by 1938 Siam consisted of seventy provinces). The passing of the old order and the decrease in the prestige of the Siamese monarchy and aristocracy directly affected the Thammayut order, especially sangha administrators in the Northeast, whose main support had come from the powerful monthon government officials.[52] High-ranking Thammayut monks who had connections with royalty were suspected of supporting the pro-monarchist group.[53]

Whereas the Boworadet rebellion decreased the prestige of the royalty, it enhanced greatly the reputation and standing of the commoner Lieutenant-Colonel Phibun, the field commander of the government forces.[54] He soon emerged as the dominant figure in the government and became prime minister from 1938 to 1944 and again from 1948 to 1957.

A second reason for the sangha head's change of attitude toward thudong Thammayut monks may be the increasing conflict, particularly after 1932, between administrative monks in the two orders, Thammayut and Mahanikai. The trouble, which started in 1854, had gotten worse since 1902, when the Thammayuts gained increasing authority over monks of other nikais. The latter resented being under the supervision of Thammayut officials, since Thammayut monks never had to report to senior Mahanikai monks. The implication was that Thammayut monks could govern Mahanikais but not vice versa.[55]

After the absolute monarchy was abolished, the new ruling elites sought to legitimize democratic government by propagating the ideals of equality, freedom, liberty, and representative government.[56] A wave of democracy swept Bangkok, and popular participation and interest in national politics grew.[57] This meant decreased sympathy toward the Thammayut order. It was in this context that the movement of Young Monks (1934–1941) first emerged in Bangkok.[58]

A third reason for Uan's approval of Thammayut thudong monks rests in the change in the status quo. In November 1938 Somdet Wannarat (Phae Tissarathera), abbot of Wat Suthat, was appointed by the government to the position of *sangharaja* (supreme patriarch).[59] This was the first time in eighty-four years that a Mahanikai elder was able to occupy the position of supreme patriarch. From 1854 to 1937 the position of Bangkok sangharaja had been held exclusively by Thammayut monks.

The Young Monks Movement and the other factors sketched above led to the reform of the sangha administration. The new government was less concerned about the Thammayut order in particular than about the fate of state Buddhism in general. Many

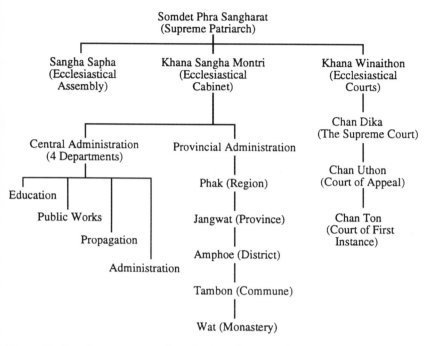

Figure 7. *Sangha structure after the Sangha Act of 1941 (Adapted from Somboon 1982, table 7)*

political leaders regarded the two sectarian rivalries as obstacles to religious progress.[60] The passage of the 1941 Sangha Act (which replaced the 1902 Act) was meant to democratize the sangha administration (see figure 7). As Jackson points out, the purpose of the act was largely to curtail the influence of the Thammayut monks over the sangha. The new Sangha Act undermined the authority of the pro-monarchist Thammayut order and transferred administrative control of the sangha in Thailand to the Mahanikai order.[61]

The Sangha Act of 1941 stipulated that the two orders were to be united within eight years. Somdet Uan, known for his administrative and political skills, had adapted so well to political change that, although a Thammayut, he was appointed the first sangha prime minister *(sangha nayok)* under the new Sangha Act. In 1942 the Phibun government established a nonsectarian monastery, Wat Simahathat, in the northern outskirts of Bangkok. The wat was meant to provide an example of unity to the sangha in Thailand. Its residents consisted of twelve Thammayut monks and twelve Mahanikai monks. The most senior monk, Somdet Uan, became abbot. However, neither the symbol of a nonsectarian monastery nor the political attempts to integrate the sangha through a Buddhist council *(sanghayana)* proved successful.[62] Eventually Wat Simahathat was taken over by the Thammayuts.

Let us backtrack and look at specific factors within the Thammayut order that led to Uan's attempt to recruit the Thammayut wandering monks. The first conflict in the Thammayut order occurred at Wat Sapathum in Bangkok, when a group of junior Thammayut monks rebelled against the authority of the abbot. This took place early in March 1932, almost three months before the overthrow of the absolute monarchy. Monks and novices led by La Sophito tried to force Abbot Nu to hand power over to them. The supreme patriarch, Chinawon, called together five senior Thammayut monks for a meeting: Somdet Wachirayanwong (M. R. Cheun), abbot of Wat Bowonniwet; Somdet Phuthakhosajan (Jaroen), abbot of Wat Thepsirin; Phrommuni (Uan), abbot of Wat Boromniwat; Satsanasophon (Jam), abbot of Wat Makutkasat; and Thamwarodom (Seng), abbot of Wat Rachathiwat.[63] The dissident monks and novices were banished from Wat Sapathum. Phrommuni (Uan) administered the wat until things calmed down. The incident prompted the senior monks to pass a decree forbidding monks to challenge their seniors' authority. Any monks who rebelled against the authority of an abbot would be punished severely and perhaps defrocked.[64] The decree did not stop the dissident monks and novices from staging another coup, however. After they were expelled from Wat Sapathum, they went to reside at another Thammayut wat in the same district, Wat Duangkhae. (As at Wat Sapathum, most of the monks and novices in this wat were from the Northeast.)

A few years later, in March 1934, La Sophito and his fellow monks took power from the abbot of Wat Duangkhae and the wat committee. This time Somdet Cheun, head of the Thammayut order, became acting supreme patriarch. He asked the director-general of the Religious Affairs Department to punish the rebellious monks according to the rules. With no investigation into the reasons for their rebellion, La and his fellow monks were defrocked. Since Phrommuni (Uan) refused to administer this wat and the senior Thammayut monks could not find a suitable abbot, they decided to close the temple.[65]

These incidents indicate that the younger generation of Thammayut Isan monks wanted changes in the sangha hierarchy. They wanted to do away with the authoritarian power of sangha officials. Their rebellion signals a conflict between the generations; it also reflects the weakening power of the Thammayut administrators in Bangkok.

These factors may have had direct bearing on Phrommuni's (Uan's) attitude toward Thammayut thudong monks. A few months after the junior Thammayut monks' rebellion in May 1932, Uan—acting as monthon sangha head—summoned the thudong monks to Khorat Province. As we saw above, he required their help in his efforts to increase the number of Thammayut monasteries and to attract more lay supporters. Note that this missionary effort was possible because the two highest administrative positions in the Northeast (the sangha heads of monthon Nakhon Ratchasima and monthon Udon Thani) were under Thammayut control. This was the first time in history that the Thammayuts had official control of the sangha administration in the Northeast.

Uan probably sensed that the Thammayut order would not be able to survive if its monks did not cooperate with the new government. The end of the old order brought hard times to many Thammayut elders. Furthermore, during the depression of the 1930s and after the end of World War II, government support for the Thammayut wats was scanty or absent. So in 1933 Uan sent the abbot of Wat Sutjinda to approach the new governor of Khorat, Phraya Kamthon Payapthit (Thaung Raksangop) and its military commander, Captain-General Roengrik Pajjamit (Dit Inthasorot), to ask for their continued support of Wat Sutjinda. Until then, the Thammayut wat had been given financial support by the monthon superintendent commissioner (who had in fact established the wat).[66] Uan had become acquainted with Captain-Major Phin Chunahawan shortly after he became the military commander of Khorat. Phin wrote later that during the Boworadet rebellion "the provinces in the Northeast were in turmoil. Phra Phrommuni (Uan) helped explain the government's objectives and policies to people in key provinces. He lectured them until they calmed down."[67] And during the years 1933 to 1944, Uan continued to cooperate with the military government to promote state Buddhism in the Northeast.[68]

A second conflict within the Thammayut order took place at Wat Phichaiyat in Thonburi, across the river from Bangkok. The dispute started in January 1938 when the abbot, Methathammarot (Sao Soriyo),[69] together with twenty-seven resident monks and thirteen novices, requested that their temple be returned to the Mahanikai order. The Thammayut senior monks not only refused to let the wat convert, they sought to defrock the abbot. When the Mahanikai somdet, Wannarat (Phae), became supreme patriarch in November 1938, the case was decided in favor of the abbot of Wat Phichaiyat and his monks. By 2 September 1939 the monks and novices at Wat Phichaiyat were legally and ceremonially returned to the Mahanikai order.

Over a month later in the Northeast, Uan, having now been promoted to the royal rank with the title Somdet Phra Maha Wirawong, officially recognized thudong monks. This is reflected in the following passage of his speech, delivered before an assembly of administrative monks in Khorat on 27 October 1939:

> Nowadays, in almost every province in the Northeast, an increasing number of monks and novices in the Mahanikai as well as the Thammayut orders follow the thudong practice. They have set up samnaks in forest cemeteries and in the forest itself. I have observed their conduct. A number of them have lived austere lives, have adhered strictly to the book of discipline [vinaya], and have been diligent in teaching people to take refuge in the Triple Gem. They have been able to convince people who had wrong beliefs, such as spirit worship, to take up the right ones. People who were wrongdoers have turned over a new leaf and taken up right livelihoods. [The thudong monks] are useful to the nation and the religion, although some of them have been arrogant and I have had to reprimand them occasionally.[70]

Although the speech was given a few years before the new Sangha Act was passed, Somdet Uan certainly knew what was coming. Since late 1937, Uan had taken part in meetings in which Thammayut and Mahanikai elders tried to negotiate and draft a new

Sangha Administrative Act. Under a democratic Sangha Act, the Thammayuts had more to lose in terms of power, since they were outnumbered by the Mahanikais. At that time (1935) there were only 260 Thammayut wats in Siam, compared with 17,305 wats in the "Mahanikai" category.[71] This means that monks following non-Thammayut traditions outnumbered Thammayut monks by more than sixty to one.

It appears that Somdet Uan had made a complete about-face in his attitude toward the thudong monks. A decade earlier he had seen the thudong monks as outlaws and ordered the district officers to chase them out. Now he urged sangha officials in the Northeast to support them: "The local administrative monks should keep watch on the thudong monks' conduct. Support them if they adhere to the vinaya and comply with the rules that I have laid out. To be prosperous, Buddhism must have both *gantha dhura* and *vipassanā dhura*. Gantha dhura is the vocation of books, and vipassanā dhura is the vocation of meditation. Nowadays the majority of monks are book learners. Therefore [we] should support those who follow the thudong practice."[72]

Sangha authorities imposed a number of rules on the thudong monks, ostensibly in order to provide them with safety, although some of the rules were also meant to keep them in line:

Monks should not travel alone, but should go at least in pairs.

They must always carry a letter from a superior. The letter should be addressed to the sangha authority in the area where the monk wishes to go on a thudong.

Thudong monks should be affiliated with a monastery of their nikai. Those without an affiliation will be considered illegal [*phra jorajat*].

Having gone on a thudong, monks should return to their monastery for the rains retreat. They should not spend the rains retreat among themselves in various places unless it is necessary. Then they should notify their monastery of their whereabouts.[73]

HEALING THE HIGH-LEVEL MONKS

Sangha authorities generally preferred settled monastics to wandering ascetics. They were especially supportive of town and urban monks who could read and write Bangkok Thai. After Uan became the sangha head of monthon Ubon Ratchathani, the study of religious texts issued from Bangkok, particularly the vinaya texts, became the main vocation of monks residing in urban monasteries. The preeminence given to Thai printed texts resulted in a shift in the understanding of what constituted authentic Buddhism. Under modern state Buddhism, the sangha authorities came to question the validity of the thudong practice—a tradition that had been transmitted verbally from teacher to disciple. Like other high-level monks, Somdet Uan shared the prejudice that the dhamma could be learned only from Bangkok texts. Even though he allowed the Thammayut thudong monks to wander and teach meditation to gain followers and thereby expand the number of Thammayut monasteries, he made no effort to learn meditation practice from them. Uan represents a classical example of the monk who studies but does not practice. His teacher Ubali (Jan), who valued both textual learning and thudong practice, tried in vain to convince Uan to practice meditation.[74] Ten years after Ubali's death, however, Uan changed his mind and decided to take up meditation practice. His decision was probably prompted by a grave illness. In 1944 Uan became so sick that he lost all appetite and had to take food intravenously. At the time he was staying at Wat Supat in Ubon.[75] To guide him in meditation, he summoned Sing (who was staying at Saensamran Forest Monastery in Warin District, Ubon), Thaung Asoko (abbot of Wat Burapha in Ubon), and Fan.

Fan, who was known among villagers in the Khorat area for his healing powers, was staying at a forest hermitage in Surin when he received the order from Uan to come to the capital town of Ubon. Fan went to spend the 1944 rains retreat at Wat Burapha, on the outskirts of the town.[76]

During the rains retreat Fan seldom had time to himself. He had to take care of the two elder monks, Uan and Pin, who were ill. Every morning Fan left Wat Burapha (in the capital district) for an almsround, then crossed the Mun River to Saensamran Forest Monastery (in Warin District) where Maha Pin was staying. After the meal Fan administered herbal medicine to Pin, who had a lung disease.[77] In the evening he crossed the river again to Wat Supat where he instructed the somdet in meditation and answered his questions regarding the practice. Finally, he returned to Wat Burapha at the opposite end of the town, two kilometers away. Often Fan did not get back to his wat before midnight.

Uan was then seventy-seven years old (Fan was forty-six) and perhaps feared imminent death. Once he asked Fan, "Will I be able to get through this rains retreat?" Fan replied, "If your holiness manages to calm your mind, you will certainly survive" (F, 103). It was then that the sangha head finally acknowledged the wandering meditation monks as worthy of respect and emulation by book-learning monks. He told Fan, "As a preceptor I have performed ordinations for numerous monks and novices, yet I never paid attention to the basic meditation practice. During this rains retreat I have begun to understand what meditation is all about."[78]

Somdet Uan admitted to Fan that for all his studies he did not understand the inner meaning of the dhamma: "As far as meditation practice is concerned," Fan relates, "he was like a novice. All the knowledge that he acquired in his Pali studies was meaningless in real life. Rank and position could not help him when he suffered from illness" (F, 103). Fan recalls that meditation practice enabled the somdet to detach himself from his painful illness and gradually recover. Fan guided Uan for several months before Uan allowed him to go to his Phu Thai village in Sakon Nakhon for a visit.

Several years later, in 1952, Somdet Uan again became seriously ill. He was then eighty-five. Again he needed further guidance in meditation. This time he summoned Li to Wat Boromniwat in Bangkok, his residence. When Li arrived the ailing abbot gave him an order, "You'll have to stay with me until I die. As long as I'm still alive, I don't want you to leave. I don't care whether or not you come to look after me. I just want to know that you are around" (Li1, 111–112). This was the second time that Li was forced to stay in Bangkok. Now that Ajan Man had passed away, Li had no teacher who could rescue him. At first he resented the senior monk's order, but he reconciled himself to it, considering that it was due to his kamma: "Sometimes I wonder about what kamma I had done that had me cooped up like this, but then I'd remember the caged dove I had dreamed about in Chanthaburi. That being the case, I'd have to stay."[79]

Somdet Uan told Li to come to his residence every day to teach him meditation. Li had him practice ānāpānasati. Here the relatively young thudong monk was teaching the elder administrator to observe inhalations and exhalations, sense objects and mind objects. They discussed a number of things while the somdet sat in meditation. The sangha head seemed both pleased and impressed with Li's explanation: "The way you say things is really different from the way other meditation monks talk. Even though I still can't put what you say into practice, I can understand you clearly and have no doubt that what you're saying is true. I used to live near Ajan Man and Ajan Sao, but I never benefited from them the way I've benefited from having you stay with me. There seem to be a lot of surprising things that occur when I sit in meditation" (Li1, 113).

Presently Uan was able to sit still for long periods of time—sometimes for two hours at a stretch. While he was meditating, he would have Li speak about dhamma to go along with his meditation. Gradually his mind was able to follow Li's guidance. As soon as Uan's mind became quiet and steady, Li recalls, "I'd start speaking—and his mind seemed to behave right in line with what I'd be saying.... From then on I never had to give him any more long talks. As soon as I'd say two or three words, he'd understand what I was referring to.... As I spent the rains there with the Somdet my mind was at ease as far as having to explain things to him was concerned" (Li1, 114).

Pleased with his progress, the senior monk finally admitted his ignorance. "I've been ordained for a long time," he told Li, "but I've never felt anything like this.... In the past I never thought that practicing samādhi was in any way necessary.... People who study and practice the dhamma get caught up on nothing more than their own opinions, which is why they never get anywhere. If everyone understood things correctly, there wouldn't be anything impossible about practicing the dhamma" (Li1, 114).

During this rains retreat (1952) the somdet asked Li to teach meditation to monks, novices, and lay followers at Wat Boromniwat.[80] It was the first time a Thammayut thudong monk from the Northeast offered meditation training to laypeople in Bangkok.[81] When the rains retreat ended, the somdet's illness had abated somewhat, and he allowed Li to go out wandering in the provinces. Li, however, ended up spending every rains retreat in Bangkok until the somdet died in 1956.

Li's account illustrates how long it can take an Isan sangha official—one who puts great emphasis on book learning and the textual tradition—to come around to the thudong monks' point of view. Somdet Uan was no exception. Colleagues of Uan's shared his initial disinterest in meditation practice and finally acquiesced only when they fell ill in old age. That is what happened with Somdet Jaroen, abbot of Wat Thepsirin (a Thammayut monastery), and Somdet Wannarat (Pheuan Tissathatata), abbot of Wat Chetuphon (Mahanikai). Somdet Jaroen was persuaded to take up meditation practice by Thammawitako (Treuk), a meditation monk known for his healing powers.[82] Somdet Pheuan was guided by Sot, abbot of Wat Paknam, in the *thammakai* method, a variety of samatha meditation.[83]

Aside from the Isan abbots, it appears that other senior Thammayut monks in Bangkok did not pay much attention to Man's disciples until 1951, when at Wat Mahathat (the center of the Mahanikai order) monks started teaching the Burmese style of vipassanā meditation to laypeople. The abbot of Wat Mahathat, Phimontham (At Assapha), was the first senior high-level monk to encourage town monks to combine book learning with meditation practice.[84] During the 1950s Mahanikai administrative monks in all regions of Thailand came to Wat Mahathat for vipassanā meditation training.

Meanwhile another Mahanikai monastery, Wat Paknam, had already become well known for popularizing thammakai meditation. During this period, too, lay meditation teachers became prominent and gained followers among the educated in Bangkok. Thus the 1950s saw a revival of meditation in Bangkok and urban areas, with different schools offering training to monks, novices, and laypeople. But lay meditation teachers were not a new species that had just evolved in this period. Historically, pha khaws (female as well as male), lay meditators, and lay ascetics have been highly respected.[85] People who followed local Buddhist traditions did not downgrade the importance of lay asceticism the way the Bangkok elite did. Both lay teachers and their followers believed that lay meditators could teach as effectively as monks.[86] It had taken the sangha authorities in Bangkok half a century to concede that meditation monks and meditation teachers, even lay ones, have their place.

CHAPTER 8

Relations

with Villagers

Sangha authorities, once suspicious of and hostile toward thudong monks, eventually recruited them. Thudong monks were no longer outlaws; they became effective promoters of the Thammayut presence in the countryside. The question now is, Why were they so effective? We shall see that the monks' exemplary lifestyle, which included both austere individual meditative practice and a willingness to work hard with others, won the villagers' respect. Furthermore, because these monks had overcome their own fear of ghosts and spirits, they were able to convince villagers that the dhamma could protect them as well. Often the villagers transferred their allegiance from mau phis to thudong monks. The monks' knowledge of the dhamma and meditation no doubt helped to establish the villagers' trust in them as healers, but so, too, did their knowledge of herbal medicine.

The thudong monks were effective for another reason: sangha authorities and government officials supported their activities. Although the efforts that thudong monks made to subdue people's fears of spirits were prompted by their goal of spreading the dhamma, these efforts coincided with government policies coming out of Bangkok. Weakening the belief in and fear of local guardian spirits was a necessary first step in the move to develop rural areas economically. Once that belief and fear diminished, local people (Lao, Phu Thai, Suai, Khmer, Yuan, Mon, etc.) would no longer be afraid of clearing large tracts of forest, and this would encourage the development of agriculture.

PROMOTING GOVERNMENT POLICIES

Much of the thudong "missionary" work took place during the Phibun regimes, which lasted from late 1938 to mid-1944 and from 1948 to 1957. As prime minister, Phibun's goal was to build a new nation *(sang chat)*—a country that belonged to the ethnic Thai and their culture rather than to other ethnic groups, particularly the economically dominant Chinese. During his first period of rule, Phibun made extensive use of the government's radio broadcasting monopoly to shape local support for his regime.[1] One of the government policies was economic development in the countryside.[2] During this period, forested land was abundant and the population was low. Forests covered more than 50 percent of the country. In the Northeast in 1937, forests covered 60 percent of the region, or about ten million hectares (40,000 square miles).[3] Such extensive forest cover meant that traveling between villages, usually by oxcart, on horseback, or on foot, was slow and difficult. And since there were few roads, people had no easy access to frontier forests. To encourage people to clear forested lands and turn them into farms, the government made it easy to stake claims *(jap jong)* to wilderness for cultivation.[4]

The sangha authorities had always gone along with government policies, whether issued by the monarchy or the military. The sangha head of Isan believed—as did the Bangkok elite—that most people in the Northeast were poor because they lacked the drive to make money. Somdet Uan was known for his articles and books advocating government policies. One of his books, *Sap nai din, sin nai nam* (Bounty in the earth, treasure in the water), encouraged people to work harder by clearing forests and expanding their paddy fields and orchards. One of Uan's personal mottoes was "We must transform the forest into a town," a slogan that was hailed as progressive at the time. Uan used the motto in an article urging monks in the Northeast to implement government policies.[5] In this article he asked administrative monks in the Northeast to take on the role of community leaders.

Fellow Isan monks, senior as well as junior, I urge you to advise laypeople to follow the right livelihood according to the guide-lines laid out by the director-general of the Ministry of Agriculture. Monks should lead people to dig ponds, construct roads, and build dams. Do whatever work you can, provided it does not violate the book of discipline [vinaya].

Basically, monks are teachers. We can't expect people to give donations if they don't have anything to give. So, first we must teach them to make a living by encouraging them to extract the treasure in the earth and in the water; that is, to turn the land into rice fields and orchards. These treasures can be found all over the region if people are diligent.[6]

Ironically, monks of local Buddhist traditions had been community leaders all along, at least until the turn of this century when modern state Buddhism began to do away with such traditions. Now the sangha authorities wanted the regional monks to resume this role, but this time pushing government policies.

The government's call for rural development initially fell on deaf ears. During the Forest-Community Period the population was sparse, and villagers were reluctant to clear forested land, believing that the trees, mountains, and ponds were guarded by powerful spirits. Although the belief in *phi* (spirits or ghosts) was widespread in all regions in Siam, the spirits that local people worshipped varied from region to region, from town to town, and from village to village. In the Northeast region, where the majority of inhabitants were Lao and Khmer, the practice of spirit worship played a major role in village life along with Buddhism. The spirits were always identified with regional or local features or with individual persons: they were the guardians of towns or villages; spirits of trees, lakes, or streams; or ghosts of the dead.[7]

One of the early problems that modern state Buddhism faced was how to deal with these local guardian spirits. In the Northeast the Thammayut sect was able to spread to the provincial capitals or district centers through the support of government officials and local elites. But Thammayut advocates could not spread their rationalized Buddhism into the countryside without first winning the hearts and minds of villagers. In 1929 senior Thammayut monks in the Northeast started recruiting thudong Thammayut monks to help convert villagers from their indigenous religious beliefs to Buddhist ones. In so doing, the wandering monks established samnaks in the hinterlands, which eventually became Thammayut monasteries.

Taking Refuge in the Triple Gem

Man and his disciples had been spreading the dhamma among the common people long before government officials in Khon Kaen sought their help in 1929 (chap. 7). The spirit beliefs that the monks encountered most often in the Northeast centered on ancestral spirits *(phi puya tayai* or *phi puta)* and guardian spirits of forests *(phi dong).* In their wanderings the thudong monks found that Lao and Khmer villagers devoted much attention and effort to appeasing or warding off one *phi* or another. They asked the spirits for favors or for their protection; they sought to escape the spirits' pranks; they searched for cures for their ills. The monks found that many villagers turned to a mau phi when they fell ill; treating illness was the most common task that these doctors performed.[8] The spirit doctors approached the spirit at the *san puta* (spirit house or shrine) in which benevolent ancestral spirits guarding the village resided. Generally located at the edge of the forest, this was usually a simple hut of wood and bamboo built on stilts.

To convert people from spirit worship, the wandering monks attempted to replace the custom of making sacrificial offerings with the custom of taking refuge in the Triple Gem—a fundamental ritual of Theravada Buddhism. Taking refuge in the Triple Gem often becomes a hollow ritual in which a person merely recites, "I go for refuge to the Buddha, I go for refuge to the dhamma, I go for refuge to the sangha." Although this may be the extent of refuge taking among urban people today, the act can be more complex and multifaceted.[9] During the Forest-Community Period, when villagers agreed to take refuge in the Triple Gem, the thudong monk would teach them meditative concentration and the five precepts (not to kill, steal, lie, commit adultery, or use intoxicants). This indispensable ritual provided the villagers with a means of protection from punishing spirits. It was more than a magical means of protection against external agents; it was a method of guarding the mind. Villagers were acquiring a means of stopping themselves from engaging in behavior that might harm others or themselves.

Neutralizing Local Spirits

But first the spirits—or rather the villagers' fears of them—had to be neutralized. Thudong monks achieved this in different ways. Monks who had overcome their own fear of spirits demonstrated that they were immune to ghost attacks. For example, they sometimes took shelter overnight in a san puta when nothing else was available. Some of these shrines were large enough for a person to lie down in, and they were good places for meditation: quiet and isolated. But as might be expected, villagers did not like the idea of anyone staying in them.

Waen recalls that was the case in 1921, when he was traveling on foot from Udon Thani to Khorat, a distance of about three hundred kilometers.[10] He went for alms in several villages along the way. Many villages, he noted, had Buddhist wats, but spirit worship still seemed to be the dominant religion. "In every village there was a san puta. Every year the community held a big sacrificial ceremony. But they also held the sacrificial rite individually when there was an illness in a family or when domestic animals got sick. The shrine was usually located at the edge of the forest near the village. No one dared to go into this forest to fell trees. The ancestral spirits would punish anyone who did" (Wn, 43).

Villagers were opposed to Waen's staying in the shrine, but he did anyway. "They were afraid that if they allowed it, the spirit would get angry and harm them. I tried to explain things to them rationally." When villagers saw that no harm had come to a monk who stayed in a forest guarded by ancestral spirits, they were impressed. Waen took the opportunity to teach them the Triple Gem and the precepts. "In those days," he recalled, "most people were mixed up about spirit worship and taking refuge in the Triple Gem."

Fan was another monk who used san putas for shelter and then made this a teaching device. In 1929, after parting from his fellow monks, Fan walked alone toward Pheu Tree Village in Nonthan Subdistrict in monthon Nakhon Ratchasima. He came across a shrine at the edge of a forest and used it as a shelter for the night.

The next day two villagers came to a nearby pond, saw the monk, and brought him water. Fan told them to notify the village headman of his presence. Shortly afterward, the headman arrived with four local people. These villagers were angry to see a monk using their spirit shrine. One man shouted, "What kind of a monk is this, living in dirt [*naun klang din, kin klang sai*]?" Another villager said, "Shoot him!" A third one said they should hit him on the head with a pestle, while the fourth urged throwing rocks at him (F, 68). The headman calmed his people and went to talk to Fan to see whether or not he was an authentic monk. Perhaps the village chief was skeptical because monks of the local traditions would not choose to sleep in a spirit shrine. Fan was tactful. He explained why he had taken shelter there: he, too, relied on the san puta for protection. Fan also pointed out that unlike the villagers who left the shrine unkempt, he had cleaned it up. After arriving, he had swept it and cleared away the fallen branches and leaves (F, 68).

The village headman then asked questions about the dhamma to test Fan's knowledge. After Fan had convinced them that he was a real monk, the villagers went home and returned with a sleeping mat and a mosquito net for him. They also invited him to spend the rains retreat in the vicinity of their village. But Fan declined, having observed a potential for flooding in the valley. He finally gave in when the villagers suggested that he stay at the forest cemetery on a hill nearby.

During this rains retreat a number of villagers were troubled by bad spirits. They believed that ghosts were possessing them and causing deaths. One woman, whose husband had traveled to Ubon by boat to sell their rice, came to Fan for help. She and her children had become lay devotees, but she was still afraid that ghosts might harm her.[11] Fan told her, "Don't be afraid. As long as you *phawana* [meditate], reciting 'buddho, buddho,' the ghosts won't be able to enter or disturb you" (F, 70). They followed the monk's instructions faithfully. Although other villagers fell ill, Fan's lay followers were spared.

A number of villagers, also afraid that sooner or later ghosts might attack them, went to see the spirit doctor. When they heard that, as usual, a sum of money would be required before a ritual could be performed, they went to the thudong monk for advice.

Fan told them, "If the mau phi is collecting money to build a wat or a facility for public use, you should pay him. If he keeps the money for himself, you should not. Everybody falls ill at some point in life. It is nonsense to believe that illness is caused by ghosts and spirits" (F, 70). Fan also encouraged the villagers to understand how even in the midst of illness they were of sound body, how the body is constantly decaying and renewing itself, and how health and illness are intertwined.

At the end of the rains retreat, Fan left the village to go to Nam Phaung District. He got as far as Wat Sijan when a group of villagers caught up with him and asked him to return. They told him that after he left every hut in the hamlet had become possessed by malevolent ghosts. When Fan returned, the headman called a meeting and all the villagers agreed to take refuge in the Triple Gem. This probably means that Fan taught them to phawana— that is, to concentrate and calm their minds—when they were afraid. Fan ended up spending another rains retreat in this village. His biographer concludes that from then on the people no longer believed in spirits. We do not know if the villagers went back to performing rituals to placate spirits after Fan left, however.

Going against spirit worship could be risky, even in a thudong monk's natal village. That was certainly Li's experience. In Li's village, like many others, spirit worship had so thoroughly meshed with the local Buddhism that the two formed a single syncretic whole.[12] Li wanted to move the people further away from the spirits and closer to the dhamma. This move, he felt, would make life easier and less wasteful. Instead of making animal sacrifices for spirits, people should make merit (by observing precepts and meditating) and transfer that merit to the spirits:

There was another practice I had seen a lot . . . which struck me as pointless . . . the belief that the ancestral spirits in the village had to eat animal flesh every year. Once a year, when the season came around, each household would have to sacrifice a chicken, a duck or a pig. Altogether this meant that in one year hundreds of living creatures had to die for the sake of the spirits, because there would also be times when people would make sacrifice to cure an illness in the family. All of these struck me as a senseless waste. If the spirits really did exist, that's not the sort of food they would eat. It would be far better to make merit and dedicate it to the spirits. If they didn't accept that, then drive them away with the authority of the Dhamma. (Li1, 13)

After the rains retreat of 1927, Li went to visit his father at his natal village (today in Amnat District, Ubon). On the way he stopped to rest overnight at a shrine in the forest near Red Pond Village (Ban Naung Daeng). His father heard the news, came out to this village to see him, and accompanied him back to their village. Li stayed in the village's cemetery in the forest, where the villagers believed the ghosts were malevolent. He stayed for several weeks, delivering sermons to people who came from the surrounding villages. Li told them that he wanted to wipe out their fear of the spirits of the ancient ruins near his village and of the ghosts in the cemetery. He set about exorcising them. "I did away with a lot of their mistaken beliefs and practices: the worship of such spirits as *phi paup, phi kraseu, phi thai, phi than,* belief in sorcery, and the use of various spells which Buddhism called 'bestial knowledge.' . . . We exorcised them by reciting Buddhist chants and spreading thoughts of good will and loving kindness throughout the area. During the day, we'd burn the ritual objects used for worshipping *phi ten, phi ram, phi mot, phi mau* and other kinds of spirits. Some days there'd be nothing but smoke the whole day long."[13]

All this made the villagers extremely nervous. They were afraid that there would be nothing to protect them in the future and that the spirits would take revenge by spreading illness. In the villagers' view, all illness had some moral or "supernatural" cause, such as an offended or angry spirit.[14] As a substitute for their animistic beliefs, Li told the villagers to take refuge in the Triple Gem. He wrote down and distributed copies of the Buddhist chants to the villagers to recite and taught them to meditate on loving-kindness.[15] He told them to leave the spirits alone, and he assured them that if they followed his instructions faithfully they would be safe.

As Li's reputation spread, some people became jealous of him and tried to drive him away. "A number of monks and laypeople in the area, thinking I was nothing but a braggart, kept trying to create trouble and misunderstanding between other monks and me."[16] When Li refused to leave, a layman claiming that he represented the householders in Yang Yongphap township went to the district education officer. Mr. Chai "denounced me as a vagrant monk [*phra jorajat*]. This simply increased my determination to stay. I haven't done anything evil or wrong since coming here. No matter how they come at me, I'm going to stick it out to the very end" (Li1, 14; Li2, 11).

One day the district officer came to the area on business and stayed overnight in the village. The headman (a relative of Li's) told the district officer what Li was doing. Since Li's teaching was compatible with government policy, which advocated the elimination of spirit worship, the officer took sides with him. "It is a rare monk who will teach the laypeople like this. Let him stay as long as he likes" (Li1, 15). From then on Li encountered no opposition in the village.

By the time Li dictated his memoirs thirty years later, he had heard that the dense forest that used to surround his village—the same forest that villagers held to be guarded by malicious spirits—had now been settled, and that the area surrounding the ancestral shrines had been planted with crops. This was proof, in Li's estimate, that the villagers had taken refuge in the Triple Gem and abandoned spirit worship.

But before a thudong monk could convert villagers he might first have to combat the most powerful figure in the village—the mau phi. Often the spirit doctor saw himself as a rival to Buddhist monks. An example from Thet's accounts reveals a clash between these two competing systems of belief. In 1931 Thet, his brother Ket (also a monk), and a number of other thudong monks spent the rains retreat at a village in Phon District (today in Khon Kaen Province). Here Thet encountered a woman spirit doctor and her dozen disciples who made their living by traveling around attending to the sick.[17] Thet challenged her belief in spirits:

> I advised her to forsake her spirit worship and to come and firmly establish herself in the Triple Gem. Her belief in spirits, I pointed out, is based in wrong view and lacks virtue and merit, whereas going for refuge to the Triple Gem really is something of merit and wholesomeness. One can then also be counted as a devotee with right view in the Buddhist Teachings.

She replied that "what she had was good" and that when she was . . . possessed by some spirit, she could be directed to find buried treasure or enabled to leap into a clump of thorny bamboo without being gashed. (T1, 116)

Thet then tried to explain the first of the five Buddhist precepts to her. He pointed out that the consequences of killing animals for sacrifice would rest on the sacrificer, even though a spirit made the request. He told her that spirits had never taught their devotees to abandon evil and cultivate good or to keep the precepts. "The only instruction they ever gave was for the person to make them an offering of the head of a pig, or a chicken or duck. After having prompted this animal sacrifice they didn't even eat it. One has to kill the animal oneself and offer it to the spirits and when they don't come and eat it then one has to eat it oneself. It isn't the spirits that will have to accept the responsibility and the evil consequences of such killing, it will all come back on the one who kills" (T1, 116). Finally the spirit doctor gave in and agreed to abandon spirit sacrifice and take refuge in the Triple Gem. Thet taught her to chant devotions and meditate. Since her skills in healing were conducive to meditation practice, it took her no time at all to get results, and she soon became convinced of the Triple Gem's protective powers.

That night, she put the teaching I had given her into practice and obtained marvellous results. That is, before going to bed she chanted her devotions to the Triple Gem and then sat in meditation. She then saw two spirit-children, a girl and a boy. They were swinging on the hand rail of the rice pounder, at the bottom of the stairs leading up to her house. They didn't say or do anything at all. This vision was as vivid as if it was happening before her very eyes but they were actually closed in meditation. She then became convinced that the spirits could no longer come and take possession of her, and that the protecting virtue and power of the Triple Gem was indeed great. (T1, 117)

Her husband, also a spirit doctor, believed that he had greater powers than the village abbot. He refused to respect the monks, and he showed his contempt by raising high his foot rather than his hands when he passed a monastery.[18] But his wife's conversion to Buddhism somehow had a mysterious effect on his powers. "That same night . . . he was unable to get to sleep. Whenever he started to doze off, he would be startled awake and become fearful, as if something threatening was near. Consequently, in the morning he asked his wife, 'What did you get from the ajan that kept me awake all night long?' His wife confirmed that the ajan had indeed given her something 'special' and that she would take her husband to see him too" (T1, 118; T2, 45). From then on, Thet says, these two old spirit doctors gave up their sorcery and took refuge in the Triple Gem.

Thudong monks were able to convert not only the spirit doctors but the spirits themselves, turning them into guardians or practitioners of the dhamma. If he had sufficient powers, a monk could establish direct contact with these deities or spirits. For example, it was believed that Ajan Man could communicate with spirits held to be responsible for much that occurs on earth. "He would sometimes communicate with invisible beings such as ghosts, demons, *nagas,* or angels of countless planes. It was this intermediate level of meditation that he used when receiving invisible guests who approached him. At other times the mind would 'separate' itself from the body and tour the celestial realms of various subtleties, from the sensual realms to the very subtle high realms. These tours sometimes would take him to the dark realms where there were beings suffering the results of their own karma."[19]

It is hardly surprising that in this region full of spirits and ghosts, the Thammayut scholars or administrative monks—contemptuous of local people and adamant that they be taught their rationalized Buddhism—were unable to win over the villagers. Villagers were not interested in listening to abstract dhamma sermons or sermons delivered in Bangkok Thai. They were more concerned about how to live successfully in an unfriendly environment of dense forests and hills guarded by spirits. Wandering meditation monks, who shared a similar cosmological view, were qualified to help. When villagers saw these monks travel through the jungle alone, or go off to meditate high up a mountain or in a forest cemetery or somewhere else that most people feared, they knew that these monks were not ordinary. They must have reached some satisfactory arrangement with the guardian spirits of the forests and caves, otherwise they would not have been able to live in such places.

It is not hard to see why the thudong tradition found acceptance in the countryside. The monks were tolerant of the belief in local spirits and ghosts, accepting it as an integral part of the villagers' world. When thudong monks preached against ghosts or spirits, it was not because they doubted their existence; rather, they opposed the practice of bribing the spirits with sacrificial offerings. Indeed, the idea that different kinds of spirits abided everywhere (in forests, trees, rivers, mountains, caves, fields, earth, sky, and animals) was convincing to wandering monks, who had experienced meetings with some of these spirits in their visions.

Many villagers were ready to abandon their beliefs in ghosts and spirits provided they could still feel protected. Taking refuge in the Triple Gem and making merit gave them this security. As Kirsch has observed, villagers "found it 'simpler' to perform general merit-making ceremonies or to call on the monkhood for assistance in warding off the malevolent attentions of 'demons' *(pret)* and 'ghosts' *(phi)*, than to propitiate a host of demons and ghosts as they impinge at unpredictable moments on one's life."[20]

Although villagers may have started meditating to protect themselves from harm or to make merit, many continued to practice meditation on their own, whether or not a monk was around to guide them (La, 30–32). In their accounts, thudong monks acknowledged that pha khaws and other lay disciples could be their equals in spiritual attainment, if they practiced seriously.[21]

The Protective Power of Meditation

In teaching villagers meditation, Thet and other thudong monks offered a "do-it-yourself" method to ward off attacking spirits. Reciting gāthās, practicing meditation, and observing precepts were techniques that villagers could use to protect themselves after the thudong monks had departed. Teaching abstract dhamma alone did not help villagers overcome their fears of spirits or ghosts, as the Thammayut authorities well knew. But meditation practice, as taught by the thudong monks, calmed their fears and gave them confidence in their own spiritual powers.

Thet gives additional examples of how village people took to meditation, sometimes with excellent results. During the 1930 rains retreat in Khon Kaen, he and three other thudong monks (Maha Pin, Phumi, and Kongma) guided a group of villagers in meditation. "Every Observance Day, all the monks, novices and visiting laypeople would apply themselves to the development of their meditation as best they could, in line with their individual abilities [and] they did achieve very satisfactory results. Some of the laypeople meditated and came to see many different and diverse things, so that they became absorbed in the meditation and forgot all about their homes and families."[22]

After the rains retreat was over, Thet and the others moved on. In Mahasarakham they taught villagers with success. Thet recalls that "some of these people achieved quite astonishing results in their meditation. They would sit in meditation in the wat and know that back in the village their children or grandchildren had been bickering and abusing each other. . . . It was miraculous how some of those who took to it seriously acquired psychic powers. Sitting at the hermitage, they 'knew' what their relatives in the village were gossiping about."[23]

Thet acknowledges that some villagers tried hard to meditate but could not succeed. They followed the precepts, however, and some even ordained as pha khaws to be with their friends. The forest hermitage that Thet and his fellow thudong monks established became a permanent monastery.

Wiriyang offers another example of how meditation helped villagers overcome their fears of spirits. In 1943 Ajan Man was spending the rains retreat in a forest hermitage at Mon Field Village (Ban Na Mon), not far from the Phu Phan Mountains in Sakon Nakhon.[24] One day four villagers came and told him that *phi paup* (vampire spirits that feed on entrails of their victims)[25] and *phi pa* (forest spirits) were continually causing deaths in their village. They asked him to go there and chase the ghosts out. Ajan Man, then seventy-three years old, sent Wiriyang instead.[26]

Wiriyang and a novice walked to the village and stayed in the forest nearby. "At night a lot of laypeople came to see me," he recalls. "They looked frightened because they were terrified of the spirits. They feared that if the spirits didn't eat them, they would eat their children. I suppose they doubted that I would be able to combat these spirits, since I looked so young. If a monk couldn't subdue the ghosts, they would attack even harder. But the lay folk seemed to have confidence that I, a disciple of a thudong master, would have the power to deal with spirits" (Wi, 91). That night Wiriyang delivered a sermon, offered refuge in the Triple Gem to the villagers, and taught them to meditate. Just before the villagers left for their homes, he said, "Tonight I will chase all kinds of spirits out of this village including the phi paups. Remember to phawana the way I taught you. If anything happens, let me know tomorrow."

The next day the villagers came to see Wiriyang and reported what had happened. "Last night the dogs howled all night long, so hardly anybody fell asleep. Everyone thought that the ajan was probably using his magical powers to subdue the ghosts. Many villagers told me about their dreams. These dreams were all alike: they saw hundreds of ghosts, with different appearances and features, carrying their children or grandchildren, leaving this village. The ghosts were grumbling, 'We have to leave. It's too hot here. We've been living in this village for so long, and nobody ever bothered us. But this time we have no strength to fight.' The ghosts seemed in a hurry to leave. In their dreams, the ghosts walked backward, unlike us people" (Wi, 91).

Wiriyang was surprised at the quick results, since he thought it might have taken a while before the villagers developed faith in him: "They really did believe that the ghosts had left their village. Confident of this, they were at peace. What a change! Within a day the atmosphere in the village changed from paranoia and distrust to lightheartedness" (Wi, 91).

As Wiriyang's reputation spread, he used this opportunity to convert the local people to his kind of Buddhism.

When people in the nearby hamlets heard that the ghosts had left this village, they thought that the ghosts would be passing through their own villages. [This] horrified them. They all came to see me. I taught them to sit in meditation and explained the dhamma to them. But they wanted me to stop the wandering ghosts from staying in their villages. So I told them they must come to listen to the sermons regularly, meditate, and observe the precepts. They agreed to do whatever I asked. In such circumstances, people's minds are most receptive to the dhamma, so I could convert them in no time at all. I performed the rituals to chase away the spirits and explained [the Buddhist concept of] right view to them. [I] stayed with them for over a week until they recovered from their fear of phi paups. They were happy now that they no longer lived in fear. (Wi, 92)

The thudong monks engaged in this missionary activity in order to spread the dhamma and help people with their fears. But one consequence, as we noted earlier, was that they helped open the forest frontier for rapid economic development. Once local people learned not to fear spirits of the forest, they were no longer reluctant to cut down trees and establish settlements.

A recollection of Juan's illustrates this point. Between 1958 and 1962 Juan was staying at Jan Tree Cave in Pink Forest (Dong Si Chomphu), Nongkhai. The Forest-Invasion Period had just begun, so remote areas such as this were still inaccessible. In this heavily forested area, villagers could move their settlements whenever they chose. But villagers who lived in Pink Forest had been reluctant to expand their fields because of their fear of spirits. Juan gradually coaxed the villagers away from their belief in guardian spirits of the forest. As a result of his teachings, local habitations increased from one tiny hamlet to several villages.

"When I first ventured into the forest" in late 1958, Juan remembers, "there were only two Khamu households. Later on people from other villages began to settle in the forest. They saw that the area around Jan Tree Cave was fertile—good soil and plenty of water. Previously the villagers believed that the area should not be cultivated because forest spirits there were malevolent. Now that they no longer held such beliefs, they cleared the forest for paddy fields and orchards" (J, 75). Later on thousands of people migrated from other provinces such as Roi-Et, Nakhon Phanom, and Ubon to settle there. Juan helped set up new villages during the five years that he stayed in his Cave. "I chose the four directions of the cave to be auspicious sites for their settlements— Golden Bamboo Village [Ban Kham Phai], Pig Pond Village [Ban Naung Mu], Salty Canal Village [Ban Khlaung Khem], and Pong Pleuai Village. With the new settlements I got plenty of food on almsround. But the area was no longer quiet or suitable for meditation practice, so I thought about leaving and seeking solitude elsewhere" (J, 75).

When the villagers found out that Juan intended to leave, they refused to let him go. "They were afraid that after I left the crops would not grow well. The rain might not fall in the proper season, as it did when I was around." Having a thudong monk around insured peace and well-being. It was almost as if the villagers were treating him like a substitute guardian spirit. But Juan left anyway, after instructing them to keep the Triple Gem and the Five Precepts in mind. "I told them to take refuge in the Triple Gem, not to kill animals or any sentient beings, not to steal, not to commit adultery, not to lie. And not to take intoxicants so that they lose sati. If everybody follows this sila, wherever they live there will be peace" (J, 75).

MONKS AS HEALERS

During the Forest Community Period most rural people relied on spirit doctors. Although thudong monks often preached against the ritual placation of spirits, they did not challenge the practice of healing through traditional herbal medicine.[27] After all, in the early days of their wandering before they learned to heal themselves, some thudong monks, like Li and Juan, were healed by local female mau phis when they fell ill in remote areas. Some thudong monks became skilled in herbal medicine, and some, like many western missionaries, served as doctors among village folk.

The monks' memoirs and biographies report many instances of a thudong monk going into the forest to find medicinal herbs for an ill villager, who takes this medicine and recovers. But that is usually only half the story, since considerably more went into the healing than meets the eye. Many wandering monks who were well versed in the medicinal value of indigenous plants also treated the psychological factors involved in illness. They healed by administering spiritual remedies as well as medicines.

Among Man's many disciples, the best known for their medicinal skills were Fan and Lui.[28] The following event, which took place in 1935, illustrates Lui's proficiency. Lui, who at the time was thirty-three years old, was wandering in Kut Bak and Phanna Nikhom Districts (in Nakhon Phanom). Here he found that villagers were suffering from *rok nep cha* (beriberi). They complained of fatigue and of numbness or weakness in the limbs and extremities, and they had no strength to plow their fields or plant their crops. Lui then remembered that in an old text, the *Bupphasikkha*,[29] the Buddha prescribed a traditional remedy called (in Thai) *ya nammut nao*. He decided to try out this medicine. The remedy called for over twenty herbs from the forest mixed together with salt and honey and the boiled urine of a gaur.[30] Lui made these herbs into a brew and distributed it to the villagers, who came with their own containers. After the patients drank this medicine, they began to recover, eventually regained their strength, and resumed their work in the fields.

Lui's reputation as a thudong monk able to cure beriberi soon spread throughout Kut Bak and Phanna Nikhom Districts. Villagers at Pheu Pond invited Lui. After Lui cured them of beriberi, they were ready to listen to whatever he taught them. As an old villager recalled, "First he taught us *dana* [generosity]—to make merit by giving alms when we had a chance. [He told us] to cook rice early in the morning, and if there's enough time, make some chili paste to accompany the rice. If there was no chili, some salt would do. If we didn't have time, he said just tell the children to offer food to the monks. . . . He also taught us how to pay respect to monks, to recite prayers, and to phawana. . . . Whatever he needed at the hermitage, we helped him with. We helped him build platforms, huts, and a hall. He taught us how to weave cloth [to make robes for the monks]."[31]

Lui stayed at Pheu Pond Village for a year until he was able to "sit in their heart."[32] The villagers became so devoted that they refused to let him go off to wander alone. Finally Lui had to flee the village.[33]

Fan, too, was also well versed in the medicinal value of indigenous herbs. Whenever he was staying in a forest or on a mountain, Fan was on the lookout for medicinal plants. In 1943 Fan was wandering in Buriram and Surin Provinces, accompanied by a few monks, novices, and village boys. Coming upon a stream in a forest of *krabao* trees, a quiet and shady area suitable for meditation, they decided to stay awhile. Here in this forest the forty-five-year-old Fan became known as a *jao phu mi bun* (a holy monk) because of his healing powers. When the inhabitants heard that a thudong monk had come to the area, they flocked to listen to his sermons and to ask for medicine. Fan's herbal medicines consisted mainly of pickled olives and chili peppers. Yet many people were cured, according to Fan's biographer. "Ajan Fan's medicine was effective for many kinds of diseases. People who had had abdominal edema for several years would come to him. After they listened to the sermon and took refuge in the Triple Gem, they received medicines. Within three days the illness was gone. Even insane people were cured after taking refuge in the Triple Gem and receiving holy water. Because of his healing powers, people flocked to see him" (F, 98).

While in Surin, Fan visited one hamlet after another in response to invitations from village folk. A forest hermitage was established in one area where Fan stayed, but he did not remain there long because soon after he had set it up, Somdet Uan ordered Fan to come to Ubon to take care of him. Later on, after Fan settled in Sakon Nakhon, village folk from Surin occasionally traveled there to visit him, a testament to the respect they had for him.

Even more than Lui and Fan, Ajan Man was renowned for his resourcefulness in curing the physical and mental illnesses of his disciples. His techniques were basically twofold: healing through teaching, and psychic or "miraculous" healing. His adeptness in psychic curing goes back to his period of prolonged solitary self-confinement in Sarika Cave in 1913 (chap. 4). After that experience, whenever Man became ill he cured himself by applying thamma osot—that is, spiritual medicine. He had little use for conventional medicines and physicians. Had he relied on them, Man believed, he would have died already. This attitude persisted even when he was weakened by old age.

An example of Man's healing ability occurred at Tham Village in Laos, across the Mekong River from the town of Nakhon Phanom. In Man's younger days, he and his teacher Sao had spent some time near this village. Just before Man's return visit, many villagers had contracted smallpox, and several were dying every day. The Lao villagers were overcome with joy to see Man arrive, and they begged him to help. They believed that the thudong monks possessed mystical healing powers. Man convened the villagers and asked them to accept the Triple Gem as their refuge instead of ghosts and spirits. "He taught them the ways of practice, such as reciting the passages of homage and recollection of the Triple Gem in the morning and at night before going to bed. This was to be done individually at home in addition to the collective recitation to be done twice a day. They readily and strictly obeyed him. He also did something to help [himself] in his own inner practice" (M1, 62). This was metta bhavana. He radiated loving-kindness during his sitting meditation three times a day:

once in the afternoon, once before going to sleep and once upon waking up. "The Ajan would first balance his mind and radiate its force to traverse the worlds in all planes, upwards, downwards and horizontally without any interruption. The radiance of his mind at that time was indescribably bright, being limitless and unobstructed, and far brighter than hundreds or thousands of suns. There is nothing brighter than the mind that is completely purified. The radiance beaming out of an absolutely purified mind illuminates the world and cools it with the tranquilizing effect it produces" (M1, 63).

According to the biographer, after Man's arrival the sick recovered speedily, the epidemic disappeared, and no more deaths were reported. The village abbot was much impressed, and from then on he made it a rule to join his hands in homage to Ajan Man and Ajan Sao whenever he mentioned their names.

This method of curing did not always work, however, as the following event (told by Waen) illustrates. During World War II, Man and two disciples, Waen and Teu, spent a rains retreat on Chiang Dao Mountain in northern Thailand. This mountain had numerous caves suitable for meditation, so each monk had a cave for himself. They convened twice a month, at the full and new moons, to listen to Man's sermons and to recite the 227 vinaya rules. During that year an epidemic was afflicting people in the area; two or three villagers were dying every day. Local people were also worried about cattle rustlers, who were raiding their cattle almost every day. The village folk turned to the thudong monks for help. Man and his two disciples meditated and repeatedly extended loving-kindness to them, but no amount of this relieved their suffering. Eventually, the thudong master decided that the villagers' kamma was too strong. No matter how much loving-kindness Man and his two disciples radiated, they could not overcome the kammic power of the thefts and other unethical acts that the villagers were still committing. The epidemic lasted about a month and killed dozens of people. As for the widespread stealing, Man taught people to distinguish between right and wrong living, but it was like "pouring water onto a tree stump": thefts remained frequent.[34]

Fan, whose skill as an herbalist we have already discussed, was also able to heal through his strong power of concentration. He demonstrated this ability when he cured himself of an illness apparently by meditation. Just before the rains retreat in 1931, Fan spent days and nights making robes for some thudong monks who were to be reordained into the Thammayut order at Wat Sijan in Khon Kaen. Although Fan was only thirty-four years old, the nonstop cutting and sewing took its toll on his health. He fell ill. His body ached all over; regardless of the bodily posture he assumed, the pain persisted. So Fan went by himself to a field and resolved to sit there and meditate on the pain, until death if necessary. As the biographer tells us, "With strong determination his mind became firmly unified. The body became light, as if there were no body at all. The painful feelings totally disappeared" (F, 76). Fan sat motionless in deep concentration from seven o'clock in the evening until the next morning. When other monks and the novices returned from almsround after nine o'clock, they went to pay him their respects. Only then did Fan come out of his samādhi and realize that he had been sitting all night long. "It felt as if I'd been meditating only a little while," he remarked (F, 77). As his biographer writes, Fan exerted himself until he "realized buddho" *(raleuk phuttho)* and fully recovered from pain. The implication is that he learned how to heal himself through meditation.

Another event provides further information about Fan's healing ability: "While meditating, as the mind reached its most refined state, Fan saw in front of him, in a nimit, a pregnant woman suffering in labor. She gave birth to a baby boy who immediately started walking and running. In the vision he also saw an Angulimala gāthā—a sacred mantra for difficult childbirth. When he came out of his samādhi, he wrote down the gāthā *sotthikhapasa.*"[35] Later an old woman brought her pregnant daughter to seek help from the thudong monk. She told Fan that her daughter had been suffering labor pains for three days and that she did not know to whom to turn. So Fan wrote this gāthā on a cigarette paper for the old woman's daughter to recite at home. A few days later, he heard that the old woman's daughter had an easy birth. From then on, village women who were expecting came to see Fan for the delivery gāthā.

Incidentally, this thudong monk's role in assisting women give birth is not unusual. Local women usually came to monks to seek help during pregnancy. In the Lao tradition, expertise in this matter was one of four kinds of practical knowledge an abbot might possess. Ideally, he should be an expert in astrology *(mau du)*, in settling disputes *(mau khwam)*, in healing *(mau tham)*, and in treatment of pregnancy *(mau tam yae)*.[36]

On another occasion Fan appeared to have healed a disciple through his powers of concentration. While he was spending the 1949 rains retreat at Phuthon Phithak Forest Monastery, in the capital town of Sakon Nakhon, many monks were suffering malaria attacks. One monk not only had fits of fever and shaking but started talking to himself nonstop. (Fan's biographer guesses that the malaria had affected the brain.) When Fan called the disciple to his hut and asked him what was wrong, the monk insisted that he was fine. Unable to bring the sick monk to his senses by questioning him, Fan concentrated his mind and directed all his attention onto the monk, even while the latter continued babbling.

> About five minutes later this monk stopped chattering. Yawning, he dropped to the floor and fell asleep in front of Fan. The ajan told another monk to bring a pillow to support his head. Then he ordered the sleeping monk to continue sleeping until he had enough rest. Ajan Fan then went about his daily activities: sweeping the ground, taking a bath, and doing walking meditation.
>
> The monk slept from three o'clock until about six. Upon waking up he wondered, "How come I'm sleeping here?" All the symptoms of illness were gone. When his fellow monks told him about his nonstop babbling, he said he had no recollection of such behavior. (F, 133–134)

Healer monks such as Man and Fan, it must be noted, were not products of the state monastic education. They learned things the way meditation monks and other ascetics always do: from their teachers and through careful observation, quiet meditation, and inner discernment.

Sometimes the mere attentive presence of a revered thudong monk was enough to provide villagers with spiritual strength. During the dry season in 1950, Fan took his disciples (a monk and a novice) to Ox Mountain in Nongkhai, where he planned to spend a rains retreat. Fan was now fifty-two years old. In those days Ox Mountain was surrounded by thick forests. To get to the mountain top they had to wade across a river and walk for half a day through a forest along a trail used mostly by elephants and tigers. Seven men from two nearby villages, Sokkam and Don Siat, guided them and carried their food. During the months that the monk and his disciples stayed on the mountain, they depended on these forest dwellers for alms. As the rainy season approached, however, the villagers found it too difficult to bring food to the monks, so Fan decided to spend the rains retreat near Don Siat. Upon arriving there, he found that many inhabitants had fallen ill, and every night mysterious bright red lights were being seen over the village, moving about at great speed. The village chief invited Fan to chant and bless his house. Afterward Fan preached to adults and children, telling them to observe right livelihood and not create bad kamma, to pay respects to the Triple Gem, and to meditate on buddho. Then he sprinkled the inhabitants with holy water. During the time that Fan stayed in the village, his biographer relates, the inhabitants recovered from their illnesses and the swiftly moving lights also disappeared. After staying with them for three days, Fan moved on.

We have already alluded to some reasons why thudong monks may have possessed healing powers. Villagers placed strong faith in the monks' abilities to cure them. Such faith can produce a healing power, which stems from both the healer's personality and the means the healer employs to stimulate faith: objects, symbols, and rites that guide the mind in a certain direction.[37] The uplifting effects of the religious rites, the deep confidence in the healing powers of the monk, the touching of limbs by the monk—all these factors, acting individually or in combination, and perhaps as a placebo, may well have been sufficient to effect a cure in the sufferer. Equally important, the monks treated everyone for free. This established their curing as an act of loving-kindness and enhanced its power in the eyes of the villagers.

MONKS AS COMMUNITY LEADERS

The miraculous and mystical events recounted in the monks' narratives derive from the special relationship that thudong monks formed with common people. An important ingredient in this relationship was the monks' social engagement. Many of them were skillful community leaders who could help villagers improve the quality of their lives.

Many of the villages the monks visited had poor nutrition, hygiene, and health.[38] Thudong monks such as Fan often taught the villagers to pay attention to these matters. In 1952, for example, Fan went wandering with his disciples in Sawang Daen Din District (Sakon Nakhon) and spent several months meditating in Pet Tree Cave on Iron Cliff Mountain (Phu Pha Lek), not far from the forest hermitage that Wan established in Songdao District. While there, Fan depended on the two villages nearby for food. Going on daily almsround enabled him to observe how the villagers lived. He noticed that many houses were dirty, and he often preached about cleanliness in his sermons or urged the headman to persuade the villagers to keep the area clean. "He also noticed that many villagers did not have enough to eat after the rice harvest, so he suggested that they grow vegetables such as chilies and eggplants. At first only a small number of inhabitants followed his advice. The result was that not only were these families able to feed themselves, they were able to sell a surplus and have some income. Soon other villagers began growing vegetables in their gardens."[39]

In another village near the cave where Fan stayed, the inhabitants grew barely enough food to live on. During the hot season they spent their time looking for bullfrogs in the mud to fill the family cooking pots.[40] When the villagers came to listen to his sermons, Fan used the opportunity to preach that they would be better off spending their time growing additional crops in their gardens. The villagers followed his advice and were able to reduce the food shortage.

These examples suggest that during the Forest-Community Period the problems of rural communities were still relatively uncomplicated. Until the late 1950s, villagers did not have to compete for land with outside interests; forested land was available to anyone willing to clear it. Thudong monks, with their good understanding of local communities, were able to advise and assist villagers. They also stayed around long enough to see whether the villagers put their advice into practice.

Another example illustrates how the thudong monks and local people were mutually supportive of each other. Early in 1954 Fan went wandering in the Phu Phan Range to search for a cave that had appeared in his vision. The local inhabitants guided him through the forest to Tamarind Cave (Tham Kham).[41] The cave was so high and access was so difficult that the villagers only went there once a year, on Songkran Day, to pour water on the Buddha image inside. Fan found it a suitable place for meditation and spent the rains retreat there, even though the nearest village was about a twenty-kilometer walk away. During his four months there, Fan went on almsround to a three-household hamlet on a nearby hill. The farmers had recently moved there to plant a chili crop. Since there was no rice, he made do without. He lived on wild bamboo shoots mixed with fish sauce and on fruit from the forest. In his sermons Fan urged the villagers to improve their life by planting bananas, sugar cane, and other crops. But mere words could not convince the villagers to try something new. The pragmatic villagers needed proof before taking action. A disciple of Fan's who was in the audience at the time recalled that "one villager argued that the land was not fertile and no crops would grow here. Ajan Fan insisted that they try first. He pointed out that the forest was full of trees, so crops should be able to grow there too. The ajan then told the villagers to bring some banana shoots and plant them on the hill. He also led the villagers in clearing the ground and supervised the planting" (F, 181). Every day villagers brought a few banana shoots to plant. Eventually the area around the cave turned into an orchard, first with bananas and later with other crops. At the end of the rains retreat, when the villagers finished working in the paddies, Fan led them in digging a pond behind the cave, so that they could have fresh water all year round. He also got them to cut a trail to the cave. From then on, Fan and other monks were able to descend to the base of the hill for their almsround; villagers would come there from the hamlet bringing food.[42]

The villagers also agreed to donate their labor to build a preaching hall *(sala)* on the mountain, provided that the thudong monks organized it. Fan supervised the construction himself.[43] In the Lao tradition, monks often supervised villagers' work and worked alongside them. Without the monks' contribution it is unlikely the villagers would have completed the job. Although Fan had converted to the Thammayut, he still followed the local monks' custom of performing manual labor whenever he had the necessary skills. According to his biographer, "It was very difficult to transport the construction materials up the hill. The monks, novices [there were now four of each], and villagers carried the timbers. Some of the logs were eleven to twelve meters long. Yet nobody complained. Village folk came to help from near and far when they heard that Ajan Fan was building a preaching hall. Eventually all the timbers were put up and the hall and a kuti were constructed. The ajan supervised the carpenters, telling them which length to cut the timbers, since the rock on which the hall was built was uneven."[44]

The construction of a samnak or wat, it seems, was a communal undertaking in which monks and novices worked alongside laypeople. Villagers willingly assisted monks who had proved their moral, spiritual, and physical strength in the solitary life of meditation and religious practice. It is also apparent that until the close of the Forest-Community Period, villagers still retained access to forest products. They had more control of their time, too. Since they had not yet become hired laborers in large monocultural plantations, they could take time off to guide the thudong monks through the forest halfway to their destinations; or they could spend the night on a mountain meditating with the monks when they could not return to the village before nightfall. The difference between then and now, in the context of the forest monastery, is that the monks always worked closely with villagers. There was little outside influence in the form of large donations from urban people. (Monks and their biographers make no mention of money, of who donated what and how much; labor and raw materials were apparently free.) Villagers felt that they were part of the monastery or hermitage that they helped build.

CONNECTING WITH VILLAGERS

For seventy-five years after the establishment (in 1860) of the first Thammayut wat in the Northeast, Thammayut scholastic administrators had little influence in the countryside. In 1925 the Northeast had only twenty-odd Thammayut monasteries, all of them in the provincial capitals or district towns.[45] Their survival depended on government officials, local nobility, merchants, and townspeople. The thudong monks changed all this. Within the next twenty-five years, nearly three hundred new Thammayut monasteries appeared. If one asks why these wandering monks succeeded when administrative monks failed, the answer will be found in the values, attitudes, and conduct of these two categories of monks.

The wandering monks and villagers in the Northeast shared similar sociocultural values. Ecclesiastical heads and villagers did not. Although many Thammayut administrators had Lao village backgrounds, they quickly became part of the Bangkok sangha hierarchy, wedded to Bangkok's language and values. When these sangha officials visited the Northeast, they generally stayed in the provincial and district towns. As we have seen, travel in rural areas was time-consuming and tedious prior to the construction of paved roads and highways in the 1960s, and few urban monks were willing to traverse the dense forests with their wild animals, bandits, and malaria. Moreover, these sangha administrators felt that the villages of their youth lay far behind them, and they sought most of their upcountry contacts among the elite monks and laypeople committed to the new values that they themselves held.[46] All this set them apart from the villagers.

Wandering forest monks, although they belonged to the same sect as the Thammayut administrators, were socially and culturally much closer to the villagers. They ate the same kind of food, got around on foot, lived in thatched huts, did hard labor, spent most of their life outdoors, got wet when it rained, caught jungle fever, had no money, wore old robes. They knew how to endure hardship. They earned the respect of villagers partly because they shared their difficult life.

They also shared a common social and cultural identity. People of various ethnic identities in the Northeast during the Forest-Community Period did not see themselves as Thai. Most of them could not read or speak Bangkok Thai.[47] They had relatives and friends in Laos, on the other side of the Mekong. Lao-speaking inhabitants on either side of the river—Nongkhai and Vientiane, Nakhon Phanom and Tha Kaek, Mukdahan and Suwannaket, Khongjiam and Pakse—had more in common with each other than they did with the Siamese urbanites in Bangkok. Many wandering monks shared a Lao background, spoke Lao, and thus could understand and be understood by villagers in a way that

others could not.[48] In the early decades of this century the thudong teachers Sao and Man and many of their disciples wandered
extensively in Laos. This older generation of wandering monks
felt that Laos and northeast Siam were part of the same region,
separated only by a river that they often crossed without much
thought. A typical remark is, "Before I knew it, I was on the other
side of the Mekong." (They do not say, "Before I knew it, I was in
Laos.")[49]

The activities of thudong monks also indicate that even though
they lived and trained in isolated forests for years on end, they
worked ceaselessly to help others. They taught all whom they met
—providing insight, humor, and guidance to local people in need
of their help. Rebutting the sangha authorities' prejudice against
forest monks, the following comment of Man's indicates that
monks who followed modern state Buddhism were the ones who
lost their inner bonds with local communities.

> Some people say that we live in the forest only to liberate our-
> selves spiritually. They say that even after we have gotten to
> "know" the dhamma, we choose to remain in the forest instead
> of coming out to help society. In fact, we have always served
> society by teaching these villagers. Villagers need both [kinds of
> monks]: those who know the dhamma superficially and those
> who understand the more subtle dhamma. We could not wait
> for the elite monks from sophisticated cities to come here and
> teach them. These scholars would not be willing to walk even a
> few kilometers. It is we who have really helped village folk.[50]

In essence, these accounts indicate that the thudong monks not
only sought spiritual liberation but also offered their services to
the community; they served both the practical and the spiritual
needs of villagers. As Man's and Sing's disciples grew more
numerous, the Thammayut authorities in Isan could no longer
ignore their popularity among local people. They recruited the
wandering monks to teach the dhamma to villagers and to build
forest samnaks—and thus expand the Thammayut presence in the
Northeast.[51] When Somdet Uan sought help from the Thammayut
wandering monks in 1932, there were only 260 Thammayut wats
all over Siam. By the end of the Forest-Community Period (a year
after Somdet Uan died in 1956), the total number of Thammayut

monasteries in Thailand had increased to 649.[52] Of these, 311 wats, or almost 50 percent, were in the northeast region. The large increase was mostly due to the thudong monks' efforts and the confidence that the local people had in them. The Bangkok government, the Thammayut authorities, and their regional representatives were no match for them.

It is historically incorrect to assume that the Thammayut thudong monks were co-opted during the Forest Community Period. Although Man and a number of his Thammayut disciples from the Northeast wandered in the North for over a decade (1929–1941), they did not set up any official monasteries. Until 1948 only one Thammayut temple existed in Chiang Mai Province: Wat Jediluang in the town of Chiang Mai. The thudong monks went wandering in the North of their own accord, not to do missionary work for the Thammayut administrators. Another twenty years passed before the Thammayuts were able to establish a second temple in Chiang Mai.[53] Man himself never wanted to establish a permanent wat nor did he want his disciples to become abbots (M3, 88). Before Man died, most of his disciples chose to pursue their thudong life rather than take up permanent residence within the walls of a wat. But this was a choice for them only so long as the forest continued to exist.

CHAPTER 9

The Forest

Invaded

Wandering meditation monks led lives on the margin. They frequented sparsely inhabited forests, and they conducted their meditative practice either in solitude or in the company of others like themselves. The outside world for them consisted, for the most part, of frontier villages, occasionally provincial towns, and rarely, and only when necessary, Bangkok. Thudong monks were quite willing to let mainstream society go its way. During the Forest-Community Period they were, for the most part, able to retain their autonomy and wander unimpeded.

But Bangkok had an agenda for them. Even during the Forest-Community Period, sangha authorities in the Northeast attempted with some success to recruit Man's disciples and turn them into settled monastics. By the end of the 1950s, however, the world outside the forest came to exert a much more significant impact on the thudong tradition and eventually dealt it a severely crippling, ultimately mortal blow. These years, comprising the Forest-Invasion and the Forest-Closure Period (late 1950s to the present), are the subject of this chapter.

In the 1950s meditation practice gained a foothold among urban Buddhists. A high-level Mahanikai Isan monk, Phimontham, started a nationwide meditation program with a center at Bangkok's Wat Mahathat. Honorific titles were bestowed on a few meditation teachers including some thudong monks. But this apparent legitimation of meditation was not to last. Political and environmental changes brought meditation into disfavor and led to the virtual demise of the wandering monk's way of life. The most significant causes of these changes were the right-wing military coups of 1957–1958 and the new government's policies of national economic development and deforestation.

AN ATTEMPT AT RELIGIOUS REFORM

By the second half of this century the sangha authorities had for the most part integrated monks of regional Buddhist traditions into Bangkok's hierarchical system. But monastic education was losing its relevance. While urban society became ever more westernized, the sangha's education system (naktham and Pali studies) remained static. Western-educated teachers increasingly saw themselves as more knowledgeable than academic or administrative monks. So while children of the poor continued to attend monastic schools, growing numbers of middle- and upper-class people educated their children in secular schools. A senior monk has estimated that as many as 70 percent of the young have turned away from Buddhism.[1] Monks in urban areas gradually lost their position as intellectual leaders and a large number of bright young monks disrobed.

During this period Phimontham (At Atsapha),[2] abbot of Wat Mahathat and the sangha minister of the interior under the Sangha Act of 1941, attempted to reform and revitalize modern state Buddhism by integrating meditation practice with book learning. Phimontham was convinced that the initiators of the sangha reforms of 1902 had made a grave error in promoting textual study at the expense of meditation practice. In his opinion "the essence of Buddhism . . . can only be found in meditation."[3] In 1949 he invited skilled meditation masters of the local traditions from Nongkhai, Khon Kaen, Khorat, and Ubon Provinces to train monks and novices in samatha meditation at Wat Mahathat.[4] To promote meditation practice among monks and laypeople he established the Vipassanā Meditation Center in 1951. Phimontham's reform was influenced by a religious revival in Burma and by Prime Minister U Nu's support of meditation for monks and laity.[5] Phimontham felt that the Burmese style of vipassanā meditation would be easy and useful for Thai urbanites. In 1952 he sent Maha Chodok Yanasithi, a Thai-Lao Mahanikai monk from the Northeast with a ninth-level Pali degree, to learn vipassanā meditation in Burma.[6] When he returned to Thailand, Chodok brought two Burmese meditation masters (one of whom was his teacher) to teach vipassanā meditation. Maha Chodok supervised Wat Mahathat's meditation center from 1953 to 1960.

This initiative by a Mahanikai administrator motivated the Thammayut elders to pay attention to their meditation monks and take advantage of this resource. In 1951 the Thammayut leader of the southern region invited Sing (Man's senior disciple) to teach meditation to monks and laypeople in Phetchaburi Province in the South. The following year the Thammayut elders recommended that ecclesiastical titles be awarded to Sing and Thet. Sing received the title of Phra Khru Yanwisit. Three years later, in 1955, Thet was given the title Phra Khru Nirotrangsi and was promoted to acting sangha head and dhamma director of three southern provinces: Phuket, Phangnga, and Krabi.[7] In 1957 the royal title of Phra Racha Khana was awarded to three disciples of Man's: Sing, Thet, and Li.[8] This was the first time since the creation of the sangha bureaucracy in 1902 that Thammayut elders recommended this royal title be given to Thammayut monks who had never taken the Pali exams.[9] Eight years earlier, the Mahanikai order had awarded a royal title, Phawanakoson Thera, to the meditation monk Sot Janthasaro, abbot of Wat Paknam (a Mahanikai wat). In 1949 Sot had become the first meditation monk in this century to be promoted to such high rank. Like the Thammayut meditation monks, Sot had never taken the Pali exams.

But it appears that many high-level administrators, Thammayut as well as Mahanikai, along with many urban elites, still did not regard meditation highly. This is reflected in Phimontham's speech to meditation monks in 1955: "As director of vipassanā meditation and as sangha minister of the interior, I want to assure you that you can always depend on me. As long as I am alive I will support you no matter what, and I will defend your right to practice and teach meditation."[10] But Phimontham's attempts at reform from within did not get very far. In 1960, as we shall see, he was removed from his position, stripped of his title, and put in jail. His meditation center at Wat Mahathat was dismantled. As for the two Burmese meditation teachers, one of them returned to Burma and the other went to teach at a meditation samnak, Wiwekasom, in Chonburi (east of Bangkok).[11] What precipitated this collapse? Political events of the late 1950s produced fundamental societal changes in Thailand, a transformation that brought the Forest-Community Period to a close.

THE FOREST-INVASION PERIOD (1957–1988)

The two coups of October 1957 and October 1958, from which General Sarit emerged unchallenged as military dictator, signified the beginning of the Forest-Invasion Period. Sarit moved against a wide range of heterogeneous groups—pedicab drivers, prostitutes, vagabonds (wandering monks were included in this category), writers, journalists, and activists—arresting or detaining them with the help of the anticommunist legislation of 1952. The small, largely Chinese, Communist Party of Thailand (CPT) was forced underground. Communists were joined by many non-Communist dissidents who feared arrest or murder at the hands of the government. What is now known in the cultural and religious history of Thailand as the "dark age" *(yuk meut)* had begun.[12] Sarit did not just abolish the constitution; with the recommendation of certain high-level monks he invalidated the democratic Sangha Act of 1941. The new Sangha Act of 1962 (figure 8), modeled after the Sangha Act of 1902, renewed state authority over the sangha and gave absolute power to the supreme patriarch.[13]

Under martial law, any nonconformist monk—whether a town monk, village monk, or forest monk, and no matter what his tradition—was at risk of being labeled a communist and imprisoned without bail or trial. In Bangkok during this period, two progressive senior monks were arrested. One was the high-level Mahanikai monk mentioned above: Phimontham (At), abbot of Wat Mahathat and former sangha minister of the interior. The other was a Thammayut monk, Phimontham's deputy minister Satsanasophon (Plaut), abbot of Wat Rachathiwat.[14] Accused of communist leanings and of sexual misconduct, both were forcibly stripped of their robes and ecclesiastical titles.[15] Phimontham, who was held in jail from 1962 until 1966, recalls that "it was very easy in those days to be accused of being a communist. 'Evidence' of the

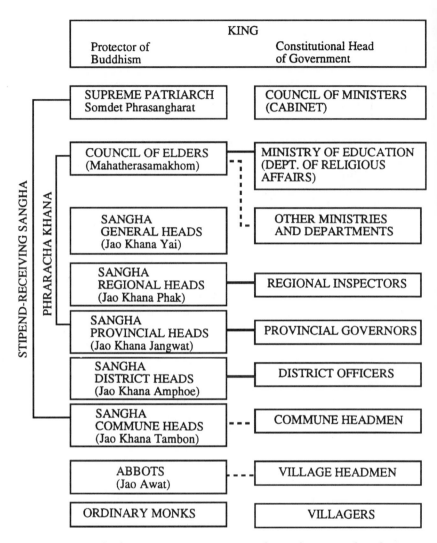

Figure 8. *Sangha bureaucratic structure and its relation to the Thai government after the Sangha Act of 1962 (Adapted from Somboon 1982, table 8)*

most tenuous kind could be produced: the fact for instance, that I am from the Northeast: an area where 90 percent of the population are poor farmers. Obviously, it was whispered, a breeding-ground for agitators. And so, in 1962, I went to prison for five years."[16]

One reason behind Phimontham's arrest as a communist sympathizer was his devoted effort to reform the modern state religion by popularizing the practice of meditation. As he explains, "I came to realize that although the form, ritual and theory of Buddhism in Thailand was in good working order, the practice was not. It was my contact with monks from Burma, who have a strong tradition of practice that gets results, that led me to realize that the situation in Thailand needed reforming. For only when the theory and practice are combined is it possible to attain the stage of Arahant."[17]

Phimontham made enemies among high-level monks, both Thammayut and Mahanikai, who disapproved of his attempts at religious reform. Eventually they conspired to get rid of him.[18] In an era of national economic development, meditation practice was seen as an obstacle to progress. The popularizing of meditation was subversive. As Phimontham put it, "General Sarit . . . as a dictator, and I, as a monk, were bound not see eye to eye. He said if everyone closed his eyes in meditation all [the] time nobody would be able to keep watch for the communists!"[19]

In this political climate it became unsafe for any wandering monks to continue living a thudong life. First-generation disciples of Man must have been aware of the danger of wandering, because many of them began to settle in one location or establish their own permanent forest wat. On the eve of the Forest-Invasion Period (1957), the fifty-nine-year-old Fan began to stay put at Kham Cave Hermitage (later called Wat Pa Tham Kham) in Phanna Nikhom District, Sakon Nakhon. He remained there for six years in a row. Also in 1957, the forty-eight-year-old La settled at Jau Kau Hill Hermitage (Wat Phu Jau Kau) in Mukdahan. A couple of years later Cha, at the age of forty-one, founded his forest samnak at Phong Pond Forest near his natal village in Ubon. Khaw also established Midday Drum Cave Hermitage in Udon Thani. In 1962 the seventy-two-year-old Waen settled into the monastery of Maepang Mountain in Chiang Mai. In 1965 the sixty-two-year-old Thet settled at Huge Rock Hermitage (later a monastery, Wat Hinmakpeng) in Nongkhai and started building a wat there two years later. Li died in 1961, three years after he established Wat Asokaram for teaching meditation (in Samut Prakan, twenty-five kilometers south of Bangkok).

Despite the increasing pressure to stay put, some of the youngest generation of Man's pupils still wanted to wander around. But the danger of being suspected as insurgents eventually forced them to give in.[20] Juan's and Wan's memoirs and other monks' life stories illustrate the impact of political, social, and environmental changes during these years.

Suspect: Juan

Economic and environmental changes came quickly to the Northeast when the construction of the first paved road began in 1960. Gravel roads linked Saraburi (central Thailand) to Nakhon Ratchasima, to Khon Kaen in central Isan, and to Udon Thani in upper Isan. But most of Isan's provinces remained isolated. In 1961, 42 percent of the Northeast was still thickly forested.[21]

In 1958 Juan set out to look for a cave suitable for solitary meditation practice. From the provincial town of Nongkhai he went by boat down the Mekong River to Beung Kan District and then walked to the hamlet of New Black-Earth Pond (Ban Naung Dindam). There he asked the villagers to guide him into the dense Pink Forest of Phon Phisai District. After Juan chose a site for his meditation, the villagers built him a platform for sitting and sleeping. They then returned to their village, having informed Juan that the nearest hamlet, about five kilometers away, consisted of two Khamu households. Juan spent the next four days without food and then decided to walk to the Khamu hamlet. As he had expected, the Khamu did not know the custom of giving food to a monk, but Juan taught them and they gave him alms regularly.

Juan found the solitude of the forest conducive to his meditation practice, so he stayed on in Jan Tree Cave. The following year an old mae chi, a male pha khaw, and a novice came to spend the rains retreat with Juan. Since the Khamu could not afford to feed all four of them, Juan resolved to subsist on water and wild vegetables (*mao* leaves). Soon the news that a thudong monk was willing to starve during the rains retreat spread to villages nearby, and many people headed into the forest to see him. Since there was no road as yet, it took them days to walk to the cave. They saw how isolated the cave was, but they resolved to bring food to Juan and his disciples once a week.[22] When the rainy season was over, Juan's three disciples returned to their natal village.

Juan lived in Pink Forest until 1962. As he became more popular among the villagers, many government officials and monks from what Juan called "the opposite side" spread the rumor that he was a communist leader.[23] One day in 1962, while traveling on foot from his cave to Ox Mountain in Beung Kan District, Nongkhai, Juan was pursued by members of the Border Patrol Police—Juan suspected they had orders to kill him. Since Juan knew the terrain better, he was able to walk faster and eventually the police lost track of him. Later on, after Juan had moved to Kratae Mountain (in the same district), four border patrolmen came to "visit" him. They told him that they were under orders to investigate whether he was a communist leader. The following dialogue between Juan and a border patrol agent suggests that the thudong monk was probably saved by his wits:

"What's a communist like?" Juan asked the policeman who was probing him for possible pro-communist sentiments.

"Among communists there is no religion, no suffering, no rich people. Everyone is equal. No private property. Only communal property," replied the policeman.

"What kind of clothes do they wear? What do they eat? Do they have a wife and children?" asked the monk.

"Yes, they have a family. They eat normal food. They wear shirts and trousers like villagers."

"How often do they eat?" Juan asked.

"Three times a day."

"Do they shave their heads?"

"No."

"So," Juan concluded, "If a communist has a wife and children, wears a shirt and trousers, eats three meals a day, does not shave his head, and carries a weapon, then how can I, who have neither a wife nor children, eat once a day, shave my head, wear robes and carry no weapon be a communist?"[24]

Although Juan was not harmed, other forest monks were not so lucky. Juan tells us about his fellow thudong monk Peng, with whom he spent several rains retreats. When Peng went to meditate in the forest on Little Lion Mountain (Phu Sing Noi) in 1964, he liked the solitude so much that he stayed on for two years. At the time there was a rumor that a group of insurgents was occupying Big Lion Mountain (Phu Sing Yai). Since Little Lion Mountain and Big Lion Mountain are part of the same range, soldiers asked Peng to spend the rains retreat elsewhere, their reason being that the monk might be in danger. So Peng went to spend the retreat with Juan in Worship Cave (Tham Bucha) on Ox Mountain. Less than a week after Peng left Little Lion Mountain, soldiers went to inspect his hermitage there. They burnt the place down to prevent insurgents from using it. As the villagers told Juan, "Every kuti was burnt down. Even the earthen jars were destroyed. All the fruit trees around the wat—mango, longan, lime, coconut—were burnt down. So were the banana and papaya trees that the pha khaws and villagers had planted so nicely. Vegetables they had planted such as chilies, eggplants, and lemon grass were rooted out and destroyed. Even the well was ruined and filled with dirt. There was nothing left of all the huts. Because the monks had to leave in a hurry, they didn't take all their requisites with them. So extra robes, chanting and dhamma books and a Buddha image were burnt, too" (J, 89). After hearing all this, Juan concluded that whoever despoiled the hermitage would accumulate bad kamma.

Shortly after leaving Pink Forest in 1962, Juan and some disciples established a forest hermitage on Ox Mountain in Nongkhai Province. The monks built their own huts, a kitchen, and a sala for meals. Since the area was isolated and quiet, only serious monks and novices came to stay in this hermitage. They lived and meditated in solitude for a few years. But increasingly the area became unsafe. In 1966 six bombs were dropped on this mountain. One bomb exploded; the other five were found unexploded in an area not far from the cave and the sala where the monks generally ate their meal. Juan sent the local people to inform the village headman, who notified government officials, who then notified the American military in Udon Province.[25]

Eventually Americans arrived by helicopter to dismantle the bombs. Juan heard that it was a common practice for American pilots to jettison bombs they had not used in their raids on North Vietnam. They simply dropped them into the jungle below on the return flight, assuming that the land beneath—Ox Mountain in this case—was uninhabited (J, 90). Juan did not know why these five bombs did not go off when they hit the ground, but he thought it might be that the power of the Triple Gem was protecting the monks.

Although Juan had been warned that the area was not safe and that he and his disciples should spend the rains retreats elsewhere, they remained on the mountain until early 1968, when the sangha head of Nongkhai told them to leave. Juan then understood that the world had changed radically. From now on it was no longer safe to wander in the forests.[26] The risk of being shot at or being identified as a communist forced Juan to find a suitable safe location. The next year he established a hermitage on Thauk Mountain (Phu Thauk), about thirty-five kilometers southwest of Beung Kan District in Nongkhai. In September of that year, the government formally declared selected districts in thirty-five provinces to be "communist-infested sensitive areas." One such area included Thauk Mountain.[27]

When local people heard that Juan had built a hermitage on the mountain, they migrated to the nearest settlement, Khamkaen Field Village (Ban Na Khamkaen). By 1968 this community had increased to ten households. Meanwhile two more villages were forming in the area, one of them only one kilometer away. More and more villagers—from Kalasin, Khon Kaen, Roi-Et, Ubon, Udon Thani, and Sakon Nakhon—migrated to the area. By 1980 the number of households had swelled to over two hundred.

In 1969 another monk arrived. Like Juan, Thui Janthakaro came to be suspected of assisting communists.[28] During the 1970s Pink Forest was classified a potential communist stronghold or "pink area" *(khet sichomphu).*

Suspect: Wan

Another disciple of Ajan Man's was searching for a permanent place in which he and his disciples might settle. In 1961 Wan and his disciples spent the rains retreat in an isolated cave on Iron Mountain (Phu Lek), part of the Phu Phan Range in Songdao District, Sakon Nakhon. The cave was between ten and twenty kilometers from the nearest villages. Mountain Monastery (Wat Doi) is what local people called the hermitage that Wan set up. It was not too far from Fan's at Kham Cave in the same mountain range (in Sawang Daendin District). Songdao, Sawang Daendin, and Wanon Niwat districts were rapidly becoming some of the most politically sensitive, insurgent-dominated districts in the entire Northeast and, not surprisingly, the site of numerous suppression operations mounted by the government. For example, a few months before the rains retreat of 1961, Khraung Chandawong, a former member of parliament from Sawang Daendin District and a headmaster of several schools in his home province, was arrested and executed in front of the district police station. After his execution, Khraung's widow and all three of his children joined the Communist Party.[29] This was the year the CPT declared its commitment to armed revolution against Sarit's dictatorship. CPT insurgents in the jungles were using armed force to oppose the military government.[30] During this period, on 5 May 1966, the Marxist historian Jit Phumisak was shot and killed in the Phu Phan area of Sakon Nakhon.[31]

Because of this violence, Wan and his fellow monks decided to stay put. From 1961 to 1974 they spent every rains retreat at their cave hermitage. When they first arrived, there were no roads. Monks and novices had to walk ten to twenty kilometers to perform ceremonies for the villagers. To make it more convenient for the villagers and the monks to travel, Wan and his followers built a seven-kilometer road connecting their samnak to the Naungluang-Kambit road (recently constructed by the government). Thereafter more villagers came to Wan's sermons.

In 1964 local government officials began to suspect that Wan was a communist sympathizer who was using the forest samnak as a supply depot for insurgents in the jungle. Meanwhile some communists suspected that Wan was a government spy.[32] Wandering forest monks were suspected by both sides principally because they formed networks. As Tambiah points out, such networks were capable of facilitating both anti-government guerrilla activity and covert pro-government counterinsurgency. A network of monks could easily—at least in the imaginations of insurgents and government officials—organize secretly and disperse into the countryside in order to collect information or mobilize the peasantry.[33]

Thudong monks such as Wan and Juan, who dwelled in deep forests or in isolated caves, were suspects because they inhabited the same terrain as the insurgents. For instance, the most important weapon-training sites used by the Dhamma Unity Organization (DUO), founded by Khraung, were Pha Lat Forest in Sawang Daendin District, Ibang Forest in Wanon Niwat District (both in Sakon Nakhon), and Pink Forest in Phon Phisai District (Nongkhai).[34] The caves where many thudong monks lived were in the Phu Phan, the same mountain range in which the CPT had concentrated its strength. DUO members, for example, stored their weapons in a large cave in the Phu Phan Range accessible only by foot.[35] Another area that Man and his disciples found suitable for meditation practice, both in terms of its people as well as its isolation, was in the mountains of Na Kae District, Nakhon Phanom.(T2, 71). Here in Na Kae the government troops and the communist insurgents had their first armed clash on 8 August 1965.

Thudong monks were also suspects because a number of communists came from the wandering monks' natal villages or from areas where thudong monks had their hermitages.[36] Hollow Palms Village (Wan's birthplace), for example, was on the local officials' list of insurgent villages. Villagers generally distrusted government officials, because such officials, whether civilians, police, or military men, were apt to treat villagers with contempt and exploit them.[37] By contrast, thudong monks like Juan and Wan were genuinely interested in helping villagers improve their lives. They were accused of being communist sympathizers because of their popularity among local people.

Wan and some of his disciples once found themselves under fire. On 15 May 1970 Wan and seven disciples went to perform a religious rite and give a sermon at an evening wedding ceremony in a village nearby. It had grown dark by the time they were ready to return to their hermitage. They were walking along a road through paddy fields only a few hundred meters from the village when some soldiers started shooting at them with M-16 rifles. The monks continued to walk until they reached their hermitage. Later on the soldiers came to see Wan and apologized, and they ceased to bother him.[38]

In the early 1970s the Thai royal family began to seek out the Thammayut forest monks in the Northeast. The royal couple made their first visit to Fan in 1972 and to Wan at his cave hermitage in 1975.[39] It was in 1975 that communists won victories in Indochina, the governments of Cambodia and South Vietnam collapsed, and the Pathet Lao consolidated its power in Laos and abolished the six-hundred-year-old Lao monarchy.[40] The following year Wan was asked to accept the royal title of Phra Racha Khana, but he declined, saying that it was not suitable for a forest monk to bear the title of a high-level monk. His plea was ignored, and in 1977 the king conferred on him the title Udomsangwonwisut.

Other Suspects

In Bangkok, Phimontham, the Mahanikai senior monk who supported the teaching of meditation, was in jail, but on the periphery many monks of local traditions continued to teach meditation and gained large followings, thereby exposing themselves to risk. Nobody knows how many monks were killed during this period. Here are two more of those who survived these years of suspicion.

Thian Jittasupho, a meditation monk of the Lao tradition, established vipassanā meditation centers at two local wats in the Chiang Khan District of Loei in the early 1960s and a meditation samnak in Laos.[41] Thian was known for his teaching of mindfulness. He preached that "awareness is the root of merit" and that it is better to develop awareness than, say, finance the construction of an ubosot. Thian's teaching was in line with other meditation masters. A similar theme is present in a sermon of Cha's: "For most monks, Buddhism is a lot of study without real practice. Everywhere, there is more interest in cutting down forests and building new temples than in developing the mind. In earlier times, this was not the case—meditation teachers lived with nature and did not try to build anything. Now, offering buildings is the religious activity that most interests laypeople."[42]

Such preachings ran counter to the mainstream belief put forth by modern state Buddhism, which equated making merit with funding monastery construction projects rather than exerting oneself spiritually. By the mid-1950s this concept of merit making had become dominant among urban laypeople and among monks who followed modern state Buddhism. Many military men and politicians sought to legitimize their power by donating large sums of money to fund the construction of elaborate monastery buildings.[43] Administrative monks gained promotions for themselves, since the main criterion for advancement within the ecclesiastical hierarchy rested on the candidate's record in furthering the construction of temples.

No doubt, Thian's criticism of this trend provoked suspicion among some members of his audience. Thian divided his audience into three categories: those who could comprehend the dhamma and become his supporters; those who opposed his teaching and tried to bring him down; and those who remained neutral and did not react to his teaching.[44] It was the people in the second category who accused Thian of being a communist. They suspected him of receiving money from communist insurgents to preach against "traditional" Thai customs. Thian was not the only one to come under surveillance: government officers arrived by helicopter to question villagers about his activities. Fortunately, the Mahanikai heads of both Loei Province and Chiang Khan District were sympathetic to Thian and defended him.[45]

Another case is that of a meditation monk named Jamnian.[46] In 1967–1968 laypeople asked Jamnian to teach at Wat Sukonthawat, in the Nasan District of the southern province of Surat Thani. Forested and mountainous areas of the South, like those of the Northeast, were a focus of prolonged and occasionally violent conflicts between government forces and the insurgents. Villagers were experiencing considerable hardship, since their villages were situated in an area of conflict. When Jamnian began teaching meditation at the wat, he was told to leave the area or risk being shot.[47] He refused. Eventually he was able to teach the dhamma to the soldiers in the town and, later still, taught insurgents in the mountains. Each side thereupon offered to "protect" his wat against the other. He replied to both sides that keeping in harmony with the true dhamma was all the protection he needed.

Needless to say, Juan, Wan, Thui, Thian, and Jamnian were not the only monks to come under scrutiny by the government or the opposition. Many other monks in the Northeast and elsewhere who worked to benefit local communities were seen as insurgents or communist sympathizers.[48]

The Real Communists

Since Siam became a modern state, two categories of monks have always been targets of the Bangkok government during times of instability: wandering monks and village monks who performed manual labor. At the turn of this century, when Bangkok authorities attempted to centralize Buddhist monks of all traditions, thudong monks were called vagabonds, and laboring monks were condemned for violating monastic rules. Bangkok authorities simply could not understand why these monks liked to live in forests or remote villages. The goals of these monks—to practice asceticism and, when possible, to help villagers—were rarely valued by Bangkok elites. During the Vietnam War and the anticommunist hysteria of the 1960s and 1970s, thudong monks who lived in forests and rural monks who worked like villagers were targeted as insurgents or communist sympathizers. To assess this claim, let us look at the historical context of the 1960s and the response of the forest monks to their accusers.

Meditation, popular in the 1950s, fell from favor largely because of government policies. Once the national economic development schemes got underway in the 1960s, the prestige of meditator monks sank to a new low in the eyes of the urban elites. With Phimontham charged with communism and in jail, meditation practice no longer had the support of high-level monks. Those at Wat Mahathat, the center of vipassanā meditation training, suffered bitterly during this period. For many monks, mae chis, and lay devotees, it seemed that everything their teacher Phimontham had striven for was now consigned to oblivion.

It is true that national economic development was not a priority for wandering forest monks. Their view of time and change was incomprehensible to the urban elites. Government leaders and sangha officials measured time in terms of material accomplishment, and accordingly they found the idea of wandering and meditating abhorrent. They perceived the thudong monks as wasting their time doing nothing beneficial. Cha's observation typifies the urban elite's perception of meditation monks during the 1960s: "Living in this world and practicing meditation, you will seem to others like a gong that has not been struck and is not producing any sound. They will consider you useless, mad, defeated; but actually just the opposite is true."[49]

A sarcastic remark made by a sangha administrator reflects the government's attitude: "Buddhism would not survive if all monks sat and closed their eyes." Juan was aware of the government officials' views: "As they see it, forest monks just sit with their eyes closed and do nothing. They consider forest monks to be obstacles to national development and to the progress of religion."[50] But in the thudong monks' view, they were the ones with the open eyes, and they were the ones carrying out the real duty of monks. Meditation teachers such as Man always urged their disciples to be mindful in everything and thereby ward off mankind's real enemies, kilesas. Responding to the sangha officials' prejudice against the thudong tradition, Wiriyang remarked that settled monastics who do not meditate "are only employees who guard the religion [*pen lukjang fao satsana*]" (M3, 129). Cha observed that those persons (including monks) who consider meditation to be a waste of time value only worldly knowledge, the kind needed to earn a living: "This is how the world is. If you try to live simply, practising the Dhamma and living peacefully, they say you are weird and anti-social. They say you're obstructing progress in society. They even intimidate you. Eventually you might even start to believe them and revert to the worldly ways, sinking deeper and deeper into the world until it's impossible to get out. . . . This is how society tends to be. It doesn't appreciate the value of Dhamma" (C2, 63).

Li explained that spreading the dhamma can be accomplished not only by word (preaching and expounding the dhamma) and by deed (offering one's own behavior as an example), it can also be communicated by thought, through *manomayā iddhi* (psychic feats) that inspire and convince receptive minds without a word being said. Many thudong monks emphasize another kind of invisible teaching, metta parami (the perfection of loving-kindness). As Li points out, a monk who sits with his eyes closed can accomplish a great deal more than a person might think.

> When goodness arises within us, we can work for the welfare of others even when we sit with our eyes closed, perfectly still. But it's the nature of ignorant people to believe that such a person is simply saving his own skin. They haven't looked deep inside. The teachers of the past thus made a comparison with thunder and rain. Some people can teach others, but they themselves have no inner goodness. Such people are called thunder without rain. They can cause others to feel awe and respect, but can give no sense of cooling refreshment. Some people are like rain with-

out thunder. They rarely speak, but spread thoughts of good will, dedicating their merit to others. They have their own full measure of inner goodness and so can give goodness and inspire conviction in the hearts of others even when simply sitting still. Those who find peace and calm in the shelter of such an influence will, in turn, feel the highest form of respect.[51]

Thet also addressed the issue of prejudice against thudong monks. In a sermon delivered in 1963 in Phuket, he identified the destroyers of religion as "those who encourage bad men to become monks, those who incite conflict and disunity among monks, those who encourage popular monks to do bad deeds, and those who encourage corruption among government officials" (T2, 285). The real "communists" (that is, subversive elements in society) are those whose activities cause laypeople to lose faith in religion: "The so-called communists who will ruin the religion are neither Chinese, Russians, nor Muslims [*jek jin, farang, khaek*]. They are the Buddhists who cannot grasp the Buddha's teachings and thus behave contrary to his teachings. Or they are educated people who, despite having a lot of knowledge, remain stubborn. They do not put their knowledge into practice. Instead they succumb to their defilements" (T2, 285).

Juan likewise was convinced that religion was being destroyed not by the communists but by people who exploited others: "If everybody helps one another, regardless of gender and no matter whether they live in the city, village, or forest, there will be no insurgents. Then there is no need to spread false rumors or accuse other people" (J, 112).

For these thudong teachers, the foundation of meditation was an ethics (sīla) based in personal transformation. They found much in the rapidly westernizing Thai society that was beyond their comprehension—local customs and ethical values were no longer cherished, and the dhamma was no longer taking root within individuals. That at least is how Wan described the situation of the 1970s.

In today's society people tend to be jealous, greedy, exploitative, and revengeful. They take advantage of others in every way— stealing, killing, accusing others of things they did not do.

Everyone wants to be a jao, and everyone finds fault with others. [Although] technologically society has progressed 100 percent, ethically it has deteriorated by 200 percent. Peace of mind has been reduced by 50 percent. Misery and unsatisfactory conditions have shot up 150 percent. This is a dark age, an age of great disaster and great upheaval, an age of ignorance. Honesty and sincerity are no longer respected. Nobody believes people who speak the truth. People with good conduct are put down. Modest people are looked down upon as old-fashioned. Those who are ethical are accused of being obstacles to progress. Those who are unethical in their thought, in their speech, and in their behavior have become respectable in modern societies. People who are tricky and corrupt gain promotion without having to work hard for it. Not only are diligent and honest people not rewarded, they often became scapegoats when things go wrong. (W, 10)

Like Juan, Wan points to kilesas as the real enemy. In a sermon delivered in 1979, about six months before he died, Wan told his audience that "in today's secular society, people who are vengeful and know how to kill, exploit, extort, oppress, and control others —such people are hailed as geniuses. But according to Buddhism, only people who are able to kill their kilesas, overcome their greed, and control their minds are considered intelligent."[52]

Finally, when the king went to visit the eighty-seven-year-old Khaw at Midday Drum Cave in the Phu Phans, he asked the old monk what the greatest problem facing the country was. To the surprise of onlookers, who expected him to say insurgency, Khaw replied that it was greed and corruption.[53] The real disruptive element in society, in the eyes of many thudong monks, was the presence of poverty, injustice, exploitation, intolerance, dictatorship, corruption, hatred, and discrimination.

THE FOREST-CLOSURE PERIOD (1989–PRESENT)

At the height of the Vietnam War (after 1964) the United States poured huge amounts of money into Thailand for military expenditures and for rural development.[54] Bangkok was now able to extend its control over rural areas. But this U.S.-backed "rural development" did not spring from people's needs; it was imposed on them through the combined forces of a strengthened police and military and a westernized educational system.[55] Paved roads, highways, electrification, and extension services resulted in the commercialization of agriculture in the rural areas. The National Social and Economic Development Plans brought about tremendous social and economic turmoil and environmental despoliation. Rural people were the main casualties. This state-led development program brought "ever-increasing income disparities between the rich and the poor, and between urban and rural dwellers. Natural resources, including forests, soil, water and biogenetic resources, have rapidly deteriorated and been depleted. Local communities, their traditions and livelihoods, especially of minority groups, have been undermined and have thus disintegrated. Conflicts over the management and use of natural resources have intensified."[56]

In particular, rapid population growth and urbanization, intensive industrial development, and the construction of large-scale hydroelectric dams, golf courses, and tourist resorts have gravely affected the environment in Thailand.[57] In 1961, 42 percent of the Northeast (51 percent of Thailand as a whole) was forest. By 1988 only 14 percent of the Northeast (19 percent of Thailand) was forest.[58] Today even less remains. Nearly gone are the Northeast's huge hardwood tracts where the wandering forest monks dwelled and trained. Forest frontiers have been replaced by roads and highways. Provincial roads increased from 2,118 km in 1960 to 27,595 km in 1989.[59] Many forest wats are now surrounded not by forests but by houses, paddies, and fields.[60] For the first time in its history, the country has faced significant demands for land. No longer is it possible for a villager to move to the frontier to carve a new farm out of the forest.

By the end of the Forest-Invasion Period most of Man's disciples had either passed away, become old and ill, or been "domesticated."[61] Since the mid 1970s, Thammayut forest monks have become so immensely popular that they have elite patrons to protect the wilderness immediately surrounding their wats. The few monks who still live in the dwindling forests are mostly non-Thammayut, and they are without influential patrons. These forest monks of today have a lot more to contend with than monks of Man's generation or his disciples' generations.

The final closure of the forest began after devastating floods occurred in southern Thailand. In November 1988 floods and landslides, triggered by rain falling on denuded hillsides, wiped out several southern villages and killed hundreds of people. For the first time the Bangkok government was forced to face the consequences of uncontrolled exploitation of the forest. Responding to an intense public outcry, the government suspended and later banned all logging activities in the country.[62] It is no surprise that such ecological disasters have struck Thailand. Three decades of rapacious land clearing had wiped out 82 percent of Thailand's forests, and in places the countryside had become a dust bowl.[63] In this context, many wandering monks decided that they had to hold their ground when they found a suitable forest. They knew that if they retreated, they risked losing it forever.

The state's policy of channeling natural resources, in this case forested land, away from local communities and into commercial sectors, has further aggravated intense local conflicts over resources.[64] Since the early 1980s several private corporations have invested in eucalyptus plantations in Thailand to meet the demands of Japanese industry. To convert native forests to eucalyptus, the government came up with the Kau Jau Kau (KJK) resettlement project, which affected nearly five million people between the mid-1980s and 1992.[65] The project relocated villagers who had been living in the forests (which had become state-owned forest preserves) and turned the evacuated land over to commercial eucalyptus plantations. In the Northeast, the KJK project began in fourteen villages in five provinces (Nakhon Ratchasima, Khon Kaen, Ubon, Sakon Nakhon, and Buriram). By September 1991, some 1,300 families had been relocated.[66]

The case of an environmentalist monk, Prajak, illustrates the plight of villagers and forest monks during the Forest-Closure Period. It also demonstrates the obstacles that an activist monk faces when he seeks to protect the forest and uphold the villagers' right to stay in the countryside rather than become migrant workers or prostitutes in Bangkok.

Prajak came of age during the decade in which eighty American military bases, scattered around the nation, brought "Americanization" to rural Thailand.[67] After his ordination he took up a thudong life and in April 1989 he and six monks wandered into Never-Dry Well Forest (Dong Hua Nam Put) in Prakham District.

The fifty-two-year-old Prajak, his fellow monks, and three novices pitched their klots and stayed for a week. This forest in Buriram, one of the poorest provinces in the now drought-stricken Northeast was the largest remaining natural forest in the region. In the 1970s, Never-Dry Well Mountain was a prized location fought over by communist insurgents and government soldiers. At the height of the conflict, the military—who saw the villagers as a frontline force against communists—offered land to those who would settle in this forest. For several difficult years villagers worked, patrolled, and fought alongside the army in counterinsurgency actions. Bullet holes in tree trunks along the dirt path leading toward Never-Dry Well bear witness to the bloody past.[68] During these years, people were told that when the trees disappeared, so would any likely insurgents, and debilitating jungle fevers as well. This belief opened the way for further national development and corporate exploitation.[69] In the 1970s the forest surrounding Never-Dry Well Mountain was burnt down as part of a military strategy to destroy refuge areas for guerrillas. The wide, dense forest of only twenty years ago had shrunk to a green island surrounded by cassava fields.

Prajak considered this island suitable for practicing meditation and set out to build a hermitage with the help of local villagers. They put up several bamboo shacks covered with thatch or plastic and a simple open shelter for prayer meetings. Prajak soon learned that although the war against the insurgents was long since over, the forest remained a battleground. The twelve villages in the area were in dispute with the military (which was backing the KJK project). The military had been using threats and intimidation to force villagers out. Once the military's mission against insurgents had been successfully completed and the villagers were no longer needed, they were told to leave—supposedly in the interest of forest conservation but actually because the military wanted to hand the land over to a private corporation. Prajak resolved to help the villagers keep their land if they would help him protect the forest.

To keep illegal timber cutters and poachers out, in June 1989 Prajak and four other monks (invited from Saraburi Province) performed a Buddhist ordination ceremony to confer sacredness on the trees.[70] A saffron robe, like that worn by monks, was reverently wrapped around each of the oldest and biggest trees in the forest. The chief monk declared to the two thousand villagers in attendance that the tree was a Ton Phraya (Great Tree), which had been sheltering all living things around and underneath its spreading branches from way back in time. Every villager and the villagers' children and grandchildren were requested "not to cut down this Phraya tree and not to harm the animals and all other living things in the 10,000-rai forest, for they are all under the protection of this tree."[71]

The ordination succeeded in deterring villagers from felling the trees, but it did not stop the unfaithful.[72] So the villagers set up a surveillance team to watch for the log poachers and to block roads that the poachers used to haul timber from the forest. Prajak sometimes took part in this surveillance work. In retaliation, the loggers threatened the monk, firing bullets into the sanctuary to intimidate him. A group of local officials also came to visit him and told him to leave. When all threats failed, officials filed a petition with the sangha head of Buriram Province to order Prajak to leave and to defrock him.[73] The Forest Department, taking the same stand as it did in 1976 when Juan set up a hermitage in the forest at Ox Mountain,[74] told Prajak that his sanctuary encroached on forest preserve. But the Mahanikai sangha head took sides with Prajak.[75]

Apart from illegal logging, the forest had been threatened by the spreading eucalyptus plantations. As Prajak tells us, speaking of the military, "What they are really after is not the timber. It all boils down to land. After the timber is gone, they will hire villagers to clear the forest. Then they will sell it to some eucalyptus companies supported by the Japanese. I've seen this happen so often during my pilgrimages. I don't think it will be different here."[76] Just as Prajak predicted, the military allowed a private company that owned paper mills to plant eucalyptus and bamboo on the villagers' land. Despite their protests, some of the villagers' crops were plowed under, and in other places they found orderly rows of another crop planted in the middle of their rice.[77] In response to such abuse, the Pakham villagers staged a mass protest against the eucalyptus plantation owners by cutting down 200,000 saplings and burning down two nurseries.[78] During an ensuing crackdown on Pakham villagers, Prajak and the village leaders were arrested and jailed. It was an unprecedented event for a monk to be jailed while still in the robes.[79] Military authorities tried to portray this forest monk, who had been living for four years in Never-Dry Well Forest, as a violent radical inciting people to revolt.

As the case of Prajak illustrates, in recent years forest monks have encountered a situation in which none of the old rules seem to apply. During the Forest-Community Period, wandering monks lived close to nature and in the company of wildlife. When encountering wild animals, the monks knew that if they calmed their minds and radiated loving-kindness, the wild beasts would not harm them. Nowadays, however, the forest monks' worst threat comes not from wild animals but from loggers, poachers, and soldiers.[80] Whenever they encountered soldiers or illegal loggers in the forest, the monks had difficulty communicating with them. No amount of loving-kindness seemed to affect these men with their guns. The forest monk Phuang remarks, "Men are more dangerous than wild animals. Animals attack only in self-defense and then run away. But men pursue us, intent on killing."[81] Forest monks and government officers, particularly the military and the police, were clearly operating from different value systems. As Prajak put it, "Sometimes I pity them. They can't tell good from evil. They don't recognize honesty. . . . I don't think they are even just doing their duty. More likely they have no morals. No rationality. No ethical conduct. They are deluded about hierarchy—about all worldly matters. I can't communicate with them. This might be because of their past kamma. We can't expect a rooster and a duck to sound the same."[82]

Fighting for the survival of the remaining forests has become the most difficult test of a monk's spiritual training. According to a government statement, deforestation results when land-starved farmers clear areas for permanent cultivation or, in the North, when hill tribes practice slash-and-burn agriculture. But in fact much of the destruction is due to the illegal felling of timber by the forest mafia.[83] Prajak tells us that "more often than not . . . it's those men in uniforms and in power that are behind forest destruction."[84] He describes his struggle to retain inner peace in the face of outer turbulence: "What I find most difficult about working to preserve the forest here is how to put my mind in the right place, a place free from anger and worry. Those emotions are a big mental trap I must constantly learn to avoid."[85]

On top of their struggle to stem the destruction of forests and wildlife, contemporary forest monks, the majority of whose samnaks are Mahanikai, have to fight battles on two other fronts—against the sangha elders and against the military. Both want the monks out of the forests. The majority of forest samnaks are "Mahanikai." Will the forest tradition be able to survive into the twenty-first century? The future of the forest monks seems precarious, especially since the sangha elders are not at all sympathetic toward their plight.[86] In 1987 the Sangha Council ordered all forest ascetics to leave the forests except for those who reside in "legal" forest wats.[87] The Forest Department, a division of the Ministry of Agriculture, has been using this law to forbid monks from living in the forests. Although the ordinance has not yet been widely enforced, its passage reflects the Sangha Council's disapproval of the forest monks' tradition.

THE WORLD THEY HAVE LOST

Forced by the turmoil of the 1960s and 1970s to come out of their secluded retreats, the thudong monks attempted to teach others about the binding link between humans and the natural world. They were unable, however, to counter the tremendous forces of modernization. People in contemporary societies seem basically insensitive to the larger meaning and value of the environment, as Rabinowitz learned while working in a forest in Thailand: "Instead, the country's natural resources were viewed simply as a commodity, a bank account to be drawn upon indefinitely."[88] Indeed, the concept that many Western environmentalists advocate, that "Nature matters because it is,"[89] not because it attracts tourists and brings in dollars, seems alien to modernized Thai society.

For the thudong monks, of course, nature did matter. The remote wilderness was a sanctuary in which they could train their minds. When they chose, they could withdraw deep into the bush where no one would be able to find them. The forest was home to wandering monks; it was their school, their training ground, and their sanctuary, and life there was safe provided the monks were mindful.

Reading the forest monks' accounts of their lives in the wilderness, one cannot help feeling that the end of the Forest-Community Period and the passing of local religious traditions has been a great cultural as well as ecological loss. The early generations of forest monks lived and thought very differently from town monks or urban people whose knowledge derived from printed texts. Wandering monks' life stories reveal their deep appreciation of nature. They tell us about forests, rivers and streams, caves, mountains, and wild creatures. Their accounts indicate that many parts of the Northeast were ecologically rich. Streams were clean, the air was cool and fresh, and caves were wide and watered by clear springs. Thudong monks saw wild water buffalo, elephant, barking deer, serow, antelope, banteng, gaur, flying lemur, gibbon, tiger, panther, leopard, bear, boar, civet, and many kinds of monkeys. Old thudong monks could identify by sound alone many of the species of wild creatures inhabiting the tropical forests—an ability they had acquired after decades of wandering.

But as the elder thudong monks settled in permanent hermitages, both the forests and its wild animals began to disappear before their eyes.[90] Bua recalls that when his samnak was established in 1955 near Tat Village in a forest in Udon Thani Province, a band of wild boars could still be seen wandering around the monks' shelters. "They roamed about fearlessly a few meters away from the walking meditation tracks, so close that they could be heard rooting around. At first some of the monks were puzzled by this and called their friends to see for themselves, but still the boars were unmoved. Before long neither the boars nor the monks paid any attention to each other, there being peace and comfort for all."[91]

By the time Bua wrote his biography of Man in 1970, the wild boars were no longer seen, "since many 'ogres' have violated the law of live and let live and have slaughtered the boars whenever possible, probably when the monks were away temporarily, or when the boars strayed into any of the nearby villages" (M1, 42; M2, 53–54). As for tigers or leopards, they were last seen at the forest hermitage in 1972.[92] At his Midday Drum Cave Hermitage in Udon Thani, Khaw noticed that tigers and wild elephants seldom came around, and he missed their "surprise visits."

During the Forest-Community Period, Thet's Huge Rock Hermitage in Si Chiang Mai District, Nongkhai, was known among local people as a place haunted by fierce spirits and wild animals such as tigers and bears. When Thet first came to check the place at the end of 1964 the jungle was still impenetrable. Thet recalls that "anyone passing by boat would remain deadly silent and not even dare look up. Such fears led to it becoming a place of isolation and solitude without anyone daring to go near."[93] But shortly after Thet settled into this spot, the surrounding population started to grow. Wild animals were forced out and gradually disappeared. By 1980 the forests in the region were almost entirely gone. When he was seventy-seven years old and had lived at Huge Rock Monastery for fourteen years, Thet said he was too old to move around as he did before. "Like other old monks, I must stay put at the wat. Even if I could go wandering again today, there are no dense forests left. They destroyed them all."[94] Thet, who had lived through the Forest-Invasion Period, mourned the lost woodland: "When I think about the [vanished] forest along the Mekong River, I still feel the solitude in my heart." Like all the wandering monks, Thet could not believe how quickly everything had disappeared.

Most of the thudong monks discussed in this book had passed away before the Forest-Closure Period began. Man died during the Forest-Community Period in 1949, a free wanderer until infirmity stopped him. The rest died as settled monastics. Li died in 1961 at the age of fifty-four. Fan died at his forest monastery in Sakon Nakhon in 1977 at the age of seventy-nine. Wan and Juan died together in an accident in 1980, Wan at fifty-eight and Juan at sixty.[95] Waen died in 1985 at the age of ninety-seven. His exact contemporary, Dun, died during the same year, after spending fifty years as a settled monastic at Wat Burapha in Surin. Cha and Thet passed away at their monasteries in 1992 and 1994 respectively. La died in January 1996 at the age of ninety-six.

Though these forest monks won the respect of the urban elite and became popular figures nationwide, they felt that their teachings hardly made a dent in contemporary Thai society. Despite their pleas, the forests in Thailand have been mostly clear-cut.

CHAPTER 10

Many Paths and

Misconceptions

Ajan Man and disciples, a lineage of peripatetics whose rise paralleled the ascent of modern state Buddhism, found themselves drawn into the turmoil of national affairs despite their wish to live secluded lives. They gradually lost their autonomy during the Forest-Invasion Period and became settled monastics. Examining their lives in detail has made it possible for us to identify and dispel some of the misunderstandings that have arisen about Buddhism in Thailand and particularly about this regional tradition.

Buddhism in Thailand has often been thought of as monolithic, that is, uniform throughout. This view derives from the fact that those who have studied religion in Siam/Thailand have done so mainly through the lens of modern state Buddhism. But the thudong monks' accounts indicate that Buddhism has always been a complex and multilayered reality. One divergence that soon meets the eye is the division into two orders, Thammayut and Mahanikai; another is the tension between two types of monk within each order: book learners and meditators. Scholars sometimes proceed as if all conflicts within Buddhism were between Thammayuts and Mahanikais or between study and practice. But this view may be too simple. The conflict is between the Thammayut order and a diversity of regional Buddhist traditions—a tension that derives from the Thammayuts' claim that their order is more authentic than others and from their refusal to perform religious rituals with non-Thammayuts. This first conflict, between modern state control and regional autonomy, crosscuts the second, between monkhood as a monasterial, text-based vocation and monkhood as a peripatetic, practice-based one. Both conflicts assume many different forms depending on the region, traditions, policies, persons, and so forth.

A second misconception is that the "important" thudong monks all belonged to the Thammayut order. This mistaken notion stems from the way the Thammayut monks of the Northeast dominated national attention when the national economic development programs were being carried out. Another misconception, that the Thai sangha is intolerant of different interpretations of the vinaya, stems from an official history that portrays Thammayut scholastic monks as representative of the pure teaching of the Buddha. These records fail to acknowledge the existence of diverse ordination lineages of monks with their own distinctive interpretations of monastic rules. The misconception that modern state Buddhism played a purifying role stems from a bias in the records of the sangha authorities at the turn of the century, records that unfailingly portray Thammayut administrators as astute and highly capable. Actually, the purveyors of modern state Buddhism may have worked to deform rather than reform local traditions.

During the past two or three decades socially engaged monks have emerged, and progressive laypeople have advocated a return to the community orientation that characterized regional Buddhism. Some monks are again becoming community leaders and addressing people's everyday concerns. The fact that the forest monks' teachings and aspirations have endured and eventually won popular support attests to their vitality and universality.

SANGHA CONFLICTS AND SOCIAL TRANSFORMATION

In discussing the centralization of the sangha, historians of Thai Buddhism usually concern themselves with religious institutions: the implementation of modern monastic education, the making of an effective sangha bureaucracy, and the prestige and authority of the "reformed" order, the Thammayut. But far more was involved in the centralization process: the interrelationships of groups of monks in an era of religious and cultural change, the establishment of a monopoly in the spheres of learning and culture and its effect on individual monks, and the reactions of local monks to the standards of discipline and the rituals of modern state Buddhism.

Modern State Buddhism versus Regional Traditions

The social organization of Buddhism in what is now Thailand underwent a massive transformation in this century, when the modern nation-state with a centralized, urban-based bureaucracy gained control over diverse community-based traditions. The 1902 Sangha Act marked the beginning of a government policy favoring religious as well as cultural homogenization. The act, based on the Western bureaucratic system, conflicted with regional Buddhist traditions. Beginning at the turn of the century, the territorial expansion of modern state Buddhism into the North and Northeast created havoc among the local traditions, which grew progressively weaker and eventually lost their earlier autonomy.

The Lao Buddhist tradition in the Northeast was the product of a different culture from that of the Siamese elites in Bangkok, and the same is true of the Buddhism of the Tai Yuan, Shan, Mon, and Khmer. Often sangha officials in the provincial and district towns followed Bangkok policies while village abbots continued to follow local traditions. The form of rationalized Buddhism that Bangkok and the new elite deemed worthy was not necessarily the kind of Buddhism that villagers wished to support.[1] Under modern state Buddhism, degrees and diplomas counted more than traditional knowledge. With the passage of the Sangha Act, moreover, Bangkok authorities assumed control over all ordinations and promotions. Preference was given to monks who had passed the centralized ecclesiastical exams, not to those with the most experience. This meant that a relatively young Thammayut monk could become a sangha leader and exercise authority over an older ajan.[2] These young sangha leaders did not always respect older ajans without title or rank. Many sangha administrators' accounts indicate that conflicts arose when a Bangkok-trained monk was sent to become the abbot of a wat in a town or village. (One such abbot recalled that it took over a decade for him to be accepted by the local people.)

In local traditions, on the other hand, abbots generally were chosen not only by seniority in the monkhood but also by a consensus of both monks and lay supporters. In the Lao tradition, as we have seen, an abbot was expected to be knowledgeable about astrology, dispute settlement, healing, and even difficult childbirth. Education in the wat was likewise dependent on traditional needs. An abbot might encourage a specialization in astrology, herbal medicine, craftsmanship, meditation, or scriptural study, depending on his own pursuits or the traditions of the monastery. Rather than pursuing formal academic study, monks of local nikais usually learned by observing and imitating their ajans. As Zack points out, much that could never be articulated was expressed by example. "What a monk saw and emulated was defined by the particular nature of the sangha around him, and especially by the individuals close to him."[3]

Thudong monks of Man's lineage followed the local traditions' customary respect for both experience and seniority. Young monks and novices learned by following the example of elder members of the monastic community, who did not hesitate to perform the same menial tasks that the young monks did. Such was still the custom during the late 1940s at the forest hermitage at Pheu Pond Village, where Ajan Man spent the last years of his life. Wan observed that "even older monks who had ten or twenty years of seniority did not pull rank. They willingly performed their duties like the younger monks. . . . This was to set an example for the junior monks. On the surface when one looked at the monks who waited on the ajan [Man], it was as if they all had more or less the same seniority. Nevertheless, in those days we did respect monks according to their seniority" (W, 45–46).

Tension developed within the Thammayut order between monks who followed the Bangkok path and monks who followed the thudong tradition. Man and his disciples were very critical of Bangkok's circumvention of the seniority principle. Many young monks with diplomas—new dhamma experts and Pali scholars—believed that they were already wise and refused to bow to old ajans without schooling. (Man himself was regarded as unqualified to teach the dhamma because he had not studied under Bangkok's system—that is, he never took a naktham or Pali exam.) In Wan's view, the "disciples of high-level monks were often overbearing. They were afraid of nobody. They looked down on elder monks, even on a preceptor, as inferior. They believed that they were better educated and wiser. They paid respects only to those monks on whom they could depend. Nobody could reprimand them. They were parasites, yet they used their authority to threaten other monks. They no longer paid attention to old monks who used to be their teachers. Far from being scholars, they were imposters" (W, 45). Many monks who came to Ajan Man fell into this category. They used their academic knowledge to argue with Ajan Man's teachings or to show off.

Settled Monasticism versus Peripatetic Forms

Although scholars have generally perceived the Thammayut order as homogeneous, the wandering monks' accounts reveal a wide gap between Thammayut administrators, who favored the ideal of a settled monastic life, and Thammayut thudong monks, who advocated the wandering ascetic ideal. Generally, a Thammayut scholar-administrator would have more in common with a Mahanikai scholar-administrator than with a Thammayut forest wanderer. Academic monks of both orders believed that learned monks were those who mastered Wachirayan's texts and knew how to recite Pali verses properly. Man was critical of the Thammayut elders of his time who wanted to turn thudong monks into settled monastics. He warned his disciples to avoid close relations with them. "These senior monks tend to look at things only from their perspective," he said. "They always think that what they are doing is beneficial. In fact, it puts others [monks] at a disadvantage. If junior monks do not follow their orders, they will be condemned. Keep this in mind if you are going to be in their circle" (M3, 88).

Wandering monks, Thammayut or not, learned the dhamma from everything around them. Often nature was their best teacher. In contrast, pariyat monks, who followed modern state Buddhism, always depended on the authority of Wachirayan's texts. The perspective of both views can be seen in the question that a Thammayut elder posed to Ajan Man and in Man's answer to it. In 1941 Man came to Bangkok and stayed briefly at Wat Boromniwat.[4] One day the abbot there, Somdet Uan, asked Man, "Living in the forests as you do, without textbooks, how did you learn the dhamma?" Man replied promptly, "For those who have pañ-ña, the dhamma is everywhere." The senior monk was puzzled and asked Man to clarify his statement. Man explained that "wisdom will arise in the mind of one who has been properly trained, even if he has not read the Tipitaka. He learns from everything he sees and from everyone who crosses his path. In an undeveloped mind true wisdom will never occur. Even though he may read the Tipitaka, he will not see the dhamma. For instance, while walking on almsround, the novice Sangkijja saw the peasants plow their fields and send water to irrigate the paddy. From this he learned that the farmer could use the soil and the water, which are external, according to his wishes. Sangkijja wondered why we do not likewise train the mind, which is internal, for our own benefit. Then he was awakened. You see, the dhamma is all around us" (M3, 132–133).

Man once told Thammayut pariyat monks that nature was his teacher: "After ordination my ajan took me wandering in the forests and on the mountains. I learned the dhamma from the trees, the grass, rivers, streams, caves, and rocks. I listened to the sounds of birds and other animals" (M2, 264).

As one might expect, a non-Thammayut forest monk like Cha had more in common with Thammayut forest monks than with scholar monks of his own order. Cha, too, instructed his disciples to learn the dhamma from things around them:

Actually in my own practice I didn't have a teacher to give as much teaching as all of you get from me. I didn't have many teachers. I was ordained in an ordinary village temple and lived in village temples for quite a few years. . . . I traveled and I looked around. I had ears so I listened, I had eyes so I looked. . . .

Sometimes I'd go to see old religious sites with ancient monastic buildings, designed by architects, built by craftsmen. In some places they would be cracked. Maybe one of my friends would remark, "Such a shame, isn't it? It's cracked." I'd answer, "If that weren't the case then there'd be no such thing as the Buddha, there'd be no Dhamma. It's cracked like this because it's perfectly in line with the Buddha's teaching. . . . If it wasn't cracked like that there wouldn't be any Buddha!"[5]

In the thudong monks' view, the humble and coarse conditions of everyday life could be better teachers of dhamma than books. Wiriyang remembers something Kongma taught him in Aranya-prathet, when they were returning from Cambodia in 1941. While looking for a place to spend the night, they came across a deserted shelter that had been occupied by Japanese soldiers during the Franco-Siamese war. The place was full of excrement, so Kongma and Wiriyang had to sweep it clean before they could use it for meditation. That night Wiriyang gave a massage to Kongma, who used the occasion, as he often did, to teach Wiriyang some dhamma. "Today," Wiriyang recalls, "I learned not to look down on dirty things. Good things come from dirt. If the Noble One had not experienced living with dirt, he would never have attained holiness. Ajan Kongma said that the shit on the floor where we lie is not as bad as the shit in our bodies. And do not be deluded by external beauty, he said. Only fools wear perfume to cover up the body's stink. 'Wiriyang,' he said, 'if their bodies were fragrant, why would they bother covering up the fragrance with perfume?' With this teaching my mind reached out for the dhamma and became oblivious to the stinky place."[6]

Thudong monks tended to dismiss scholastic learning as little more than rote memorization of texts and secondhand knowledge. Ajan Man thought that scholastic Buddhism was a lower path than meditation. When Waen first met Man, the latter told him, "Leave your knowledge in a cabinet and put all your energy into practicing meditation" (Wn, 28). Similarly, when Fan walked from Sakon Nakhon to Ban Pheu District in Udon Thani to see Man in 1921, the thudong master asked him if he still wanted to study "the big books."[7] Upon hearing that this was indeed Fan's intention, Man said, "Fan, don't bother going to Ubon to study. Stay here with me. I'll teach you all I know. If you're still not satisfied, then you can go study" (F, 25). Fan decided to take up meditation training with Man and never went to study in Ubon.

Another comment of Man's, made in 1943, could very well refer to the sangha authorities' attempt to mold all monks regardless of ability into the same form through the study of Bangkok's curriculum. "Do not look for the dhamma outside yourself. The dhamma is neither in palm-leaf books nor in a wat. A monastery is merely a place where monks reside. Neither is dhamma in the air or in the forest. The dhamma is within ourselves" (Wi, 78).

Cha shared this same conviction: "If you don't practice, you won't know," he said. "Frankly speaking, you won't know the Dhamma by just reading it or studying it. Or if you do know it your knowledge is still defective" (C1, 30). Above all, thudong monks valued wisdom gained from experience, and their teachings generally reflect this. Doctrinal knowledge with no practice to back it up is useless. In Wan's words, "He who has not realized dhamma within himself cannot say that he knows. The knowledge that one gains from memorizing is superfluous for it is merely *sañña* [perception]. . . . Therefore we should not mistake perceptions for our knowledge. But that does not mean that the knowledge we acquired was worthless. . . . Someone who has learned from books will have his memory of the dhamma to serve as a foundation for his meditation practice. If he keeps up with the practice, eventually the knowledge that he possesses will be confirmed. Only then can he say that his knowledge comes from his personal experience" (W, 53).

The tensions between scholastic Thammayut administrators and Thammayut wandering monks appear between the lines on the pages of the thudong monks' memoirs and the biographies written by their disciples. These tensions can be detected in the monks' accounts of their relations with their superiors: between Man and Abbot Ubali, Waen and Ubali, Dun and sangha head Uan, Fan and Uan, Thet and Uan, Li and Abbot Nu, Li and Uan, Wan and district sangha heads. Here it is important to remind ourselves of the cultural context in which these monks lived. As Wyatt points out, "it was frowned on to demonstrate anger openly, or overtly to criticize superiors. This did not mean that anger (or pain or disappointment) was simply suppressed: subtlety is called for."[8]

Provincial and Local Rivalries

When nonlocal monks went to a new territory to spread their form of Buddhism, they often found themselves subject to the animosity of local monks. Thudong as well as other meditation monks encountered this kind of conflict as their efforts brought them growing popularity. Accounts by Thet, Li, and Sot provide us with a vivid glimpse of the hostility that nonlocal monks aroused when they began to attract supporters.

In 1950 Thet and his fellow thudong monks went wandering in

southern Thailand. This territory was new to them. When they arrived in Phuket ten days before the 1950 rains retreat, they found that many administrative monks in the province were hostile toward them. As Thet recalls,

> A party of people together with a group of local monks schemed together to prevent our residing there. They tried various ways to frustrate us: setting fire to our huts, poisoning our food, throwing stones at us and forbidding the people to give us alms. When we were out on almsround, they would sometimes head straight towards us on a collision course.
>
> As we were the visitors in their territory, we tried to be as conciliatory as possible. We went to see their head and pleaded to be allowed at least to spend the coming Rains Retreat there, for it was already so close. But he wouldn't permit this and further accused us of being vagrant monks. Whatever explanations and reasons I put forward were adamantly rejected, until finally he let out that it was really his superiors who would not allow us to stay. (This referred to his superiors in Bangkok.) I therefore told him quite frankly that although he might have his superiors, I also had mine. Afterwards, I learnt that he had set down this serious challenge: "If the Thammayut monks were able to spend the rains retreat in Phuket and Phangnga, he would 'put on trousers.' "[9]

This incident lends itself to an interpretation in terms of sectarian rivalry: the local Mahanikai monks did not want the Thammayuts' influence to spread to their area. (At that time there was no Thammayut wat in Phuket.) But what happened next indicates otherwise. After encountering the local monks' resistance, Thet's lay devotees succeeded in arranging hermitages for him and his group of fifteen monks and novices at Khok Loi, in Phangnga.[10] Here they encountered another type of resistance, this time from monks of their own order. Thet found that the provincial Thammayut administrators' opinion of them was similar to that of their Mahanikai counterparts. They did not want thudong monks here either: "It was during this Rains Retreat that we ... were also affected by pressure from 'undercurrents.' I refer here to other monks of our own Thammayut group who started clamouring against us. They accused us of: 'not keeping the disciplinary Rule';

'that our practice was outside what the scriptural authorities set down'; 'that we didn't observe the Patimokkha Sangha duties inside an official *Ubosotha* Hall' " (T1, 200).

Thet was stunned to be accused of not reciting the patimok in an ordination hall, which their new samnaks did not even have. He had heard, furthermore, that Thammayut administrators had remarked sarcastically that anyone who wants to be enlightened should "go over to Ajan Thet." Thet knew that "this sarcasm was probably directed at their own disciples who had come over to me." He went on to say, "If such an opinion came from newly ordained monks it would have been understandable, since they were ignorant. But these [administrative] monks were senior and learned. I pitied them because their knowledge came from books only; they had no experience of meditation practice" (T1, 89).

The hostile and disdainful attitudes that both the Thammayut and Mahanikai administrators held toward wandering monks had not changed much since the 1902 act was passed. One explanation may be that they harbored a sense of cultural superiority—a certain ethnic chauvinism—with regard to the Lao-speaking people of the Northeast. A comment of Thet's suggests such a prejudice:

> At the time there were not many Isan laborers in Phuket. The locals feared them as if they were somehow monsters or tigers. This originated in various rumours about Isan people, how "they were brutal and cruel, catching, killing and eating children."
>
> I had been on the island for a year before more Isan laborers started heading here. They arrived walking in file along the road and became an object of intense interest to the townspeople. Meanwhile, people out on the town's outskirts or in the countryside who saw them would flee to the shelter of their home. Anyone out in the forest ducked and hid themselves in the trees. I didn't witness this with my own eyes but it was reported to me later. (T1, 197–198; T2, 88)

Another explanation for the hostility that thudong monks encountered can be attributed to the provincial administrative monks' dislike of wandering monks in general. The arrival of thudong monks in town, their teaching of meditation, and their ability to draw popular support were seen as a threat.

When thudong monks arrived with the support of government officials they were especially likely to encounter hostility from local monks. One example of this, a conflict between a Thammayut thudong monk (from Ubon) and local monks in the Northeast (in Khorat), illustrates the damaging effect government support could have.

In 1933 Li went to Salawan Forest Monastery in Khorat on the assumption that Abbot Sing knew where to find Ajan Man. While Li was there, the district officer of Krathok District (now Chok Chai District) came to the wat to invite a Thammayut monk to spend the rains retreat in his district. Abbot Sing sent Li and a couple of other monks. During the first rains retreat Li stayed at a hut in the cemetery of Bongchi Forest. One evening, while Li was delivering a sermon at the district officer's house, two laymen came looking for Li. They told the district officer that a disciple of Li's, Phra Yen, had been stabbed. Li learned from the police investigation that local monks had felt threatened by the thudong monks' presence.

> Since my coming to spend the rains retreat there at Bong Chi Cemetery Hermitage, the way I and other monks in the wat had conducted ourselves had received a great deal of praise from the District Official, civil servants, townspeople and most of the people in the nearby villages. Other temples in the area had become jealous as a result and, not wanting us to stay on there, had laid plans to frighten us away by doing us bodily harm.
> ... What happened was ... that Phra Yen had taken a chair and a sewing machine that evening and placed them on the porch of his hut, which was about a meter off the ground. As he was sitting in the chair, sewing his robes, the attacker standing on the ground tried to stab him in the left shoulder with a long-handled scythe. The handle struck the chair, though, so the scythe left only a surface wound.[11]

A second example illustrates how conflicts arose when sangha authorities appointed monks to serve as abbots of wats where they were outsiders. Such appointments often ignored villagers' preference for local monks. Sot Janthasaro, a native of Suphanburi, lived a thudong life in the Central Plains before he was sent by his superior in 1916 to Wat Paknam in Thonburi, across the river from Bangkok.[12] When Sot first arrived, he did not know anybody in Thonburi and had no one to turn to. "It's like being in exile," Sot thought. Seeing that the resident monks of Wat Paknam were lax, he set out to discipline them. He told them, "I know many monks who have been ordained for decades, yet they lack the knowledge to teach others. Though they depend on Buddhism to survive, they contribute nothing to the religion. They bring no gain for themselves or for others. These monks are like parasites. Why were they ordained? I was sent here and I intend to follow the path of dhamma-vinaya strictly. You monks are welcome to join me, or you may decide not to join me if you wish. I don't mind, so long as you don't interfere with my work. I believe in live-and-let-live as long as you stick to the rules of the wat."[13]

But Sot's attempt to discipline the monks in the wat made enemies. Although he encouraged monks and novices to study naktham and Pali, if that was what they wanted, he personally taught meditation. From 1920 on, students came to study under him, mainly from other towns or districts. Because he sought to popularize meditation, a practice that no official wat followed at the time, he made enemies both of the higher level administrators and local monks. His superior, a Mahanikai elder, saw him as going against the sangha authorities.

Sot gained considerable popularity with laypeople, however, which apparently made some people jealous enough to try to kill him. One night after he finished teaching meditation, he stepped out of the preaching hall followed by a lay disciple. An unidentified man fired two shots at him. Sot narrowly escaped injury. One bullet went through his robe and the other hit the disciple in the face.[14]

Thudong Monks and the Thammayut Connection

Ajan Sao and Ajan Man are sometimes considered to be the originators of the forest meditation lineage in the Northeast. This belief stems from an assumption that an earlier forest tradition had died out and that Sao and Man revived it. Historically this is inaccurate, since the thudong way was practiced in many local Buddhist traditions that existed in Siam. It is true that the *Thammayut* forest tradition did come into being in the late nineteenth century with Sao, since Thammayuts do not acknowledge non-

Thammayuts as their ajans. (Sao's meditation teachers came from Lao traditions, and Sao himself belonged to one such tradition before he converted to the Thammayut order. These Lao teachers were not acknowledged by Sao's or Man's followers simply because they were not Thammayuts.)

Although a lineage of forest monks reciting the 227 monastic rules may have begun with Sao and Man, wandering forest monks of local traditions preceded them. Thudong monks from regional traditions followed different sets of disciplinary rules that allowed them to store food in a cave, gather fruits and vegetables, make their own herbal medicines, and the like. Many of these activities were forbidden by the Thammayuts' monastic rules. The result is that monks belonging to the non-Thammayut nikais were often thought to be lax in discipline and were dismissed by Bangkok authorities as inauthentic. Many of Man's and Sao's disciples started out in local Buddhist traditions before they converted, but we do not know the details of their early meditation teachers' lives. Some of them may have been as strict as the Thammayuts, perhaps, but about different issues. Cha, who was trained under several thudong teachers, including Thammayut ones, confirms that some non-Thammayut thudong monks were no less strict than Thammayut ones, although they were not as famous. By now they have all passed away.

People today tend to think of forest meditation monks as Thammayut. This is because of the attention that many Thammayut forest monks have received both from the government and the media in the 1970s. A story or picture featuring a thudong monk appearing in a newspaper or magazine or on television may reach millions of people. In addition, some monks' memoirs or biographies have been published and republished, often for free distribution as cremation volumes at funerals. Since book publishing is costly, only monks who had upper- or middle-class lay support had their life stories published. Thammayut forest monks had this kind of support.

Publicity and media attention have shaped our understanding of the thudong tradition. Only a minority of wandering monks have become well known nationwide. Several reasons account for the obscurity of most forest monks: (1) they lived in the era before the mass media brought forest monks to the attention of urban people, and so died unnoticed; (2) they adhered to local traditions and were not acknowledged; (3) often they did not teach or had few disciples; (4) many never had their life stories published, whether for personal reasons or because their supporters were mainly local people who could not afford the publishing costs; (5) many shunned publicity for fear of being disturbed by urban tourists; and (6) most were not visited by the royal family.

Throughout the first half of this century, sangha authorities considered the thudong practice to be inferior to Pali studies. Thammayut pariyat monks certainly shared this attitude. Man's experience as acting abbot of Wat Jediluang in Chiang Mai during a rains retreat in the early 1930s confirmed this prejudice. Man recalled that the Thammayut monks and novices at the wat had little desire to meditate and were not especially taken with his teaching. "No matter how hard I tried to teach them, nobody took the practice seriously. I don't understand their attitude. Even though I explained it in sermons and demonstrated it, nobody thought practicing meditation was important. I kept thinking that it was a waste of time to stay here."[15]

Later on Man left his administrative post to resume the thudong life. When Thet went to Wat Jediluang in 1932 to inquire into his teacher's whereabouts, he found that the Thammayut administrators there were scornful of thudong monks of their own order: "Worse than that, some of the [scholastic] monks there even referred to him [Ajan Man] with dismissive contempt" (T1, 128).

A wide cultural gap existed within the Thammayut order between the Lao thudong monks and the Bangkok-trained pariyat monks, who considered themselves to be more sophisticated. Bua's recollection of an occasion when thudong monks were invited to participate in a cremation ceremony with urban Thammayut monks is illustrative.

Taking part in a religious ceremony along with other, more sophisticated monks, the thudong monks looked clumsy. Until then they had been living among forest dwellers, who did not have these rituals and ceremonies. Having no experience in these rites, the thudong monks did not know the procedure. They were at a loss to know in which hand they should hold the holy thread or the fan. Some of the thudong monks did not even know which side of the ceremonial fan was the front. In a chanting ceremony some thudong monks held the fan backward, with the back of the fan turned toward the audience. Some laypeople and disciples felt so embarrassed that they turned their faces aside. But these mistakes did not bother the thudong monks; they retained their equanimity. Many of them had no idea that what they did was wrong, and they continued the ceremony as if nothing had happened. The sight of the thudong monks committing these errors, which any urban child would know about, embarrassed their disciples to death. Some of the hostesses probably lost face. They were afraid that the honored guests in the audience might feel offended.[16]

Such behavior was typical of Man's disciples when they were asked to take part in formal religious ceremonies instituted by Bangkok. When the thudong monks were invited to have a meal at a formal ceremony and ate directly from their bowls, the practice drew stares from Thammayut town monks and urban people.[17] The acute discomfort of the urban laity as well as monks contrasted strikingly with the forest monks' lack of concern.

The attitude that thudong monks were bumpkins was particularly strong among Bangkok-trained Thammayut monks. Why then did Man and his disciples join the Thammayut order when there was such prejudice? To find out, we need to examine the thudong monks' accounts of their early years.

In the late nineteenth century, prior to centralization of the sangha in the Northeast, the Thammayut abbots in meuang Ubon were meditation monks who emphasized ascetic practice and adhered strictly to the 227 monastic rules. They forbade monks to participate in local festivals, which persisted in outlying areas for several decades after the passage of the 1902 Sangha Act. Sao and Man were impressed by these Thammayut monks' discipline, which was reinforced by the fortnightly recitation of the patimok (one of the many rituals required by the sangha authorities from Bangkok). So Sao, who was abbot of Wat Liap in Ubon, converted his wat to the Thammayut order, and Sao's disciple, Man, likewise was ordained in the Thammayut order.

Once they were reordained in the Thammayut order, the monks

were freed from tasks that local monks in the Lao or Khmer Buddhist traditions (later dubbed "Mahanikai") were obliged to perform. Because the sangha elders forbade monks from engaging in village festivals and discouraged them from doing major construction and maintenance work—activities that Thammayuts considered secular—time was freed up for meditation. (This was not exactly what the Bangkok Thammayut elders had in mind; they wanted monks to study Bangkok's texts.)

Sao did not mind working on construction projects, but Man hated it. Man was a loner who shunned communal activities, preferring to spend his time wandering and meditating. Dun, likewise, decided to leave Surin and go to study Pali in Ubon because he got tired of building bullock-carts and looking after oxen in the local wat. Li left his village wat and converted to the Thammayut order because he disliked the tasks expected of indigenous monks such as participating in local festivals and doing manual work. Kongma gave similar reasons for fleeing his local ajan: "In the evening monks often spent time pulling weeds or felling trees to clear the forest. It's against the vinaya, but we had to do it."[18]

But it was, of course, the search for a teacher that brought monks to Man and thus to the Thammayut order. Early on, monks of local traditions came to practice meditation under Sao's and Man's guidance. Many of them converted to the Thammayut order only after they became Man's disciples.

Waen, for example, originally was ordained in a Lao tradition. When he first met Man, around 1918, Man greeted him with pleasure and allowed him to attend his sermons. Waen benefited from his teaching and appreciated the ajan's kindness. At first, he did not become a formal disciple, which would have entailed his undergoing a new ordination as a Thammayut. Like all Thammayut monks in those days, Man would not allow a non-Thammayut disciple to join him in the recitation of the patimok. Before beginning this ritual, Man asked the non-Thammayut disciples to leave the area. After the recitation was over, the non-Thammayut monks were called in to recite among themselves. Waen, the only non-Thammayut, felt left out.

Not all thudong monks who knew Man converted, however.[19] Waen and Teu, who had wandered on their own for twenty years, saw no immediate reason to convert. Waen finally converted in the late 1920s while in Chiang Mai, but only because he could not go against the wishes of Ubali (Jan), abbot of Wat Jediluang in Chiang Mai at the time. Soon after, his close friend Teu also converted. When a non-Thammayut monk converted to the Thammayut, he lost his monastic seniority. Even though Waen (and Teu as well) had been ordained in his local tradition for twenty years, his number of rains retreats *(phansa)* within the Thammayut order was only one.

For much of his life, Man was not officially an upatcha; he had no authority to ordain monks.[20] Thudong monks who wanted to convert to the Thammayut had to be reordained by administrative monks. In 1926 as many as twenty thudong monks went through a reordination ceremony performed by Phra Khru Chinowat (Jum Phanthulo) at a village in Nakhon Phanom. For the monks of a Lao tradition, the conversion was not easy because of the requirement that they recite the 227 monastic rules. The rules were printed in Bangkok Thai script. Juan and Thet could master this task without difficulty, since they had studied Thai during their school years. But Kongma, who had formerly been a buffalo trader and who could not read Thai, had a hard time reading the patimok text (which monks in local traditions were not required to recite). He persevered out of his desire to be "a true disciple" of Man's. Kongma recalls what a tremendous struggle it was: "It is very difficult to practice meditation, yet I've made progress. Why should I feel discouraged trying to memorize the patimok? For days and nights I kept on deciphering the text. I even asked other monks who knew Thai to read it to me. For several months I worked hard. Finally I mastered the patimok, here at Sam Phong Village in Phanao Forest" (Wi, 11–12).

Man, however, did not insist that all his disciples become Thammayut. His reasoning was that if all the thudong monks became Thammayut, no one would be left to guide those in other traditions: "The path to enlightenment does not depend on belonging to a particular nikai" (Wn, 32). Man wanted good thudong monks in every nikai, since that way there would be a better chance for the tradition to survive.

Some of Man's disciples believed strongly that the Thammayut order was purer than the Mahanikai. Lui went through the reordination ceremony a second time because he was not sure that the first one had been done properly. But many other thudong monks, such as Waen, Teu, Kongma, Phuang, and Aunsi, held no such conviction. And many Thammayut thudong converts, like Phuang and Aunsi, respected their local preceptors and kept in contact with them long after their conversions.[21] Aunsi was converted along with other disciples of Man's in 1932, when Sing and a large number of thudong monks were staying in Nakhon Ratchasima. Aunsi felt he had to explain his reordination to his lay devotees. "I want you to know that I was not reordained in the Thammayut order because I think the Mahanikai is unworthy. In fact, my Mahanikai preceptor is highly respected and filled with loving-kindness. I was reordained so that it would be convenient for me to practice meditation [under the guidance of teachers who are Thammayut]."[22] It is understandable that thudong monks like Aunsi felt they had to justify converting. By and large, apart from wanting to be in the same nikai as Ajan Man, they saw no reason to convert. For those thudong monks who did convert, the conversion was often in name only, since their thudong practice did not change.

It is instructive that Cha, who espoused Man's teachings and practiced them for most of his life, never became a Thammayut. When Cha met Man for the first time in 1947, Man asked him about the meditation teacher under whom he had practiced. Upon hearing that Cha had been trained at Wongkot Hill under a Khmer disciple of Ajan Phao's, Man approved. "Good," he said. "Ajan Phao is an authentic monk" (C3, 23). Man evidently judged a monk not by the order to which he belonged but by the depth of his meditation practice. Cha once asked Man if it was necessary for him to convert to the Thammayut order. Man told him that it made no difference which nikai a thudong monk belonged to.[23]

A Different Interpretation of Monastic Rules

A related misconception in the literature is that Theravada Buddhists in general and Thai Buddhists in particular are intolerant of different, non-Theravada interpretations of the vinaya. Actually, it is modern state Buddhism that has been intolerant of other traditions and lineages.

Prior to the imposition of standard Buddhist practices, each local monk identified with the monastery where he studied and with his teachers, whose lineage had stretched back many generations. Different nikais held dissimilar opinions on interpreting the dhamma, the rules of conduct, and religious rituals.[24] Each popular and well-established lineage had its own monastic practices and its own history. As Reynolds explains, "Such histories were not always committed to writing, but that made them nonetheless real in the minds of the nikai's adherents."[25]

Within the Thammayut order, the two categories of monks differed in their interpretations of monastic rules. Wandering monks, whose practices evolved in the context of their local traditions, took pride in the austerity of thudong practice. But urban Thammayut monks, whose custom evolved from Bangkok's court, did not share the thudong monks' criteria of strictness. They saw the thudong monks as lax because they did not always recite the patimok. When, for example, Man arrived in Bangkok in 1941 (he was coming from Chiang Mai to catch a train for the Northeast), Somdet Uan told him to stay at Wat Boromniwat. Pariyat monks at this wat used the opportunity to ply Man with questions.

> "I've heard that you keep only one rule, not the 227 precepts like us. Is it true?" asked an academic monk.
>
> "Yes, I observe only one, and that is the mind," replied Man.
>
> "What about the 227 rules?"
>
> "I guard the mind so that it will not think, speak, or act in violation of the Buddha's disciplinary rules. It does not matter if the discipline consists of 227 rules or even more. Being mindful prevents me from violating the vinaya. Anybody who thinks that I do not observe the 227 precepts is entitled to his opinion."
> (M2, 262-263)

Man's reply indicates his preference for mental discipline over rules of behavior. He believed that if one is mindful at all times—which requires meditation—then one will not violate the rules of moral conduct. Awareness will transmute and transform one's whole being to the extent that observing the precepts will become natural to one's character instead of a mechanical adherence to rules.

Conversations such as this, between the meditation master and the academic monk, suggest that monks learned in texts and monks skilled in meditation interpreted vinaya rules differently. To thudong monks, discipline must come from within; it cannot be imposed from the outside. Discipline should be based on a clear awareness of its value and also a certain degree of introspection and mindfulness. At the turn of this century, sangha authorities, claiming that monks of local traditions were remiss in not reciting the 227 precepts, insisted upon rigid observance of the whole patimok, which was henceforth to be recited in its entirety once every two weeks. In practice, this meant that the letter of the vinaya could be observed "religiously" without necessarily heeding the meaning of the precepts.[26]

From the meditation monks' perspective, discipline was a natural outgrowth of deep meditation practice and an advanced stage of self-purification. Vinaya texts were only words, Man told a disciple. "It's not so much that we must know every single training rule, if we know how to train our own minds. . . . You should try to bring the teachings of the Buddha into your mind" (C1, 10). Cha recalls what he learned about practicing the vinaya from Ajan Man: "The Pubbasikkha [text] . . . was too much. I didn't know which was the essence and which was the trimming, I had just taken all of it. When I understood more fully I let it drop off because it was too heavy. I just put my attention into my own mind and gradually did away with the texts."[27] Meditation monks generally saw no point in memorizing every single rule of the vinaya. Like Man, Cha recommended guarding and training the mind in order to achieve right behavior: "At first we trained the body and speech to be free of taints, which is *sila*. Some people think that to have *sila* you must memorize Pali scriptures and chant all day and all night, but really all you have to do is make your body and speech blameless, and that's *sila*" (C2, 105).

In their memoirs and biographical accounts, the thudong monks emphasized repeatedly that their practices did not go against the vinaya rules. They believed that the spiritual community of the Buddha's disciples consisted originally of peripatetics. Ajan Man praised the thirteen ascetic practices. Li often pointed out that living in a cemetery or in a cave was not against the vinaya. Cha, too, kept saying that "living at the foot of a tree isn't against the precepts" (C1, 85). As late as 1977, Bua still had to defend the thudong practices: "All thirteen ascetic practices are tools for subduing the defilements of those who follow them. There's nothing about them that anyone can criticize—except for Devadatta and his gang."[28]

Had Bangkok authorities not insisted that the only proper monks are settled monastics, thudong monks would not have been so defensive. Putting the sangha authority's attitude toward religious discipline into perspective, Cha defines thudong conduct as "practices that are hard to do" (C1, 85). Referring to the extreme disparity between learning the dhamma from books and learning it from thudong practice, he says that "the real foundation of the teaching is in order to see *attā*, the self, as being empty, having no fixed identity. It's void of intrinsic being. But people come to the study of Dhamma to increase their self-view, so they don't want to experience suffering or difficulty. They want everything to be cozy" (C1, 128). Thudong monks were of the opinion that awarding honorific titles and dignitary fans to monks who conformed to state Buddhism simply increased attā or *moha* (delusion). As they saw it, the awarding of honorific titles stood in conflict with the fundamental Buddhist tenet that urged monks to turn away from worldly distinctions of authority, status, and wealth. In his memoirs, Thet comments that it is not proper for a meditation monk to have a title conferred on him. He expressed this same opinion verbally as well as in a private letter to a Thammayut elder (Thet did not mention his name). But his plea was ignored and he was asked to accept the title for "the benefit of the sangha administration as a whole." Thet compared the conferring of a title on a monk to hanging jewelry around the neck of a monkey—it doesn't mean anything to the monkey. "Although," Thet admitted, "some other monkey will think that the jewelry has turned it into a human."[29]

At least one Bangkok aristocrat would have agreed with the forest monks. Prince Damrong felt ambivalent about ecclesiastical status. He expressed this opinion in 1934 to a Thammayut elder. "The dhamma is universal," Damrong said. "It can be practiced by all kinds of people in any country. The vinaya as codified, however, is tailored to the specific culture. Here is an analogy. Had Gotama Buddha lived in Siam, the code of discipline that he came up with would have been more or less different from that in

India; his intention was that the vinaya that the monks followed should suit the local customs. . . . If the Buddha were to proclaim the vinaya today, I wonder if he would allow the monks to receive honorific titles and dignitary fans."[30]

In fact, adherence to rules and regulations laid down by Bangkok was seen by meditation masters as commitment to the lowest level of morality, a level that requires no meditation at all, since it needs only "rules and somebody to swing the stick."[31] Monks who had trained their minds through meditation had a higher level of morality; they followed the numerous precepts faithfully whether anyone was watching or not.

Many revered ajans or khubas of regional traditions, whose spiritual lives were modeled on the bodhisatta ideal,[32] were on the whole deeply aware of ethical considerations. When circumstances demanded it, they did not hesitate to increase, modify, and even abolish the minor rules, particularly if the promotion of the spiritual welfare of the community required it. Although they may have never recited the patimok, many village abbots were full of compassion and answered the needs of the community. Yet Bangkok authorities considered them bad because they did not follow the Theravada precepts strictly.

COMMUNITY CONCERNS IN REGIONAL TRADITIONS

During the past two decades, progressive monks and laypeople have advocated a return to "traditional" Buddhist values and practices. These values and practices include allowing monks to serve as community leaders, teaching the dhamma in a lively manner, recognizing meditation as relevant to everyday life, and granting women full participation in religion.

Monks as Community Leaders

Abbots of local traditions were often viewed as community leaders as well as heads of monasteries. In many regional Buddhist traditions, the division between the spiritual and the secular worlds was difficult to draw. Modern state Buddhism has not been as effective as a community religion because it undermined the wat as a local institution.[33] Sangha authorities wanted local monks to obey decrees issued from the center, decrees that the officials believed would strengthen Buddhism throughout Siam. Unintentionally, these decrees undermined wat-village relations that had evolved over centuries. As the sangha regulations pulled monks into a national institution, the wat became peripheral to local societies. In O'Connor's words, Buddhism moved from a wat-localized to a Sangha-centered religion.[34]

In the mid-1960s the military government and the sangha authorities decided that monks should take part in rural development to help combat the threat of communism. In an effort to win over villagers, the Thai government attempted to make the monks' roles more relevant to the daily lives and problems of rural people by allowing monks to perform tasks that would contribute to community development.[35] Ironically, modern state Buddhism had previously condemned monks who were involved in these matters (see chap. 1). But now young monks trained at the Buddhist universities in Bangkok were assigned to up-country posts to participate in government development projects. These monks were called *phra nak phatthana* (development monks). But the effort was unsuccessful because policy making remained in the same hands as in 1902: urban people with little awareness of villagers' needs and even less respect for local cultures. This attempt to recover the monk's role as a community leader was tried only in form, not in spirit.

During the 1970s a more genuine movement of socially engaged monks emerged. These monks were mostly from rural areas in all regions of Thailand; some were progressive provincial or district sangha heads. They met voluntarily from time to time in small forums convened by nongovernmental organizations and thereby got to know one another personally. They realized that some sort of return to older religious values was needed to help villagers get back on their feet. "In traditional Buddhism," Seri states, "monks have always been community leaders."[36] As we know, this "traditional Buddhism" to which nongovernmental organization workers refer is in fact a plurality of local Buddhist traditions. Although these workers may not be acquainted with the actual history of Buddhism in Thailand, many recognize that monks in the rural areas today have to find ways to regain the confidence of local people.[37]

Socially engaged monks realized that after twenty years of living under the government's national socioeconomic development plans, many villagers were worse off than before. Particularly in the Northeast, vast tracts of forest had been turned into single-crop plantations producing food for export. Having lost their farms, villagers had left to work as migrant laborers or prostitutes in the cities. Socially engaged monks understood the connection between the modernization of agriculture and the disintegration of village cultures. They began to search—and still are searching—for an alternative model of development based on local Buddhist traditions. They seek to devise ways to rebuild rural communities in conformity with the Buddhist principle of right livelihood. For example, these monks have helped villagers create producers' cooperatives, credit unions, child care centers, buffalo banks, and forest conservation measures. They also teach that income derived from home agricultural production should not be wasted in buying unnecessary commodities as status symbols.[38]

Revered monks of regional Buddhist traditions had always regarded work as a means of practicing the dhamma. They taught by example, by living simply, working hard, and acting ethically. In Ajan Man's forest hermitages, the old as well as the young were engaged in the same kind of work; no distinctions were made. Manual labor such as chopping wood, hauling water, cleaning latrines, sweeping the ground, and thatching roofs was seen as training for mindfulness. Progressive monks today have returned to these qualities. Perhaps the greatest flaw of modern state Buddhism is revealed in the poor habits that have been cultivated in the average monk. Panyanantha (b. 1911), a pariyat monk with much sympathy for the forest tradition, offered this advice to fellow monks: "After graduation we should work. Pariyat monks often complain that 'nobody assigned us any work, and we were not told what to do.' Why must we wait [for the senior monks] to give us an order? Why wait for work to be assigned to us? This is a flaw in today's monks' thinking—that we must have an order to get to work. Look around, there are lots of things that need to be done. In fact, the amount of work is overwhelming. The problem is that there are not enough monks to tackle all this work. . . . We don't have to wait for anybody's order. We, monks, take orders directly from the Buddha."[39]

Teaching Dhamma with Drama

During the late 1970s, when socially engaged monks attempted to recover their role as community leaders, new preaching monks emerged. The most unconventional of them is Phayom Kalayano (b. 1949), the Mahanikai abbot of Wat Suan Kaew in Nonthaburi. Phayom refused to follow the sangha authorities' standard, which held that monks should base their sermons on Bangkok's texts, that the sermons should be delivered solemnly, and that the audience should listen quietly and respectfully. While staying at Suan Mokkhabalarama, Buddhadasa's monastery in southern Thailand, Phayom noticed that young people in Chaiya District would stay up all night watching shadow theater. Phayom resolved to make his Buddhist sermons compel the same degree of attention from the youth. Drawing on his fine oratorical skills, Phayom is able to preach dhamma in a style not unlike that which modern state Buddhism had tried to suppress for almost a century. Like the sermons once delivered by monks of diverse regional traditions, Phayom's are not bookish; they are meant to be heard live rather than read. His mastery of rhyme, combined with an unusual sense of humor and great boldness, have enabled him to capture a massive youth audience.

Like the preachers of old traditions, Phayom is sensitive to the deeper vibrations moving through his society. He is able to adapt his dhamma talks to bear on the problems that confront people struggling to cope with rapid socioeconomic change: high rates of homicide, domestic violence, teenage pregnancy, child abuse, child prostitution, child and migrant labor, contempt for hard work, a desire for commodities, corruption, crime, addictions of all kinds (drinking, smoking, gambling, drugs, sex), and bad examples set by those paid to enforce the law—government officials, the military, and the police.

Phayom is well aware of the display of waste in religious rituals and ceremonies and the absurdity of the rules about preaching styles imposed by the sangha authorities. He pokes fun at the pomp and solemnity of the dry, standardized sermons that sangha administrators deliver. Unlike other abbots or sangha administrators, who draw only upon ancient stories about the Buddha's time to teach dhamma, Phayom draws examples from daily newspapers. His ability to frame and interpret these stories to teach dhamma reveals the insight and understated wit characteristic of the sermons of popular local preachers long ago.[40] By the late 1970s he had succeeded in persuading Thai youth that Buddhist sermons can be really "cool," and other sectors of society were also willing to hear him out.

The success of Phayom's sermons suggests that the regional style of preaching can be as effective with the urban youth of today as it was for audiences of all ages in the nineteenth century. Phayom's success is all the more striking since young people, especially in urban centers, have been strongly influenced by Western popular culture and tend to regard religion as irrelevant. Being effective as a preacher is considerably more difficult today than it was four decades ago, before radios, movies, television, and cassette players came on the scene. Nowadays Buddhist sermons must compete with high-tech entertainment, and unless a sermon is exciting or relevant to everyday life, it will not capture people's attention.

Naturally Phayom's popularity brought him criticism, much of it severe, from sangha authorities and government officials. Detractors contemptuously labeled Phayom a "teenage idol." The Department of Religious Affairs criticized him for using improper, earthy language to explain dhamma and for lack of seriousness in his delivery. He was, in short, crude and disorderly *(mai riap roi)*. But Nakhon Khemapali (titled Amonmethajan), the rector of Maha Chulalongkorn Buddhist University, came to his defense: "Some people criticize Phra Phayom for the 'crude' language that he uses in his sermons. But such people should not bother to listen if they can't take it. Let the people who can take it listen to it. It's unrealistic to expect all monks to preach the same way. There are different sorts of people in this society who like different kinds of preaching. The main thing is that his teaching can have some effect on people's behavior."[41]

Phayom in some respects resembles Ajan Man. First, Phayom has been criticized for failing to teach formal doctrine. (Man, too, was considered unqualified to teach because he lacked a theoretical background.)[42] Second, both preachers' sermons are meant to be heard, not read. In his teaching, Man used word play, riddles, puns, innuendoes and metaphors.[43] The use of extemporaneous puns and rhymes was common among skilled preachers of the Lao tradition. Thudong monks spoke highly of their Ajan's preaching skills, recalling that Man's sermons were inspiring and uplifting. Man's disciples admit that they could never match the master's oratorical skill.[44] Third, despite the differences in content and style, both Man's and Phayom's sermons have a strictly pragmatic value: their function is to facilitate the realization of the dhamma. Finally, personal experiences supplied both Man and Phayom with much of the material for their sermons. The sangha authorities, today as well as in Man's time, look at the content of these sermons as doctrinal statements with which they may agree or disagree on purely theoretical grounds. Seizing the letter of the teaching, they miss its spirit.[45] In this regard the sangha elders' attitudes have changed little since the turn of the century.

Meditation Is for Ordinary People

For most of this century, meditation has been misunderstood as a mysterious practice reserved for ascetics and hermits, not for ordinary people. This misunderstanding has prevailed among western-educated urbanites since the turn of this century when modern state Buddhism became dominant and book learning overshadowed meditation. Sangha authorities perpetuated the stereotype. Young monks with ambition saw no future in learning meditation practice from the old ajans. They followed Bangkok's example by focusing on academic learning, taking naktham and Pali exams, and earning diplomas that would come in handy should they decide to disrobe—they could always find a job in the civil service. By the middle of the twentieth century, specialization had been taken to extremes. In outlying regions, however, monks, novices, and pha khaws (male as well as female) continued to meditate, to practice the dhamma seriously, and to teach local people.

Clearly meditation practice was not beyond the reach of lay folk. The first meditation monk who tried to prove this point to high-level Bangkok monks was Abbot Sot of Wat Paknam. Sot cared greatly for laypeople and personally taught them to meditate alongside the monks. To convince them that meditation was not a difficult or ascetic practice, he taught children to meditate. Before Sot started popularizing meditation there, people in that town had seen only monks and mae chis meditate.

Thudong monks, of course, knew that meditation was good for all people everywhere. In their wandering in the North, the Northeast, and Laos they met many villagers who were eager to try meditation. Man found widespread interest in "Phu Thai villages, Black Tai villages, Lao Song villages. All of them were Buddhists. The Phu Thai had stronger faith than other groups. In meditation practice they could easily attain a one-pointed mind. But the Lao Song were not so good at it. In any case, they all supported thudong monks."[46]

When thudong monks said people came to learn the dhamma, they often meant learning meditation. "People in this area are keen about learning the dhamma," Man told Wiriyang as the two were walking through Na Kae District (Nakhon Phanom Province) in 1943. "Everywhere we have stayed, people have always come with flower offerings to ask the monks to teach them to phawana" (M3, 69). Man recalled that wherever he and his teacher went, village monks, novices, and laypeople came to practice meditation under their guidance. "Many laypeople who worked hard in their meditation practice were able to reach more advanced levels than monks. This fact made the monks work harder, since they did not want to lag behind the laypeople" (M3, 67–68). Meditation practice appealed to villagers because it is practical and the results are concrete. It gave them confidence in their powers of concentration, and this confidence served to fend off their fear of tigers, ghosts, or spirits. Villagers saw that thudong monks were able to travel through tiger-infested areas and stay in caves inhabited by spirits. They believed that the monks were speaking the truth when they told them that if they concentrated their minds and meditated upon buddho, they would not be attacked by ghosts.

Meditation also enabled people to understand the dhamma without reading texts. Some of Man's disciples, monks as well as laypeople, were illiterate, yet they could understand and teach the dhamma competently because their knowledge came from the depth of their meditation practice.[47] One old man from Phon Village in Chiang Khwang, who had learned the dhamma from practicing meditation, was able to teach meditation to other disciples. He had never studied texts, but he was well respected among thudong monks. An illiterate monk named Niam, a close disciple of Man's and a skilled meditator, was likewise much respected.

Niam was able to help less experienced monks solve problems that arose in their meditation practice, a skill that some literate thudong monks did not have (Wi, 87–89).

The importance of meditation practice is evident in the local term for knowledge acquired in monastic life: *wicha akhom* (magical knowledge). Magical knowledge was highly valued in environments where spirit worship was prominent.[48] One acquired it by living an ascetic life, observing the required precepts, and practicing meditation. A monk's knowledge remained intact after he disrobed, provided that he continued to live an ascetic life. Such a person could become a healer, a mau tham, and help people overcome their fear of spirits.[49]

Like their contemporaries in the nineteenth-century West, the rationalist leaders of Siam did not appreciate the value of meditation and made a conscious turn away from "superstition" toward "science."[50] Local Buddhist traditions, which emphasized meditation, were associated with mysticism, and meditation fell from favor among the urban elites.

Women as Spiritual Equals

One consequence of modern state Buddhism's preference for study over practice is that it devalued lay asceticism. Meditation practice was, in principle, open to anyone—monks, novices, male and female pha khaws, lay practitioners, illiterate persons, and children. Bua compared his meditation tradition to a forest university which "covers a vast area, far longer and wider than any other secular university. Moreover, it can accept more students— men and women, bhikkhus and lay disciples, irrespective of nationality, caste, sex, age and prior academic qualities. It is open all day and every day throughout the year . . . day and night, seven days of the week."[51] By contrast, the study of religious texts was an activity restricted to monks and novices. While men who wanted to receive education could become monks, this avenue was not open to women. Their limited opportunity for Buddhist education has meant that women assumed an inferior status. Under the dominance of modern state Buddhism, women's prestige in religious communities declined. This is most noticeable in the changing views concerning ordination and merit making, in the practice of going for refuge in the Triple Gem, and in the taking of precepts.

Modern state Buddhism places great emphasis on the correctness of the ordination rituals, which have to be performed in official temples, within the proper boundary-stone markers, by Bangkok-appointed preceptors, and accompanied by the proper Pali recitation. Among regional traditions, ordination was more informal; it consisted of going for refuge in the Triple Gem and being recognized and acknowledged by the religious community. Laymen and laywomen could receive (lay) ordination—as pha khaws.[52] These renunciates enjoyed a higher status than the pha khaws we see in monasteries today. They felt that they were full members of the religious community, not just supporters of monks and temples.

In regional traditions there were prominent women renunciates but their identities and teachings do not appear in official records because they were devoted to meditation rather than scholastic training.[53] Nevertheless, some of these women ascetics remained in the memory of elderly people and monks. There is plenty of evidence that teachers of regional Buddhist traditions held female ascetics in high esteem.

At the turn of this century, female pha khaws still followed their local tradition of pilgrimaging. A Westerner surveying northern Siam once came across a group of these white-robed women traveling about the countryside. They were carrying their belongings and camping out on their own, much like wandering monks. "Leaving Chiang Dao, I met four old ladies on a pilgrimage to Taptao Cave," McCarthy writes. "The youngest one was over sixty. Dressed in white, in a habit like a nun's, they had walked from Lakawn, and had been to Prabat [Phrabat, the Buddha's Footprint] Si Roi. They told me they would not be sorry if they died when making their pilgrimage. To lighten their burdens, I undertook the care of some few things they were carrying, and promised to have them safely delivered at the cave."[54] During the first half of this century, the isolated settings of caves or hermitages provided an environment conducive to intensive religious practice, and the earnestness of the white-robed ascetics in their spiritual endeavors was greatly appreciated by the lay community.

In their accounts, thudong monks acknowledged that laypeople who observed the eight precepts could attain higher levels of meditation than monks if they practiced seriously.[55] They generally admitted, too, that women have a high capacity for understanding the dhamma and can attain high levels of jhāna and supernormal knowledge. In their wandering lives, thudong monks met many laywomen and mae chis (or *mae khaw*, as they were also called) who surpassed monks in their meditation. Lui recollects meeting two mae chis of a local tradition in the Northeast who were spiritually more advanced than himself. The encounter took place in 1933, when he was spending the rains retreat in a cave on a mountain near Phon-ngam Village in Kut Bak District, Sakon Nakhon. One day Lui went to the village for almsround. Villagers told him about two mae chis named Jan and Yau, who resided at a wat near Songkhon Forest Village. They believed that the two had supernormal powers. When the rains retreat was over and Lui had an opportunity to discuss dhamma with the two mae chis, he realized that their understanding of the dhamma, derived from meditation practice, was deeper than his own. He was deeply impressed. Back at his cave, he kept thinking, "If these women can master it [their meditation technique], why can't I?"[56] So he worked harder in his meditation, day and night, until he mastered the meditation method that the two renunciates had been practicing.

In his wandering through remote villages, Man occasionally came across women ascetics. For example, in the mid 1940s at Pheu Tree Village, where the inhabitants were Yau, Man met an eighty-year-old white-robed laywoman. He recognized her high attainment and told his disciples that she had surpassed many monks.[57] Discussions she held with Man about the experience of meditation fascinated the less advanced monks and novices (who, however, believed she possessed the psychic power to read a person's character, and therefore kept their guard).

Thudong monks often supervised the meditation of female practitioners, sometimes their own mothers. Man's, Thet's, and Juan's mothers were all ordained as mae chis and stayed with their sons during rains retreats. As a mae chi, Man's mother stayed with him for six years. Before he left for the North in 1926, she traveled with him on foot from Sakon Nakhon to a village in Ubon, accompanied by a number of thudong monks and novices. Thet's mother, too, was ordained as a mae chi and learned meditation from her son. Thet's recollection of his mother's attitude toward illness indicates that she had made considerable progress in her meditation practice. She stayed with him during the year 1947, shortly before she died from infected sores and ulcers. Thet believed that the reason his mother did not suffer greatly was the mindfulness that she had developed under his supervision. Having practiced meditation at the wat and learned how to contend with the pain and disease, she calmly accepted her approaching death. Juan's mother, too, became a mae chi and spent a rains retreat with him. He converted his mother from her belief in spirit-worship by teaching her to meditate. After she died in 1949, Juan's teacher, Khaw, told him that she had attained the level of anāgāmī, only a step away from complete enlightenment (J, 40–41).

Before or beyond Bangkok's influence, women actively participated in their religious communities as skilled meditators, healers, or teachers and were highly respected by local people. Meditation masters generally held female practitioners in high esteem, considering them comparable to monks.[58] Buddhadasa recalls that in the 1920s in Chaiya district (Surat Thani) several mae chis resided in one of the five village monasteries in the subdistrict. The most revered mae chi continued her practice of daily almsround. "Phak, who was about the same age as my mother, used to live a thudong life. [In Phumriang] she was the only mae chi who went on almsround. She was much revered by the village folk. During her almsround she got more food than the monks. When I was ordained she was quite old and no longer went wandering. She used to follow her ajan on a thudong along with a male pha khaw. Now she stays put and takes care of the wat. She is beloved by the villagers. Whenever she wants something, her lay supporters comply."[59]

In many local traditions, female renunciates were respected by monks as well as local laypeople, and they attracted many personal followers. The existence of several highly respected independent samnaks run by women renunciates in Ratchaburi and Phetburi (provinces southwest of Bangkok) is testimony to the high status of women in regional traditions. Two of the foremost women meditation teachers in this century were Ki Nanayon (1901–1978) and Naeb Mahaniranon (1897–1983). Ki, a native of Ratchaburi, taught meditation to laywomen in her meditation samnak at Suan Luang Hill in Ratchaburi Province.[60] Naeb was born in Kanchanaburi, a province on the border of Thailand and Burma, and in her thirties began meditation practice under the guidance of Thanta Wilasa, the Burmese abbot of Wat Prok in Bangkok. At the time Wat Prok was a monastery of a Burmese tradition; the abbot spoke Burmese and Shan but not Thai (today the abbot is Thai). Naeb, who became well known for her teaching of vipassanā meditation and abhidhamma, established meditation centers in many parts of Suphanburi Province. By the 1970s she headed over twenty meditation centers throughout central as well as eastern Thailand. Many monks and novices studied meditation under Naeb's guidance and recognized her as their main dhamma teacher.[61]

Regional abbots publicly recognized female renunciates who had advanced far in their practice. If conditions were right, some abbots would not hesitate to give full ordination to women, making them *bhikkhunī* (nuns). After the passage of the 1902 Sangha Act, however, abbots of local traditions lost this power. One such preceptor, the abbot of Yoi Mountain Monastery (Wat Khao Yoi) in Phetburi (southern Thailand) continued to follow the local tradition.[62] In 1932, three decades after the passage of the Sangha Act, this abbot ordained two *sāmaṇerī* (female novices)—they were sisters—as bhikkhunīs.[63] Their father, who had supported their ordination first as sāmaṇerīs in 1928 and then as bhikkhunīs, had built them a temple, Wat Nariwong ("Female Lineage Monastery").

Sangha authorities in Bangkok, however, ordered the two bhikkhunīs to disrobe and declared the ordination invalid. Two members of the Sangha Council—Phra Satsanasophon of Wat Makut (Thammayut) and Somdet Phuthakhosajan of Wat Suthat (Mahanikai)—commented that ordaining women as bhikkhunīs could only be the act of a crazy person. The abbot who was suspected of giving the ordination was defrocked.

Before they were compelled to disrobe, the two women continued to follow their own local tradition. From the South they traveled to various provinces in the Central Plains. People offered them food on almsround, which suggests that female monastics were not an unfamiliar sight. People in Saraburi, for example, treated them with respect. They stayed at the Buddha's Footprint Monastery, Wat Phra Phutthabat. Here "it was local custom for laypeople to put only cooked rice in the bowl, placing other dishes on a tray held by the temple boy who followed the monks on alms-rounds. The bhikkhunis had no temple boy to follow them, and for the first three days they received only cooked rice. When the local people realized this, they assured them that food would be brought for them to the temple. Other [mae chis] joined them, and together they formed a group of eight."[64]

Although some temples offered them shelter (they stayed with the local mae chis), others refused for fear of reprisal from the authorities. In Suphanburi Province, the abbot of Dhamma Wheel Monastery (Wat Kongchak), acting against the wishes of sangha authorities in Bangkok, allowed the two bhikkhunīs to stay in his wat. The abbot explained that it was a custom of his wat—a custom according to local tradition, that is—to give shelter to any monastics who followed good practice. He saw no reason to turn down these two well-behaved women.

In recent decades, Buddhist feminists have advocated opening up the religious sphere to more participation by women. Chatsumarn, for example, comments that Thai Buddhism is traditionally conservative. She points out that many Thai women have wanted to receive full ordination, but the Thai Sangha Council opposes the idea of renewing the bhikkhunī lineage. Sangha elders in Bangkok have always insisted that the bhikkhunī lineage in Theravada Buddhism is extinct and cannot be renewed. They refer to the Pali vinaya rule stating that five senior bhikkhunīs must be present in addition to five bhikkhus if the bhikkhunī ordination is to be valid.

If we look at this event in the context of so-called Thai Buddhism (that is, modern state Buddhism), the Buddhist feminist is right to assert that the Thai sangha is narrow-minded. Regional Buddhist traditions were much more flexible and open-minded, however. Although he violated a literal reading of the vinaya, the local abbot who performed the bhikkhunī ordination in 1932 probably believed that full ordination for women would benefit not only the women themselves but also the monastery, the sangha, and the community as a whole.

In the forest tradition, many thudong masters believed that women were capable of the highest spiritual attainment. They often referred to female monastics as exemplary teachers. Perhaps the most telling account is from Juan, who in 1955 had a vision of an enlightened bhikkhunī coming to instruct him. "One night I had a vision in which a bhikkhunī appeared. She was magnificent. Before she started preaching dhamma, I asked her who she was. She told me who she was and revealed that she was an arahat. Then she bowed to me. I was taken aback. Having learned that she was an arahat I was about to bow to her in return, but she stopped me. Her gesture reminded me of a vinaya rule in which the Buddha requires a bhikkhunī to bow to a monk, even when the bhikkhunī is an arahat and the monk has been ordained for only a day."[65] Juan says that her dhamma, which she taught him with much compassion, moved him deeply.

Sangha authorities, who favored monasticism in the purely formal sense, did not share local people's attitude toward female renunciates. They eventually suppressed the custom of female ascetics going wandering or going on almsround. When the Thammayut elders later came around to approving thudong practice in 1939, their recognition did not extend to mae chis. They continued to admonish any monk who took mae chis along on wanderings or pilgrimages.[66]

From the sangha authorities' perspective, women posed a threat to the monks' purity. But meditation masters observed that the reverse was also true: "For women who would cultivate their hearts to a purity that transcends all suffering, they should contemplate the dangers of the opposite sex, the male, which forms their object of physical gratification. By seeing the fault and harm in this way they will also come to dispassion, as in the case of the elder Upalavanna Bhikkhuni who once declared something to the effect that . . . 'I have seen the harm of all sensual desires. Whenever sensual desire besets someone's heart it obscures and blinds them.' "[67]

FROM TRADITION TO FASHION

Although urban people recently have begun to admire ascetic monks, at the turn of this century educated urbanites perceived the thudong practice as backward, uncivilized, old-fashioned, and standing in the way of westernization and modernization. The thudong monks' ignorance of status distinctions and elite manners made them contemptible. The life they led in the forest was not only irrelevant but foolish.

Whereas the urban dwellers' feelings ranged from condescension to indifference to adoration depending on the fashion, rural people's regard for thudong monks, especially in remote areas, did not change. They generally revered forest ascetics or meditation monks. Forest monks' accounts indicate that no matter how low townspeople's opinions of thudong monks might fall, villagers of various ethnic identities were unstinting in their support for the wandering ascetics. Forest-dwelling villagers provided the milieu in which the thudong tradition could exist and thrive. Certainly the credit for the survival of the thudong tradition belongs to the villagers[68] and not to the urban elite who eventually "discovered" the tradition and then claimed the monks as their own.

Within the Thammayut order during the early decades of this century, the sangha leader Uan was known for his disdain of thudong monks regardless of their nikais.[69] When he eventually came around to support thudong monks, pariyat monks of the same order were appalled. This happened when Somdet Uan became convinced of the importance of meditation practice (through the influence of Fan and Li). In 1953 Uan asked Li to train monks, novices, and lay followers at Wat Boromniwat in Bangkok, and a number of laypeople, monks, and novices from other temples started coming. When even more laypeople came the following year, some book-learning monks residing in this Thammayut wat schemed to get rid of him. "A number of bad events began to interfere," Li recalls. "Some monks became envious and started looking for ways to spoil things. I'd rather not name names."[70]

Until the early 1950s, the Thammayut elders in Bangkok did not really see these Lao thudong monks of the Northeast as a significant part of the Thammayut order.[71] In Thet's opinion, local people began to support meditation monks in the 1950s because of the way Wat Mahathat, the center of Mahanikai order, was promoting meditation practice. "Phra Ajan Man's disciples have been practicing meditation for over fifty years. But we never advertised. When the other side [Wat Mahathat] promoted meditation practice, inevitably it affected us. We became famous [in Phuket]" (T2, 94). An anonymous source confirmed Thet's opinion: "Seeing the success of Phimontham's program of popularizing *Vipassana* meditation throughout the country, Wat Bovonniwet [headquarters of the Thammayut order] engaged in the counter-campaign of popularising and celebrating the achievements of the provincial forest meditation teachers like Acharn Mun, Acharn Fun, Luang Pu Waen, and Acharn Maha Boowa, who are all of the Thammayut sect."[72]

In the mid 1970s after the royal family visited some of Man's disciples, the forest monks became well known nationwide. The upper echelon of society (military officers, politicians, business owners, and corporate heads) began to seek them out. Within less than a century, thudong monks had risen from the bottom of the national sangha hierarchy to the top, and from being despised as vagabonds (by urban elites) to being venerated as saints. The unsophisticated bumpkins were now fashionable and "in." Forest monks' cremations, attended by the royal family and several million people, were grander than those of the Sangha Council's members.

Although the regional tradition of pilgrimages was condemned by Bangkok authorities at the turn of this century, today this religious activity has become popular, albeit in a different form. Before state Buddhism became dominant monks and laypeople of local traditions would walk to pilgrimage sites in their region. In recent decades, urban people have begun to flock to the forest monasteries in the Northeast where the forest monks' ashes or relics are kept. This is not a walking pilgrimage, nor an exercise in ascetic living along the way, but a quick tour in an air-conditioned bus. Among urban Thai people this is called "looking for merit."[73] It entails visiting the forest monasteries, paying respects to venerated teachers (or to their relics), and making offerings. Within a week or ten days, pilgrims can visit as many as seven forest monasteries. (One can almost hear, "If today is Tuesday, this must be Wat Pa Phong, and tomorrow is Wat Phu Jau Kau.") Cha, abbot of Wat Pa Phong, finds little of value in dhamma tours. He sees them as proof, if proof were needed, that Thai society has degenerated.

> These days people are going all over the place looking for merit. Wat Pa Phong has become a stopover point. Some people are in such a hurry I don't even get a chance to see or speak to them. Most of them are looking for merit. I don't see many looking for a way out of wrongdoing. They're so intent on get-

ting merit they don't know where they're going to put it. It's like trying to dye a dirty unwashed cloth. . . .

Sometimes they go looking for merit by the busload. Maybe they even argue on the bus, or they're drunk. Ask them where they're going and they say they're looking for merit. They want merit but they don't give up vice. They'll never find merit that way.

. . . If the mind is virtuous and skillful we don't have to take a bus all over the countryside looking for merit. Even sitting at home we can attain to merit. But most people just go looking for merit all over the countryside without giving up their vices. (C2, 1–3)

All of Man's disciples discussed in this book became meditation masters in their own right with their own lineages and followers. Thudong monks such as Li, Thet, Bua, and Cha had Western disciples who spread this meditation tradition to Western countries. For example, by 1976 Cha's disciples had established over twenty branch samnaks in the Northeast. Another wat near Wat Pa Phong, the International Forest Monastery (Wat Pa Nanachat), was especially designed for Western monks and students. By 1988 over eighty monasteries in Cha's lineage had been established in the Northeast as well as several branch monasteries and associated centers in Western countries. Most notable among the latter is the large monastery in Hemel Hempstead, England.[74] In the United States, a forest monastery has been established in California, run by an American monk of Li's lineage.[75] The appeal of these thudong masters' teachings to people of different nationalities and walks of life attests to their universal message.

Conclusion

The wandering forest monk tradition, whose history spans three generations from the formation of the modern Thai state until the present, developed within a specific natural and sociocultural ecosystem. When that ecosystem changed—when the forests disappeared and the forest communities vanished or were transformed—the tradition could no longer persist. Those forest monks of Ajan Man's lineage who survived into the 1990s were all settled in monasteries. No longer were they encountering opposition from "mainstream" Buddhism; instead they were receiving ample material support, high status, and frequent praise. This loss of autonomy and isolation had an impact on the monks, of course. As Thanissaro Bhikkhu points out, the forest tradition's very popularity may soon lead to its demise.[1]

It appears that although urban people like having forest monks to venerate, they tend to venerate them as symbols and remain unaffected by the message that the monks hope to convey. The habits of city or town dwellers and their lack of interest in the dhamma have puzzled many forest monks. The thudong masters have found it strange that urban people in general expect spiritual rewards to come their way without the expenditure of effort. Unlike villagers of local traditions, townspeople hope to learn the dhamma or to acquire merit without practicing meditation or observing precepts. They expect monks to cater to their whims by giving them hints on lottery numbers, sacralizing their amulets, or sprinkling them with holy water—anything but practicing the dhamma. Cha, in particular, was discouraged with the general level of interest Thai people had in the dhamma. He felt that people from Bangkok and other provinces flocked to his forest wat merely to take a look at him. According to a Western disciple, Cha often said he felt like a monkey on a string. People came to gawk at him, poke him, and watch him jump. "When I get tired maybe they throw me a banana."[2]

Our understanding of the thudong monks' lives has relied heavily on their recollections, observations, and expressions of feeling or opinion. Of course these monks had their own outlooks, agendas, and biases. The task was to see exactly what these were, and how they compared to those of bureaucratic or scholarly monks. I have not given equal time to these other monks for the simple reason that they have already received thorough treatment in writing. Nor have I attempted to assemble the often fragmentary information about regional Buddhist traditions into a coherent picture. I have assumed, along with Reginald Ray, that we can best understand Buddhism in Thailand "not by arriving at some supposedly balanced and objective overview, but rather by hearing clearly the different voices that have spoken—without being too put off by contrary perspectives or trying too hard to resolve contradictions."[3]

I hope this study will encourage further research into the character and shape of early Buddhist traditions and various local monastic communities in Siam/Thailand. The questions raised here —What kind of evidence should be used to understand Buddhism in Thailand? Does modern state Buddhism represent a departure from or a continuation of preexisting cultural traditions? What essentially constituted the early traditions?—are large and contentious ones. Unless we acknowledge the existence of regional diversity and study religious groups and traditions in relation to one another and to the state, we cannot hope to understand fully the dynamics of Buddhist practices in Thailand (or of Theravada Buddhism in general).

The portrait of the sangha in Thailand as drawn from the wandering monks' and village monks' accounts is a complex one. Several hundred Buddhist nikais coexisted in Siam before the country became a modern nation-state, and in remote parts of the country these regional traditions continued until the latter half of this century. One of the most important factors allowing peoples of various ethnic affiliations to maintain their culture, languages, and religious customs was their isolation and the absence of modern technology. The conformity to a single type or pattern visible today—a "Thai" Buddhism—is neither traditional nor natural. It is a historical product. Today's hierarchical and bureaucratic national sangha is, in terms of the cultural histories of ethnic groups in Siam, an aberration; it is the legacy of the 1902 Sangha Act, which sought to mold diverse cultural and religious traditions into a single, centralized, and uniform type. This standardized Buddhism, which undermined existing traditions, is often mistakenly seen as "traditional" Thai Buddhism.

People generally think that Buddhism in Thailand today is fragmenting into various factions, and they attribute religious divisiveness to some external force like capitalism or modernization. The unexamined assumption here, common in scholarly work as well as in official government and mass media writings, is that the diversity is new. O'Connor contends that this consensus about diversity and its causes is remarkable in light of the religious diversity of just a century ago: "It shows people of differing pasts are becoming one. As they acquire a common past, they learn to identify a religious 'change' by whatever deviates from *the* 'traditional' religion, even if this fixed point was not their tradition."[4] As O'Connor observes, what everyone identifies as traditional Buddhism "is not how religion actually was. It is an imagined religion, a past already 'corrected' by the 1902 Sangha Act."[5] My examination of the lives of wandering meditation monks shows that Buddhism in Thailand was diversified from the start and remained so as recently as fifty years ago.

Throughout this book I have tried to avoid using such problematic terms as "traditional Buddhism," "modern Buddhism," "sangha reform," or "Thai Buddhism." These terms are vague and have led to considerable confusion about the origin of Buddhism in present-day Thailand. To be historically correct, the origin of this contemporary Buddhism—the Buddhism associated with the modern Thai state—dates back only a century and a half, when the Thammayut sect was established and called itself a reformed order. This sect became the model for modern state Buddhism and the basis for standardization and reform. Local religious practices and cultural values were first undermined by the legal code of the 1902 Sangha Act; later they were wholly transformed by three decades of the National Social and Economic Development Plans starting in 1961. Once Bangkok imposed modern state Buddhism on the local traditions, much of the preexisting diversity went unrecorded, was dismissed as degenerate, was ignored or trivialized by "official" histories, and is now largely forgotten.[6]

The conventional distinction between what is "mainstream" and what is "deviant" in Thai Buddhism is largely a fiction created by official history. If we look at "traditional" Buddhism through the lens of the modern Thai state and take the centralization reforms as "an agent of continuity,"[7] we are likely to treat local Buddhist customs as aberrant, just as official inspectors did. In fact, these ethnic groups embodied values that are, in many ways, quintessentially Buddhist. As this book has suggested, it is precisely that which has seemed the most strange, caused the most offense, and was the hardest to digest that was really most significant and creative.

The so-called centralizing reforms meant different things to those doing the reforming and those being reformed. To the reformers, the goal was to put monks of various ethnic affiliations under Bangkok's regulations, bring them closer to the Pali texts (as interpreted by the sangha authorities), and free the country from what they regarded as superstition. By imposing Bangkok's standard texts, rituals, and monastic rules, the sangha authorities assumed that there could be a single way of understanding or interpreting the Buddha's teachings. To those being reformed—the monks and laypeople of different ethnic identities—reforms meant the disruption of their religious customs and practices. Modern state Buddhism imposed a particular way of seeing and being; its symbols, values, and customs, its language and laws, were alien to the monks and villagers of the territories that Bangkok brought under its control.[8]

In Thailand today, diversity in Buddhist conduct is looked upon with suspicion. This might be because scholars as well as popular writers, both past and present, argue that Buddhist practices in outlying areas were corrupt and impure. Thai people today see one superstar monk after another fall from grace; they then assume that regional monks of the past must have been equally bad.[9] As a consequence, people tend to confuse diversity with laxity. In fact, diversity within the sangha is crucial to the survival of Buddhism. Since society is comprised of people from various backgrounds with diverse needs, it makes sense that there be all kinds of monks to serve those spiritual needs.[10] As a leader of a student council of monks observes, "It is better to allow several nikais to exist than to put all monks under one nikai. The weakness of limiting monks to one nikai is that there are no other nikais to compare with. A variety of nikais does not necessarily lead to religious deterioration. Nor does it mean that monks are not unified. Actually, when there are several nikais they serve as checks on one another. Monks of each nikai would try their best to uphold their own practices and principles. Each nikai would strive to improve itself to be relevant to change in society so it would not die out."[11]

A balanced history of Buddhism in Siam/Thailand must take a variety of local traditions into account. Important questions should be asked: Why did local monks and people follow particular forms of Buddhism? What bearing did the local tradition have on spiritual life? How did following the Buddhist path help people? To answer these questions, we need intensive studies of monks as well as lay ascetics in various nikais or lineages. Living in regions that had absorbed diverse religious traditions, local monks were bound to be both more tolerant and more innovative. For example, Lao and Khmer village abbots, known for their skill in magical arts, were much respected wherever people believed in the power of spirits. These magician monks *(keji ajans)* helped people cope with spirits and manage their fears. Many of these revered ajans followed ascetic practices, carved amulets by hand, possessed healing powers, and thus were able to persuade people to live out the dhamma. These monks were very different from the present-day keji ajans who routinely bless factory-made amulets. Other abbots of local traditions were great preachers known for their oratorical skills and their mastery of storytelling in local languages. They became abbots because of their practical skills, their expertise in local customs, and their ability to frame religious teachings in the context of folk culture. We need studies of these and other local traditions, studies that will be sensitive to multiple dimensions and rooted in local histories. Although in official histories, government records, and newspapers or popular magazines these local monks (now deceased) are usually perceived or portrayed as "Thai" or as natives of particular provinces, their distinct cultural or ethnic characteristics must be recognized.

The wandering monks and their meditation tradition perhaps have something to teach us, here in the West. For one thing, these monks advocated meditation in action. They tested their skills in challenging environments, and they made human suffering—illness, pain, fear, fatigue, other hardships—essential to their discipline. Although we may not wish to follow this path, we should recognize it as a valid religious calling. Another thing we learn from the forest monks is that people's lives connect deeply to nature —to prominent themes in the social, cultural, and environmental history of a community. We hear the forest monks say that wilderness is indispensable to culture. Having lived in areas where nature was left undisturbed, these monks have an accurate sense of the impact of modernization upon it. National economic development and the population explosion changed most of the Northeast from a territory covered with dense forests to a treeless, barren expanse. The history of religion in twentieth century Thailand is inextricably connected to this ecological destruction—a major transformation of the human relationship with nonhuman nature. As a monk who helped create a strong local forest preservation movement tells us, "Through protecting the forests we are simultaneously protecting the animals and the well-being of communities, the essential basis for morality to grow."[12]

In ways that usually go unnoticed, the forest monks' view of nature is accessible to the present age. The thudong monks approached wild animals with respect and humility. They realized that it was they who were trespassing in the animals' territory. They believed that animals are fellow beings in samsara and deserve equal opportunity to gain kammic merit. This conviction runs counter to the prevailing attitude among people, monks included, who live in urban areas and have little or no connection with nature. Thudong monks, who were at home in the wild, knew of their kinship with nature.

This historical study has done more than set the wandering forest monks in their local contexts: it has redefined the very nature of the evidence used to construct the history of the sangha in Thailand. Such a history cannot rely solely on written documents left by sangha officials, on scriptures, or on other authoritative texts. It must also make the best possible use of the wealth of detailed information contained in the life stories of town and village monks, the recollections of village elders, and the histories of local wats and settlements. Since local religious practices were often passed on orally, the most obvious place to find out how religion worked and changed is in the memories of elderly monks and villagers, wherever they may live and whatever their ethnic identity.

We have seen that Buddhism survived and flourished among ethnic groups in Siam because it was a grassroots, community-based religion combining spiritual pursuits with practical concerns. Revered abbots of local traditions—Lao, Mon, Khmer, Shan, Yuan, Siamese—were known for their ingenuity, adaptability, flexibility, tolerance, and their ability to make the dhamma relevant to everyday life. These ajans were each representative of a Buddhist tradition of a particular time and place. Differences among these traditions reflect the diverse ways in which the Buddha's teachings have been experienced through the ages. Studying the ajans and their traditions will contribute to a clearer understanding of the long history of Buddhism and of the historical role of religious diversity. We therefore ought not dismiss these monks as "marginal" or "deviant." Their individual qualities, their local knowledge, and their experiential wisdom deserve our serious consideration. They are an important link in our understanding of contemporary Buddhist societies in Thailand and its neighbors. We have much to learn from them.

Abbreviations

Citations of frequently used works—monks' memoirs, autobiographies, biographies, recollections, and teachings—are made parenthetically in the text and notes. The works are identified by the following abbreviations:

C1   Chah [Cha], Ajahn. *Food for the Heart.* Ubon, 1992.

C2   Chah [Cha], Ajahn. *Living Dhamma.* Ubon, 1992.

C3   *Suphatthanuson chut Phothiyan Thera* [Biography of Phra Ajan Cha]. Ubon, 1976.

F   Suphon Nachom, *Chiwa prawat lae patipatha Phra Ajan Fan Ajaro* [Biography of Phra Ajan Fan Ajaro]. Bangkok, 1977.

J   Juan Kulachetto, "Attano prawat" [My life]. Bangkok, 1981.

La   La Khempatato, Phra. *Chiwa prawat Luang Pu La Khempatato* [Memoirs of Ven. Grandfather La]. Bangkok, 1989.

Li1 Lee [Li] Dhammadaro. *The Autobiography of Phra Ajaan Lee.* Nonthaburi, 1992.

Li2 Li Thammatharo. *Chiwa prawat khaung Phra Sutthithamrangsi (Than Phau Li)* [Memoirs of Ven. Father Li]. Bangkok, 1962.

M1   Boowa [Bua] Nyannasampanno. *The Venerable Phra Acharn Mun Bhuridatta Thera.* Bangkok, 1982.

M2   Bua Yannasampanno, Phra Ajan. *Prawat Than Phra Ajan Man Phurithatta Thera* [Biography of Phra Ajan Man]. Bangkok, 1971.

M3 Wiriyang Sirintharo [Yanwiriyajan], Phra. "Prawat Phra Ajan Man." Bangkok, 1978.

T1 Tate [Thet], Ajahn. *The Autobiography of a Forest Monk.* Bangkok, 1993.

T2 Thet Thetrangsi, Phra Ajan. *Attano prawat lae thammathetsana* [My life and dhamma teachings]. Bangkok, 1981.

W Wan Uttamo. "Atta chiwa prawat" [My life]. Bangkok, 1981.

Wi Wiriyang Sirintharo [Yanwiriyajan], Phra. "Tai saman samneuk" [With common sense]. Bangkok, 1978.

Wn *Anuson Luang Pu Waen Sujinno* [Biography of Ven. Grandfather Waen]. Chiang mai, 1985.

Notes

INTRODUCTION

1. The name of the country was changed to Thailand in 1941 during the Phibun regime. I will use the terms "Siam" and "Siamese" to refer to the country and to the ethnic Thai in pre-1941 contexts, and "Thailand" and "Thai" in post-1941 contexts. As a result of the nationalist policy of the Phibun government, the term "Thai" came to encompass all ethnic groups in Thailand and not just the Siamese, who were concentrated in the Central Plains. (Here I am following Thongchai Winichakul, *Siam Mapped: A History of the Geo-Body of a Nation* [Honolulu: University of Hawai'i Press, 1994], 18.)

2. In this study the terms *wandering monk, thudong monk,* and *kammathan monk* will be used interchangeably, following the monks' own usage. The Thai *thudong* comes from the Pali *dhūtanga,* which denotes ascetic or austere practices. The literal meaning, according to Nyanatiloka, is a "means of shaking off" mental defilements. The thirteen practices are wearing patched-up robes, possessing only three robes, going out for alms, not omitting any houses on the almsround, having only one meal a day, eating out of the alms bowl, not accepting food presented afterward, dwelling in forest areas, dwelling under a tree, staying in the open or in caves or abandoned houses, visiting or staying in a cemetery, being content with whatever shelter is provided, and sleeping in the sitting position. See Nyanatiloka, *Buddhist Dictionary* (Kandy:

Buddhist Publication Society, 1980), 59; also Boowa [Bua] Nyanasam-panno, "An Account on the Dhūtaṅga Kammaṭṭhāna Bhikkhus," in *Bud-dhism in Thailand* (Bangkok: World Fellowship of Buddhists, 1980), 71–72. *Kammathan* (from the Pali *kammaṭṭhāna)* refers to meditation subjects.

3. The vinaya comprises the disciplinary rules for all monks. People today tend to associate Buddhism in Thailand with Theravada monks who recite the vinaya's 227 rules.

4. As Craig Reynolds puts it, "Each abbot was to a large extent mas-ter of his own realm. . . . The quality of monastic leadership in combi-nation with the attention the monastery received from the community determined its prosperity and influence." Craig J. Reynolds, "The Bud-dhist Monkhood in Nineteenth Century Thailand" (Ph.D. diss., Cornell University, 1972), 26.

5. Scholars screen out diversity when they construct, for the purpose of comparison, a monolithic "Thai" Buddhism. See, for example, Geof-frey Samuel's comparison of Tibetan and Theravada societies in *Civil-ized Shamans: Buddhism in Tibetan Societies* (Washington, D.C.: Smith-sonian Institution Press, 1993), 24–36, 308.

6. See Thongchai, *Siam Mapped.*

7. David Wyatt writes the following about the meuang as it existed in the pre-modern state. Meuang "is a term that defies translation, for it denotes as much personal as spatial relationships. When it is used in ancient chronicles to refer to a principality, it can mean both the town located at the hub of a network of interrelated villages and also the total-ity of town and villages which was ruled by a single *chao* 'lord'." David K. Wyatt, *Thailand: A Short History* (New Haven: Yale University Press, 1982), 7.

8. Thongchai, *Siam Mapped,* 99–100.

9. Before Tai-speaking people gained dominance in the ninth and tenth centuries, Khmer-speaking people and Khmer civilization domi-nated much of what is now Thailand. In the eighteenth century, signifi-cant numbers of new Khmer migrated into the area. William A. Smalley, *Linguistic Diversity and National Unity: Language Ecology in Thailand* (Chicago: University of Chicago Press, 1994), 137. The following discus-sion of languages draws on Smalley's work.

10. Mon people were most numerous in Pathum Thani, Nonthaburi, and Ratchaburi. They settled there as a result of wars between the Siamese of Ayuthaya and the Burmese kingdoms, wars that lasted into the early years of the nineteenth century. King Taksin (1767–1782) of Thonburi and Rama I (1782–1809) of Bangkok conferred noble titles on

the leaders of Mon settlers and drew them into the ranks of Siamese officials and the aristocracy. Reynolds, "Buddhist Monkhood," 226.

11. Lan Na is the name of an ancient northern kingdom. The term "Lanna Thai" is now gaining usage to refer to the people of the northern region of Thailand. The language they speak among themselves is called Kham Meuang. It has several major subregional dialects, of which the most important is spoken in Chiang Mai and its environs. See Smalley, *Linguistic Diversity,* 81, 85–86.

12. These were the Chiang Mai nikai, Chiang Saen nikai, Nan nikai, Lawa nikai, Mon nikai, Yaung nikai, Phrae nikai, Ngiew nikai, Mae Pala nikai, Luang nikai, the Khoen nikai, etc. See Sommai Premchit, *A List of Old Temples and Religious Sects in Chiang Mai* (Chiang Mai: Department of Sociology and Anthropology, Chiang Mai University, 1975). The name of a nikai often indicated its origin. In the nikais bearing the names Man, Thai, Mon, and Lawa, for example, Man is an ajan's name, while Thai, Mon, and Lawa are names of ethnic groups. Sommai Premchit, interview by author, 18 August 1995.

13. My current research on village abbots in regional Buddhist traditions provides evidence of this.

14. See, for example, Reynolds, "Buddhist Monkhood"; Stanley J. Tambiah, *World Conqueror and World Renouncer: A Study of Buddhism and Polity in Thailand against a Historical Background* (Cambridge: Cambridge University Press, 1976).

15. Wyatt, *Thailand,* 175.

16. Reynolds, "Buddhist Monkhood," 90.

17. Ibid., 65.

18. An exception was the Raman nikai, a Mon nikai that Mongkut treated as a distinct category. Later, however, this nikai came to be included in the Mahanikai category.

19. Wyatt, *Thailand,* 176. Monks in regional Buddhist traditions did indeed follow what their teachers had taught them.

20. During his twenty-seven years in the monkhood (1824–1851), Mongkut came into contact with a number of American and French missionaries. With them he studied Western languages and sciences: Latin, English, mathematics, and astronomy (Wyatt, *Thailand,* 177).

21. The most important kingdoms—Chiang Mai (whose ruling family also controlled Lamphun principality), Nakhon Ratchasima (Khorat), and Phuket—were the first in their respective regions to be put under the authority of the royal commissioners sent from Bangkok (ibid.).

22. The term "Tai" refers to an ethnolinguistic family of related peoples scattered from South China westward to Assam and southward

to the Malay peninsula. Within the borders of Thailand, Tai peoples include the Siamese, Yuan (northern Thai), Shan, Lu, and Lao. Richard O'Connor, "Interpreting Thai Religious Change: Temples, Sangha Reform and Social Change," *Journal of Southeast Asian Studies* 24, no. 2 (September 1993): 330.

23. Smalley observes that Thailand is a country with eighty languages *(Linguistic Diversity,* 1). In the nineteenth century it was probably even more diversified.

24. Smalley notes that the word "Thai" is used loosely both in Thai and in English. He proposes using "Standard Thai" for the Thai that has become the national language (ibid., 14). I depart from this suggestion by using "Bangkok Thai" instead. Since many residents of Bangkok speak nonstandard dialects of Thai, Bangkok Thai should be understood as referring to the dialect standardized by Bangkok and especially by the Royal Institute.

25. The Thammayut order has been politically dominant in Bangkok since the mid-nineteenth century, when its founder succeeded to the throne as Rama IV.

26. Steven J. Zack, "Buddhist Education under Prince Wachirayan Warorot" (Ph.D. diss., Cornell University, 1977), 187.

27. These periods are based partly on Mongkhon Danthanin, *Pa chumchon isan kap khau jau khau* [Forest communities in Isan and the KJK] (Bangkok: Local Development Institute, 1991), 10–12. The year 1957 corresponds to the beginning of the Sarit regime (see chap. 9). Prayong Nettayarak and Banthon Aundam see the Forest-Invasion Period as ending in 1977, not 1988, and the Forest-Closure Period as extending from 1978 to the present. They choose the 1978 date because that was the first year of the official policy of forest closure. See Prayong Nettayarak and Banthon Aundam, "Wiwatthanakan khaung kanbukboek thidin thamkin nai khetpa phak thawanauk chiang neua" [Growth of forest clearance for subsistence in the forests of the northeast region], in *Wiwatthanakan khaung kanbukbeuk thidin thamkin nai khetpa,* ed. Joemsak Pinthaung (Bangkok: Local Development Institute, 1991), 201. But in reality the forests continued to be invaded until 1989, when Thailand banned logging within its own boundaries and began coveting the timber resources of its neighbors. See Mark Mardon, "Tropical Forests: Maneuvers in the Teak Wars," *Sierra,* May/June 1991, 32.

28. Tambiah, *Buddhist Saints of the Forest and the Cult of Amulets* (New York: Cambridge University Press, 1984).

29. Ibid., 358 n. 3.

30. Bibliographical materials in Thai include Phra Ajan Bua Yannasampanno, *Prawat Than Phra Ajan Man Phurithatta Thera* [Biography

of Phra Ajan Man] (Bangkok: Si Sappada, 1971), hereafter cited as M2; *Ubon mani* [Jewel of Ubon] (Bangkok: Khurusapha, 1992); "Chiwa prawat lae patipatha Phra Ajan Wan [Life and conduct of Phra Ajan Wan]," in *Phra Udomsangwonwisut Thera (Phra Ajan Wan Uttamo)* (Bangkok: Crem. vol. Aphaidamrong Cave Wat, 1981); Phra Nanthapanyaphon, *Chiwa prawat thammanuson khaung Phra Ratwutthajan (Luang Pu Dun)* [Biography of Ven. Grandfather Dun] (Surin: Crem. vol. Luang Pu Dun, Wat Burapharam, 1985); Prajiat Khongsatra, *Luang Pu Waen Sujinno* [Ven. Grandfather Waen Sujinno] (Bangkok: Namo special issue, 1985); *Anuson Luang Pu Waen Sujinno* [Biography of Ven. Grandfather Waen] (Chiang Mai: Crem. vol. Luang Pu Waen Sujinno, Wat Doi Maepung, 1985), hereafter cited as Wn; *Suphatthanuson chut Phothiyan Thera* [Biography of Phra Ajan Cha] (Ubon Ratchathani: Vol. commemorating construction of ordination hall, Phong Forest Wat, 1976), hereafter cited as C3; Suphon Nachom, *Chiwa prawat lae patipatha Phra Ajan Fan Ajaro* [Biography of Phra Ajan Fan Ajaro] (Bangkok: Kanphim Phranakhon, 1977), hereafter cited as F; Suriphan Maniwat, "Phra Ajan Juan Kulachettho: Chiwa prawat patipatha [Biography of Phra Ajan Juan]," in Suriphan, *Phra Ajan Juan Kulachettho: chiwa prawat patipatha lae thammathetsana* (Bangkok: Crem. vol. Thauk Mountain Wat, 1981); and Phra Wiriyang Sirintharo, "Prawat Phra Ajan Man," in *Prawat Phra Ajan Man chabap sombun* [Complete biography of Phra Ajan Man] (Bangkok: Crem. vol. Grandmother Man Bunthrikun, 1978), hereafter cited as M3. Memoirs in Thai include Juan Kulachettho, "Attano prawat" [My life], in Suriphan, *Phra Ajan Juan,* hereafter cited as J; Phra La Khempatato, *Chiwa prawat Luang Pu La Khempatato* [Memoirs of Ven. Grandfather La Khempatato] (Bangkok: Sinlapa Sayam, 1989), hereafter cited as La; Li Thammatharo. *Chiwa prawat khaung Phra Sutthithamrangsi (Than Phau Li)* [Memoirs of Ven. Father Li] (Bangkok: Kathin ceremony vol. Wat Asokaram, 1962), hereafter cited as Li2; Phra Ajan Thet Thetrangsi, *Attano prawat lae thammathetsana* [My life and dhamma teachings] (Bangkok: Amarin Kanphim, 1981), hereafter cited as T2; Wan Uttamo, "Atta chiwa prawat" [My life], in *Phra Udomsangwonwisut Thera (Phra Ajan Wan Uttamo)* (Bangkok: Crem. vol. Aphaidamrong Cave Wat, 1981), hereafter cited as W; and Wiriyang, "Tai saman samneuk" [With common sense], in *Prawat Phra Ajan Man chabap sombun,* hereafter cited as Wi.

31. J. L. Taylor, *Forest Monks and the Nation-State: An Anthropological and Historical Study in Northeastern Thailand* (Singapore: Institute of Southeast Asian Studies, 1993).

32. See O. W. Wolters, *History, Culture, and Region in Southeast Asian Perspectives* (Singapore: Institute of Southeast Asian Studies, 1982).

33. A. Thomas Kirsch, "Text and Context: Buddhist Sex Roles/Culture of Gender Revisited," *American Ethnologist* 12 (May 1985): 317.

34. "The ten kinds of recollection are these: the recollection of the Buddha (the Enlightened One), recollection of the Dhamma (the Law), recollection of the Sangha (the Community), recollection of virtue, recollection of generosity, recollection of deities, recollection (or mindfulness) of death, mindfulness occupied with the body, mindfulness of breathing and recollection of peace." Buddhaghosa, *The Path of Purification (Visuddhimagga),* trans. Nyanamoli (Kandy: Buddhist Publication Society, 1979), 112.

35. The almsround (Thai: *bindabat;* Pali: *pindapada*) is the early-morning visit that a monk makes to houses where he can expect to receive a small amount of food, perhaps only rice. The monk lifts the lid of his bowl, and the lay supporter—most often a woman—places the food inside.

36. In contrast, an administrative monk's life story reads like a job resumé. The emphasis is on outer forms: titles, positions, projects. Likewise, the autobiography of a book-learning monk who has yet to develop an individual perspective stands little chance of holding our attention.

37. Thet gave this reason for giving permission to publish his memoir: "I am a truthful person. So I don't want anybody to write the story of my life after I die. I decided to write it myself because I know my life better than anyone. Otherwise after my death other people will write about it. If the person doesn't like me, he might write it according to his negative perception. He might magnify my weaknesses out of hatred. By contrast, if the author loves me he might exaggerate my goodness beyond reality." Thet, *Attano prawat,* 19.

38. La apologizes that he wrote down his recollections as they came to mind, so they are not chronological. He says he wrote about "what the mind actually sees and feels," and he hopes that nobody will take his work to "Sanam Luang" (a humorous way of asserting he would not like to be examined and graded on it). La, *Chiwa prawat,* 12–13. La's inexperience with writing makes his life story colorful and creative. He did not know what was supposed to go into a "proper" memoir.

39. Suriphan, *Phra Ajan Juan,* 2.

40. Wan's cremation volume, *Phra Udomsangwonwisut Thera,* is divided into two parts. The first, a memoir of seventy-seven pages, is henceforth cited as Wan, "Atta chiwa prawat." The second part, "Chiwa prawat lae patipatha Phra Ajan Wan" [Life and conduct of Phra Ajan Wan], is a biography compiled by a disciple.

41. Incidents mentioned in a given monk's story as it appears in a

popular magazine can be cross-checked against the incidents recounted in the biographies or memoirs published by the monks' lay followers. Articles in these popular magazines can also be used to identify monks who go unnamed in Ajan Man's biographies. Information found in these popular accounts, such as the identity of a monk who supposedly trained under Ajan Man, can be checked for discrepancies by looking at dates of birth or ordination dates. If a disciple was ordained after Man died, obviously he could not have been trained under Man's guidance.

42. Quoted in Jack Kornfield, *Living Buddhist Masters* (Kandy: Buddhist Publication Society, 1977), 163. Panyawattho, a British monk, was the first translator of Bua's dhamma talks.

CHAPTER 1: BUDDHIST TRADITIONS IN SIAM/THAILAND

1. John Calderazzo, "Meditation in a Thai Forest," *Audubon,* January 1990, 89.

2. Monthon Chanthaburi consisted of three meuangs: Chanthaburi, Rayong and Trat. Monthon Prachinburi consisted of four meuangs: Prachinburi, Chachoengsao, Nakhon Nayok, and Phanom Sarakham. See Tej Bunnag, *The Provincial Administration of Siam 1892–1915* (Kuala Lumpur: Oxford University Press, 1977), 271.

3. Monthon Phuket included the meuangs of Phuket, Krabi, Phangnga, Ranong, Takua Pa, and Trang. Tej, *Provincial Administration,* 271.

4. Monthon Nakhon Ratchasima consisted of three meuangs: Nakhon Ratchasima, Buriram, and Chaiyaphum. Monthon Ubon held four: Ubon Ratchathani, Khukhan, Sisaket, and Surin. Ibid., 271–272.

5. The northeastern region covers an area of 168,854 square kilometers, one-third of Thailand's area, about the size of the state of Washington. Prior to the 1960s more than half of it was covered with deciduous forest. Paitoon Pongsabutra, ed. *Illustrated Landforms of Thailand* (Bangkok: Chulalongkorn University Press, 1991), 66–67.

6. *Si Ubonrattanaram* [Wat Sithaung, Ubon] (Bangkok: Rongphim Mitthai, 1968), 28.

7. Khaneungnit Janthabutra, ed., *Khon di meuang Ubon* [Good people in Ubon] (Ubon: Ubon Cultural Center, 1984), 31.

8. The average age of the sangha directors was forty. The majority were Thammayut. Reynolds, "Buddhist Monkhood," 248.

9. Richard A. O'Connor, "Cultural Notes on Trade and the Tai," in *Ritual, Power and Economy: Upland-Lowland Contrasts in Mainland Southeast Asia,* ed. Susan D. Russell (De Kalb: Center for Southeast Asian Studies, Northern Illinois University, 1989), 45–46.

10. Many sangha inspectors reported such activities. They noted that

in several monasteries laypeople were not able to feed the monks because of poor crop yields. For example, in monthon Phuket, less than half of the forty-eight monasteries inspected were supported by the laity. From the education-director's report, monthon Phuket. *Ratchakijjanubeksa* [Royal Thai government gazette] 18 (5 December 1900): 62.

11. Education directors' reports. *Ratchakijjanubeksa* 16–18 (1899–1901).

12. The area around the village was first settled by three families. When the plowing season arrived, everybody who had worked in the field fell ill with fever and some people died. Believing that they were being punished by evil spirits who lived in the fields, the villagers invited monks from a monastery, Wat Pho Nachai, to work in the fields and to perform religious ceremonies to clear out the bad spirits. Since people thereafter were able to work in the fields without falling sick, they named the place Monk Field Village. Prani Bancheun, *Khwammai lae prawat tambon muban jangwat Loei* [Meanings and history of communes and villages in Loei Province] (Bangkok: O. S. Printing House, 1984), n.p.

13. Report of Phra Thepmuni, sangha head of monthon Nakhon Ratchasima. *Ratchakijjanubeksa* 17 (2 June 1901): 156.

14. For a modern expression of this idea, see Rita Gross, "After Patriarchy: Sacredness and Everyday Life," *Tricycle: The Buddhist Review* 2, no. 2 (winter 1992): 62.

15. This was at Chaiya in the southern province of Surat Thani. Samphan Kaungsamut, *Prawat chiwit lae phon-ngan khaung Phra Thepwisuthimethi* [Life and work of Buddhadasa] (Bangkok: Odian Printing, 1987), 168.

16. Li2, 4. The village wat was in Yangyophap Commune; today it is in Muang Samsip District, Ubon Ratchathani.

17. Wan does not explain what exactly the monks in his village did in their solitary retreats in their huts. Every year, many village monks went through this religious ritual (W, 36).

18. The Thai term comes from the Pali *parivasa kamma*. See Sommai Premchit and Amphay Dore, *The Lan Na Twelve-Month Traditions* (Chiang Mai: So Sap Kan Phim), 134–135. According to Sommai, who interviewed abbots in the North, today only a few monasteries continue to observe this ceremony. It became too difficult to organize the ritual, which required much support and cooperation from local people.

19. Mani Phayomyong, *Prapheni sipsaung deun lan na thai* [Twelve festivals in Lan Na Thai] (Chiang Mai: S. Sapkanphim, 1990), 77.

20. See Toem Wiphakphotjanakit, *Prawatsat Isan* [History of Isan] (Bangkok: Thammasat University Press, 1987), 605–606, 613–614.

21. Mani, *Prapheni*, 76–77.

22. Charles F. Keyes, *Thailand: Buddhist Kingdom as Modern Nation-State* (Boulder: Westview Press, 1987), 178.

23. For a discussion of the twelve festivals in the Lao tradition, see Phra Maha Kowit Siriwanno et al., *Moradok Isan* [Heritage of Isan] (Bangkok: Mahachula Buddhist University, 1990). For the most detailed discussion of the twelve festivals in the Yuan tradition see Mani, *Prapheni*.

24. James McCarthy, *Surveying and Exploring in Siam* (London: William Clowes and Sons, 1990), 76. McCarthy made this observation in meuang Phichai, monthon Phitsanulok.

25. O'Connor, "Cultural Notes," 40. O'Connor contrasts the Lao search for fertility with what he sees as a Siamese preoccupation with ranking and order. But rank and order may be more a concern for Bangkok elites than for Siamese villagers.

26. Ibid., 40. Here O'Connor cites C. Archaimbault, "Religious Structures in Laos," *Journal of the Siam Society* 52, no. 1 (1964).

27. Sujit Wongthes, "Samoson sinlapa watthanatham: bantheuk kansamruat khaung James McCarthy" [Art and culture club: Record of James McCarthy's surveys], *Sinlapa Watthanatham* 5, no. 1 (November 1983): 57.

28. The inspectors particularly singled out meuang Suphanburi in monthon Nakhon Chaisi and meuangs Ratchaburi and Samut Songkhram in monthon Ratchaburi.

29. O'Connor, "Cultural Notes," 40.

30. This is according to Sathirakoses, cited in Pranee Wongthes, "Phithikamkhabot pheua phaunkhlai khwamteungkhriat" [Rebellion rituals serving to release stress], *Sinlapa Watthanatham* 5, no. 7 (1984): 13–14.

31. Pranee, "Rebellion rituals," 15.

32. In 1940 the Thai government adopted the Western calendar and changed New Year's Day to January 1. Wyatt, *Thailand*, 255.

33. Sommai and Dore, *Lan Na Traditions*, 176.

34. Ibid., 175.

35. Boat racing during the rainy season is a tradition that Lan Na Buddhists inherited from the Yue (Sommai and Dore, *Lan Na Traditions*, 23). The drum beating competition is Lao. Monks skilled in drum making were much respected by local people (Sobin Namto, interview by author, 29 January 1996). Although Bangkok authorities forbade monks to engage in these games, the practices continued in remote villages. During the 1940s, when Sobin was a novice at a village wat in Mahasarakham, monks there still participated in these competitions. As for chess, Buddhadasa (b. 1906–1993) says that he "would include

Thai chess in the education curriculum for the young. Chess playing would help them learn how to think for themselves, to be alert,
quick thinking, astute, and shrewd. It would train them to have mindfulness and clear comprehension" (Samphan, *Prawat Phra Thepwisuthimethi*, 158).

36. This was witnessed in 1925 by Li Thammatharo, a monk at Double Marsh Village, Yangyophap Commune, Muang Samsip District,
Ubon Ratchathani. See Lee Dhammadaro [Li Thammatharo], *The Autobiography of Phra Ajaan Lee*, trans. Thanissaro Bhikkhu (Nonthaburi:
Thepphrathan, 1992), 4. Hereafter cited as Li1.

37. People were especially afraid of ghosts during wakes. Today this
is less true; people now want the monks to leave as soon as the funeral
rites are over so that they can drink and gamble. Phra Palad Wanna
Wanno, abbot of Wat Lak Hok, Damnoen Saduak District, Ratchaburi,
interview by author, 16 April 1989. In the past, the monks traveled to
laypeople's houses by rowboat. Today few monks know how to row.

38. McCarthy, *Surveying and Exploring*, 76.

39. Ariyakawi (Aun Thammarakhitto), abbot of Wat Sithaung (Thammayut) and the sangha head of meuang Ubon, forbade monks and
novices to take part in the Bun Bangfai (bamboo rocket) festival or in
drum-beating *(seng klaung)* competitions, boat racing, and horse raising.
Toem, *Prawatsat Isan*, 552.

40. Sommai and Dore, *Lan Na Traditions*, 192.

41. Juan says that the Moei and Yau monks did not seem to be concerned about the vinaya (J, 98). The Moei and Yau left Laos after the
French colonization and settled in what is now Nongkhai Province. Juan
recalls that "in the old days, these people were called *lao kaut* [the hug-
ging Lao] or *lao kum* [the holding Lao] because of a peculiar tradition. If
a visitor did not kiss, hug, or hold a daughter of the house after arriving,
the hosts considered him *phit phi* [in violation of custom] and he would
be fined. He was not allowed to go beyond touching her, however. This
tradition disappeared after the area became accessible by roads."

42. The sangha inspectors' reports on monasteries in all monthons
provide evidence of this.

43. John P. Ferguson, "The Symbolic Dimensions of the Burmese
Sangha" (Ph.D. diss., Cornell University, 1975), 19.

44. Education director's report on monthon Ayuthaya. This report
and those cited below were published in *Ratchakijjanubeksa* 16–18
(1899–1901).

45. Education directors' reports on monthons Ratchaburi, Chumphon, Phuket, Nakhon Sawan, and Chaisi. The *Questions of King*

Milinda (Pali: *Milindapañha)*, an important noncanonical Theravada work, takes the form of a dialog between a monk named Nagasena and the Greek Menander.

46. Paraphrased from education directors' reports on monthons Isan and Nakhon Ratchasima. Here the sangha officials did not make a distinction between the various types of oral narratives. They considered myths, legends, and folktales all the same.

47. Sommai and Dore, *Lan Na Traditions*, 77.

48. Ibid., 88.

49. Mani recalled his experience of learning to recite the Wetsandon Chadok as a novice at Wat Khilek Noi in Mae Rim District, Chiang Mai, in 1944. Mani, *Prapheni*, 51–52.

50. Ibid., 50.

51. Ibid., 38.

52. In the Central Plains the inspectors singled out meuang Suphanburi, meuang Ratchaburi, and meuang Samut Songkhram; in the Southeastern region, meuang Prachinburi and meuang Chachoengsao.

53. Mani, *Prapheni*, 51–52, quoting Chai Phayomyong, a monk and teacher of Princess Dara Ratsami in Chiang Mai from 1917 to 1935, and Abbot Khamtan Thammathinno, Wat Nuangkhong, Sankampaeng District, Chiang Mai.

54. Sangharakshita, *A Survey of Buddhism* (Glasgow: Windhorse, 1993), 432, 437.

55. Ferguson, "Symbolic Dimensions," 18.

56. Chatsumarn Kabilsingh, "Early Buddhist Views on Nature," in *Dharma Gaia: A Harvest of Essays in Buddhism and Ecology*, ed. Allan Hunt Badiner (Berkeley: Parallax Press, 1990), 8–13.

57. "Luang Phau Khian, Wat Samnak Khunen, Phichit," *Phra Aphinya*, no. 1 (n.d.): 26.

58. "Luang Phau Noi, Wat Thammasala, tambon Thammasala, Nakhon Pathom," *Phra Aphinya*, no. 5 (n.d.): 96.

59. Andrew Schelling, "Jataka Mind: Cross-Species Compassion," *Tricycle* 1, no. 1 (fall 1991): 11.

60. Paraphrased from education directors' reports from the following monthons: Nakhon Chaisi, Phuket, Chumphon, Nakhon Sawan, Krungkao (Ayuthaya), Isan, and Nakhon Ratchasima (*Ratchakijjanubeksa* 16–18).

61. Makha Bucha, literally worship on the full moon day of Magha (Pali), the third lunar month, which occurs sometime in February or early March. The Bangkok government declared Makha Bucha a national holiday commemorating an event believed to have taken place

2,500 years ago: 1,250 arahats assembled without notification to hear the Buddha deliver a summary of his teachings. See Sommai and Dore, *Lan Na Traditions,* 129.

62. Wisakha Bucha literally means the worship on the full moon day of Visakha, the sixth lunar month, which occurs in May. This day, during which a star named Visakha moves closest to the moon at midnight, has been regarded as auspicious since early times. Before modern state Buddhism was imposed on regional Buddhists, however, most monasteries outside Bangkok did not have Wisakha Bucha on their calendars (see sangha inspectors' reports for 1899 to 1901). The day was fixed in the Bangkok calendar by King Rama II to commemorate the Buddha's birth, enlightenment, and death; and it was introduced to all regions of Siam by Rama V in the late nineteenth century. In the Lan Na (or Yuan) and the Lao traditions, although the full moon of the sixth lunar month was religiously important, it was not associated with the Buddha's birth, enlightenment, and death. For example, in the Yuan tradition, where it was called *paweni wai phra that* (festival of paying respect to sacred relics), people went on pilgrimage to stupas holding sacred relics (ibid., 199, 201).

63. The Mahābhinikkhamāna Sutta, or the Discourse on the Great Renunciation, describes the going forth of Prince Siddhattha (later the Buddha) into the homeless life. The Mahāparinibbāna sutta, the Discourse on the Complete Nibbana (nirvana), contains an account of the Buddha's last days. See U Thittila, "The Fundamental Principles of Theravada Buddhism," in *The Path of the Buddha,* ed. K. W. Morgan (New York: Ronald Press, 1956), 68.

64. Education director's report, monthon Phuket. *Ratchakijjanubeksa* 18 (5 December 1900): 54–55.

65. La Janthophaso (1898–1994) was abbot of Teung Forest Monastery, San Kamphaeng District, Chiang Mai. In addition to being a skilled storyteller, he was a healer and a craftsman (he painted, sculpted, built dhamma box seats in the local style, and repaired buildings in his wat). For more details about his life and work see Withaya Chupan, *Khamsaun Luang Pu La* [Luang Pu La's Teachings] (Chiang Mai: Thai News, 1989).

66. For example, see the report by the sangha head of monthon Isan. *Ratchakijjanubeksa* 18 (8 September 1901): 22.

67. Phra Thepsumethi, "Hok kheun nai Pakthongchai" [Six nights in Pakthongchai], in *Prachum krawi* [Collection of poems] (Bangkok: Crem. vol. Wat Simahathat, 1979), 13. Thepsumethi (Sawaeng Wimalo) wrote this on 28 November 1934, when he was a junior administrative monk. Eventually he became abbot of Wat Simahathat, a Thammayut monastery in the outskirts of Bangkok.

68. Ibid., 13–14.

69. See Bhasit Chitrabhasa, "Pai fang thet Wetsandon Chadok thinai" [Where can you hear a recitation of the Wetsandon Chadok?], *Sinlapa Watthanatham* 7, no. 1 (May 1990): 16–18. Although the Vessantara story is still a living force in village life, in Bhasit's opinion, contemporary Great Birth recitations (no longer in the indigenous languages) are artless. In Chiang Mai the recital of Vessantara story reached the peak of its popularity before World War II. See John Ferguson and Shalardchai Ramitanondh, "Monks and Hierarchy in Northern Thailand," *Journal of the Siam Society* 64, part 1 (January 1976): 131.

70. Thanissaro Bhikkhu, *The Buddhist Monastic Code* (Berkeley: DharmaNet International, 1993) 13.

71. Recalled by Khruba In Intho (b. 1903), abbot of Wat Falang, Sanhin Village, Chiang Mai, in *Prawat lae khamsaun khaung Luang Pu Khruba In* [Life and teachings of Ven. Grandfather Khruba In] (Chiang Mai: Khraungchang, 1991), 14–17.

72. Sangha officials reported this on their inspection trips in 1899–1901. The rains retreat (Thai: *phansa*) is the three-month period from July to October, corresponding to the rainy season, in which a monk is required to stay in a single place (usually a monastery) and not wander.

73. Information concerning this tradition comes from Mani, *Prapheni*, 69–77, and from Sommai and Dore, *Lan Na Traditions*, 104–111.

74. Sommai and Dore, *Lan Na Traditions*, 309.

75. Regional Buddhists believed that the presence of monks in the cemetery would release the spirits of the dead dwelling there. Sitting around the cremation pyre, monks asked the souls of the dead to accept the merit made on their behalf. Local people believed that the monks' merit—gained from observing precepts and practicing meditation— would carry the spirits to heaven.

76. Phra Phothirangsi, abbot of Wat Phantaung, Chiang Mai, interview by author, 10 July 1989.

77. When Bangkok authorities told abbots of regional Buddhism to compile a list of resident monks, the abbots typically listed monks pursuing meditation (*vipassana dhura*) first and those pursuing studies (*gantha dhura*) second. Sangha officials of modern state Buddhism do just the opposite.

78. Zack, "Buddhist Education," 187.

79. O'Connor, "Cultural Notes," 43.

80. Ibid., 43, citing K. Kingshill, *Ku Daeng—The Red Tomb: A Village Study in Northern Thailand* (Chiang Mai: Prince Royal's College, 1960), 141.

81. Reynolds, "Buddhist Monkhood," 272.

82. Richard A. O'Connor, "Siamese Tai in Tai Context: The Impact of a Ruling Order," *Crossroads* 3, no. 1 (1990): 10

83. For a detailed discussion of this topic, see Christine Gray, "Thailand: The Soteriological State in the 1970s" (Ph.D. diss., University of Chicago, 1986). Kathin ceremonies were the preeminent rituals in the Siamese courts of the past—that of Sukhothai (thirteenth to fifteenth centuries) and Ayuthaya (fourteenth to eighteenth centuries). O'Connor, "Cultural Notes," 44.

84. See *Thera prawat Phra Suphrom Yannathera* (Khruba Phromma Phromjakako) [Biography of Khruba Phromma] (Lamphun: Wat Phra Phuthabat Takpha, 1980), 15–16. The monk who wrote this biography does not reveal his identity. Leaving cloth anonymously for the monks to sew into robes was a common practice in local traditions.

85. O'Connor, "Cultural Notes," 48.

86. W, 36. In the Siamese Bangkok custom, as O'Connor observes ("Cultural Notes," 48), "What counts now is not what all gave together but who gave how much."

87. Sommai and Dore, *Lan Na Traditions,* 102, citing Mani, *Prapheni.*

88. In the Northeast, Lao Buddhists made pilgrimages to Phra That Phanom and other shrines holding sacred relics. In the North, people in Chiang Mai went to Phra That Doi Suthep, in Lamphun to Phra That Hariphunchai, in Nan to Phra That Cha Haeng, and in Mae Hong Son to Phra That Doi Kaungmu.

89. O'Connor, "Cultural Notes," 46.

90. Keyes, *Thailand,* 17.

91. The Lan Na kingdom comprised a group of principalities in the North, among which Chiang Mai was preeminent. These principalities were either independent or autonomous from the Bangkok court until the late nineteenth century. Keyes, *Thailand,* 17–18.

92. O'Connor, "Interpreting Thai Religious Change," 333.

93. In Northeast Thailand as well as in Laos, the song nam pha period might last between five to fifteen days. Sommai and Dore, *Lan Na Traditions,* 189, 191.

94. Report of Phra Yanrakhit (Jan Sirijantho), education director of monthon Isan. *Ratchakijjanubeksa* 18 (September 8, 1900).

95. O'Connor, "Interpreting Thai Religious Change," 334.

96. O'Connor, "Cultural Notes," 45.

97. Wachirayan designed the monastic studies syllabus and written examinations known as *Sanam Luang.* Bangkok's new monastic education system consisted of the naktham and the pariyat tham (dhamma

teachings) exams, leading to *parian* titles (from the Pali, *pariññā*: learned in Pali studies). In order of increasing difficulty, the naktham levels are *tri, tho,* and *ek* (3, 2, and 1). Naktham studies form the foundation of Bangkok's monastic education system and are a precondition for Pali studies. Piyasilo, *Buddhist Currents: A Brief Social Analysis of Buddhism in Sri Lanka and Siam* (Petaling Jaya, Malaysia: Community of Dharmafarers, 1992), 104–105.

98. Quoted in Jane Bunnag, "The Way of the Monk and the Way of the World: Buddhism in Thailand, Laos and Cambodia," in *The World of Buddhism,* ed. Heinz Bechert and Richard Gombrich (London: Thames and Hudson, 1984), 162.

99. As Charles Keyes points out, the architects of centralization were not concerned about how these peoples thought about themselves. Keyes, "Hegemony and Resistance in Northeastern Thailand," in *Regions and National Integration in Thailand, 1892–1992,* ed. Volker Grabowsky (Wiesbaden, Germany: Harrassowitz, 1995), 156.

100. See O'Connor, "Interpreting Thai Religious Change," 333.

101. Reynolds, "Buddhist Monkhood," 258.

102. According to Sommai, in the North there were as many as eighteen nikais in and around Chiang Mai. A nikai in Chiang Mai usage includes all monks who have had the same preceptor. Monks of different nikais and from different traditions often performed the religious ceremonies together. Under Bangkok's influence, however, monks of the Thammayut order refused to perform group rituals with monks of other orders. Sommai Premchit, *A List of Old Temples and Religious Sects in Chiang Mai* (Chiang Mai: Department of Sociology and Anthropology, Chiang Mai University, 1975), 2–3.

103. See Charles Keyes, "Buddhism and National Integration in Thailand," *Journal of Asian Studies,* vol. 30, no. 3, 551–568. For a discussion of Siwichai and the sangha authorites see Rujaya Abhakorn, "Change in the Administrative System of Northern Siam, 1884–1933," in *Changes in Northern Thailand and the Shan States,* ed. Prakai Nontawasee (Singapore: Southeast Asian Studies Program, 1988), 95–97.

104. Batson makes an apt analogy when he says that the expansion of central government control to areas remote from the center "was in many respects similar to colonial regimes in neighboring countries, and the Thai official sent from Bangkok to supervise the administration in Chiang Mai or Ubon was only somewhat less 'foreign' than the British district officer in Malaya or the French resident in Indochina." Benjamin A. Batson, *The End of Absolute Monarchy in Siam* (Singapore: Oxford University Press, 1986), 12.

105. See Phra Thammakosajan (sangha head of monthon Phayap) to minister of religious affairs, 1 August 1935, and minister of religious affairs to prime minister, 3 February 1936, "Khwamkhatyaeng rawang Phra Siwichai kap khana song" [Conflict between Phra Siwichai and the sangha], S.R. 0202.10/61, National Archives, Bangkok.

106. Thammakosajan to minister of religious affairs, "Khwam khat yaeng." The fact that there was hardly any crime in Li District may be a testimony to the effectiveness of Siwichai's teachings.

107. At the time the abbot of Wat Benjamabophit (a Mahanikai wat), Phra Thammakosajan (Plot Kittisophano), was the sangha head of the North (monthon Phayap). Later, from 1960 to 1962, he served as supreme patriarch.

108. La Janthophaso (1897–1994), abbot of Tung Forest Monastery, Auntai Commune, Chiangmai, interview by author, 13 July 1989. After Siwichai died, his body was kept for six years. On his cremation day in 1944, Siwichai's followers came to his funeral in Lamphun from as far away as Sipsong Panna (now in China) and Chiang Saen (the northernmost district of Chiang Rai Province). Some came from various hill-tribe villages in Chiang Mai and Lamphun. The sangha provincial heads of Lamphun and Chiang Mai, however, refused to attend the cremation. Phra Phothirangsi, abbot of Wat Phantaung, Chiang Mai, interview by author, 10 July 1989. (Phothirangsi attended Siwichai's cremation.)

109. Keyes, *Thailand*, 58.

110. Phra Khru Wiratham-sunthon, letter to Phra Thammakosajan, sangha head of monthon Phayap. *Thalaengkan khana song* [Bulletin of sangha affairs], no. 24 (May 1935): 447. During Wachirayan's time, the supreme patriarch would have sent the monthon sangha head to inspect wats in Mae Hong Son, not a junior official.

111. See Tej Bunnag, *Kabot R.S. 121* [Uprisings of 1902] (Bangkok: Thai Watthanaphanit, 1987) for a detailed discussion of these uprisings.

112. In the age before mass media, *mau lam* (folk opera singers) were respected and appreciated by local people. Traditionally, they were regarded as the "soul" of the Northeast. Traditional mau lam were farmers as well as indigenous intellectuals and artists. Particularly during the dry season, they would travel from village to village and perform. Most male mau lam were either ex-monks of the Lao tradition or had studied with monks. They were knowledgeable about Buddhist stories, dhamma teachings, local history, literature, and contemporary events. In their singing, mau lam conveyed ethics as well as religious and secular knowledge through poetic tales with entertaining skills. Jiraporn Witayasakpan, "Nationalism and the Transformation of Aesthetic Concepts: Theatre in Thailand during the Phibun Period" (Ph.D. diss., Cornell Uni-

versity, 1992), 281-287. For bibliographical information about the rebellions see Keyes, *Thailand,* 67 n. 12.

113. Volker Grabowsky, introduction to *Regions and National Integration,* 6.

CHAPTER 2: THE PATH TO THE FOREST

1. Volker Grabowsky interprets Kao as a combination of Kuai (Kui) and Lao, the two largest ethnic groups in Champasak (in Laos) and the southeastern parts of the Khorat Plateau. See "The Isan up to Its Integration into the Siamese State," in Grabowsky, *Regions and National Integration in Thailand,* 113 n. 21.

2. Monthon Nakhon Ratchasima took the name of its major town. *Isan* means northeast, and *udon* means north.

3. Grabowsky, "Isan up to Its Integration," 107 n. 1.

4. Grabowsky, introduction to *Regions and National Integration,* 6. Lao is the name of the people and language of Laos. It is also the regional language of the Northeast of Thailand, or Isan. Compared to other regions in Thailand, the Northeast has a greater number of different Tai languages and dialects. Non-Tai languages spoken there include Northern Khmer and Kui. Lao (a Tai language) consists of numerous dialects in three major groups. The Luang Prabang or northern group extends down into Loei Province. The Vientiane or central group straddles the border east and south of Loei. (Luang Prabang and Vientiane are cities in Laos; Loei is in Thailand.) The southern group extends into southern Laos. Within these Lao dialect groupings in the Northeast, various towns and villages have minor differences of dialect. Smalley, *Linguistic Diversity,* 89, 92.

5. None of the monks described their families or the villagers as poor.

6. Tate [Thet], Ajahn, *The Autobiography of a Forest Monk,* ed. Ariyesako Bhikkhu (Bangkok: Amarin Printing, 1993), 32. Hereafter cited as T1.

7. Two and a half *rai* equal one acre.

8. There used to be four different ways of writing Lao in the Northeast. *Tua tham* (Tham script) was for Buddhist texts. It was similar to the Yuan script used in the North. The Khom script (an ancient Khmer script) is no longer used except in amulets, tattoos, charms, and fortune tellers' charts. The Lao script was for writing local poetic and romantic literature. The Bangkok Thai script was recently introduced to the Northeast by the Bangkok schooling system. See Smalley, *Linguistic Diversity,* 89, 92.

9. Keyes, "Hegemony and Resistance," 159.

10. In 1921 the Siamese king enacted a compulsory education law, requiring all boys and girls between the ages of seven and fourteen to attend elementary school for four years. But initially the law could be enforced in only 45 percent of the country. Wyatt, *Thailand,* 229.

11. Thanet Chareonmuang, "When the Young Cannot Speak Their Own Mother Tongue: Explaining a Legacy of Cultural Domination in Lan Na," in *Religion and National Integration,* 86–87.

12. *Ubon mani,* 468.

13. According to Bua, in this kind of competition singers compose songs extemporaneously. Neither side can prepare in advance since the topic is selected on stage, after which each must immediately sing, converse, or pretend to quarrel with the other, always using verse. One contestant delivers a verse, and then the opponent must compose another verse that rhymes with it. The competitor who stammers, hesitates, or is simply less fluent than his opponent is considered the loser. The trick is to end your verse with a word for which it is difficult to find a rhyme. Boowa [Bua] Nyanasampanno, *The Venerable Phra Aeharn Mun Bhuridatta Thera,* translated by Siri Buddhasukh (Bangkok: Funny Publishing, 1982), 165. Hereafter cited as M1.

14. All distances are measured by the paved roads constructed during recent decades.

15. These were the village wats of Sangthau, Weruwan, Big Kheng Tree (Kheng Yai), Big Bamboo (Phai Yai), and Post Pond (Naung Lak). The latter two wats are in Muang Samsip District (W, 24). This was before Wachirayan replaced the traditional texts with the naktham texts used today. The monastic education at Big Bamboo Wat and Post Pond Wat conformed to a Siamese tradition brought to Ubon by Phra Ariyawongsajan (Sui), a native of Ubon who went to study at Wat Saket in Bangkok. See *Ubon Ratchathani 200 pi* [Ubon Ratchathani, 200 Years] (Bangkok: Chuan Phim, 1992), 167.

16. The local ruler, named Muang and titled Phraya Surin, persuaded Dun's grandfather to settle in this area. After Muang died in 1891, his brother was selected as governor of Surin by the Bangkok royal high commissioner, Prince Pichit-Prichakhon. Nanthapanyaphon, *Chiwa prawat Luang Pu Dun,* 2.

17. These *lakhuan nauk* performances were sponsored by the governor of meuang Surin. In those days all the roles were played by men. Good-looking young men were offered female roles (ibid., 3). Among the plays in which Dun played female characters were *Chaiyachet, Laksanawong,* and *Janthakuman.*

18. Ibid., 4.

19. Ibid., 7. Dun's biographer does not identify this tradition, but nei-

ther does he mention Dun being ordained in the Mahanikai order. The local tradition could be either Lao or Khmer in origin. Seventy percent of the population in Surin was Khmer in 1988; during the early twentieth century the percentage was probably higher (Grabowsky, "Isan up to Its Integration," 108 n. 5). The kasina meditations are designed to strengthen the power of concentration or "one-pointedness." They involve concentrating on one thing, such as a colored disk or on the flame of a candle, and excluding everything else from the mind. See Michael Carrithers, *The Forest Monks of Sri Lanka* (Delhi: Oxford University Press, 1983), 225.

20. Although a monk could practice mindfulness and awareness while building bullock carts, in the case of an inexperienced meditator like Dun such mundane activities were invitations to mindlessness and distraction. See Gross, "After Patriarchy," 62.

21. An upatcha is a monk who performs the ordination ceremony.

22. Wat Suthat was the third Thammayut wat established in Ubon, after Wat Supat and Wat Sithaung. All three were built before 1866.

23. Sing Khantayakamo (1888–1961) was ordained as a novice at Log Pond Village (Ban Naung Khaun, today in Amnat Charoen District, Ubon). In 1909 he was ordained as a monk in the Thammayut order at Wat Suthat. The sangha supervisor of monthon Isan (Uan Tisso) was his preceptor. Sing met Ajan Man when the latter spent the rains retreat at Wat Burapha on the outskirts of Ubon. See Suriphan Maniwat, *Chiwa prawat Phra Khun Jao Luang Pu Lui Janthasaro* [Biography of Ven. Grandfather Lui] (Bangkok: P. Samphanphanit, 1990), 38. Sing became a thudong monk in spite of his preceptor's protest. Eventually, he became abbot of Salawan Forest Wat in Nakhon Ratchasima.

24. Paitoon Mikusol, "Administrative Reforms and National Integration: The Case of the Northeast," in *Regions and National Integration,* ed. Grabowsky, 149.

25. When his children reached maturity, Fan's father moved out of Egg Mango Village. Together with several Phu Thai families they reestablished a community in another location in the same district. The new village was called Ban Bathaung, so named after the big *thaunglang* trees in the area. As Fan recounts, the new location was more fertile for rice and other crops as well as for cattle grazing. It was also suitable for raising silkworms. Fan's father, a headman before the move, was elected village chief in Ban Bathaung. Fan was ordained as a novice at the village wat (F, 6–7).

26. Paitoon, "Administrative Reforms," 150.

27. Thet had no recollection of his Lao Phuan grandfathers, both of whom died when his parents were young. His grandmother was among

the Phuan people from Chiang Khwang who were taken into captivity by Siamese troops sent by King Rama III during the first half of the nineteenth century. Some of the Phuan were settled in Fang in Uttaradit, where his mother was born. Eventually Thet's mother and other relatives moved to Loei and set up the village where Thet was born. Thet gives an account of his ancestors in Tate, *Autobiography*, 27–31. For a detailed discussion of the fate of the Phuan see Sanit Samuckarn and Kennon Breazeale, *A Culture in Search of Survival: The Phuan of Thailand and Laos* (New Haven: Yale University Southeast Asia Studies, 1988).

28. Li1, 2. After a while his father remarried, and life at home became more bearable.

29. His relatives (elder brothers, sisters, and brothers-in-law) seemed glad that Li became a monk. After Li's ordination they borrowed most of his money to buy water buffaloes and land and to use in trading (Li1, 4).

30. La explains that he took the third-level naktham exam twice because he had disrobed after being a novice. When he was ordained as a monk he had to take the exam again. La was married twice. The first marriage broke up after a year. His second marriage, less than a year later, produced two sons and lasted nine years until his wife died of an illness. La returned to the robes and left his wife's property (rice fields, a house, and three water buffaloes) to her elder sister, who gladly adopted his children (La, 17–18).

31. La, 20. La appreciated that the village abbot did not encourage him to behave like the other monks. The strictness of the wandering monk whom La met when he was a boy had, it seems, made a lasting impression on him.

32. In those days the schools were often quite far from the village, and the walk there and back every day would be too exhausting for younger children.

33. In the local traditions, a mae chi (or *mae khaw*) observed eight or ten precepts continually. This was a form of lay ordination.

34. Khamphaung Tiso was born in 1921 in Songpleuai Commune (today in Kheuan Khamkaew District, Ubon). He was ordained at Wat Mahachai in Udon Thani. Khamphaung's personality was similar to that of Teu, Wan, and Maha Bua: straightforward, outspoken, and undesirous of pleasing laypeople. See *Ruam phapchut lae prawat yau 80 phra kammathan* [Brief biographies of eighty kammathan monks] (Bangkok: Sisayam Kanphim, n.d.), 112.

35. Wan took the exam in Bunthrik Commune in Ubon Province. He ranked first. Taking the exam with him were four monks who had all flunked in previous years. One of them had taken the exam once before;

another had taken it three times; a third, four times; and the fourth, five times. Wan was the only one who had not taken it before. Before writing this exam, Wan tutored the others. This time they all passed (W, 28).

36. Uan Tisso (Phra Phrommuni), *Prawat patipatha lae ngan khaung phra maha thera paet rup* [Biography of eight senior monks] (Bangkok: Mahamakut University Press, 1990), 4–5.

37. After the passage of the 1902 Sangha Act, however, academic monks replaced meditation monks as abbots. See Reynolds, "The Buddhist Monkhood," 220. Wat Saket ceased to be a monastery known for its meditation practice until Phra Phimontham revived meditation practice in Bangkok (see chap. 9).

38. Phra Ariyakawi (Aun) was Man's preceptor, Phra Khru Sitha was the announcing teacher, and Phra Khru Prajak-ubonkun (Sui) was the instructing teacher. Aun was appointed sangha head of meuang Ubon by the Siamese king in 1891. See Toem, *Prawasat Isan,* 372. Later on Man went on a thudong with Sitha, who was fond of wandering. Prajak was a craftsman. Since Man came to Wat Liap before the wat was converted to the Thammayut, most likely Man was ordained as a monk in the Lao tradition, like his teacher Sao, before he became a Thammayut.

39. Sao Kantasilo (1861–1942) was born in Khakhom Village (today in Kheuang Nai District, Ubon). He was ordained as a monk in the Lao tradition (his preceptor resided in Champasak, Laos). Ten years later, after becoming abbot of Wat Liap, he converted to the Thammayut order. Since 1899 this wat has belonged to the Thammayut. Sao died while sitting in meditation at Wat Ammat in Champasak, southern Laos. His corpse was transported to Wat Burapha in Ubon, where the cremation took place. Recalled by Lui in Suriphan, *Chiwa prawat Luang Pu Lui,* 54–55. See also "Prawat Phra Ajan Sao Kantasilo," in Uan, *Prawat pathipatha,* 83–85. In 1899 five wats in Ubon—Wat Tai, Wat Liap, Wat Burapha, Wat Ban Khumeuang, and Wat Ban Hwang (today in Warin District)—were converted to the Thammayut order. At the time Nu Thitapanyo was abbot of Wat Tai. Wat Burapha was previously deserted before it became a Thammayut wat (*Si Ubonrattanaram,* 21; see also Khaneungnit, *Khon di meuang Ubon,* 26).

40. Aya Khu Tham was trained in the Phu Thai tradition. He was born into a Phu Thai family in Egg Mango Village in 1884. Because his birth coincided with the death of his maternal grandfather, the villagers believed that he was his grandfather's reincarnation (F, 11). After Bangkok integrated the Lao and Khmer monks into the national sangha hierarchy, Aya Khu Tham was given the title Phra Khru Sakon Samanakit. He was appointed sangha head of Sakon Nakhon.

41. Despite the imposition of modern state Buddhism, many village

abbots (particularly in remote areas) continued to follow regional traditions: going on a thudong between rains retreats and training monks and novices in meditation.

42. Sing Khantayakamo was a disciple of Ajan Man's.

43. T1, 46. Thet was also grateful that Sing taught him to read and write (probably in Bangkok Thai, since Thet had already learned to read and write in Lao from his brother).

44. It took them over a month to reach Log Pond Village in Amnat Charoen District, Ubon. Sing stayed there for three months to teach his mother in spiritual matters. Here he arranged for Thet to be ordained as a novice at a village wat of Big Kheng Tree. Thet was then eighteen years old.

45. The textbooks that Thet used—books of sermons, the vinaya, and the *Navakovada* (an elementary textbook with advice for new monks)—were written by Wachirayan. See David K. Wyatt, "The Beginnings of Modern Education in Thailand, 1868–1910" (Ph.D. diss., Cornell University, 1966), 318.

46. Pin Panyapalo (1892–1946), unlike his brother Sing, wanted to be an academic monk. Although in his early years Pin had met Ajan Man, like many ambitious monks of his generation, he preferred to go to Bangkok and study Wachirayan's texts. He passed Pali exams up to the fifth level. In 1922 he returned to Ubon to attend his mother's funeral and spent the rains retreat at Wat Suthat. While there he learned meditation practice from Sing and became a thudong monk. He died at Sansamran Forest Monastery in Warin Chamrap District, Ubon (F, 66).

47. T1, 63. After he passes the first three of nine Pali exams, a monk is referred to as a maha—for example, Maha Pin.

48. Li1, 5. Although sangha officials forbade monks from participating in festivals, many village abbots continued to do so.

49. Li himself could not always follow the vinaya rules. On one occasion he was invited to deliver the Mahachat sermon at Wat Non Daeng in Big Bamboo Commune: "It so happened that my turn to read the sermon came at 11:00 A.M. By the time I was finished, it was afternoon, so it was too late to eat. On the way home I was accompanied by a temple boy carrying some rice and grilled fish in his shoulder bag. A little after 1 P.M., feeling really tired and hungry, I told the boy to show me what was in his bag. Seeing the food, I couldn't resist sitting right down and finishing it off under the shade of a tree" (Li1, 5). On another occasion, Li went to the forest to help drag wood back to the wat for building a meeting hall. Feeling hungry in the evening, again he ate. Li tells us that his fellow monks also ate supper at one time or another, although they did not tell others.

50. Khampha's account reflects the Isan monks' feeling that Laos and Isan were part of the same region. He told La's father, "I was meditating as I was walking, and before I knew it I had already crossed the Mekong" (La, 14–15).

51. Juan does not reveal the wandering monk's name.

52. Copies of this book, whose title may be translated as "The Triple Gem and techniques of meditation," were widely distributed to young monks and people who could read Thai. See J. L. Taylor, "From Wandering to Monastic Domestication," *Journal of Siam the Society* 76 (1988): 82. The book was published after Sing, Man's senior disciple, became abbot of Salawan Forest Monastery in Nakhon Ratchasima.

53. Juan does not say why he thought that he had to convert to the Thammayut in order to become a thudong monk. It may be that the wandering monk whom Juan met earlier was Thammayut.

54. A series of events at a Thammayut wat, including his being implicated in corruption while staying at Sutthawat Forest Monastery, led to Wan's disillusionment with academic and administrative life (W, 25–26, 29).

55. At the time Prince Wachirayan had just been appointed supreme patriarch, but one would not know it from reading Man's biography. Man had little interest in Bangkok ecclesiastics and their world.

56. Waen walked through the districts of Muang Samsip (in Ubon Province), Kham Kheuan Kaew, Yasothon, Loeng Nok Tha (today all in Yasothon Province), Khamcha-i (today in Mukdahan), Na Kae (in Nakhon Phanom), Phanna Nikhom and Sawang Daendin (in Sakon Nakhon), and Naung Han (in Udon Thani), arriving finally in Pheu Tree Village.

57. Aya Khu Di was abbot of Wat Phochai in Egg Mango Village. Fan had studied with him as a child. Ku Thammathinno (1900–1953) was ordained at Wat Phochai in Egg Mango Village. From the beginning he followed the Phu Thai tradition. He preferred living in the forest and practicing meditation. After he met Man in 1923 he converted to the Thammayut order. He died while sitting in meditation in Jao Phuka Cave (F, 12–13, 36).

58. Ibid., 15. It is interesting to note that the local monks Di, Ku, and Fan thought that Man's ability to articulate the dhamma to villagers was a result of the local *texts* that Man had studied in Ubon (the Prathomkap, Prathommun, and Mulakatjai). It was in Ubon that Bangkok's monastic education system first took root and that Wachirayan's texts replaced local Pali ones.

59. In the old days, thudong gear (klots, kettles, large bowls) was not readily available. Monks had to make or acquire it themselves.

60. Jum Phanthulo (1888–1962) was born in Uthen Landing Village (today in Nakhon Phanom). He was ordained in the Thammayut order at Wat Mahachai, Udon Thani, in 1907. He followed his teacher to study at Wat Liap in Ubon where Sao and Man were then residing. Like many young, ambitious monks, Jum was not interested in meditation practice. He went to study in Bangkok at Wat Thepsirin and passed the third-level Pali exam. By the time La met Jum, the latter had already turned to meditation practice (F, 33).

61. Afraid that Ajan Man would not accept him as a disciple, La wandered on his own to meditate (La, 26–29).

62. Maha Seng Pusso, deputy to the sangha head of the Isan region, was inspecting Thammayut wats in the region. Maha Seng knew Juan's preceptor, Maha Dusit, who told him that Juan wished to meet Ajan Man (J, 28). Seng was born in 1908 in Khon Kaen Province. He was ordained as a novice in 1922 at Sutthawat Forest Wat in Sakon Nakhon. Then he went to Bangkok for Pali studies. In 1929 he was ordained as a monk at Wat Samphanthawong (Wat Kau), sponsored by Jao Khun Ubali (Jan), abbot of Wat Boromniwat. His preceptor was Somdet M. R. Cheun, who became supreme patriarch in 1945 (the year that Seng came to inspect Thammayut wats in Isan). In his later years, Seng resigned from the assistant abbotcy of Wat Phra Simahathat. The reason he gave was "poor health." See "Phra Ariya Khunathan (Seng Pusso)," in *Ruam phap 80 phra kammathan*, 230–231.

63. Man's forest hermitage near Pheu Pond Village was far from the main road. At the time, the only way to get there was by foot or by oxcart. On foot it took three to four hours to reach the village. Following a more indirect route by oxcart took more than eight hours (M3, 137). Juan does not say which route they took.

64. The largest number of Lao Phuan people resided in Banmi District, Lopburi Province. Wongkot Hill Village (Ban Khao Wongkot) is one of the Phuan communities in Banmi District. See Pho Samlamjiak, *Tamnan Thai Phuan* [Stories of the Thai Phuan] (Bangkok: Samakkhisan, 1994), 21.

65. This teacher was Phao Phuttasaro (1872–1946). Ordained in 1892 in Nakhon Sawan, Phao was known as a strict meditation teacher. While wandering in Lopburi in 1925, he came upon Wongkot Hill and set up a forest hermitage there. See *Ruam phap 80 phra kammathan*, 182–183.

66. He recalled that when he was still a novice he had seen a thudong monk carry a rosary *(luk pat)* for use in meditation. Deciding to make a rosary, he found a *tabaek* tree, whose oval nuts could be used for beads. Fear of violating the vinaya prevented him from climbing the tree to pick

the nuts, however. But one day a troop of monkeys climbed into the tree, and their movements shook the nuts from the branches. As Cha recalls, his rosary practice was of short duration. "Each *phawana* [repetition of a thought or word] ends with a drop of a nut into a tin can until all 108 nuts are gone. Having practiced this repeatedly for three nights, I felt that this is not the way. It's no different from a Chinaman counting and selling betel nuts in the market." Cha dropped the method (C3, 20). Calming the mind by counting a rosary with 108 beads is an old method practiced by many meditation monks. Fan, too, learned it from a village abbot when the two went wandering in 1920. Here is how Fan describes it: "The rosary is tied around the wrists. While practicing sitting, lying, or walking meditation, one recites 'buddho . . . buddho' and counts the beads one by one: 'buddho one, buddho two, buddho three' up to 'buddho one hundred and eight.' Then a second and third round reciting 'dhammo' and 'sangho' respectively. Miscounting means that the mind is not calm. Then one must start all over again from 'buddho one' " (F, 11).

67. Cha did not say why he had to leave so soon. He merely mentions that there were certain obstacles to staying.

68. Taylor, *Forest Monks,* 90.

69. Ajahn Chah [Cha], *Living Dhamma* (Ubon, Thailand: Bung Wai Forest Monastery, 1992), 63. Hereafter cited as C2.

70. Boowa, "Dhūtaṅga Kammaṭṭhāna Bhikkhus," 72.

CHAPTER 3: FACING FEAR

1. Gaurs (Thai: *krathing*) and bantengs *(wua daeng)* are species of wild oxen. Their charge could be fatal. Today both animals are listed as endangered species. See *Samsip pi kananurak satpa thai* [Thirty years of wildlife conservation in Thailand] (Bangkok: Seub Nakhasathian Foundation, 1990), 63.

2. Kilesas include craving, aversion, and delusion in their various forms, including greed, malevolence, anger, hypocrisy, arrogance, envy, miserliness, dishonesty, obstinacy, violence, pride, and fear.

3. Boowa, "Dhūtaṅga Kammaṭṭhāna Bhikkhus," 87.

4. Phra Ajaan Thate Desaransi [Thet Thetrangsi], "Steps along the Path" (Berkeley: DharmaNet International, 1994), 4; DharmaNet electronic document, available from DharmaNet Electronic Files Archive (DEFA) at sunsite.unc.edu.

5. As Bua explains, "Whichever method is used it should suit one's character, for characters differ, and to teach that everyone should use only one type of meditation may well prove to be a hindrance to some

people, thus preventing their attaining beneficial results from their practice." See Boowa [Bua], "Wisdom Develops Samadhi," in *Living Buddhist Masters*, ed. Jack Kornfield (Kandy: Buddhist Publication Society, 1977), 167.

6. Tracks for walking meditation were cleared by lay devotees, one track for each monk. Each track was about ten to twenty meters long. These tracks were used by the monks day and night (M1, 51).

7. These small raised platforms were usually made of pieces of split bamboo. This kind of bed was about two meters long, and one or one and a half meters wide. Such a platform was intended to be used by one person only. Each platform was about thirty to forty meters away from the next one, depending on the size of the meditation site at each forest locality. In a wider area the platforms would be much further apart. As Man's biographer explained, the smaller the number of the monks in a given area, the greater would be the distance between them, so that only the occasional cough or sneeze could be heard by the others. The trees and bushes between each platform were left intact so that a monk would not be able to see other monks staying near him (M1, 50–51).

8. See, for example, Boowa, "Dhūtaṅga Kammaṭṭhāna Bhikkhus," 74.

9. M1, 66. Although Man often stayed in places where tigers were plentiful, he seemed never to have been bothered by them, nor does he mention anything about his own fears. Most likely he had been around tigers enough so that his fear had dissipated.

10. Although tigers prefer to hunt at night, dawn and dusk are also favored times. Simon Barnes, *Tiger!* (New York: St. Martin's Press, 1994), 19.

11. C3, 36–37. The ellipsis points in the quotation are Cha's. *Citta* (Pali) means "mind" or "heart."

12. Li1, 39. In those days when wildlife was abundant, the wandering monks could tell time by listening to wild jungle fowl. As Man told his disciples, wild roosters usually crowed every three hours. They were loudest in the early morning when a large number of them crowed at the same time. This was around 3 A.M., when the monks normally got up. Today hardly any wild jungle fowl can be found in the few remaining forests of Thailand.

13. T2, 76. Thudong monks referred to the Lahu people as the Muser, which means hunters (the first Lahu settlers were mainly hunters).

14. Chaup personally related this story to Bua (M2, 390–400). Although the biographer does not indicate in what year this event took place, it was probably in 1937 that Chaup wandered into the Shan states.

Chaup, Thet's exact contemporary, was born in 1902 in Mon Hill Village (Ban Khok Mon), today in Wang Saphung District, Loei Province. He was the first-born in a family of four children. He began to shoulder adult responsibilities at the age of ten after his father died (in 1912). His mother and other relatives then settled in the village of Chiang Phin (today in Makkhaeng District, Udon Thani). In 1915, when he was fourteen, Chaup met Pha, a disciple of Ajan Man's who had pitched his klot near the village wat. Chaup was assigned by his family to attend the thudong monk, who taught him the dhamma. Young Chaup was so impressed with Pha that he decided to wear white robes (as a lay renunciate), observe the eight precepts, and leave home to wander with his teacher. Four years later Chaup, at the age of nineteen, was ordained as a novice at Kae Field Village Monastery in his uncle's village (in Naung Bua Lamphu District, Udon Thani). As a novice he wandered around and studied with many teachers. He was ordained as a monk at the age of twenty-three at Wat Sangsok (today in Yasothon Province). Four years later he met Man at Samphong Village, Si Songkhram District, Nakhon Phanom. Afterward Chaup was reordained in the Thammayut order at the same time as his fellow wandering monk, Khaw Analayo. See Suriphan Maniwat, *Chiwa prawat Phra Khun Jao Luang Pu Chaup Thansamo* [Biography of Ven. Grandfather Chaup] (Bangkok: Commemoration of Chaup's eighty-eighth birthday, 1990), 1–39.

15. M2, 392. When Chaup entered into jhāna, his mind became impervious to fear. Pains in the body (from standing still for several hours) were also without significance.

16. As an expert on tigers explains, "Like those of most mammals, a tiger's eyes are less efficient than the human eye at giving information about shape, but very acute indeed at spotting movement. . . . Stillness is one of the great acquired virtues of jungle life, and that holds good for naturalists, predators and prey. Movement is, often quite literally, a dead giveaway." Barnes, *Tiger!* 19.

17. At the time (1953–1955) there was no road. To go from Golden Pot Forest (Dong Mau Thong, in Wanon Niwat District, Sakon Nakhon) to the district town, one had to spend the night on the way. Between the rains retreats the monks wandered to other mountains. From Golden Pot Forest to Ox Mountain was a three-day walk; to Loei province it took nine days (J, 99).

18. J, 55. The story was also related by Bua, although Bua does not reveal the identity of the monk. See Phra Ajan Bua Yannasampanno, *Patipatha phra thudong kammathan* [Thudong kammathan monks' conduct] (Bangkok: Crem. vol. Chu Sitachit, Wat Thepsirin, 1973), 226. The tigers may have been cubs. The affectionate tone of Khaw's scolding may not come across in my translation.

19. J, 58. In the queue for the latrine the order of seniority was disregarded.

20. The biographer, as usual, does not identify the location where this

event took place. Maha Thaungsuk eventually settled at Sutthawat Monastery in Sakon Nakhon Province. This account was related by Maha Thaungsuk in M2, 200–203. Khaw Analayo (1888–1983), born in Chanaeng Pond Village (today in Amnat Jaroen District, Ubon Province), was a married farmer with seven children. At one point he traveled to Bangkok to find work. When he returned to his village he caught his wife having an affair with another man. Khaw threatened to kill her and her lover but managed to control himself. He fled to the village wat, ordained as a monk in the local tradition in 1919, and spent six years there before becoming a thudong monk. In 1958, at the age of seventy, he settled at Midday Drum Cave (Tham Klaung Phen) in the Phu Phan Range (Udon Thani Province), which later became the site of Tham Klaung Phen Monastery. For more information about Khaw's life see Taylor, *Forest Monks*, 156–157.

    21. M1, 160, slightly modified.

    22. J, 52. At the time Juan was thirty years old; he had been wandering for nine years.

    23. In local traditions, pha khaws are either laymen *(phau khaw)* or laywomen *(mae khaw* or *mae chi)* who observe eight or ten precepts. Some pha khaws used to wander on their own or in the company of thudong monks; others stayed in wats or at hermitages.

    24. Man told his disciples that sometimes he could read the thoughts of birds, monkeys, elephants and other animals (M1, 161).

    25. M2, 395. There are, of course, more naturalistic ways of explaining the tiger's tolerance of Chaup. The tiger may have been young (an eighteen-month-old cub can be as large as a mature animal), or it may have already made its kill and was resting.

    26. M1, 67–68. Although the thudong monks believed that they were saved by the dhamma's power, another way of explaining their survival is in terms of animal behavior. Tigers, experts tell us, are not as well equipped with senses as one might expect. They depend on their hearing while hunting. Their eyesight is not particularly good, and they seem unable to spot prey until it moves. They avoid man as much as possible. They are quiet, solitary animals when well fed. Jim Corbett, an expert on tigers, points out that most cases of tigers killing people can be attributed to the animal's old age or injuries; tigers turn to eating human flesh only when forced into it. Hunters who wound a tiger and fail to kill it may therefore be condemning a number of fellow humans to terrible deaths. Most of the man-eaters Corbett hunted were found to be partially incapacitated when finally destroyed. See Roger A. Caras, *Dangerous to Man* (New York: Holt, Rinehart and Winston, 1975), 7–16. The same point was made by Thai hunters. See Chali Iamkrasin, *Pa nai adit*

[Forests in the past] (Bangkok: Tonmai, 1991), 33–48. (Monks use the Thai word "seua" to refer to both tigers and leopards.)

27. Related by Khamdi Panyaphaso (who went wandering with Phuang), in Damrong Phuraya, "Luang Pu Phuang Akinjano," *Lokthip* 7, no. 134 (15 July 1988): 41. Phuang Akinjano (1897–1982) was a disciple of Dun's. He was recalling his experiences at Thammajedi Mountain (in Sakon Nakhon) during the 1950s. In those days the forest held many striped tigers and herds of elephants. Today the area is deforested and the tigers have been wiped out.

28. Wild water buffaloes *(khwai pa)* are bigger and faster than domestic water buffaloes. The latter used to be called *khwai pla* (free-living water buffaloes) because in the old days they were let loose in the wilds to fend for themselves after the plowing season. The khwai pa, once abundant, are now almost extinct. Due to excessive hunting and loss of habitats, Thailand's wild water buffalo population was down to between thirty and forty head as early as 1965. Thiraphat Prayunsit, "Endangered Species," in *Sat pa meuang thai khaun ja leua phiang khwam song jam* [Wild animals in Thailand before they became just a memory], ed. Sudara Sujachara (Bangkok: Thirakanphim, 1988), 64–66.

29. This was recounted by Phra Chote, one of the novices who accompanied Dun, in Nanthapanyaphon, *Chiwa prawat Luang Pu Dun,* 27.

30. Khaung, an older thudong monk, personally told this story to Juan when they spent a meditation retreat together at Golden Pot Forest in Sakon Nakhon. Khaung died prior to 1980, when Juan's life story was transcribed (his recollections were on tape). Suriphan, *Phra Ajan Juan,* 101.

31. Boowa, "Dhūtaṅga Kammaṭṭhāna Bhikkhus," 87, slightly edited.

32. Boowa [Bua] Nyanasampanno, *Things as They Are: A Collection of Talks on the Training of the Mind,* trans. Thanissaro Bhikkhu (Udon Thani, Thailand: Ban Tat Forest Monastery, 1994), 56.

33. Reported by Fan, Li, and La. See, for example, F, 70; Li2, 50; La, 92.

34. See M1, 44–47. The biographer, as usual, does not identify the location where this event took place.

35. C1, 71. Most villagers will refuse to sleep on bamboo that has been used as a stretcher to carry a corpse; they believe that the ghost will haunt them at night. The fact that they used this bamboo for a monk's bed (without asking his permission first) suggests that they think monks do not fear ghosts. Sometimes they are right. Phim, abbot of Wat Suthat, Ubon Ratchathani, remarks that it is wasteful to burn up a good wooden coffin with a corpse. He says he has often removed the corpse from a coffin (especially a teak one) before cremating the body, and

afterward he has used the wood to build a table or a chair. His disciples and temple boys were afraid to use this furniture, though. They said that at night they sometimes heard the chair or the table being tapped, and they thought that the ghost was wanting its coffin back. Phra Khru Suthat (Phim), interview by author, 20 June 1989.

36. C1, 73–74. What Cha heard may have been a large wild animal or, possibly, a spirit doctor from the village who wanted to test the thudong monk's courage.

37. C1, 61. When the fear was gone the figure that stood outside the klot also went away. See "Phra Ajan Cha taun tamha Phra Ajan Man" [Phra Ajan Cha in search of Ajan Man], in *Muttothai* (Bangkok: Chuanphim, 1972), 195.

38. C1, 75–76. *Paccattaṁ veditabbo viññuhi* (to be experienced individually by the wise) is traditionally listed as one of the excellent qualities of the dhamma.

39. "Phra Ajan Cha taun tamha," 195.

40. Jiw, abbot of Nature Forest Monastery (Wat Pa Thammachat), Beung District, Chonburi, interview by author, 5 April 1991. Jiw, a native of Surin Province, learned these rules when he was a novice accompanying his teacher on a thudong in Isan. He recalled that a novice had died mysteriously after leaving his klot to investigate a strange sound.

41. Li1, 44.

42. Li1, 44. Like Chaup when he faced the tigers, Li entered into deep concentration and his mind became impervious to fear.

43. In those days, a secluded and peaceful place was easy to find, even in a provincial town.

44. Li had to have permission before he could spend the rains retreat in the cemetery. He sought approval from the sangha head of Chanthaburi Province, who refused his request. One of Li's followers, a former government official, appealed higher up, to the sangha head of the southeast region, the abbot of Wat Thepsirin in Bangkok. This sangha official approved the plan and sent a letter to the provincial head instructing him to give Li permission. It is curious that the high-level Thammayut monk did not object to Li's spending the rains retreat in the cemetery. Senior administrative monks maintained that the rules decreed that monks should spend the rains retreat in a wat. Perhaps the senior monk did not want to go against the local lay devotees' wishes. (Administrative Thammayut monks, whose main support came from the nobility, began to lose their power after the end of absolute monarchy in 1932.)

45. Sitha Chetawan, "Phra Ajan Suthi Thitayanno," *Lokthip* 10, no. 196 (March 1991): 33. This is an interview with Phra Suthi Thitayanno (b. 1928) of Phuttawatrangsi Forest Monastery, Na Yai Commune, Suwannaphum District, Roi-Et .

46. Finally, it is worth noting again that the context in which these wandering monks trained their minds during their early years no longer exists. Monks can no longer find remote forests inhabited by tigers or isolated caves where they can stay for long periods undisturbed. The few tracts of wilderness that remain have been declared national forests, and these preserves have been declared off-limits to forest monks.

47. Boowa, *Things as They Are,* 56–57.

CHAPTER 4: OVERCOMING BODILY SUFFERING

1. This treatment must be distinguished from the practice of some urban people who, according to newspaper reports in 1995, drank so-called holy monks' urine in the belief that it would cure their illnesses. Thudong monks and pha khaws drank only their own urine, and only when ill. (Traditional Vedic medicines in the Buddha's time were often pickled in cow's urine.)

2. Thamma osot is the curing of sickness through the practice of dhamma using the healing power of virtue and meditation (T1, 191).

3. For most of his life Man was a peripatetic. Not until he was in his seventies did he settle down to teach.

4. C1, 99. The Four Noble Truths are the truth of suffering *(dukkha sacca),* the truth of its cause *(samudaya sacca),* the truth of its cessation *(nirodha sacca),* and the truth of the way *(magga sacca)* leading to cessation.

5. Many monks knowledgeable in Pali went to Man to check him out. Some expected him to alleviate their problems or to make them feel good.

6. Boowa [Bua] Nyannasampanno, *Straight from the Heart: Thirteen Talks on the Practice of Meditation,* trans. Thanissaro Bhikkhu (Bangkok: P. Samphan Panich, 1987), 49.

7. Although Sao strictly followed the thudong practices, he was lenient with his disciples. Perhaps Man saw that when a teacher is not strict, disciples become lax, since they do not fear the teacher. Therefore Man took a different approach in teaching. See Bua, *Patipatha phra thudong kammathan,* 288.

8. M2, 249–250. The five meditation themes *(kammathan ha)* to which Man refers are the five externally visible parts of the body: head

hair, body hair, nails, teeth, and skin. In all there are thirty-two body parts in the meditation on the repulsiveness of the body. The first five are external; the other twenty-seven are internal.

9. C2, 39–40. When Fan fell ill while wandering in Sakon Nakhon in 1926, Man told him to meditate all night long using the interior body as the object of meditation. Fan followed the instruction, and the next morning he recovered from his illness. Fan, however, does not reveal the details of the meditation method (F, 41).

10. In his memoirs Wan, too, recalls how he and his companion would keep walking despite their high fevers and weakness (W, 24–28).

11. Bua and La met while staying with Ajan Man at Pheu Pond Hermitage. They soon left the hermitage to wander on their own. Later Bua wrote a biography of Man.

12. By the time La took up a wandering life, modern drugs for malaria had become available and many people were relying on them for recovery. Quinine had been available in Thailand since the turn of the century, but people in rural areas had no access to such modern medicines until after World War II. A record of a modern doctor, Phraya Wibunayurawet (Sek Thammarot), who accompanied the Bangkok military campaign to Chiang Kham during the Shan rebellion in 1902, reveals that the military medicinal supplies included quinine as well as herbal medicines. See Vikan Phongphanitanon, "100 pi rongrian phaet ratchawithayalai" [Ratchawithayalai on the one-hundredth anniversary of the medical school], in *Sinlapa Watthanatham* 11, no. 2 (September 1990): 84.

13. La, 88. Bua's comment was probably a local expression, meaning that poor La really did not need the allergy on top of the malaria.

14. Phan, a monk with seventh-level Pali, had the same preceptor as Bua and La, namely Thepkawi (Jum), abbot of Wat Phothisomphon in Udon Thani.

15. During World War II, troops had been stationed near Naweng Stupa in Sakon Nakhon. Wan, who was a monk at Hollow Palms Village Wat in the same province, was called up for service in the military in 1943 (W, 29).

16. La, 101. Fan's empathy for La probably stemmed from his own bout with malaria as well as his experience of nursing the sick. Two or three years earlier, Fan and other monks had gone wandering in Udon Thani. Upon reaching the forest hermitage of Hill Village, one of the monks came down with malaria. This was in 1945, during World War II, and it was difficult to find medicine. Fan took the sick monk back to Weng Field Monastery and nursed him until he recovered. Fan himself suffered from recurrent malaria for over ten years before he got used to

it. Until then he always carried along some herbal medicine when he went wandering (F, 118).

17. Wn, 52. Barami (Pali: *pārami*) refers to a level of spiritual perfection achieved by those who are determined to become an arahat.

18. Wn, 52. Nagas (Thai: *nak*) are the serpent deities of the underworld that control water. Garudas (Thai: *khrut*) are mythical figures, part bird and part human, that symbolize the sun and destroy serpents. This recollection of Waen's reflects the local religious practices: deference to the forces of the natural world and faith in the power of deities and mystical animals. It also demonstrates his belief that the pure motives and intentions of the ascetic have a force of their own.

19. W, 70-71. A nimit (Pali: *nimitta*) is an image that appears in meditation, in dreaming, or in other visionary experiences.

20. Thate, "Steps along the Path," 10, 12. "Jhāna" has been translated as meditative absorption, trance, rapture, or ecstasy, none of which are suitable. According to Gunaratana, jhāna is a state of deep mental unification characterized by a total immersion of the mind in its object (*The Path of Serenity and Insight* [Delhi: Motilal Banarsidass, 1985], 3–4).

21. This was Dun's eighth year in the monkhood; he was about thirty years old and had not yet converted to the Thammayut order. Nu was later appointed abbot of Wat Sapathum in Bangkok.

22. Nanthapanyaphon, *Chiwa prawat Luang Pu Dun,* 14.

23. Ibid., 16.

24. Not to be confused with the other Nu, Dun's companion.

25. Thate, "Steps along the Path," 10.

26. Man probably could locate and identify the roots he needed, but he observed the precept that forbids a monk from digging up plants.

27. M1, 22. *Upacāra samādhi,* or access concentration, is the degree of concentration required in order to enter any of the jhānas.

28. Paraphrased from M3, 23–24.

29. At this point, Bua apologizes to his readers that he was unable to quote everything that Man told him. See M1, 22.

30. Man's visualized struggle with a demon bears some resemblance to the Tibetan meditation practice *chod,* wherein similar visualizations are cultivated in a deliberate and methodical way for the purpose of destroying attachment to the body.

31. The third stage of enlightenment. According to Bua, although anāgāmī is not yet the full and final stage of attainment, it is upon this infrastructure that the superstructure can be firmly constructed, with all the defilements totally annihilated in the long run. Boowa, "Dhūtaṅga Kammaṭṭhāna Bhikkhus," 85.

32. Letters written to supreme patriarchs during the next half-century,

from 1910 to 1957, reflect this same attitude (National Archives, Bangkok). Sometimes, however, "too ill to remain in the monkhood" was used as a pretext to disrobe. Administrative monks knew that if they used reasons other than illness, senior monks would try to talk them out of leaving the monastic life.

33. Ajahn Chah [Cha], *Bodhinyana: A Collection of Dhamma Talks* (Bangkok: Funny Press, 1982), 58.

34. According to meditation teachers, a sensation is anything that one feels at the physical level—pleasant or unpleasant, gross or subtle, intense or feeble. The sensation *(vedanā)* and the mind *(citta)* can be analyzed and separated from each other. Through the advanced development of mindfulness and wisdom, the body *(kāya)* is recognized not as one's self, but as a mere kāya. The same is true of vedanā and citta, each being recognized as such, i.e., not as one's self but as mere vedanā and mere citta. The false idea of self ceases to exist. The body, thoughts, and feelings become the truth. It is through attaining this realization that the wonder and the power of the mind can be experienced: its power to divorce itself absolutely from the sensations and become absolutely fearless of the threat of death. Boowa, "Dhūtaṅga Kammaṭṭhāna Bhikkhus," 85.

CHAPTER 5: BATTLING SEXUAL DESIRE

1. Thate Desaransi [Thet Thetrangsi], Phra Ajaan. "Buddho" (Berkeley: DharmaNet International, 1994), 16; DharmaNet electronic document, available from DharmaNet Electronic Files Archive (DEFA) at sunsite.unc.edu.

2. This would have been sometime between 1900 and 1920—Waen does not say. Although the Mekong River was the political border between Siam and Laos, this did not stop local people from crossing. Inhabitants on both banks of the river shared similar ethnic backgrounds.

3. Waen does not explain this meditation method, but Thet has a clarification: "The opposite sex or any object stimulating sensual pleasure can . . . be made into something that promotes the conditions necessary for a person to discern the harm of all sensuality. Those objects will then be seen as great facilitators in liberating oneself from the sensual realm" (T1, 137).

4. Ubali (Jan Sirijantho) was born in 1855 in Lai Pond Village, about twenty kilometers from the town of Ubon. He died in 1932, a year after Fan and Sing's visit. For a detailed discussion of why the wandering monks were in Khorat Province and why they went to Bangkok, see chapter 7.

5. Panyaphisan (Nu Thitapanyo) was born in 1864 in the town of Ubon. Like Jan, Nu was ordained in the Thammayut order at Wat Sithaung in his hometown. Their preceptor was Thewathammi (Maw). He died in 1944 (F, 82, 84).

6. This account comes from Lui Janthasaro, a fellow wandering monk. See Suriphan , *Chiwa prawat Luang Pu Lui,* 30–31. Fan's biographer, however, describes it more gently: Ajan Sing told Fan to stay in the ordination hall and to put more effort into his meditation.

7. F, 85. According to local beliefs, if a man and a woman were married in a previous life, they are likely to meet and marry again in their present life because they are soul mates. Wajuppa Tossa, ed., *Phadaeng Nang Ai: A Translation of a Thai-Isan Folk Epic in Verse* (London: Associated University Press, 1990), 112.

8. Ch3, 31. At first Cha's biographer (a lay disciple) was reluctant to include this incident, even expressed in such an understated way. But when consulted, Cha said, "Without the story of this battle there won't be a biography." As might be expected, when his life story was first published in 1968, it was heavily criticized. Cha's reaction was "Let them complain."

9. Cha did not learn these things from other monks, they occurred to him in the course of his practice. He tells us, "I would sit in meditation and reflect on sensual pleasure as being like a nest of red ants. Someone takes a piece of wood and pokes the nest until the ants come running out, crawling down the wood and into their faces, biting their eyes and ears. And yet they still don't see the difficulty they are in" (C1, 55–56). In the Northeast, incidentally, people do on occasion raid the nests of red ants. Both the ants and their eggs are used for food.

10. Wat Sapathum was the name thudong monks used for Wat Pathum Wanaram, because the Lao inhabitants in the area called it that. The wat was established in 1853 by King Mongkut. Its location is near the Sapathum Palace. At the time the area was surrounded by rice fields with abundant lotus flowers in the water. Hence it was named *sa pathum* (lotus pond). All but one abbot of this wat came from the Northeast. Phra Khru Wisuthiyansunthon, "Lao thi Wat Pathum Wanaram" [The Lao at Wat Pathum Wanaram], *Sinlapa Watthanatham* 12, no. 9 (July 1991): 52–58. Hereafter we shall refer to Wat Pathum Wanaram as Wat Sapathum.

11. Li1, 29–30; Li2, 22. Waen also complained that when he was staying at Wat Boromniwat (in the early 1930s) he hardly got enough food on his almsround. Many monks from the rural areas who came to Bangkok for a visit or to study Pali had similar experiences. This might be because a large number of people in Bangkok at the time were non-Buddhist Chinese.

12. Li1, 31; Li2, 22. All the incidents mentioned here were important in changing Li's thinking, as he tells us: "I have to beg the reader's pardon for mentioning them . . . because there's nothing at all pleasant about them. But since they were good lessons, I feel they should go on record" (Li1, 29).

13. Li1, 30; Li2, 22–23. A conflict with which Li struggled in the urban Thammayut wat, and which led him to consider leaving the monkhood is discussed at length in chapter 7.

14. T1, 133. According to the monastic discipline that Thet followed, a monk cannot be alone with a woman.

15. Ibid. Before secular education became widespread, young men would normally ordain for a number of years before marrying. The woman was probably trying to find out if that was Thet's intention.

16. T1, 134. Thet does not give the place or the year of this episode. It might have been in the early 1920s when he was staying at Wat Suthat, a Thammayut monastery in the town of Ubon. He was then about twenty years old. In those days this was still a rural area without electricity, and people went about on foot.

17. J, 10. The custom of not covering the breasts was common in rural Siam at the time. Bangkok people, however, frowned upon it. A government official in Bangkok, who traveled to the Northeast region in 1930 to conduct an economic survey, recalled that at the time young women in a village about twenty kilometers from the provincial town of Sisaket still went topless: "They do not feel embarrassed," he writes. "Some of us [from Bangkok] sneakily took photos of them." See Bamratnaradun, "Kham wai alai naiphaet Chi Sitajit" [In memory of Physician Chu Sitajit], in Bua, *Patipatha phra thudong kammathan,* 13. Perhaps this is why wandering meditation monks avoided staying near a village any longer than necessary.

18. J, 36. Juan was about twenty-eight years old then and was in his sixth year of monkhood.

19. J, 35. It is interesting that Juan thought about the teachings of Ubali (Jan Sirijantho), since Juan had never met him in person. Ubali died in 1932 when Juan was only twelve years old. He may have known about Ubali through his Thammayut preceptor, who was a nephew of Ubali's. Juan, however, tells us that the night before, while meditating, he had a vision that he was with his teacher, Man, and Ubali came to see them and gave him this particular advice.

20. Thet remarks that with all these monks gathered for the rains retreat, it would be difficult to find a better group of dhamma companions (T1, 176, 180).

21. Kheuang was a native of Kam Field Village (Ban Na Kham), That Phanom District, Nakhon Phanom Province (T1, 179–180; T2, 78).

22. Nanthapanyaphon, *Luang Pu fak wai: bantheuk khati tham* [A collection of Luang Pu Dun's Dhamma] (Bangkok: Kledthai, 1990), 62–63.

23. Agehananda Bharati, *The Ochre Robe: An Autobiography* (Santa Barbara: Ross-Erikson, 1980), 148.

24. Seng, a deputy to the sangha head of the Northeast, took Juan in 1945 to Pheu Pond Forest Hermitage (Sakon Nakhon) and introduced him to Ajan Man.

25. Suriphan, *Chiwa prawat Luang Pu Lui,* 120.

26. Many other Thammayut meditation monks disrobed, but the circumstances have not been published. High-level Thammayut monks have carefully guarded the stories of those Thammayut monks who quit the monastic life because they could not resist sexual desire, hoping that the facts would be known only within their immediate circle. They were probably afraid that if such information were made public, their image as a strict order would be tarnished. Sulak Sivaraksa, personal communication, 28 April 1992.

27. Thate, "Steps along the Path," 8.

28. Kornfield, Jack, and Paul Breiter, eds. *A Still Forest Pool: The Insight Meditation of Achaan Chah* (Wheaton, Ill.: Theosophical Publishing House, 1985), 82.

CHAPTER 6: WANDERING AND HARDSHIP

1. Bua, *Patipatha phra thudong kammathan,* 5–6.

2. T1, 125. Thet drew up these rules before setting out to the northern region to find Ajan Man.

3. Man's disciples took his instructions seriously. Li was thinking about going to Keng Tung to look for Man, but he was afraid that if he found him, Man might scold him for not taking advantage of the solitude that these caves offered.

4. The Chiang Dao Range is of considerable height and contains many sharp peaks. Chiang Dao Cave is one of the largest limestone caves in the country. The cavern consists of an intricate system of underground passages linking several small caves (Paitoon, *Landforms of Thailand,* 23, 35). Man liked the solitude of this area so much that he returned in the early 1940s, accompanied by Waen and Teu. Each of them stayed in a separate cave. They got together only twice a month on holy days. Chiang Dao Cave was later turned into a tourist attraction. A six-kilometer road was built linking the cave to the town of Chiang Dao, seventy-two kilometers from Chiang Mai. In the 1980s Waen lamented that Chiang Dao had ceased to exist as an isolated area suitable for meditation retreat (Wn, 78).

5. Bua, *Patipatha phra thudong kammathan,* 5–6. Anne Klein makes a similar point about monks in Tibet. She points out that in Tibet renunciates are rarely alone "in the sense that a Westerner in an apartment in a city to which she had just moved and knows no one is alone" (*Meeting the Great Bliss Queen: Buddhists, Feminists, and the Art of the Self* [Boston: Beacon Press, 1995], 40).

6. Chaup's biographer offers no details of Chaup's interaction with the mountain dwellers.

7. Boowa, "Dhūtaṅga Kammaṭṭhāna Bhikkhus," 80.

8. Wn, 36. The Yao people migrated from China to northern Siam by way of Laos and Burma in the 1890s. They call themselves Mien or Iu Mien and are concentrated in the northern provinces, mainly in Chiang Rai, Chiang Mai, Lampang and Nan. See John McKinnon and Bernard Vienne, eds., *Hill Tribes Today: Problems in Change* (Bangkok: White Lotus-Orstom, 1989), 10; Chob Kacha-ananda, "Yao: Migration, Settlements, and Land," in *Highlanders of Thailand,* ed. John McKinnon and Wanat Bhruksasri (Kuala Lumpur: Oxford University Press, 1983), 212–213.

9. Wn, 37. Monks who adhere to the 227 disciplinary rules are not supposed to ask for food or any requisites.

10. Li1, 54. Such concern with getting food might seem petty. But the wandering monk never knew where his next meal would come from or whether he would get any food at all. Li's, Waen's, and Thet's accounts contradict a widely believed myth that a thudong monk did not mind going without food for several days.

11. Li accepted the food but refused to go into the woman's house. He sat down in a grove near her home, and she brought out two trays of food plus a basket of glutinous rice. When he finished he chanted blessings for her and then was on his way (Li1, 55; Li2, 41). Li's recollection of the meal is not insignificant. Monks retain vivid memories of meals they have received, especially if they have not eaten enough for several days.

12. Wn, 55. This custom is similar to that of the Lahu, whose villages are usually situated at very high elevations.

13. T1, 147–148. From there they crossed over a mountain, passed a Karen village, and descended to the district of Phrao in Chiang Mai. Here they were relieved to hear that Man was staying not far away.

14. Wn, 34. Waen comments that he did not know which ethnic group these villagers belonged to. Although he could not understand their language, the men understood him quite well. He thought this was because the men traded with other tribes or other ethnic groups and thus had learned several languages, whereas the women stayed home and knew only their own language.

15. Further north, in China, the Buddhist vinaya prohibits meat eating, taking as its authority the Brahmajāla Sūtra and the Lankāvatāra Sūtra. See Xu-Yun, *Empty Cloud: The Autobiography of the Chinese Zen Master* (Shaftesbury, Dorset: Element Books, 1988), 30 n. 3.

16. Kongma Jirapunyo (1900-1962) was born in Khok Village (today in Tongkhom Subdistrict, Sakon Nakhon). His father was a trader; Kongma, a buffalo trader. He married a local woman. When she died during pregnancy, Kongma was filled with sorrow and ordained as a monk in a Lao tradition. He first met Ajan Man in 1926 at Wat Burapha in Ubon, became his disciple, and converted to the Thammayut order a few years later (at the same time as Li). Their upatcha was Panyaphisan (Nu). In 1933 Kongma established a samnak near a village in Nakhon Ratchasima. At this samnak Wiriyang became a disciple of his and went thudong with him to Chanthaburi Province, eastern Siam. In 1942 they traveled on foot from Chanthaburi to Pheu Tree Village in Sakon Nakhon to see Man. See Damrong Phuraya, "Luang Pu Kongma Jirapunyo," *Lokthip* 3, no. 40 (September 1984): 8–27. For details of their thudong life see Wi, 17–40.

17. Wi, 28. During the early-morning almsround in the Northeast, the villagers' custom was to give only rice to the monks and then have boys bring other food to accompany it to wherever the monks were sitting. The boys served while the monks ate.

18. T1, 141–142. Thet is referring to the Buddhist ethnic groups in the Shan states.

19. Wi, 25. The Lao thudong monk's bowl is a bit larger than the local town monk's.

20. Thongchai makes a similar point with reference to the "Thai" state (*Siam Mapped,* 164).

21. Wi, 8–9. Man was forty-one in 1911. He went wandering into the Shan states with a monk named Bunman. In his younger days Man went wandering in Burma to search for meditation teachers. The brief account recorded in Wiriyang's biography is discussed in chapter 2.

22. Suriphan, *Chiwa prawat Luang Pu Chaup,* 69. Suriphan writes that Chaup could speak *phama* and Chaup believed that he was a phama in one of his previous lives. *Phama* is a generic term that Bangkok people use to refer both to anyone living in Burma, regardless of actual ethnicity, and to the official language, Burmese. The more correct term for this ethnic group is Shan or Tai-Yai.

23. Ibid., 71. Later, when Chaup told this story to lay disciples in Thailand, he added, "Whoever wants to be reborn with fine features and a light complexion must observe the five precepts." Evidently Chaup shared the commonly held view that light-skinned women are more blessed.

24. Li1, 63; Li2, 46–47. This was probably a Mahayana monastery. The local monk had no objection to Li and his disciples staying in his temple, although they were followers of a different tradition. In contrast, many Thai abbots who followed modern state Buddhism were not always hospitable to visiting monks whose religious customs differed from theirs. Such abbots would check visitors' identification papers first before allowing them to stay.

25. Li1, 63; Li2, 47. In the English version the distance is incorrectly given as thirty kilometers. (Li records the distance as eighty *sen;* one kilometer equals twenty-five sens.)

26. In November 1940, under the Phibun regime, Thailand invaded western Cambodia as well as Lao territories. The Japanese mediated between Thailand and Indochina and forced a settlement. Consequently, the Cambodian provinces of Battambang and Siem Reap were annexed by Thailand (Wyatt, *Thailand,* 256). After World War II the two provinces were returned to Cambodia.

27. Wi, 24. Wiriyang's impression of the Kula's progress in meditation is similar to Man's and Thet's impressions of the hill tribes in the North (see below).

28. Among the disciples with Man in the North were Thet, Khaw, Aunsi, Manu, San, and Maha Thaungsuk. See Damrong Phuraya, "Phra Ajan Maha Thaungsuk Sujitto," *Lokthip* 3, no. 4 (November 1984): 26–33. Man's biographers give few details about the highlanders Man encountered during a decade of wandering in the North. Moreover, they seldom record the exact year that Man spent a rains retreat in a certain area, although they describe some incidents in detail.

29. Thudong monks depended on the generosity and goodwill of forest people for alms. If there were too few households in a village, a monk, unless specifically invited, would be reluctant to stay there so as not to impose on them. See T1, 156.

30. Most of the Lahu live at fairly high altitudes in the provinces of Chiang Mai, Mae Hong Son, and Chiang Rai. They comprise several cultural-linguistic subgroups, all speaking the Lahu language. See Anthony R. Walker, "The Lahu People: An Introduction," in *Highlanders of Thailand,* ed. McKinnon and Bhruksasri, 231. Local people call them Muser, meaning "hunters," because the first Lahu to reach Lan Na in the 1880s were mainly hunters and gatherers.

31. Today few villages are self-sufficient in food. During the Forest-Invasion Period (1958–1988) the impact of market forces and development projects combined with the diminishing availability of land—a result of government intervention and population increase—have led to ecological impoverishment. The number of cultivated plants has decreased,

and the old system of multiple cropping has given way to monoculture. Commercial development has brought farmers hardship by making them dependent on markets over which they have no control. Chantaboon Sutthi, "Highland Agriculture: From Better to Worse," in *Hill Tribes Today: Problems in Change,* ed. John McKinnon and Bernard Vienne (Bangkok: White Lotus-Orstom, 1989), 107.

32. See T1, 157. Thet adds that "wild yams, taros and other potato-type tubers were widely found and eaten throughout the northern region. In the Northeast they were considered more a famine food."

33. Bua writes that Man learned all of this through his psychic powers.

34. Bua adds that lay disciples who have faith and obedience are able to develop psychic abilities better than monks or learned men. Scholars' intellectual knowledge seems to stand in the way of their attainment of these special powers. Even in the attainment of insight meditation, they often proved to be no match for the humble, unsophisticated lay devotees. M1, 154–155.

35. M2, 163–164. Here is a typical remark by a sangha official from Bangkok: "In this village [Bau Luang Village, Hot District, Chiang Mai], the inhabitants are Lua (Lawa). There are about two hundred of them. They have dark skin. Quite barbaric. They don't know how to make merit or give alms." Phra Khru Wiratham-sunthon, report to the sangha head of monthon Phayap, May 1935, *Thalaengkan khana song* 24 (1936): 425–478.

36. For details of Man's attaining enlightenment see M2, 139–147.

37. Thet became acquainted with the Mlabri, learned about their culture, and explained why they were called *phi* (spirits) by the Lahu. For a detailed account of Thet's encounter with the Mlabri, see T1, 162–167. The Mlabri lost their traditional way of life after the extensive forests disappeared. Today their descendants, no longer subsistence hunters and gatherers, have been integrated into the outside world. A survey taken in September 1988 shows that in Nan Province the population of the Mlabri or Phi Taung Leuang was 138 persons living in 26 households. In Phrae Province there were 34 persons in 7 households. They have no legal status as hill-tribe people. McKinnon and Vienne, *Hill Tribes Today,* 7, 426.

38. This was in 1937 when Man was in Mae Suai District, Chiang Rai (M3, 124).

39. Wn, 57. Ubosot days, every full and new moon, are so named because on these days monks recite the patimok in the ubosot.

40. Ibid. The abhidhamma that the Shan monks discussed dissects transcendental or supermundane *(lokuttara)* mental states. According to abhidhamma, the supermundane "path" *(magga)* designates the moment

that the meditator enters into one of the four stages of mental purification. It is produced by insight into the impermanence, unsatisfactoriness, and impersonality of existence (Nyanatiloka, *Buddhist Dictionary,* 23–26, 109). Abhidhamma is the subject matter of the third basket of the Tipitaka, the Abhidhamma Pitaka, a scholastic elaboration of doctrine regarding the analysis of mind (Richard Gombrich, *Theravada Buddhism* [New York: Routledge and Kegan Paul, 1988], 4).

41. Li1, 50. Li and Khian did not stay for the rains retreat.

42. Shigeharu Tanabe, *Nung leuang, nung dam* [Wearing yellow, wearing black] (Bangkok: Sangsan, 1986), 249.

43. Li1, 50–51. It was not unusual for wandering thudong monks to encounter an ascetic who had befriended wild animals.

44. Li1, 64. It is curious that Li mentions that there was no conflict. One wonders whether he was expecting to have a heated argument with the Khmer scholar monk.

45. Li1, 65. Li does not say in what language he communicated with the Chinese monk. It is not surprising that Li hit it off so well with the Chinese monk, though the two were of different traditions, Theravada and Mahayana. Both were wandering monks and probably had more in common with one another than with administrative monks of their own sects. Li, we know, had little in common with the Thammayut book-learning monks of Bangkok (see chap. 7).

46. Thudong monks are considerate in this respect. If younger monks or novices refuse to stay in a certain place, an older monk will not force them. Perhaps this is why Waen preferred not to take young disciples with him.

47. During the early 1930s a large number of Thai monks and novices followed Phra Lokanat, an Italian monk, to Burma. At first they were supported by the Siamese King (Prachathipok) who gave each monk fifty baht and issued them all passports. They left Bangkok on 14 January 1933 for Ayuthaya, Lopburi, Nakhon Sawan, and Sukhothai. From Tak Province a group of monks (ten of them from the South) went on their separate ways to Burma. Unlike the thudong monks, these monks did not seek solitude to practice meditation. They usually stayed in wats along the way. See Panyanantha, *Chiwit khaung khapphajao* [My Life] (Bangkok: Commemoration of sixtieth birthday, 1972), 54–56, 60–61. It is interesting that a Thammayut monk should have traveled with Pan, a Mahanikai monk. Pan was later to be known nationwide for his oratorical skills under his Pali name Panyanantha.

48. Panyanantha (Pan) became abbot of Wat Cholaprathan (in Nonthaburi) in 1960. He told this story to laypeople who came to listen to his sermon. Later it was published in Panyanantha, *Chiwit khaung*

khapphajao. Obviously the experience changed this Thai monk's perception of Mahayana monks. A *wai* is a respectful greeting made by bringing the palms and fingers of both hands together and raising them to the level of the chin (or higher or lower depending on the degree of respect).

49. The Thammajarik monks worked among the Meo, Yao, Lisu, Lahu, Akha, and Karen hill peoples. For the use of Thammajarik monks (during the Forest-Invasion Period) as instruments of national policy to undermine hill-tribe culture, see Charles F. Keyes, "Buddhism and National Integration in Thailand," *Journal of Asian Studies* 30, no. 3 (1971): 551–568.

CHAPTER 7: RELATIONS WITH SANGHA OFFICIALS

1. Uan and Jan were active participants in Wachirayan's monastic education reforms in the Northeast. Christine Gray observes that Uan and Jan were "either heroes or traitors to the Isan people, depending upon with whom one talks (i.e., whether the speaker is affiliated with the Thammayut or Mahanikai orders of Isan)." Uan, in particular, rose higher in the sangha hierarchy than any Lao-speaking monk had done (Gray, "Thailand," 294).

2. See Kitirat Sihaban, "Kan ruam khana song isan khao kap khana song thai" [Integrating the Isan sangha into the Thai sangha] (master's thesis, Thammasat University, 1990), 137–145.

3. Uan (1867–1956) was born in Khaen Pond Village (Ban Naung Khaen), Red Ants Hill, meuang Ubon Ratchathani. His father was a jailer in meuang Lao Khaw Lao Phuan. At the age of nineteen he was ordained as a novice in a Lao tradition at Wat Sawang (now in Warin District, Ubon). In 1887 he received higher ordination in the Thammayut order at Wat Si Thaung with Thewathammi (Maw) as his preceptor and Phra Maha Jan Sirijantho as his ordination instructor. Uan accompanied Jan to study in Bangkok in 1890 after his preceptor died. After passing the fifth-level Pali exam, he returned to Ubon to establish Pali studies at Wat Supat in 1897. He became the sangha head of monthon Isan in 1904 when his teacher, Jan, gave up the post. Uan accompanied Wachirayan (who had become the supreme patriarch in 1910) on his inspection trip to monthon Ayuthaya (central Siam) in 1914–1915. For a detailed account of Uan's life see Uan, *Prawat patipatha,* 25–45.

4. This monastery was established in 1906 by Pho Nethipho (titled Phraya Sisuriraj), the first governor of meuang Udon. Villagers were ordered to clear the forest and donate labor to build the wat. The next governor, Uap Paorohit (Phraya Mokhamontri), built an ordination hall and expanded the temple in 1916. In 1923 he converted the monastery

to the Thammayut order and asked the supreme patriarch to send an academic monk to become abbot.

Prior to this, a Thammayut wat had been established in 1898 in meuang Kamutsai-Buriram (now called Naung Bua Lamphu District in Udon Thani Province). It was established after Saeng, a native of Kamutsai-Buriram, came to meuang Ubon with a group of local monks and converted to the Thammayut order at Wat Sithaung. The monks studied with the preceptor, Abbot Maw, before returning to Kamutsai-Buriram. At first they had no wat to stay in, so they wandered around teaching meditation. The ruler of Kamutsai-Buriram was impressed with their conduct and invited them to reside at Wat Mahachai. Later they set up a branch wat in Kumphawapi (today a district in Udon Thani), and three other branches in Loei and Khon Kaen. None of these Thammayut monasteries that Saeng set up are located in towns. Their isolated locations protected them from outside influences, and as a result Saeng and his fellow monks remained independent of Thammayut administrators. Saeng appointed himself a preceptor, ordained monks at will, and did not report to the Thammayut authorities in Ubon Ratchathani. (This was all before the Sangha Administrative Act was enforced in Udon Thani in 1908.) See Kitirat, "Kan ruam khana song isan," 83–84.

5. Jum Phanthulo, a native of Nakhon Phanom, went to Bangkok as a novice to study under the state monastic system, residing at Wat Thepsirin (a royal Thammayut monastery). He was sent to Wat Phothisomphon fifteen years later and was appointed abbot (with the title of Phra Khru Sanghawutthikonwat) at thirty-five—a relatively young age for the position (F, 29, 33).

6. For brief biographies of Sing and Maha Pin, see chapter 2.

7. F, 79. It is well documented that thudong monks preferred developing self-knowledge and mental stability to studying texts and preparing for exams.

8. Abbot Jum (then titled Phra Khru Chinowathamrong) was the preceptor (appointed by Bangkok authorities to perform ordination for the Thammayuts), Sing the announcing teacher (recommending the candidate's acceptance into the community of monks), and Maha Pin the instructing teacher. After the passage of the Sangha Act of 1902, local senior monks who were not appointed by Bangkok lost the power to ordain monks into their lineages.

9. Phra Thepsumethi (Sing Suthajitto), abbot of Wat Si Ubon, interview by author, 12 June 1989. The abbot was a young boy at Chaneng Pond Village (Ban Bau Chaneng) when Man's disciples came there in 1926. A few years later, he was ordained as a novice and followed Ku (a disciple of Man's) on a thudong in northeastern and northern Siam.

10. This was not the only time Sing was confronted by Uan, who was his preceptor. At times Sing was so annoyed that he went wandering outside Siam, according to Fan (F, 79).

11. Aun Yansiri was born in 1902 in Udon Thani and was ordained as a monk in 1921 at Wat Pakho, Kumphawapi District. He went wandering in 1922, met Sao and Man in 1923 at Kau Village Monastery, Ban Pheu District in Udon, and converted to the Thammayut order in 1924. Jum Phanthulo was his preceptor (F, 55). Koeng Athimuttako (1887–1965) was born in Samphong Village (today in Nakhon Phanom Province), and in 1907 was ordained as a monk at his village wat. He searched for a meditation teacher and found Man wandering in Sakon Nakhon in 1926. He invited Man to his village and was reordained into the Thammayut order the same time as Fan. He died at Wat Phochai in his village, at the age of seventy-eight (F, 49). Sila Issaro (1886–1967) was born in a village in Wayai Commune (today in Wanon Niwat District, Sakon Nakhon). In 1909 he was ordained as a monk in the tradition of his village wat. He met Koeng in 1926, and together they went to meet Man when the latter came to Sakon Nakhon. Sila converted to the Thammayut order at the same time as Koeng and Fan (F, 50).

12. F, 52. This was probably how the sangha authorities obtained records of thudong monks. Such records enabled the sangha authorities to locate thudong monks when necessary.

13. This is a method that Man and his disciples employed when there was insufficient knowledge to draw a conclusion. They would enter deep concentration, silence the self, and then form a judgment.

14. T1, 93. The ellipsis points in the quotation are Thet's. Ariyesako Bhikkhu, the editor of this translation, believes that Thet put them there because he thought it best not to go further into the matter.

15. In 1914 Ubon Ratchathani and Nakhon Ratchasima became the centers of pariyat tham. See Kitirat, "Kanruam khana song isan," 96, 144.

16. F, 49. *Jai* is sometimes translated as "mind." See Boowa, "Wisdom Develops Samadhi," in Kornfield, *Living Buddhist Masters,* 164–165.

17. Wat Jediluang, previously abandoned, was restored during Ubali's time as the first Thammayut wat in the North. Ubali wanted an abbot who was strict in the vinaya to teach the local monks, whom he considered lax. At Wat Jediluang monks were required to study as well as practice meditation. But Man found that the town monks were not interested in practicing meditation. When Ubali died, Man fled the wat without notifying sangha authorities (M3, 87–88).

18. While in Ubon Man took his mother to Chaneng Pond Village.

Once settled in that village she was to be cared for by a disciple of Man's (F, 58).

19. At Wat Burapha, Nu reordained a number of thudong monks, including Kongma and Li, into the Thammayut order. Ajan Man was a witness of the ceremony. Before becoming abbot of Wat Sapathum in Bangkok, Nu had been abbot of Wat Tai, located near Wat Liap in the capital town of Ubon. Both Wat Tai (under Nu) and Wat Liap (under Sao) were converted to the Thammayut order in 1896. See Phra Maha Saun Si-ek, *Prawat kankaukoet Thammayut nikai, prawat Wat Supat, prawat Wat Si Ubon* [History of the Thammayut order, Wat Supat, and Wat Si Ubon] (Ubon: Saphasan, 1979), 26.

20. Prachuap Sanklang, "Botbat khaung phra song fai vipassana thura thi mi tau sangkhom Isan neua: seuksa korani sai Phra Ajan Man Phurithatto" [Role of vipassanā monks in upper Isan: Phra Ajan Man's lineage] (master's thesis, Srinakkharinwirot University, 1988), 30.

21. Monthon Isan was abolished and was replaced by monthon Nakhon Ratchasima. Nakhon Ratchasima is more popularly called Khorat.

22. Suriphan, *Chiwa prawat Luang Pu Lui*, 36–37. According to Fan's biographer, Sing and his disciples were wandering in Nam Phaung District (in Khon Kaen) when they received the order to go to Khorat.

23. Khorat, a center of cattle trading in the Northeast, had a reputation for bandits and violence (T2, 45).

24. F, 90. This new samnak, called Marum Village Hermitage, was located between Fak Village and Nongna Village in Phon Songkhram Commune. Kamdi Praphaso established another samnak, Sakaerat Hermitage, in Pak Thong Chai District. Lui left Khorat at the end of the 1932 rains retreat and went wandering in Sakon Nakhon. There he spent the 1933 and 1934 rains retreat in Phongam Village Cave in Kut Bak District. Suriphan, *Chiwa prawat Luang Pu Lui*, 37, 39.

25. See Taylor, *Forest Monks*, 120.

26. A report from Prince Wachirayan to King Chulalongkorn mentions that Nakhon Ratchasima presented a particular problem for sangha "reforms." Ibid., 120.

27. Wi, 1–3. Given his background, Kongma would have had no difficulties relating to local people. Kongma had been a cattle trader before being ordained in a Lao tradition and later converting to the Thammayut. Note that Kongma followed the Bangkok-imposed custom according to which monks chant together daily.

28. Fan's biographer does not say when he met Phin, who was later promoted to lieutenant-general. It was probably after sangha head Uan became acquainted with the captain-major in 1933, when the latter took

command of the Suranari Garrison in Khorat. For these recollections of Phin's, see *An somdet* [Read the somdet] (Bangkok: Crem. vol. Somdet Phra Maha Wirawong Tissathera, Wat Boromniwat, 1956), 47. Phin had fought in the Indochina War, was commander of the Third Division of the Northern Army in the northern campaign, and was in charge during the capture of Chiang Tung (in the Shan states). In 1941 the Siamese government gained control of Chiang Tung and Phin was stationed there. He then wanted the meditation monks Sing, Maha Pin, and Fan to go there to teach the dhamma and vinaya to the Shan monks. The plan did not materialize, however. At the end of World War II the Japanese were defeated and Chiang Tung was returned to Burma. In November 1947 Phin was one of the instigators of the coup that seized power from the Bangkok government.

29. F, 95–97. Literally, *phra jao chu* means "monk with many lovers."

30. Among the thudong monks who spent the 1932 rains retreat at Sattharuam Forest Monastery were Fan, Phumi, Lui, Kongma, and Thet.

31. It appears that Sing wanted Thet to continue doing samatha meditation, whereas Thet thought he had gone beyond that level. Thet realized then that he could no longer depend on Sing. He thought that only Ajan Man could help him. As well, he disliked living in a group and wanted to get away (T1, 124).

32. For details of Thet's and Aunsi's search for Ajan Man, see chapter 6.

33. Phim Thammaro (1896–1974) was born in Sawang Village, Warin District, meuang Ubon. From the beginning he was ordained as a novice in the Thammayut order at Wat Supat and took higher ordination there in 1917. His preceptor was Uan (titled Ratchamuni at the time). In 1965 Phim received the title of Somdet Phra Maha Wirawong, a title that previously belonged to Uan (F, 97). Du Pond Village was a Mon community, and the monks in this monastery were strict in keeping disciplinary rules. The eighty-year-old abbot, who was revered for his supernatural powers, had been converted to the Thammayut order by thudong monks who had stayed there. At first the senior Thammayut monk, Phim, wanted to send Aun, who was visiting Man in Chiang Mai in 1937, to teach the Mon monks. But Aun managed to avoid Phim's call and returned to the Northeast. So it was Thet who took up the teaching duty (T2, 78–79; F, 97; Taylor, *Forest Monks*, 83–84).

34. Thet does not tell us why he became a settled monastic at Wat Aranyawasi. Possibly he had to comply with the request of a senior monk such as Thepkawi (Jum Phanthulo), the sangha head of monthon Udon Thani (whose authority included Nongkhai Province). Although

in his memoirs Thet does not explicitly say he was an abbot, the responsibilities expected of him were those of an abbot.

35. When he finished his sermon he would ask the audience what he had been speaking about and if it made any sense. The laypeople answered that they could understand it very well, just as they always did (T1, 187). It seems that the laypeople here liked Thet.

36. Khao Salakphat is an annual festival in the Northeast during which villagers present offerings to the monks to make merit for the dead. Distribution of the gifts to the monks is done by drawing lots (T1, 189).

37. According to the biographer, although Dun would have preferred to go wandering, he went along with his preceptor's wishes. Dun's preceptor was short of funds and needed Dun's help to solicit donations. Uan, the monthon sangha head, had had his eye on Dun since the early 1920s, when Dun was studying for the naktham exam at Wat Suthat in Ubon. He was one of the first local monks to pass the naktham exam. At the time Dun had not yet converted to the Thammayut order (Nanthapanyaphon, *Chiwa prawat luang pu Dun,* 9, 31). Dun managed to avoid the sangha head's demand until 1934.

38. As Lui put it, Sing, having been appointed abbot of Salawan Forest Monastery in Khorat, received "unanticipated rewards" (Suriphan, *Chiwa prawat Luang Pu Lui,* 38).

39. Jan Sirijantho (1856–1932) was born in Lai Pond Village (Ban Naung Lai), about twenty kilometers from the town of Ubon and not far from Man's natal village. At the age of twelve he was ordained a novice in a Lao tradition at his village wat. The following year a relative of his, a Thammayut monk in Ubon, came home for a visit. The Thammayut monk then took Jan with him to study at Wat Sithaung in Ubon. The abbot of this wat, Thewathammi (Maw), a disciple of Mongkut's, was Jan's cousin. Jan disrobed at the age of nineteen to help his mother plow the paddy fields (his father had been conscripted into the army to fight the Haw). In 1878 his cousin, an abbot, sent a layman to his village to take him to Ubon to be ordained in the Thammayut order. After the 1902 Sangha Act was passed, Jan was appointed the sangha head of monthon Isan. He resigned from the position in 1903 so he could go on a thudong in the Shan states, but Wachirayan appointed him abbot of Wat Boromniwat in 1904. Although Jan disliked administrative work, he had to accept the abbotcy in Bangkok. See Jan Sirijantho, "Attano prawat" [My Life], reprinted in *Si Ubonrattanaram,* 5–6. For discussion of the rise of Ubali (Jan) in the sangha hierarchy see Taylor, *Forest Monks,* 53–58.

Nu Thitapanyo (1864–1944) was born in the town of Ubon. A disciple of Jan's, he was ordained at Wat Sithaung in Ubon by Thewathammi (Maw). See F, 82, 84.

40. The earliest date mentioned in Man's biography is 1912 (M3, 10). This was the year that Wachirayan went to inspect monasteries in southern Siam.

41. In those days Wat Sapathum was on the outskirts of the city. It was a long walk, and Man passed paddies and orchards on his way to Wat Boromniwat. Man used the occasion to do his walking meditation (M3, 41). Today this temple is in the middle of the city, with shopping malls, several cinemas, and nightclubs nearby.

42. Waen converted to the Thammayut order in 1927 at Wat Jediluang in Chiang Mai. Ubali, who spent the rains retreat there from 1927–1930, was his preceptor.

43. Without adequate nourishment it is difficult to meditate, Waen told his disciples (Wn, 59). Li's experience was similar to Waen's: he got very little food during almsround. This might be because Bangkok had a large number of Chinese residents who did not follow the custom of giving food to monks on almsround.

44. Li1, 20. Li gives no details of the "worldly matters" that his fellow monks had been discussing. It is not clear if Li knew that after he had left Bangkok, these urban Thammayut monks, led by La Sothito (not to be confused with our thudong monk, La Khempatato), took power from Abbot Nu in March 1932. For more details see below.

45. Li1, 20. Li remarks that "the whole affair was my preceptor's fault. One morning he had been invited to accept some donations on the day following a cremation at the house of a nobleman, but his ceremonial fan and shoulder bag were kept in my room, and since I had gone out for alms and taken the key with me, he couldn't get to them. So from then on he told me to leave the key with Nai Bun [a temple boy] every morning before going out for alms, and this was how the money had disappeared. I was lucky that Nai Bun had admitted his guilt."

46. As one Mahanikai abbot in Isan remarked, "Although in public Thammayut monks do not touch money, privately if they catch a temple boy spending their money they often beat him severely. In a similar situation, the Mahanikai abbot, who is outwardly less strict since he may handle money, will not punish the temple boy so harshly." Phra Kittiyansophon (b. 1927), abbot of Wat Maha Wanaram, Ubon Ratchathani, interview by author, 6 June 1989.

47. Li1, 22. Since we know little about Abbot Nu's personality, a comment of Sao's might give us a clue. In his younger days, Nu used to go wandering with Sao. But Nu had problems with his meditation that Sao could not resolve. In Sao's opinion, "It's beyond [my] capability to

rescue him from going berserk, because he has been crazy since birth."
Sao expressed this opinion to Lui when the two went wandering
together (Suriphan, *Chiwa prawat Luang Pu Lui,* 55–56).

48. Man had come to Bangkok to visit Ubali, who had broken his leg
and was laid up at Wat Boromniwat. While in Bangkok, Man made a
point of attending Lady Noi's funeral services at Wat Thepsirin. Lady
Noi, mother of Phraya Mukkhamontri, was one of Man's supporters
when he was staying in Udon Thani (Li1, 32). Lady Noi met Man in
1924 at Wat Phothisomphon in Udon Thani when they were attending a
ceremony consecrating the wat's boundary stones. Impressed by Man's
sermons, she became a lay supporter (T2, 25). Noi was also a lay supporter of Somdet Phra Phuthakhosajan (Jaroen), abbot of Wat Thepsirin
and sangha head of monthon Prachinburi, although she died before he
received the somdet title (see Dulaphaksuwaman, *Somdet upatcha* [Bang-
kok: Mahamakut University Press, 1988], 10).

49. Eighty baht was a lot of money in those days. For example, a
clerk in a drug store in Bangkok was paid twenty baht per month.
Monthly rent for a room was four baht (Li2, 18).

50. The death of Ubali, a senior Thammayut monk who appreciated
the thudong tradition, probably had more personal impact on Man and
his disciples than the coup d'état. Thet, however, points out that the
establishment of the first two Thammayut forest monasteries in Khorat
in 1932 coincided with the end of absolute monarchy in Thailand
(T2, 46).

51. Boworadet, a grandson of Chulalongkorn (Rama V), had been
minister of war under Prachathipok (Rama VII). Early in October 1933,
he appeared at the head of a provincial army revolt, having incited the
Nakhon Ratchasima garrison to rebel. Several other provincial garrisons
joined the revolt. The government's military response to the rebels was
organized by Lieutenant-Colonel Phibun. After intense fighting, the
rebellion was broken. When the government troops approached, Boworadet fled into exile in French Indochina (Wyatt, *Thailand,* 248).

52. Early in 1934 the king went abroad for medical treatment, and in
March of 1935 he abdicated. Although the monarchy was still present in
form, in practice the new king was absent. For a quarter century, during
which time King Rama VIII (Ananda) and King Rama IX (Bhumibol)
were studying in Europe, Thailand was without a monarch as a focus of
power. Other incidents further decreased the power and prestige of the
nobility. In January 1939 Phibun, who had become prime minister the
month before, arrested some forty people including members of the
royal family and other nobles. He executed eighteen of them on charges
of plotting against the government. He also moved against the monar-

chy, prohibiting the display of pictures of the former king Prachathipok and suing him for misuse of crown property. This period marks the lowest point in the prestige of the monarchy (ibid., 153).

53. See Peter Jackson, *Buddhism, Legitimation, and Conflict: The Political Functions of Urban Thai Buddhism* (Singapore: Institute of Southeast Asian Studies, 1989), 28, and Sawaeng Udomsi, *Kanpokkhraung khana song thai* [Administration of the Thai sangha] (Bangkok: Mahachula University Press, 1991), 138. One Thammayut senior monk who may have been suspected by the new government was Somdet Wachirayanwong (Cheun), abbot of Wat Bowon and head of the Thammayut order. His brother—Phraya Senasongkhram (M R. Ee Nophawong)—was a participant in the Boworadet rebellion. Another possible suspect was Somdet Phuthakhosajan (Jaroen), abbot of Wat Thepsirin, who was close to Prince Damrong and corresponded with him after he went into exile in Penang. In one of his letters to Somdet Jaroen (dated 6 June 1934), the prince wrote, "In summary, you know me better than most people." Sulak Sivaraksa "Khamnam" [Introduction], in *Sam somdet* [Three somdets] (Bangkok: Kledthai, 1980), 11; Damrong's letter appears in *Sam somdet,* 68. Damrong was never in sympathy with the new government. It was widely believed that he was one of the nobles who opposed political change in the last months of the absolute monarchy. Shortly after the Boworadet rebellion in November 1933, he went to live in Penang, Malaya. He did not receive official permission to return to Bangkok until 1942. Batson, *End of the Monarchy,* 256–258.

54. Wyatt, *Thailand,* 248.

55. See a discussion of the conflicts between senior Thammayut and Mahanikai administrative monks during this period in Sawaeng, *Kanpokkhraung khana song thai,* 131–195.

56. Somboon Suksamran, *Buddhism and Politics in Thailand: A Study of Socio-Political Change and Political Activism of the Thai Sangha* (Singapore: Institute of Southeast Asian Studies, 1982), 41. The revolution, however, did not lead to any substantial restructuring of Thai society. It merely replaced the royal segment of the bureaucratic elite with the nonaristocratic bureaucrats. Phibun's democratic forms often masked quite autocratic actions. Jackson, *Buddhism, Legitimation, and Conflict,* 27, 30.

57. Wyatt, *Thailand,* 252.

58. The young Mahanikai monks who secretly organized the movement in Bangkok were supported by monks in several provinces, particularly the central and southern provinces. On 5 March 1935, for example, 2,080 monks (including 110 abbots and 45 academic monks) from 368 monasteries in twelve southern provinces submitted a petition to

Prime Minister Phahon to reform the sangha administration. In the Northeast, only monks from Khon Kaen openly supported the movement. This might be because the high-level administrative posts in the Northeast were controlled by the Thammayuts. After Wachirayan's death the two highest administrative positions in the Northeast (the sangha heads of monthon Nakhon Ratchasima and monthon Udon Thani) were under the Thammayuts' supervision.

During the years that the movement took place, the Sangha Act of 1902 was still in force. The Young Monks took considerable risks, since the Sangha Council was controlled by Thammayut elders. In Bangkok those participants in the movement who were caught were either defrocked or punished as severely as criminals. For a comprehensive account of the Young Monks movement, based partly on interviews, see Khaneungnit Janthabutra, *Kankhleuanwai khaung yuwasong thai runraek,* 2477–2484 [The first movement of Thai Young Monks, 1934–1941] (Bangkok: Thammasat University Press, 1985).

59. Somdet Phae was eighty-two then. He died in 1944.

60. For example, Pridi Phanomyong (at the time minister of the interior) was most sympathetic to the Young Monks movement. He met with leaders and agreed to help them. Afterward he shielded them from police arrest. Another supporter of the movement was Thawan Rithidet (an ex-Thammayut monk from Wat Samphanthawong), who in 1933 sued King Prachathipok for libel (this was before the Boworadet rebellion). However, Pridi's and Thawan's support backfired when the royalists later accused the two of infiltrating the sangha institution to spread communist ideas. Khaneungnit, *Kankhleuanwai,* 117–119, 192–193.

61. Jackson, *Buddhism, Legitimation, and Conflict,* 27–28, 30.

62. Ibid., 74.

63. Khaneungnit, *Kankhleuanwai,* 182.

64. The announcement was published in *Thalaengkan khana song* 20 (1932): 452–464. For the entire document see Sawaeng, *Kan pokkhraung khana song thai,* 136–139.

65. See the correspondence between the senior Thammayut monks and the director-general in Sawaeng, *Kanpokkhraung khana song thai,* 139–142. Townsfolk in the area later appealed for the wat to be reinstated (Khaneungnit, *Kankhleuanwai,* 66).

66. Phra Khru Winaikoson, *Reuang arai di* [Stories worth telling] (Chiang Mai: Wat Jediluang, 1954), 10–11. In 1933, when the new government abolished the monthon system, the superintendent commissioner was replaced by a new governor.

Wat Sutjinda was established by Dan Rakprajit (titled Phraya Phetprani), superintendent commissioner of monthon Nakhon Ratchasima.

Dan told people in Nakhon Ratchasima, Buriram, and Chaiyaphum (the three meuangs in monthon Nakhon Ratchasima) to donate money to build the wat. He combined two small local monasteries in the provincial town and converted them to a Thammayut wat. The construction of the ordination hall was completed in 1925. The monthon sangha head, Uan, was invited to be abbot of Wat Sutjinda in 1927. Uan was later appointed abbot of Wat Boromniwat in Bangkok (Uan, *Prawat pathipatha*, 37).

67. *An somdet*, 48.

68. This was Phin Chunahawan's opinion, expressed in *An somdet*, 47–49. During the period between 1933 (when General Phahon became prime minister) and 1944 (when Phibun fell) the army held political power.

69. Sao Soriyo was a disciple of Ubali (Jan). Ubali had considered him trustworthy. See Ubali's autobiography, "Attano prawat," in Uan, *Prawat patipatha*, 80.

70. Uan Tisso (Somdet Phra Maha Wirawong Tissathera), *Niphon bang reuang* [Somdet's writings] (Bangkok: Crem. vol. Phra Maha Wirawong, 1956), 29. The speech is titled "Support the nation and the religion."

71. *Thalaengkan khana song* 23 (1935), cited in Khaneungnit, *Kan khleuan wai*, 81–82.

72. Uan, *Niphon bang reuang*, 32.

73. Ibid., 30–31.

74. Ubali expressed this concern to his brother, Thepworakhun (Um Phatharawutho), abbot of Sirijan's Vision Wat (formerly Beautiful Buddha Image Hill Monastery) in Lopburi. According to Um (in *An somdet*, 35), Ubali was afraid that Uan might never learn how to meditate.

75. Uan went to stay in Ubon because of allied bombing raids on Bangkok. But Ubon Province also became a target. During World War II a large number of Japanese soldiers were stationed all over Ubon. Allied planes dropped bombs onto strategic targets several times a week. Most people in the town moved out to the rural areas where there were no Japanese troops. Those who remained in town often went with their children to seek shelter in monasteries during the air raids. During these frightened times Fan kept people calm by having them recite "buddho, buddho" to concentrate their minds (F, 106–107).

76. In those days part of Wat Burapha was a building for dhamma study; another part was a forested area with five or six huts for monks and novices practicing meditation. Fan stayed in the forested area for the entire rains retreat (F, 103).

77. This was during World War II and modern medicine was difficult

to get. Fan managed to find various herbal medicines for Pin's ailment (F, 104). Pin died in 1946 at Saensamran Forest Monastery.

78. F, 103–104. In the ordination ceremonies the ordinands must learn the five basic meditation themes (Pali: *pañcakammaṭṭhāna*). This is a meditation on the first five of the thirty-two parts considered to make up the body: head hair, body hair, nails, teeth, and skin. Some students and educated people snigger to themselves when they hear this part of the ordination ceremony (C2, 9).

79. Li1, 112. Li is referring to the dream he had fifteen years earlier when he was staying at Prawn Canal Hermitage in Chanthaburi.

80. The English version of Li's autobiography gives the year as 1953. But the Thai version gives B.E. 2495 (Li2, 85), so 1952 is correct.

81. Since then, Wat Boromniwat has offered meditation training to monks, novices, and laypeople. "Somdet Phra Maha Wirawong (Uan Tisso), 1867–1956," *Lokthip* 3, no. 34 (June 1984): 40. This was the year after Phimontham (At Assapha Thera) and his meditation teacher, Phawanaphiram Thera (Suk), set up a meditation center at Wat Mahathat. *Phra niphon lae niphon somdet* [Somdet's writings] (Bangkok: Crem. vol. Somdet Phra Phutthajan, Wat Mahathat, 1990), 141.

82. According to Treuk's biography, Somdet Jaroen (1872–1951) did not pay attention to meditation practice until he fell ill. From then on, he often asked Treuk to direct him in meditation. For details of Treuk Thammawitako's life (1887–1971) see T. Liangphibun, *Anuson Thammawitako* [Commemoration of Thammawitako] (Bangkok: Rungreuangsan, 1972) and Atheuk Sawadimongkhon, *Prawat phra phiksu phraya Norarat Ratmanit* [Biography of Phra Norarat] (Chonburi: Young Buddhist Association, 1971). It is not clear if Treuk met Ajan Man when Man came to a funeral service at Wat Thepsirin in 1931.

83. When Somdet Wannarat (Pheuan) (1876–1947) fell ill in 1946, Sot dispatched some of his disciples to cure him by meditation techniques. Only then did the somdet think it was worthwhile to read Sot's sermon on Thammakai meditation, compiled and published by a lay follower. Sot assisted the somdet in practicing meditation, and as a result the somdet became convinced that meditation practice was worthwhile. For details of Sot's life (1884–1959) and thammakai meditation, see T. Magness, *The Life and Teachings of the Ven. Chao Khun Mongkolthepmuni (Late Abbot of Wat Paknam Bhasicharoen)* [Bangkok: Croake, n.d.], and Pun Punyasiri (Somdet Phra Wannarat), *Phra Mongkhonthepmuni* (Bangkok: One-hundredth anniversary of Ven. Father Sot, Wat Paknam, 1984).

84. In 1952 Phimontham sent Chodok, a Mahanikai monk from the Northeast with a ninth-level Pali degree, to take up vipassanā meditation

practice in Burma. On his return trip Chodok brought two Burmese monks to teach vipassanā meditation at Wat Mahathat.

85. Several elderly monks whom I interviewed confirmed that lay meditation teachers were common in local Buddhist traditions. Most local traditions valued lay asceticism, although this varied greatly from region to region.

86. Chua Jantrupon, Bunkanjanaram Meditation Center, Chonburi, Thailand, interview by author, 23 June 1989. Chua, a lay meditation teacher, was a student of Naeb Mahaniranon (see chap. 10).

CHAPTER 8: RELATIONS WITH VILLAGERS

1. He was the first public figure in Siam/Thailand to use radio to propagate government policies. Wyatt, *Thailand*, 253.

2. One of the best known government's radio programs during this period was "Conversations between Mr. Man Chuchat and Mr. Khong Rakthai" [Bot sonthana rawang nai Man Chuchat kap nai Khong Rakthai]. The discussants (Man and Khong) were fictitious. Aside from exchanges about the war (propaganda against the Allies) and about the cultural mandates issued by the government between 1939 and 1942, the two discussants urged the audience to build the nation by growing their own food and by providing food supplies for the Japanese. Transcripts of the daily broadcasts of government policies from 8 December 1941 (the day Japanese troops entered Thailand) to 28 February 1942 were published in *Pramuan hetkan nai yuk mai khaung thai* [Events of the new era in Thailand] (Bangkok: Crem. vol. Hoksui Sapsunthon, 1942).

3. Seri Phongphit and Kevin Hewison, *Thai Village Life: Culture and Transition in the Northeast* (Bangkok: Mooban Press, 1990), 5.

4. This policy was broadcast on 16 February 1942 and published in *Pramuan hetkan*, 324.

5. *An somdet*, 129. Uan coined this motto when he was the sangha leader of monthon Isan, according to Kasem Bunsi ("Reuang Somdet," in *An somdet*, 52).

In September 1941 the director-general of the Ministry of Agriculture, Chuang Kasetsinlapakon, and another officer came to see Somdet Uan at Wat Boromniwat. They asked the somdet to write an article advocating the government's agricultural policies. Uan, *Niphon bang reuang*, 52.

6. Excerpted from Uan Tisso (Somdet Phra Maha Wirawong), "Ngoen din ngoen deuan" (Self-employment and salaries), in Uan, *Niphon bang reuang*, 52–53.

7. This was still the case in rural Lao villages in the 1950s and 1960s. See Georges Condominas, "Phiban Cults in Rural Laos," in *Change and Persistence in Thai Society,* ed. G. William Skinner and A. Thomas Kirsch (Ithaca: Cornell University Press, 1975), 252–273. Such beliefs were also intact in Lao villages in the Northeast as recently as the 1960s. See A. Thomas Kirsch, "Phu Thai Religious Syncretism: A Case Study of Thai Religion" (Ph.D. diss., Harvard University, 1967), 372.

8. In the early 1960s this was still the case in many Lao villages, for example in Naung Sung Village in Mukdahan District, Nakhon Phanom, as observed by Kirsch ("Phu Thai Religious Syncretism," 385).

9. For a rich discussion of this topic, see Sangharakshita, *The History of My Going for Refuge* (Glasgow: Windhorse Publications, 1988), and Thanissaro, "Going for Refuge," *Insight,* spring 1996, 30–31.

10. Over forty years later, in the early 1960s, the practice of spirit worship was still widespread. A census in the commune of Naung Sung (then in Nakhon Phanom, now in Mukdahan Province) showed that there were fifty-five mau phis in that commune. See Kirsch, "Phu Thai Religious Syncretism," 376.

11. In those days, due to the difficulties of traveling, a man on a business trip might be absent from his family for several months each year. It appears that women in general, and in particular women whose husbands were away, were more likely to fear ghost attacks. Spirits were believed to attack those who manifest the least "self-control": those with "tender" *khwan* (spirit or life force), namely children, women, and ill people. See Kirsch, "Phu Thai Religious Syncretism," 387, 407.

12. This is similar to what Condominas has observed in the villages in Laos: "The *vat* [wat] answers the needs of the people as members of a spiritual community, and it is the place of assembly for the group as a social and political entity. The jurisdiction of the *ho phiban* [spirit shrine], on the other hand, is not the community as a social entity but rather the natural ecological system that nurtures its members, above all the land which provides food, shelter, and clothing. The *phiban* belongs to the world of nature, and it is there that it takes refuge." Condominas, "Phiban Cults in Rural Laos," 272–273.

13. Li1, 13; Li2, 9–10. Curiously, Li does not mention how the village abbot felt about his coming there as a Thammayut monk and preaching against local beliefs.

14. Kirsch, "Phu Thai Religious Syncretism," 345. These offended spirits were believed to be deceased relatives or neighbors, not anonymous spirits wandering around performing malevolent acts (ibid., 373).

15. One reason why thudong monks like Li taught loving-kindness

meditation to villagers is that they believed it to be an effective way of healing oneself. The process of generating strong feelings of empathy, compassion, and love toward others had, in their view, a purifying effect on the mind. When such strong positive feelings are invoked in a mind that has become relatively calm and stable through intensive meditation practice, these feelings can then be effectively directed toward others.

16. Li was not explicit about who these people were. Most likely the jealous laypeople were mau phi and their followers, who would lose their income if villagers abandoned spirit worship. As for the monks, they were probably of local origin and sympathetic to spirit worship. Li's stance toward spirits might be characterized as one of blunt opposition. He compelled the spirits to go away. Li's superior mystical powers (compared to village monks) supposedly enabled him to thwart the capricious spirits. See Kirsch, "Phu Thai Religious Syncretism," 389.

17. Thet does not say whether her disciples were male or female.

18. T1, 118. Thet apologizes to readers for even mentioning this coarse act. Feet, as the translator Ariyesako explains, are considered unmentionably low and contemptible in polite society.

19. M1, 90. As Seri put it, "spirit beliefs were 'true' because they were meaningful to the villagers" as well as forest monks. Seri Phongphit, *Religion in a Changing Society: Buddhism, Reform and the Role of Monks in Community Development in Thailand* (Hong Kong: Arena Press, 1988), 34.

20. Kirsch, "Phu Thai Religious Syncretism," 368–369.

21. See, for example, Suriphan, *Chiwa prawat Luang Pu Lui*, 43–45; Suriphan, *Chiwa prawat Luang Pu Chaup*, 59–61.

22. T1, 113. This was in 1930. The location was Phra Khreu Village in Khon Kaen.

23. T1, 115; T2, 43–44. The location here was near Thauk Pan Lake, Mahasarakham.

24. It had been over a year since Man returned to the Northeast after more than a decade of wandering in northern Siam.

25. Villagers who believed that they or their children were possessed by phi paups were prepared to give anything to spirit doctors to expel the spirits. For details see Pricha Phinthong, *Saranukrom phasa: Isan Thai–English Dictionary* (Ubon: Siritham Press, 1989), 536.

26. Wiriyang wondered why Man did not choose some older disciple who had more experience than he. He thought perhaps Man wanted to test him (Wi, 90).

27. Often the role of herbalist and spirit doctor were conjoined in the same person, who performed one or the other therapeutic role depend-

ing on his or her diagnosis. This was also the case in Burma as observed by Melford E. Spiro, *Burmese Supernaturalism* (Philadelphia: Prentice-Hall, 1978), 149.

28. Lui Janthasaro (1902–1989) was a native of Loei. His parents, who were Lao, named him Wau. His father, the son of the local lord of meuang Kaenthao in Laos, died in 1909, when Wau was seven years old. After Wau finished the third year of elementary school in his village in 1917 he moved to Chiang Khan District to be trained as a clerk under his brother-in-law, a revenue auditor of the district. While living in Chiang Khan, Wau worked as a servant to French people. There he converted to Christianity, after which his uncle called him Lui (after Saint Louis). In 1921 Lui moved to Sangbadan (now called Thawatburi District) in Roi-Et to work as a clerk for the district attorney, but he found the job unpleasant and left. In 1923 he was ordained as a Buddhist monk. Lui became a thudong monk after he was exempted from conscription. When he arrived at Wuasau Pond District in Udon Thani, he heard that a thudong monk, Bun Panyawuttho, had led some villagers from Ubon Ratchathani to settle in Lao Field Village (Ban Na Lao), and establish a forest hermitage. It was Bun who converted Lui to the Thammayut order in 1925. A year later Bun took Lui to visit Man at Thabau, Si Chiang Mai District, Nongkhai. From 1926 to 1930 Lui spent five rains retreats with Bun at the forest wat of Wuasau Pond in Udon Thani. For more details of Lui's life story see Suriphan, *Chiwa prawat Luang Pu Lui.*

29. The *Bupphasikkha* (Pali: *Pubbasikkha*) is a detailed interpretation of the vinaya. The older generation of thudong masters such as Sao carried this vinaya text with them. It was eventually replaced by the *Winaimuk* (Pali: *Vinayamukha,* Entrance to the Vinaya), Wachirayan's three-volume summary of the vinaya texts, which came out in 1913. For the origin of the *Buphasikkha* see Taylor, *Forest Monks,* 134–135.

30. The wild herbs in the remedy included *makham pom* (Indian gooseberry), *samau* (chebulic myrobalam), *kha* (galangal), ginger, garlic, *boraphet (Tinospora tuberculata), krachai* (galingale), black pepper, *dipli* (Indian long pepper), large pepper, lemon grass, kaffir lime leaves, lime, tamarind, *manglak* (hairy basil), *sadao* (neem), *songfa* (feather fern), *nauk* (Asiatic pennywort), and *ilauk* (an araceous plant with purple flowers). Lui emphasized that the boiled urine of a gaur was the most important ingredient (Suriphan, *Chiwa prawat Luang Pu Lui,* 50–51). Gaur urine apparently has curative properties for diabetes. Other ingredients, dipli for example, are used as carminatives, tonics, treatments for hemorrhoids, etc. See *Thai Book of Genesis: Herbal Medicine in Paedi-*

atrics, trans. Jean Mulholland (Canberra: Australian National University, 1989), 254, 325.

31. From an interview with Bu, an old monk at Pheu Pond Forest Wat, by Suriphan (*Chiwa prawat Luang Pu Lui*, 48–49). Bu was a young man when Lui came to his village in 1935. He attended to Lui, became a lay devotee, and then was ordained as a monk.

32. See Seri, *Religion in a Changing Society*, 78. Lui said he could *thauraman* villagers: make them do whatever he wanted.

33. Lui did not return to Pheu Pond Village again until nine years later, when he went to spend the rains retreat there. He then schemed with the villagers to invite Ajan Man to stay permanently at the hermitage when the latter came for a visit. Man accepted the villagers' invitation, believing it was a deserted wat. It was here that Man spent the last years of his life. Man had never lived in one place for such a long time. Suriphan, *Chiwa prawat Luang Pu Lui*, 51.

34. Wn, 75. According to Waen, it was not until the war ended and government officials clamped down on bandits that peace returned to Chiang Dao.

35. F, 77. In Pali *sotthikhapasa* means "may there be well-being for the unborn child." The entire gāthā is: "I, sister, am not aware of having intentionally deprived any living thing of life since I was born of the ariyan birth. By this truth may there be well-being for you, well-being for the unborn child." See Spiro, *Buddhism and Society*, 267. Thudong monks believe that gāthās are communicated to them by deities *(thewada)* during visions. It is also possible, of course, that Fan had heard this gāthā at some earlier time and that it arose from buried memory, prompted perhaps by his concern for the dangerous childbirth.

36. The therapeutic role provided by a local abbot included interpreting a woman's dream about pregnancy, giving an appropriate name to the child, and taking care of the spiritual well-being of the expectant mother. The task of assisting the actual childbirth, however, belonged to the midwife (also called a *mau tam yae*). Sobin Namto and Phra Maha Thanat Inthisan, interview by author, 31 March 1996.

37. Lama Anagarika Govinda, *The Way of the White Clouds: A Buddhist Pilgrim in Tibet* (Boston: Shambhala, 1988), 94.

38. This was still the case in the Phu Thai region in the 1960s, as observed by Kirsch, "Phu Thai Religious Syncretism," 345.

39. Suphon, *Chiwa prawat Phra Ajan Fan*, 159. That same year, it is interesting to note, an article by Uan Tisso (Somdet Phra Maha Wirawong), "Kasikam pen maebot khaung ngan" [Farming, the mother of all professions], was published in the newspaper *Kasikon* [Farmers]. The

article was written at the request of the head of the Agriculture Education Division to urge people to do agricultural work. In the article he stressed the Phibun government's concern about poverty in the Northeast. He suggested that "the people should ease the government's worries by growing palm trees and tamarind trees (both of which grow well in the soil of that region). Each family should grow fifty to one hundred of these trees." Reprinted in Uan, *Niphon bang reuang,* 64–65.

40. Suphon, *Chiwa prawat Phra Ajan Fan,* 159. Frogs are eaten in a dish called *om,* accompanied by ground rice, chilies and any available vegetables. Tadpoles are usually prepared with chili into a spicy *lap,* mixed with fermented fish or wrapped in banana leaves and roasted. In the Forest-Invasion Period, the use of fertilizers, herbicides, and pesticides (pushed by the Ministry of Agriculture) killed many fish, frogs, and snails. Those that lived were of questionable food value because of the high concentration of toxins.

41. When Fan first arrived here, the cave was called Tiger Cave. A tiger lived in it until Fan built his hut at the entrance (F, 171).

42. This was a common practice. Whenever the thudong monks stayed in an isolated cave, they would suggest that the villagers cut a trail and meet them halfway to give alms. That way, neither party had to walk too far, the villagers could return to their fields sooner, and the monks would get to eat before noontime. Man, however, discouraged this habit. He was afraid that a trail would make the cave too accessible to laypeople and thus deprive the monks of their solitude.

43. F, 172. Fan's biographer, Suphon Nachom, was one of the four monks who spent the rains retreat of 1955 with Fan at Tamarind Cave. The construction of a preaching hall turned the place into a samnak. From 1957 to 1962 Fan spent the rains retreats in this hermitage. In spite of their orchards, the villagers were poor. Fan found that the inhabitants could not afford to feed more than fifteen monks at a time. So he limited the number to between six and nine monks and novices (F, 184).

44. F, 173, 178. Instead of cutting down a large tamarind tree that was on the site, the hall was built around it.

Initially laypeople from Bangkok had to hire an oxcart to visit Tamarind Cave. In 1964 an engineer who had ordained temporarily came to the samnak and spent a rains retreat. While there he surveyed the mountain, and after disrobing he helped construct a paved road to the cave.

45. Kitirat, "Kan ruam khana song isan," 137.

46. See Richard O'Connor, "Urbanism and Religion: Community, Hierarchy and Sanctity in Urban Thai Buddhist Temples" (Ph.D. diss., Cornell University, 1978), 235.

47. Administrative monks, however, wanted to integrate people of

various ethnic groups into Bangkok culture by making them learn Thai. A telling example is Somdet Uan's account of how he established the first government school in meuang Surin. When meeting with commune and village headmen, Uan noticed that they were displeased to hear that they must learn the Thai script. At the time the Bangkok government had just announced that the old currency was going to be taken out of circulation. Uan used this recent news to threaten the headmen: "It's just like keeping old coins *(ngoen duang)* which have been made obsolete once the government issues new ones. If you people in Surin continue to learn Khom [Khmer] after the government has gone over to the Thai script, officials who know Thai will be sent here. Wouldn't you rather have local people who speak [Bangkok] Thai govern you instead of outsiders? If you don't want non-native officials to govern you, you must all learn Thai." Evidently this threat worked. The first government school for the teaching of Bangkok Thai to Surin natives was established at Wat Burapha, where Dun was abbot. Reported by Phra Thamthitiyan, "Somdet lae chao surin" [Somdet and Surin People], in *An somdet,* 137–138.

48. Quite a few of these wandering forest monks, such as Sao and Aunsi, died in Laos. When Sao died in Jampasak in 1941, his body was transported across the border and was cremated in Sakon Nakhon. Aunsi died and was cremated in Vientiane (Laos) in 1956. See J, 62.

49. They usually wandered in the areas of Tha Khaek (across the river from Nakhon Phanom), Vientiane, Buffalo Mountain (Phu Khao Khwai), and Luang Prabang. They especially liked Tha Khaek with its vast forests, isolated caves, and many wild animals. Even though the country was under French control, Sao, Man, and many of their disciples managed to wander in Laos at one time or another.

50. Man made this comment to Wiriyang when the latter returned to Pheu Pond Hermitage after helping the villagers drive the ghosts from their villages (Wi, 92). Wiriyang, however, does not identify the "some people" that Man referred to. Most likely they were sangha administrators who disliked thudong monks.

51. It should be emphasized that these samnaks were not full-blown forest monasteries as we see today but rather places where people could gather and hear the dhamma.

52. This represents an increase of 250 percent, more than double the rate of increase of "Mahanikai" wats, although more "Mahanikai" wats were actually built. (Non-Thammayut wats increased from 17,315 in 1935 to 20,295 in 1957.) See Phra Wanna Wanno, *Prawat Thammayut lae Mahanikai* [A history of Thammayut and Mahanikai] (Bangkok: Rungreuangsan, 1985), 237–341, and Uan, *Prawat patipatha,* 12, 20.

53. This is Wat Santhitham. Its first abbot, Sim, was a disciple of

Man's. Later on several more Thammayut forest wats were established in Chiang Mai Province. By 1976 there were nine in Chiang Mai and one in Lamphun. See Ferguson and Shalardchai, "Monks and Hierarchy." In this article the monks whom the authors interviewed indicate that all the unregistered Thammayut wats (they were actually samnaks) in Chiang Mai Province (whether located outside villages and towns or within) followed Ajan Man's tradition. These samnaks, however, were established after Man left the North, not through Man's own efforts. Wat Santhitham, like many Thammayut wats established by Man's disciples, has evolved into a more conventional Thammayut temple. Its abbot today is a disciple of Sim's.

CHAPTER 9: THE FOREST INVADED

1. This was Phimontham's opinion, according to Steven Carr, "An Ambassador of Buddhism to the West," in *Buddhism in Europe,* ed. Aad Verboom (Crem. vol. Somdet Phra Phutthajan, Wat Mahathat, 1990), 10. The Buddhism that Phimontham was referring to is modern state Buddhism.

2. At Atsapha (1903–1989) was born in Ton Village in Banton Commune (today in Khon Kaen Province). In 1916, he was ordained in the local tradition as a novice at Wat Sijan. His preceptor, Ya Khu Nau, taught him to read dhamma script *(tua tham)* from palm-leaf texts. At sixteen he attended a training course for teachers at the government school, passed the exam, and became a teacher at an elementary school in Wat Klang, Meuang Kao Commune. At the age of eighteen, in 1920, he resigned from his teaching job and went to Bangkok for Pali studies. He stayed at Wat Chanasongkhram and about a year later moved to Wat Mahathat, where he was ordained as a monk in 1923. His preceptor was the abbot of Wat Mahathat, Heng Khemajari (titled Thammatrailokajan, later to become Somdet Phra Wannarat). In 1929 he passed the level eight Pali exam, and six years later, at the age of thirty-two, he was appointed abbot of Wat Suwandaram in Ayuthaya. He became abbot of Wat Mahathat in 1948. During this year, he was appointed sangha minister of the interior under the democratic Sangha Act of 1941. A year later he received the title Phimontham. For more details see *Phra niphon lae niphon somdet.* At Atsapha is usually referred to by his title, Phimontham.

3. Carr, "Ambassador of Buddhism," 11.

4. Sobin Namto, interview by author, 31 March 1996. In 1949 Sobin, a nineteen-year-old novice, underwent the intensive meditation training

at Wat Mahathat. He was the only novice to do so; the rest of the meditators were monks. Each monk and novice lived and meditated in a tiny room for many months (seven in Sobin's case).

5. U Nu was premier of Burma from 1947 to 1958. Among the most respected vipassanā meditation teachers were Mahasi Sayadaw and U Ba Khin. Mahasi administered the Thathana Yeiktha meditation center in Rangoon, which served as a model for many others throughout Burma. U Ba Khin was a lay meditation teacher and also the head of the auditing department of the Burmese government. For a discussion of the U Nu government's promotion of meditation see E. Michael Mendelson, *Sangha and State in Burma: A Study of Monastic Sectarianism and Leadership,* ed. John P. Ferguson (Ithaca: Cornell University Press, 1975), 314–318.

6. Chodok (1918–1988) was born in Khon Kaen. His father was a farmer, carpenter, blacksmith, and folk doctor in his Lao village. After being ordained as a novice, Chodok went to study Pali in Bangkok, where he was ordained as a monk at Wat Mahathat. He returned to Khon Kaen to teach naktham and Pali from 1943 to 1949. He was called back to Wat Mahathat when Phimontham (At) became abbot. It was then that he took up vipassanā meditation under the guidance of the meditation master Suk (Phawanaphiram Thera) of Wat Rakhang. In 1951 he passed the highest Pali level—the only monk to do so during that year. The following year Phimontham sent him to Mahasi Sayadaw's center in Rangoon. Since the beginning of 1953, Wat Mahathat has been offering the Burmese style of meditation training to people from all walks of life. Mahanikai monks from other provinces came to this wat for meditation retreats until 1960, when the meditation hall was destroyed by the police on the orders of Sarit. For more details about how Wat Mahathat became the center of vipassanā meditation training, see Chodok Yanasithi (Phra Thamthirarat Mahamuni), *Lak patibat samatha-vipassana kammathan* [Practice of samatha-vipassanā meditation] (Bangkok: Crem. vol. Phra Thamthirarat, Wat Mahathat, 1988), 11–25.

7. In addition to teaching meditation, Thet set up naktham schools in the wats and encouraged monks to take the exams. This is what Phimontham, sangha minister of the interior at the time, had been promoting—combining study with meditation practice.

8. Phra Racha Khana is a title of deputy somdet rank. Monks so titled are often referred to as Jao Khun.

9. In 1964 Thet was promoted from acting sangha head to full sangha head of Phuket, Phangnga, and Krabi. By then Thet and other disciples of Man had established eleven wats in these southern prov-

inces. In 1965 he returned to the Northeast, ending fifteen years at Phuket. He also resigned from his position as sangha head. He settled permanently at Hinmakpeng in Nongkhai Province.

10. Opening speech to the first conference of meditation monks at Wat Mahathat, 20 November 1955, in *Phra niphon lae niphon somdet,* 138.

11. Phra Thepsithimuni, "Preface," in *Phajon Mara: Bantheuk ha pi nai haungkhang* [Confronting Mara: Phra Phimontham's diary of five years in jail] (Bangkok: Bandit-kanphim, 1987), 8–9.

12. Craig J. Reynolds, *Thai Radical Discourse: The Real Face of Thai Feudalism Today* (Ithaca: Southeast Asia Program, 1987), 36.

13. Taylor, *Forest Monks,* 314; Somboon, *Buddhism,* 39.

14. Satsanasophon (Plaut Atthakari) was one of the few senior Thammayut monks who supported Buddhadasa's work at Suan Mokkhabalarama. Phra Pracha Pasanathammo, ed., *Phap chiwit 80 pi Buddhadasa* [Photographs from Buddhadasa's eighty years] (Bangkok: Phonphan Kanphim, 1986), 113.

15. Somdet Phra Wannarat (Plot Kittisophano), the supreme patriarch during this period, allowed these charges to stand. For details on the persecution of Phimontham see Jackson, *Buddhism, Legitimation, and Conflict,* 94–111. Although Satsanasophon was Thammayut, he was close to Phimontham as deputy sangha minister of the interior and was therefore perceived by Thammayut elders as more like a Mahanikai.

16. Carr, "Ambassador of Buddhism," 10. Only those aspects of Phimontham's case that relate to the sangha elders' attitude toward meditation in the 1960s will be discussed here.

17. Ibid.

18. According to Phimontham, "This was not appreciated in certain quarters, it being the idea that the King or the Sangharaja has the authority to initiate religious reforms. Those who opposed me—the abbots of Wat Benjamabophit [Mahanikai] and Wat Makutkasat Thiyaram [Thammayut], both in line for the position of Phra Sangharaja, along with [me]—did so for personal reasons." Ibid., 9–10. See Tambiah, *Buddhist Saints and Cult,* 166–167; Gray, "Thailand," 563–564.

19. Carr, "Ambassador of Buddhism," 10.

20. J. L. Taylor, "Living on the Rim: Ecology and Forest Monks in Northeastern Thailand," *Sojourn* 6, no. 1 (February 1991): 113.

21. Joemsak Pinthaung, ed., *Wiwatthanakan khaung kanbukboek thidin thamkin* [Study of conservation forest area demarcation, protection, and occupancy in Thailand] (Bangkok: Institute of Rural Community Development, 1991), 170.

22. The laypeople included the district doctor in Beung Kan, who

probably heard about Juan from the villagers. He also arranged to have food transported to the monk.

23. It is not clear if "the opposite side" designated Thammayut administrators (who disliked wandering monks), Mahanikai monks, or monks supporting the dictatorship. Juan does not mention any names (J, 73).

24. J, 74. The Border Patrol Police was a counterinsurgency force whose main task at the time was to fight communists in rural Thailand. It operated not only along Thailand's borders but everywhere within the country. Thongchai, *Siam Mapped,* 170.

25. J, 90. This was during the war in Vietnam. The planes were probably returning to one of the bases in Thailand. After March 1964 U.S. aircraft were based at Takhli airfield in Nakhon Sawan Province, 255 kilometers due north of Bangkok. After the Gulf of Tonkin incident in August of that year, additional U.S. aircraft were based at Khorat, while other military contingents, operating out of Nakhon Phanom, were directed mainly against the Ho Chi Minh Trail region of southeastern Laos. Wyatt, *Thailand,* 277–288.

26. From the late 1960s to the early 1970s the government carried out massive search-and-destroy operations against the insurgents, but the number of communist supporters continued to increase rather than decline. The number of armed clashes increased partly because the government's suppression forces were seeking out the insurgents more aggressively. David Morell and Chai-anan Samudavanija, *Political Conflict in Thailand: Reform, Reaction, Revolution* (Cambridge, Mass.: Oelgeschlager, Gunn and Hain, 1981), 83, 85.

27. Fourteen of the thirty-five provinces were in the Northeast: Nongkhai, Sakon Nakhon, Nakhon Phanom, Udon Thani, Loei, Buriram, Chaiyaphum, Kalasin, Khon Kaen, Nakhon Ratchasima, Mahasarakham, Roi-Et, Sisaket, and Ubon Ratchathani (ibid., 83).

28. Thui was a disciple of Bua Siripunyo (Saeng Pond Forest Wat, Udon Thani) and later of Khaw and Bua Yannasampanno. Thui's links with influential elite figures probably saved him from being charged with insurgency. For a discussion of Thui see Taylor, "Living on the Rim," 114–116, 117. Shortly after Thui founded his Thammayut wat, the villagers built another one, Kham Field Village Wat, for the "Mahanikai" order.

29. Khraung Chandawong (1908–1961) was born in Sakon Nakhon; both of his parents were Lao-Yau (or Yo). For details of Khraung's life and activities see Khomsan Matukham [pseud.], *Dong Phra Jao, daen morana* [Lord Buddha Forest, a deadly region] (Bangkok: Phithakpracha, 1977).

30. For a discussion of the causes of insurgency in Thailand, see Morell and Chai-anan, *Political Conflict in Thailand*, 84–87.

31. Jit Phumisak (1930–1965), author of *The Real Face of Thai Feudalism Today* (1957), was accused of sympathizing with communists. Reynolds, *Thai Radical Discourse*, 38.

32. "Chiwa prawat Ajan Wan," 17.

33. Tambiah contends that charismatic ascetic monks believed to have supernormal power could become rallying points for either millenarian cults or radical movements. Tambiah, *Buddhist Saints and Cult*, 334.

34. Khomsan Matukham [pseud.], *Khraung Jandawong, khao kheu khrai* [Khraung Jandawong, who is he?] (Bangkok: Phithakpracha, 1978), 208. Khraung started the DUO in the Northeast in 1958. He encouraged collective farming and advocated a union of Thailand's Northeast with Laos. Morell and Chai-anan, *Political Conflict in Thailand*, 90.

35. Khomsan, *Khraung Jandawong*, 208.

36. See Khomsan, *Dong Phra Jao*, 157–158, 196, 203; also *Thi rareuk ngan phraratchathan phloengsop wiraburut thi sia chiwit naikan paungkan lae prappram phu kaukanrai communit* [Cremation volume in memory of the heroes who were killed by communists] (Bangkok: Wat Phra Simahathat, 1969), 9, 33–39, 48–50, 63.

37. Morell and Chai-anan, *Political Conflict in Thailand*, 90.

38. In those days there was a curfew in the district of Songdao and people were forbidden to travel at night ("Chiwa prawat Ajan Wan," 18).

39. Ibid. The king and the queen also made their first visit to Khaw at his hermitage in Midday Drum Cave, Udon Thani Province.

40. Wyatt, *Thailand*, 301. By late 1975, about one hundred activists within the broad student movement (the National Student Center of Thailand, the Secondary School Students Center of Thailand, and various student unions in major universities) were working full time for revolution. Morell and Chai-anan, *Political Conflict in Thailand*, 290–291.

41. Thian Jittasupho (1911–1988) was born in Buhom Village in Chiang Khan District, Loei. At the age of ten he became a novice in one of the Lao traditions, attending his uncle, a monk, and studying meditation, prayer, and magic under him. After a year and a half, Thian disrobed to help his parents in rice growing and trading. When he reached the necessary age, he was ordained as a monk for six months, disrobed, got married, and later became the village chief. He started practicing meditation seriously in 1957 and was ordained as a monk in the local tradition for the second time in 1960 at the age of forty-eight. Thian spoke Lao. He never attended a government school (there was none in his natal village) and could neither read nor speak Thai. For more details of his life story see *Pokati: Luang Phau Thian Jittasupho lae sing thi fak*

wai [Ven. Father Thian: Biography and teachings] (Bangkok: Thian Sawangtham, 1989).

42. Kornfield and Breiter, *Still Forest Pool*, 121–122.

43. Sathianphong, an ex-monk and Pali scholar, points out that in the
years following World War II a large portion of the Thai sangha consisted of monks who were using it to fulfill their personal ambitions. He
is critical of how the Thai sangha changed during these three decades
(1946–1971), noting that high-level monks, who held teaching and writing in low esteem, would rather confer honorific titles *(samanasak)* on
monks involved with construction. "Nowadays," he tells us, "the monks
are losing their important function as spiritual leaders. They have become the followers of lay society, which is preoccupied with status and is
greedy for power, prestige, and wealth. . . . Some unworthy monks were
awarded honorific titles because they were the favorites of influential
sangha authorities. Apart from these privileged monks, priority is given
to [those who have the] ability to promote the construction of ordination halls or preaching halls. It has become common practice for a monk
who has built an ordination hall to be given a preceptor position, and
building a preaching hall can be exchanged for a Phra Khru title." Maha
Sathianphong, "Phra song thai nai raup 25 pi" [Thai sangha over 25
years], *Sangkhomsat parithat 9*, no. 6 (December 1971): 22–23, quoted
in Somboon, *Buddhism and Politics in Thailand*, 24. Sathianphong, a
parian 9 monk, left the monastic life and is now teaching at Sinlapakhon
University.

44. *Pokati: Luang Phau Thian*, 46.

45. A dozen letters were sent to the sangha provincial head and
sangha district head asking them to dismiss Thian. The senior Mahanikai monks showed the letters to Thian (ibid., 47).

46. Jamnian Silasetho, the fifth of seven children, was born in
Paknam, a fishing village in Nakhon Si Thammarat. After his father left
the household to become a wandering monk, Jamnian and his siblings
lived with their grandfather. At the age of twenty Jamnian was ordained
at Wat Naripradit, Tharai Commune, in the same province. He passed
the lowest naktham level but wanted to live a thudong life like his father.
Nevertheless, he stayed at this wat for seven years before he went wandering in Trang Province in search of meditation teachers. "Phra Ajan
Jamnian Silasetho," in *Ruam phap chut 80 phra kammathan*.

47. The source (Kornfield, *Living Buddhist Masters*, 273–274) does
not say whether Jamnian was told this by government officials, by soldiers, or by insurgents. After ten years of living at this wat Jamnian went
to the Northeast to visit Ajan Cha at Phong Pond Forest Wat in Ubon.
Then he wandered in the South and came upon Tiger Cave in Krabi

Province. He found it suitable for meditation practice and established a samnak there, later to become Tiger Cave Monastery.

48. For biographies and activities of abbots in the Northeast who were suspects during this period see Seri, *Religion in a Changing Society.*

49. Kornfield and Breiter, *Still Forest Pool,* 181.

50. J, 112. In response to the urban elites' accusation, Juan pointed out that the Buddha himself urged monks to find solitude in forests, under trees, and in caves or deserted huts.

51. Lee [Li] Dhammadharo, *Frames of Reference,* trans. Thanissaro Bhikkhu (Bangkok: P. Samphanphanit, 1987), 99–100.

52. A sermon to monks, novices, and laypeople, "Kan triam tua phawana [Preparation for meditation]," 10 September 1979, in *Phra Udomsangwonwisut Thera (Phra Ajan Wan Uttamo)* (Bangkok: Crem. vol. Wat Tham Aphaidamrong, 1981).

53. As Taylor remarks, Khaw's reply was a thinly veiled criticism of Thai institutions (*Forest Monks,* 175).

54. Total U.S. "regular military assistance" to the Thai armed forces between 1951 and 1971 amounted to $935,900,000, a sum equal to 59 percent of the Thai government's entire military budget for that period. A further $250,000,000 was spent for the construction of air and naval bases in rural Thailand. Another $850,000,000 poured in from American servicemen who came to Thailand for "rest and recreation." John L. S. Girling, *Thailand: Society and Politics* (Ithaca: Cornell University Press, 1981), 236; cited in Anderson, introduction to *In the Mirror: Literature and Politics in Siam in the American Era,* 21 n. 8.

55. Between 1950 and 1975, the United States provided Thailand with $650,000,000 in support of economic development programs. Most of the money was granted in the years after General Sarit came to power. Girling, *Thailand,* 235.

56. Vitoon Panyakul, ed. *People Centered Development* (Bangkok: Local Development Institute, 1992), 36. The government plans referred to are the *Phaen phatthana sangkhom lae setthakit haeng chat.*

57. *Population growth:* The population grew at some 3 percent per year, from 26.6 million in 1960 to 42.3 million in 1975 (Morell and Chai-anan, *Political Conflict in Thailand,* 76). *Hydroelectric dams:* There are around thirty large-scale hydroelectric dams in Thailand. Dams and reservoirs are often built on floodplains where land is fertile and supports tropical forest. Construction inevitably forces local communities to relocate and produces deforestation. Negative effects of dam construction include water pollution, loss of habitat for wildlife, and the destruction of sacred sites. Deforestation associated with dams is the main cause of the decline of rainfall in recent times. In addition, 1989

figures indicate that one-third of the Thai population (located in Bangkok and the Central Plains) consumes over three-quarters of the total electricity produced (Vitoon, "Failures of Hydroelectric Dams," in *People Centered Development,* 79-83). *Golf courses:* At present 182 golf courses are either in operation or under construction in Thailand. Between 65 to 75 percent of them are located on agricultural land, 13.5 to 26 percent in forested areas, and the rest are on unoccupied land. Most of the new golf courses require large amounts of land, since they include hotels and garden resorts. This brings the total land taken up by a golf course to as much as 2,500–5,000 acres. The largest golf course in Thailand is Kang Krajan Country Club in Phetchaburi, with 87,500 acres (Ponchai Termwaree, "Agricultural Land Crisis in the Period of High Land Prices," in Vitoon, *People Centered Development,* 108).

58. Joemsak, *Wiwatthanakan,* 170.

59. During the height of the Vietnam War, road length totaled 5,891 km in 1970; 7,439 km in 1975; 14,257 km in 1980; 21,017 in 1985; and 27,595 in 1989. Constance M. Wilson, *Thailand: A Handbook of Historical Statistics* (Boston: G. K. Hall, 1983), 172–175. These roads were built primarily for military purposes, to move troops and equipment to rural areas.

60. For example, when Ajan Man was cremated in 1950 at Wat Sutthawat in Sakon Nakhon, the monastery, two kilometers outside of town, was surrounded by forest. In 1980 the town had extended as far as the wat and the forest had disappeared (Wi, 38).

61. For a detailed discussion of the domestication of Thammayut forest monks during the last three decades, see Taylor, *Forest Monks.*

62. Although the rainy season had ended in other regions, heavy rains continued in the southern part of the country. In areas that had been heavily logged and rapidly deforested, the bare, degraded soils could no longer regulate the natural flow of the rain water. Overnight, thousands of legally and illegally felled logs were swept downhill into several villages. Whole villages (including village wats) were buried under the logs. The circumstances and the magnitude of the disaster outraged the Thai people, and the government was forced to take action. An immediate result of the ban on logging was a sudden steep increase in the price of timber. This in turn made illegal timber cutting more profitable. Alan Rabinowitz, *Chasing the Dragon's Tail: The Struggle to Save Thailand's Wild Cats* (New York: Doubleday, 1991), 210.

63. Mardon, "Tropical Forests," 32. Another source estimates that in 1989 no more than 10 to 13 percent of the country's natural forest was left (Rabinowitz, *Chasing the Dragon's Tail,* 186).

64. Vitoon, *People Centered Development,* 37–38.

65. As Joe Franke points out, these eucalyptus plantations were backed by the World Bank and the United Nations Food and Agriculture Agency. The plantations are seen by the Thai business community and the international lending institutions as a means of integrating Thailand into world economy. Joe Franke, "Tiger in the Forest," *Shambhala Sun,* November 1995, 51.

66. P. Charasdamrong and S. Raksakul, "Villagers Split: Saving the Forests or Axing a Way of Life?" *Bangkok Post,* 5 January 1992.

67. Prajak Khuttajitto (b. 1939) was born in Phae Village, Pak Khaosan Commune, Nakhon Ratchasima. His parents with their seven children later moved to Saraburi. While attending government school, Prajak helped his parents earn money by peddling ice cream and bread. He finished elementary education at the age of fifteen and opened a small coffee shop with his sister near a temple. Later he worked as houseboy, waiter, and assistant chef in a restaurant catering mostly to Americans working on the construction of the Saraburi-Khorat Friendship Highway. At nineteen he was ordained as a novice, and he stayed in robes for two years before returning to restaurant work, this time on the Phitsanulok-Lomsak highway project. After this highway was completed, Prajak went to Nakhon Ratchasima to work at the American Air Force base; then he moved to U-Taphao base, to an F-105 base, to Bang Saray and from there to Pattaya (in Chonburi Province) to work as a waiter in a newly built hotel. The turning point of his life came when he went home to Saraburi to visit his family (he had married at the age of twenty-one and had four children). One day, when he went to collect money he had loaned to a friend, the friend got angry and shot Prajak. While being carried in an ambulance to the Saraburi hospital, he resolved that if he survived the gunshot wounds, he would be ordained as a monk to make merit for his mother. At the age of thirty-five, Prajak was ordained in the "Mahanikai" order at Wat Bamrungtham in Saraburi—the same wat near which he had operated a coffee shop during his adolescent years. His teacher, Khamtan, taught him to meditate. Together they went to stay for a while at Bodhisatta Cave (Tham Phothisat) in Saraburi. In the mid-1970s they went wandering in Udon Thani and Loei. At one point his teacher left him alone in Nonviolence Cave (Tham Ahingsa) in Udon Thani. During his fifth year as a monk he met Buddhadasa and his disciple Pracha Pasanthammo. For more details of his background see the interview with Prajak in *Kheu Luang Phau Prajak rak pa dong yai* [Interview, life and conservation work of Ven. Father Prajak] (Bangkok: Wanaphithak, n.d.), 6–16.

68. Sanitsuda Ekachai, "When the Yellow Robe Faces Arrest," *Bangkok Post,* 22 January 1991, section 3, p. 1.

69. Taylor, "Living on the Rim," 116.

70. This practice originated in Phayao Province in the North in 1988. Since then tree ordination rites have been performed in other forests in different parts of the country: in Buriram and Chaiyaphum (in the Northeast) and in the rain forest of Klongyan, Surat Thani (in the South). Pongpet McKloy, "Stopping the Chainsaws with Sacred Robes," *Bangkok Post,* 29 March 1991, section 3, pp. 27–28.

71. Suda Kanjanawanawan, "Losing the Forest They Love," *Nation* (Bangkok), 6 June 1989, section 3, p. 28. There seems to be some discrepancy over the size of the forest. Sanitsuda says that Never–Dry Well Mountain covered 20,000 rai. See "Yellow Robe Faces Arrest," 25.

72. In Great Mountain (Phu Luang) Forest in Chaiyaphum Province, loggers simply tore the yellow robes off the trees and cut them down. McKloy, "Stopping the Chainsaws," 28.

73. Sanitsuda, "Yellow Robe Faces Arrest," 25.

74. After Juan died in 1980, his disciples were ordered to move his hermitage, Samnak Sanaen, out of the national forest. Suriphan, *Phra Ajan Juan,* 406-411.

75. Sanitsuda, "Yellow Robe Faces Arrest," 25. It is significant that the local sangha head announced, after an investigation, that the sanctuary and Prajak's presence helped preserve the forest.

76. Ibid. 25.

77. Joan MacNab, "The Thai Media and Environment Issues," *Friends of Thailand News* (Vancouver) 4, nos. 4–5 (May 1992): 4, 9. (MacNab, a journalist, covers AIDS and the environment for the *Nation* [Bangkok].) According to environmentalists, eucalyptus trees may be fine for Australia but they are bad for Thailand. In the Northeast, where the original forests have been mostly clear-cut, eucalypti destroy the soil and deplete water resources. They suck out what little water remains in the soil, pollute the soil with their natural herbicides, and deprive wild animals and birds of food. In addition, large-scale planting of eucalypti robs villagers of local economic autonomy by making the area dependent on the plantations. Franke, "Tiger in the Forest, 51; see also "Human Rights in Siam: The Case of Phra Phrachak and Prof. Sulak Sivaraksa," *Seeds of Peace* 8, no. 1, 28.

78. Sanitsuda, "Yellow Robe Faces Arrest," 25.

79. When Phimontham was arrested in 1960, General Sarit compelled him to disrobe before he was actually jailed. Phimontham refused, so a police officer forcibly removed his robe. Phimontham also refused to wear prison clothes and wore dark robes instead. In his mind he remained a monk, since he had never spoken the formula for leaving the sangha. Carr, "Ambassador of Buddhism," 10.

80. Poachers and illegal tree cutters often carried M-16s and AK-47s, had police connections, and were backed by money from wealthy businessmen or highly placed officials in Bangkok. Alan Rabinowitz, "In Memory of a Warrior: Seub Nakhasathian (1949–1990)," *Wildlife Conservation,* January/February 1991, 31.

81. Quoted in Damrong, "Luang Pu Phuang Akinjano," 53. Phuang (1897–1982) was born in a village of Phlai Commune (Prasat District, Surin). In 1937 he met some thudong monks in the forest where he had gone to find food. At the age of forty he left the householder's life and was ordained in the local tradition at Wat Jampa in Prakhonchai District, Surin. He did not start a thudong life until his sixth year in the monastic life in 1943. Phuang converted to the Thammayut order after he met Dun. (His reason, like that of many non-Thammayut thudong monks, was his desire to take part in sangha rituals with his teacher and fellow disciples, all of whom were Thammayut.) He accompanied Dun to attend Ajan Man's cremation at Sutthawat Wat in Sakon Nakhon. There he met Fan, whom he later followed on thudong to Ox Mountain and Lanka Mountain. For more details of his life see Damrong, "Luang Pu Phuang Akinjano."

82. *Kheu Luang Phau Prajak,* n.p. Prajak was speaking in an interview with *Mattichon* journalists after his arrest and release on bail.

83. See Sippanondha, *Middle Path,* 47; Vitoon, *People Centered Development,* 40–41.

84. Sanitsuda, "Yellow Robe Faces Arrest," 25.

85. Ibid. Prajak disrobed in July 1994 ending his seventeen years as a monk. At this writing he has been freed from jail and is awaiting trial. He says that if prison is his kamma, he will accept it. Franke, "Tiger in the Forest," 53.

86. See Sawaeng Udomsi, "Pa mai kap phra song" [Forests and monks], *Phutthajak* 45, no. 5 (May 1991): 29–35.

87. See Sathianphong Wannapok, "Khanchaung song phra pi phae" [Mirror of the sangha in the year of the goat], *Thai Rat,* 31 December 1991, 8. The wandering Thammayut monks, who were perceived as vagabonds in the past, now have become respectable. Their wats, built by elite or middle-class lay supporters, are spacious, comfortable, and legal. Land surrounding many of the wats has been designated as national forest.

88. Alan Rabinowitz, "Eye of the Tiger," *Wildlife Conservation,* November/December 1991, 54. Rabinowitz, a field zoologist for Wildlife Conservation International, conducted research in 1987 on leopards, tigers, and civets at Huai Kha Khaeng, a wildlife sanctuary in Uthai

Thani. While there, he discovered that the same government employees who hired him to protect the forest routinely aided in its destruction: "Publicly, the Forest Department was touting massive reforestation programs and intensified forest and wildlife protection, but in reality all their talk amounted to nothing." For example, some natural forest outside of Huai Kha Khaeng was actually being cut down and "reforested" (with Forestry Department approval) because there was more money per acre available for government-sponsored replanting than there was for the protection and maintenance of an already existing forest. Reforestation was often being used as an excuse to give control of forest reserve land to private businesses. Rabinowitz, *Chasing the Dragon's Tail*, 186.

89. Bill McKibben, "Bio Essay: Tuned-in but out of Touch", *Wildlife Conservation*, September/October 1992, 67.

90. Although a Wildlife Conservation Act was passed in 1960 and implemented a year later, wild animals continue to be killed (for food or for their supposed medicinal value) or captured and exported. See *Samsip pi kan anurak*, 11.

91. M1, 42. Some hunters thought that wild boars were more dangerous than tigers. See Chali, *Pa nai adit*, 149–151, 169–173.

92. According to Panyawattho in Geoffrey Beardsley, *A Magic Interlude: Visiting the Forest Monasteries of Thailand* (Casehayes, Devon, England, 1982), 110. Now tigers, leopards and panthers are so rare that they are a national treasure. See McNeely, *Soul of the Tiger*, 194.

93. T1, 217. The wat got its name from three huge rocks on the bank of the Mekong River. According to local history, the three rocks belong to three kingdoms: the northern rock to Luang Prabang, the middle rock to Bangkok, and the southern rock to Vientiane (T1, 219).

94. This statement was written in 1979 in his memoir after he became a settled monastic (in T1, 109). Thet, however, was not explicit about who destroyed the forests.

95. Juan and Wan were killed in a plane crash along with three other forest monks from Sakon Nakhon and Ubon on their way to the palace in Bangkok to bless the king and queen on their wedding anniversary.

CHAPTER 10: MANY PATHS AND MISCONCEPTIONS

1. Rujaya Abhakorn and David Wyatt, "Administrative Reforms and National Integration in Northern Thailand," in Grabowsky, *Regions and National Integration*, 76.

2. An example is Wachirayan's appointment of Maha Uan as sangha head of a Northeast monthon in the early 1900s, when Uan was only

thirty-seven. It was unprecedented for such a young monk to be given authority over older, respected teachers. When he died in 1956, Uan had been a sangha leader for over fifty years.

3. Zack, "Buddhist Education," 48.

4. This was on the eve of the passage of the new Sangha Administrative Act (1941), which stipulated that the two factions, Mahanikai and Thammayut, be united within eight years.

5. Cha remarks, "Really down inside I was also sad to see those buildings cracked but I'd throw off my sentimentality and try to say something which would be of use to my friends, and to myself. Even though I also felt that it was a pity, still I tended towards the Dhamma" (C1, 118).

6. A few decades later, while telling this story to his young disciples, Wiriyang reminded them that giving a massage to the teacher is a good way to learn the dhamma. If one is not too afraid of the teacher, it provides a good opportunity to question him (Wi, 26).

7. "The big books" *(nangseu yai)* that Man was referring to are the Prathomkap, the Prathommun, and the Mulakatjai, which were taught in the monasteries in Ubon at the time (F, 25). For details see Pricha, *Saranukrom phasa,* 841–842.

8. David K. Wyatt, "Presidential Address: Five Voices from Southeast Asia's Past," *Journal of Asian Studies* 53, no. 4 (November 1994): 1085.

9. T1, 198–199. As it turned out, Thet and his fellow wandering monks stayed in Phuket and Phangnga from 1950 to 1965.

10. The wandering Thammayut monks in Thet's party numbered eighteen and included a few southern monks of a different lineage from that of Thet and his disciples. They divided into three groups and stayed in Khok Loi, Takua Thung, and Thai Meuang.

11. According to Li, a chief suspect in the attack, a man named In, was a scoundrel from way back. Li had given him errands to run such as collecting firewood for the wat. Since Li considered In a follower of his, he asked the police to let him go. From then on, In was willing to do any work for the wat.

After this incident, the local people who had once resented the thudong monks' presence began to hold them in awe. The word got around that if a scythe could not pierce the skin of a disciple of Li's, Li himself must have even greater protective powers. "If his disciple is that invulnerable, just think what he's like!" (Li1, 58–60).

12. There was then no bridge connecting Thonburi to Bangkok. Wat Paknam, a half-deserted wat in Phasi Charoen District, was quite isolated from Bangkok.

13. Thamwarodom, *Prawat Jao Khun Phra Mongkhon Thepmuni,* 12.

14. Ibid., 15.

15. Recalled by Wiriyang in M3, 87. Later, in 1932, some monks and laypeople who took up meditation practice experienced great peace and calm, and their testimony convinced others to come to Man. But the number of practitioners remained small (M3, 104).

16. Bua, *Patipatha phra thudong kammathan*, 312–313. Quite probably, the thudong monks who held their fans backward did not know that the Thai words printed on one side of the fan should face the audience. Indeed, they may not have been able to read the Thai script.

17. When a disciple told Man about his experience, Man responded that he should follow the Buddha, not urban people's values or judgments (M3, 75–76).

18. Wi, 9. Kongma's teacher, Ajan Wankham, whose monastery was near the Phu Phan range, was probably from a Lao Buddhist tradition.

19. Among the thudong monks who did not convert to Thammayut were Ajan Kinnari Janathiyo (b. 1885) and Thaungrat Kantasilo, both of whom were Cha's teachers. Among Thaungrat's disciples were Bunmak Thitapanyo (abbot of Wat Phumaro in Laos) and Ki Thammutatamo (Wat Sanamchai, Phibun Mangsahan District, Ubon Ratchathani). In their younger days Kinnari and Thaungrat went wandering together in Laos and the Shan states. Kinnari stayed in Burma for twelve years and was fluent in the local language. *Ruam phap 80 phra kammathan*, 100–101, 150–151.

20. Only when Man was appointed abbot of Wat Jediluang did he have the authority to ordain monks.

21. Phuang's reason for converting, like that of other thudong monks, was to be able to take part in communal rituals with his teacher and fellow disciples, all of whom were Thammayut. For a biography of Phuang see Damrong, "Luang Pu Phuang Akinjano," 30–59.

22. Aunsi had been in the local tradition for three years. The reordination ceremony, which took place at Wat Sutjinda, was performed by Thammapamok (Uan Tisso). Sing and Maha Pin also participated in the ceremony. Damrong Phuraya, "Luang Pu Aunsi Sumetho," *Lokthip* 5, no. 76 (March 1986): 24.

23. "Phra Ajan Cha taun tamha," 193.

24. Zack, "Buddhist Education," 50-51.

25. Reynolds, "Buddhist Monkhood," 26.

26. Sangharakshita, *Survey of Buddhism*, 170.

27. C1, 11. The *Pubbasikkha vannana* (Elementary training) is a Thai commentary on dhamma-vinaya based on the Pali commentaries. Although Cha says he dropped it, he still taught it to monks at his forest wat (C1, 9 n. 7).

28. Boowa, *Things As They Are,* 57. Devadatta, the Buddha's cousin, was a monk who tried to bring about a schism in the sangha.

29. T1, 211; T2, 95. Li, who was awarded a title during the same year as Thet, also objected to it.

30. Prince Damrong, letter to Somdet Phuthakhosajan (Jaroen), abbot of Wat Thepsirin in Bangkok, 6 June 1934, in *Sam somdet,* 68–69. Damrong, Chulalongkorn's half-brother, was an architect of the modern Thai state. He went into exile in Penang after the revolution ended the absolute monarchy in 1932. He wrote this letter in Penang.

31. This is the lowest level in Gunaratana's three categories of morality. Henepola Gunaratana, *Mindfulness in Plain English,* 26–27.

32. In many local traditions, Buddhist sermons focused more on people who led ascetic lives and followed the bodhisatta ideal. The historical Buddha's life story was less prominent in their sermons (see chap. 1).

33. O'Connor, "Interpreting Thai Religious Change," 300.

34. Ibid., 333, 336.

35. A. Thomas Kirsch, "Modernizing Implications of Nineteenth Century Reforms in the Thai Sangha," in *Religion and Legitimation of Power in Thailand, Laos, and Burma,* ed. Bardwell L. Smith (Chambersburg, Pa.: Anima Books, 1978), 63.

36. Seri, *Religion in Changing Society,* 16. The grassroots community development movement had no founder and was neither supported nor imposed by the state. As Seri points out, it is not easy to determine the exact number of monks who are engaged in social action today.

37. Ibid., 19.

38. Sippanondha Ketudat, *The Middle Path for the Future of Thailand* (Honolulu: East-West Center, 1990), 73.

39. Phra Panyanantha, "Khwam yu raut khaung phra phutthasatsana [Survival of Buddhism]," *Dhammapadip* 20 (May-June 1995): 12–13.

40. Phayom's sermons are available on cassettes at Wat Suan Kaew, Nonthaburi.

41. Phirot Yumonthian, *Phra Fipak Kla: Chiwit lae kan tausu khaung Phra Phayom* [A bold preacher-monk: Life and struggle of Phra Phayom] (Bangkok: Amnuaiwep Printing, 1990), 235. The preaching style practiced among regional traditions was often humorous, but the humor arose from problems people faced in everyday life and the sermons contained clear ethical rules and instructions, just as in Phayom's sermons today.

42. See Phra Phaisan Visalo, "The Forest Monastery and Its Relevance to Modern Thai Society," in *Radical Conservatism: Buddhism in the Contemporary World,* ed. Nicholas P. Kohler (Bangkok: Sathirakoses-Nagapradipa Foundation, 1990), 290–291.

43. Taylor, *Forest Monks,* 76. Thudong monks' memoirs confirm this point. It is likely that Man's mode of teaching was influenced by the rhetorical style of *mau lam* (folk-opera singers), which he learned in his younger days.

44. Normally Ajan Man did not allow anyone to record his sermons, let alone print them. Perhaps he knew that once such a sermon is written down, it loses its power. Worse yet, copies of sermons were likely to invite criticism from the scholastic-administrative monks of his time. Wiriyang decided to take the risk and wrote down some discourses of Man's that he heard in 1943, however (Wi, 52–53).

45. Sangharakshita, *Survey of Buddhism,* 437.

46. Man encountered these groups while wandering along the Mekong River in his younger days. Wiriyang, "Prawat Phra Ajan Man," 6.

47. With regard to proficiency in insight meditation, Man and his disciples believed that persons with strong intellects were often no match for the humble, unsophisticated lay devotees (M1, 154–155).

48. Sommai Premchit and Sobin Namto (two ex-monks from the Northeast) confirm this point (personal communications, 14 February 1993 and 22 January 1996).

49. Sobin Namto's father, an ex-monk, was respected as a mau tham even after he disrobed. Villagers believed that he had the power to heal people who were possessed by phi paup, spirits believed to eat the entrails of their victims. Interview by author, 31 March 1996.

50. Zack, "Buddhist Education," 221.

51. Boowa, "Dhūtaṅga Kammaṭṭhāna Bhikkhus," 72.

52. In regional Buddhist traditions female renunciates—like male ones—shaved their heads, wore white robes and observed eight or ten precepts: not killing, not stealing, not lying, not using intoxicants, not eating after noontime, not taking part in entertainment, not using ornaments, not sleeping on high beds, not accepting gold, silver, or money, and remaining celibate.

53. Thanissaro makes a similar point in his introduction to Ubasika Kee [Ki] Nanayon, *An Untangled Knowing: The Teachings of a Thai Buddhist Lay Woman,* trans. Thanissaro (Barre, Mass.: Dhamma Dana Publications, 1995), vii.

54. McCarthy, *Surveying and Exploring,* 126–127.

55. See, for example, Suriphan, *Chiwa prawat Luang Pu Lui,* 43–45; Suriphan, *Chiwa prawat Luang Pu Chaup,* 59–61.

56. Suriphan, *Chiwa prawat Luang Pu Lui,* 45. Lui called the mae chis' meditation practice *mangkai;* this is a meditation on the thirty-two parts of the body.

57. Man spent the last five years of his life at Pheu Tree Village.

According to Man's biographer, one of the reasons Ajan Man stayed there for such a long time was because of this old white-robed lay devotee and her attainment (M2, 313).

58. Among these meditation teachers are Buddhadasa (1906-1993), Luang Phau Sot (1884-1959) of Wat Paknam, Ajan Man, and many of his disciples who later on became meditation masters in their own right.

59. Phra Pracha Pasannathammo, *Lao wai meua wai sonthaya: atta chiwa prawat khaung than Buddhadasa* [Memoir of Buddhadasa's early years] (Bangkok: Komon Khimthaung Foundation, 1986), 69. Three decades ago in Chonburi, eastern Thailand, *mae chis* could be seen on almsround. In the late 1950s I used to offer food to them.

60. For a biography of Ki, known as K. Khao-suan-luang, see Thanissaro, introduction to Kee, *An Untangled Knowing.* Thanissaro attributes the high regard that inhabitants of Ratchaburi and Phetburi have for women ascetics (whom he calls lay nuns) to the influence of Mon culture. The Buddhism practiced in this area was probably that of the Mon Buddhist tradition.

61. Naeb's followers also included teachers, government employees, and people in business. For a discussion of Naeb and another woman meditation teacher, Suchin Borihanwanakhet, see John Van Esterik, "Women Meditation Teachers in Thailand," in *Women of Southeast Asia,* ed. Penny Van Esterik (De Kalb: Center for Southeast Asian Studies, Northern Illinois University, 1982), 42–53. Sobin Namto, a student of Naeb's when he was a novice and now a lay meditation teacher himself, confirms that monks and novices who studied under Ajan Naeb did not see anything unusual about their having a woman as a teacher. They knew that she was spiritually superior to them. (Sobin Namto, interview by author, 29 January, 1996.)

62. The area around Yoi Mountain (now called Khao Yoi District) was largely inhabited by Lao Song (or Phu Thai) people from Laos. These Phu Thai continued to observe many customs that they inherited from their ancestors in northern Laos. See Pho, *Tamnan Thai Phuan,* 109–110. Sobin Namto, who visited this area when he was a monk, believes that the ancestors of the Phu Thai followed a Buddhist tradition similar to Mahayana Buddhism (which acknowledges the existence of a bhikkhunī lineage). It is likely the abbot of Yoi Mountain Monastery who performed the bhikkhunī ordination was merely following a Phu Thai Buddhist tradition.

The Lao thudong monks in the Northeast knew this area well. After Ajan Man's cremation in 1950, some of his disciples went to spend rains retreats at Yoi Mountain Cave. One of the reasons Thet decided to wander into the South was to look over some of the famous meditation samnaks in Phetburi and Ratchaburi. T2, 87.

63. A sāmaṇerī is a female novice who observes ten precepts; a bhikkhunī is a fully ordained nun. Both sāmaṇerīs and bhikkhunīs wore robes of the same ochre color as monks' robes. For further information about the two bhikkhunīs and the bhikkhunī movement in Thailand, see Chatsumarn Kabilsingh, *Thai Women in Buddhism* (Berkeley: Parallax Press, 1991), 45–48.

64. Ibid., 46.

65. J, 59. According to Chatsumarn (*Thai Women in Buddhism*, 29) a bhikkhunī's subordination to bhikkhus was a strategy to insure their protection in the Sangha, given the social climate of India during the Buddha's time. Juan's vision of being instructed by an enlightened and inspiring bhikkhunī is significant, considering that it occurred in 1955 when the Sangha Council still refused to acknowledge the importance of female monastics.

66. This is evident in a speech that Somdet Uan gave on 27 October 1939 to provincial administrative monks. "Do not act in violation of the vinaya," he warned the monks. "Do not take mae chis or lay female practitioners along on a thudong." "Phadung chat satsana" [Support the nation and the religion], in Uan, *Niphon bang reuang*, 197.

67. T1, 136. Uppalavanna was an eminent disciple of the Buddha, an arahat and foremost in psychic powers among women.

68. See James Placzek, "The Thai Forest Tradition," in *Southeast Asia: Women, Changing Structure and Cultural Continuity*, ed. Geoffrey B. Hainsworth (Ottawa: University of Ottawa Press, 1981), 180.

69. See Taylor, *Forest Monks*, 138–139.

70. Thao Satyanurak was a female attendant in the royal household who came to practice meditation under Li's guidance. While staying at Nekkhamma House, a home for mae chis at Wat Boromniwat, she attained such unusual realizations that she decided to stay at the wat until death (Li1, 114–115).

71. Thet remarked that senior Thammayut monks did not pay much attention to him or to his fellow thudong monks until after they had become popular in Phuket in the early 1950s: "Our presence on Phuket Island drew the attention of the senior [Thammayut] monks in Bangkok" (T2, 94).

72. Quoted in Tambiah, *Buddhist Saints and Cult*, 155.

73. C2, 2. Among the "must see" sites for pilgrims on dhamma tours is Juan's hermitage (established in 1969) on Phu Thauk, a sandstone mountain, thirty-five kilometers southwest of Beung Kan District in Nongkhai.

74. The first abbot of Amaravati was Sumedho, Cha's senior Western disciple. For a collection of biographies of English-speaking monks in Ajan Cha's lineage see *Seeing the Way: Buddhist Reflections on the Spir-*

itual Life, (Great Gaddesden, Hertfordshire, England: Amaravati Publications, 1989).

75. Thanissaro Bhikkhu of Metta Forest Monastery, near San Diego.

CONCLUSION

1. Thanissaro "Introduction," Kee, *An Untangled Knowing,* viii.

2. Paul Breiter, *Venerable Father: A Life with Ahjahn Chah* (Bangkok: Funny Publishing, 1993), 58. Breiter was ordained as a monk and trained under Ajan Cha's guidance for five years.

3. Reginald A. Ray, *Buddhist Saints in India: A Study in Buddhist Values and Orientations* (New York: Oxford University Press, 1994), viii.

4. O'Connor, "Interpreting Thai Religious Change," 338.

5. Ibid., 335.

6. As Kirsch comments, the lost folk elements served functions that [modern state] Buddhism must now meet unmediated. A. Thomas Kirsch, "Complexity in the Thai Religious System," *Journal of Asian Studies* 36, 2 (1977): 265–266.

7. O'Connor, "Interpreting Thai Religious Change," 335.

8. Grabowsky refers to Siam's administrative control of outer regions as "inner colonialism." From the regional perspective, he points out, "Siam behaved not unlike an indigenous colonial power." Grabowsky, *Regions and National Integration,* 8–9.

9. See Sanitsuda Ekachai, "Falling from Grace," *Bangkok Post,* 5 September 1995, Outlook section, 27–28. Three popular monks—Nikon, Yantra, and Phawanaphutho—all attracted large followings within a short time and then became the subject of scandal. In the late 1980s they gained renown nationwide through the media. Their popularity and massive lay support, which perhaps came too early in their careers, led to the erosion of their self-discipline and ultimately to their downfall.

10. This point is made by Phra Maha Prayun Miroek (titled Methithammaphon), dean of Graduate Studies at Mahachulalongkorn Buddhist University. Saowarop Panyacheewin, "In Search of the Old Buddhist Values" *Bangkok Post,* 4 December 1990, sec. 3, p. 1.

11. Phra Maha David Yodsi, "Wikritkan borihan kan pokkhraung khraung khana song thai" [A Crisis in the Thai Sangha's Administration], *Nation Weekend* [Bangkok], 3–9 March 1995, 24–25.

12. Phra Phongsak Techathammo, quoted in "Religion in the New Society," *Bangkok Post,* 10 July 1990, 25. Phongsak received the Global 500 Award for 1990 from the United Nations Environmental Program.

Glossary

Terms in italics are Thai unless otherwise noted. Translations of dhamma terms give the meanings accepted by forest monks and monks of other regional traditions. These may depart from standard definitions.

abhidhamma (Pali): Buddhist higher psychology

ajan: Teacher, abbot (Pali: *acariya*)

anāgāmī (Pali): Nonreturner, one who has reached the third of the four stages of holiness

ānāpānasati (Pali): Meditation technique based on noting the coming and going of the breath

arahat (Pali): One who has reached the highest stage of holiness, having completely eradicated all defilements *(kilesa)*

ban: Village or community. In the past a village was a natural community. Today it is the smallest administrative unit in Thailand. Several villages make up a commune or subdistrict *(tambon);* tambons in turn make up a district *(amphoe)*. A number of districts make up a province *(jangwat)*. The provincial capital, itself a district (the *amphoe meuang*) usually has the same name as the province. A number of provinces make up a region *(phak)*. (Prior to 1938 a number of *meuang* made up a *monthon.*)

barami: Perfection; quality leading to Buddhahood (Pali: *pārami*)

381

bhikkhu (Pali): Buddhist male monk

bhikkhunī (Pali): Fully ordained nun, the approximate female equivalent of *bhikkhu*

bodhisatta (Pali): A future Buddha, one who aspires to be a Buddha (Sanskrit: *bodhisattva;* Thai: *phothisat*)

buddho (Pali): Word (referring to the Buddha) used as a mantra in meditation (Thai: *phuttho*)

bun: Merit (Pali: *puñña*)

Bun Phawet (Lao): Festival of reading the Wetsandon Chadok (Vessantara Jataka), popular in the Northeast

dhamma (Pali): Truth, nature of things, teachings of the Buddha

dukkha (Pali): Suffering, unsatisfactoriness of conditioned existence, stress, conflict, pain

gāthā (Pali): Mantra, verse (Thai: *khatha*)

Isan: Term coined in this century to refer to a *monthon* in the northeastern region of Thailand; today refers to the entire Northeast and to its dominantly Lao-speaking people

jao: Lord or master, as in *jao meuang,* ruler of the domain, governor of a province; *jao nai,* government officials who wield power invested in them by the state; or *jao awat,* abbot

jhāna (Pali): State of deep mental unification characterized by a total immersion of the mind in its object

kamma (Pali): Morally relevant actions; intentional actions that result in future states of being; in Thai usage, consequences of morally relevant actions of the past, including past lives (Thai: *kam;* Sanskrit: *karma*)

kammathan: Subjects of meditation, meditation exercises; act of meditating or contemplating (Pali: *kammaṭṭhāna*)

kilesa (Pali): Defilement, a mental factor associated with unwholesome states of mind

klot: Large umbrella equipped with a mosquito net, used for meditation or as a tent

kuti: Monk's hut or room

mae chi or *mae khaw:* Female white-robed renunciate (see also *pha khaw*)

Maha: Prefix in the name of a monk who has passed the third level of Pali exams

Mahanikai: The "large order" *(maha nikai)* of monks. The term was coined after the establishment of the Thammayut order in the nineteenth century. Monks of diverse traditions in Siam were lumped together in this category.

Makha Bucha: Worship on the full moon day of Magha (Pali), the third lunar month, which occurs in February or early March, commemorating the assembly of 1,250 arahats who assembled without notification to hear the Buddha deliver a summary of his teachings

mau: Expert, as in *mau phi,* expert in communicating with spirits; *mau tham,* expert in healing; *mau tamyae,* expert in midwifery; *mau du,* astrologer; *mau lam,* folk opera singer

metta (Pali): Loving-kindness; type of meditation that extends acceptance and kindness to all beings

meuang: Kingdom or principality; in ancient chronicles, designates both a town located at the hub of a network of interrelated villages and all the towns and villages ruled by a single lord

monthon: Previously an administrative unit comprising several *meuang* (see *ban*)

naktham: Formal dhamma curriculum, created by Prince Wachirayan (literally, "expert in dhamma")

nikai: Sect, order, or lineage (see also Mahanikai, Thammayut)

nimit: Internal mental image or object that arises when the mind becomes concentrated, including visions; dream image (Pali: *nimitta*)

Pali: Language in which the scriptures and related texts of Theravada Buddhism are written. In Bangkok, Pali texts are written and printed in Bangkok Thai script; regional Buddhist texts were written in Khmer or Yuan scripts.

parian: A monk who has passed a certain level of the graded Pali exams, the ninth being the highest

pariyat monk: Book-learning monk, one who specializes in *pariyat tham* (Pali: *pariyatti dhamma,* wording of the teachings)

patimok: Monks' disciplinary code of 227 precepts (Pali: *pātimokkha*) *pha khaw:* White-robed renunciate; lay practitioner, male *(phau khaw)* or female *(mae khaw),* who follows eight precepts and wears white robes

phawana: Meditate (Pali: *bhāvanā,* meditation, mental development)

phi: Spirit or ghost

Phra: Title used for sacred persons, Buddha images, or relics; title for a Buddhist monk

Phra Khru: The lowest title of monastic rank awarded through the national sangha hierarchy

phu mi bun: Persons with great merit; holy men

samādhi (Pali): State of concentration attained by meditation practice. It has many levels depending on the degree of mental absorption in the object of the meditation.

samatha (Pali): Tranquillity, calm; type of meditation that develops high levels of concentration and tranquillity

samnak: Hermitage, unofficial *wat* (without an ordination hall) usually consisting of a few huts *(kuti)* and an open hall (see also *wat)*

san puta: Shrine for local ancestral spirits

sangha (Pali): The monastic community; in official usage, the institution of Buddhist monks and novices (Thai: *song)*

sangharāja: Supreme patriarch of the Thai sangha

sati (Pali): Mindfulness, attention, recollection; the quality of mind that notices what is happening in the present moment without clinging or aversion

Siamese: Ethnic Thai people concentrated in the Central Plains of Siam (as Thailand was called before 1941)

sīla (Pali): Virtue or self-discipline; moral training rules

Somdet: Initial element in the titles of some royalty and high-ranking monks of the national sangha hierarchy; connotes sacral dignity

sutta (Pali): Discourse (of the Buddha)

Tai: Ethnolinguistic family of related peoples scattered from South China westward to Assam and southward to the Malay peninsula. Within the borders of Thailand, Tai peoples include the Siamese, Yuan (northern Thai), Shan, Lu, and Lao.

Thammayut: Sect or order of Buddhist monks and novices founded by Prince Mongkut (see also Mahanikai)

thudong: Ascetic practices (Pali: *dhutānga*)

Tipitaka: Buddhist Canon; lit., the "three baskets" of *vinaya, sutta,* and *abhidhamma*

ubosot: Ordination hall; building in a *wat* where important religious ceremonies and rituals are performed (also called *bot*)

vinaya (Pali): Disciplinary rules for the monastic community; section of the Tipitaka dealing with monastic rules

vipassanā (Pali): Insight; type of meditation that develops mental clarity and intuitive understanding of the nature of things

wat: Monastic residence of members of the sangha; a center of Buddhist religious practice. Officially a wat is a temple with an ordination hall and/or a shrine hall. Forest monks, on the other hand, often casually refer to a cluster of *kuti* (huts) and a *sala* (hall) as a *wat,* although the administrative monks call it a *samnak.*

wat pa: Forest wat, forest hermitage

Wetsandon chadok: Story of the Buddha's last rebirth as the *bodhisatta* Wetsandon (Pali: *Vessantara jātaka*)

Wisakha Bucha: Worship on the full moon day of Vesakha (Pali), the sixth lunar month, which occurs in May, commemorating the Buddha's birth, enlightenment, and death

Bibliography

An somdet [Read the somdet]. Bangkok: Crem. vol. Somdet Phra Maha Wirawong Tissathera, Wat Boromniwat, 1956.

Anderson, Benedict. Introduction to *In the Mirror: Literature and Politics in Siam in the American Era,* edited by Benedict Anderson and Ruchira Mendiones. Bangkok: Duang Kamol, 1985.

Anuman Rajadhon. *Essays on Thai Folklore.* Bangkok: Social Science Association Press, 1968.

Anuson Luang Pu Waen Sujinno [Biography of Ven. Grandfather Waen]. Chiang Mai: Crem. vol. Luang Pu Waen Sujinno, Wat Doi Maepang, 1985.

Anuson ngan phuk phathasima [Commemoration of establishing the boundary stone]. Ubon: Wat Bau Chaneng, 1988.

Anuson ngan sop Somdet Phra Yotkaeo [Commemoration of Somdet Phra Yotkaeo]. Bangkok: Crem. vol. Supreme Patriarch of Laos, Wat Thepsirin, 1985.

Badiner, Allan Hunt, ed. *Dharma Gaia: A Harvest of Essays in Buddhism and Ecology.* Berkeley: Parallax Press, 1990.

Barnes, Simon. *Tiger!* New York: St. Martin's Press, 1994.

Batson, Benjamin A. *The End of the Absolute Monarchy in Siam.* Singapore: Oxford University Press, 1986.

Beardsley, Geoffrey. *A Magic Interlude: Visiting the Forest Monasteries of Thailand.* Casehayes, Devon, England, 1982.

Bharati, Agehananda. *The Ochre Robe: An Autobiography.* Santa Barbara: Ross-Erikson, 1980.

Bhasit Chitrabhasa. "Pai fang thet Wetsandon chadok thinai" [Where can you hear a recitation of the Wetsandon chadok?]. *Sinlapa Wattha-natham* 7, no. 1 (May 1990): 16–18.

Boowa [Bua] Nyanasampanno. "An Account on the Dhūtaṅga Kammaṭ-ṭhāna Bhikkhus." In *Buddhism in Thailand*. Bangkok: 30th Anniversary of the World Fellowship of Buddhists, 1980.

———. *The Dhamma Teaching of Acariya Maha Boowa in London*. Translated by Phra Panyawattho. Bangkok: Chuan Printing Press, 1980.

———. *Straight from the Heart: Thirteen Talks on the Practice of Meditation*. Translated by Thanissaro Bhikkhu. Bangkok: P. Samphan Panich, 1987.

———. *Things as They Are: A Collection of Talks on the Training of the Mind*. Translated by Thanissaro Bhikkhu. Udon Thani, Thailand: Ban Tat Forest Monastery, 1994.

———. *The Venerable Phra Acharn Mun Bhuridatta Thera*. Translated by Siri Buddhasukh. Bangkok: Funny Publishing, 1982.

———. "Wisdom Develops Samadhi." In *Living Buddhist Masters*, edited by Jack Kornfield. Kandy: Buddhist Publication Society, 1977.

Breiter, Paul. *Venerable Father: A Life with Ahjahn Chah*. Bangkok: Funny Publishing, 1993.

Bua Yannasampanno, Phra Ajan. *Patipatha phra thudong kammathan* [Thudong kammathan monks' conduct]. Bangkok: Crem. vol. Chu Sitachit, Wat Thepsirin, 1973.

———. *Prawat Than Phra Ajan Man Phurithatta Thera* [Biography of Phra Ajan Man]. Bangkok: Si Sappada, 1971.

Bua, Ajahn. *The Biography of Ajhan Man (1871–1949)*. Translated by Ruth-Inge Heinze. Taiwan: Chinese Association for Folklore, 1976.

Buddhaghosa. *The Path of Purification (Visuddhimagga)*. Translated by Nyanamoli. Kandy: Buddhist Publication Society, 1979.

Bunnag, Jane. "The Way of the Monk and the Way of the World: Buddhism in Thailand, Laos and Cambodia." In *The World of Buddhism*, edited by Heinz Bechert and Richard Gombrich. London: Thames and Hudson, 1984.

Calderazzo, John. "Meditation in a Thai Forest." *Audubon*, January 1990, 85–91.

Caras, Roger A. *Dangerous to Man: The Definitive Story of Wildlife's Reputed Dangers*. New York: Holt, Rinehart and Winston, 1975.

Carr, Stephen. "An Ambassador of Buddhism to the West." In *Buddhism in Europe*, edited by Aad Verboom. Bangkok: Crem. vol. Somdet Phra Phutthajan, Wat Mahathat, 1990).

Carrithers, Michael. *The Buddha*. Oxford: Oxford University Press, 1983.

———. *The Forest Monks of Sri Lanka*. Delhi: Oxford University Press, 1983.

Chah [Cha], Ajahn. *Bodhinyana: A Collection of Dhamma Talks*. Bangkok: Funny Press, 1982.

———. *Food for the Heart*. Ubon, Thailand: Wat Pah Nanachat, 1992.

———. *Living Dhamma*. Ubon, Thailand: Bung Wai Forest Monastery, 1992.

———. *A Taste of Freedom*. Bangkok: Funny Press, 1980.

———. *Tuccho Pothila: Nurturing Buddhism through Contemplation of Mind*. Bangkok: Funny Press, 1985.

Chali Iamkrasin. *Pa nai adit* [Forests in the past]. Bangkok: Tonmai, 1991.

Chandler, David P. *A History of Cambodia*. Boulder, Colorado: Westview Press, 1983.

Chantaboon Sutthi. "Highland Agriculture: From Better to Worse." In *Hill Tribes Today: Problems in Change*, edited by John McKinnon and Bernard Vienne. Bangkok: White Lotus-Orstom, 1989.

Chatsumarn Kabilsingh. "Early Buddhist Views on Nature." In *Dharma Gaia: A Harvest of Essays in Buddhism and Ecology*, edited by Allan Hunt Badiner. Berkeley: Parallax Press, 1990.

———. *Thai Women in Buddhism*. Berkeley: Parallax Press, 1991.

"Chiwa prawat lae patipatha Phra Ajan Wan [Life and conduct of Phra Ajan Wan." In *Phra Udomsangwonwisut Thera (Phra Ajan Wan Uttamo)*. Bangkok: Crem. vol. Aphaidamrong Cave Wat (Sakon Nakhon), 1981.

Chob Kacha-ananda. "Yao: Migration, Settlements, and Land." In *Highlanders of Thailand*, edited by John McKinnon and Wanat Bhruksasri. Kuala Lumpur: Oxford University Press, 1983.

Chodok Yanasithi (Thamthirarat Mahamuni), Phra. *Lak patibat samatha-vipassana kammathan* [Practice of samatha-vipassana meditation]. Bangkok: Crem. vol. Phra Thamthirarat, Wat Mahathat, 1988.

Condominas, Georges. "Phiban Cults in Rural Laos." In *Change and Persistence in Thai Society*, edited by G. William Skinner and A. Thomas Kirsch. Ithaca: Cornell University Press, 1975.

Damrong Phuraya. "Luang Pu Aunsi Sumetho." *Lokthip* 5, no. 76 (March 1986): 14–48.

———. "Luang Pu Phuang Akinjano." *Lokthip* 7, no. 134 (15 July, 1988): 30–59.

———. "Phra Ajan Maha Thaungsuk Sujitto." *Lokthip* 3, no. 44 (November 1984): 26–33.

———. "Phra Ajan Sing Khantayamo." *Lokthip* 3, no. 24 (January 1984).

Damrong Rajanuphap, Krom Phraya. *Thiaw tam thang rotfai* [Travel by train]. Nakhon Ratchasima: Crem. vol. Phraya Ratbamrung, 1962.

De Berval, Rene, ed. *Kingdom of Laos*. France: A. Bontemps, 1959.

Ferguson, John P. "The Symbolic Dimensions of the Burmese Sangha." Ph.D. diss., Cornell University, 1975.

Ferguson, John P., and Shalardchai Ramitanondh. "Monks and Hierarchy in Northern Thailand." *Journal of the Siam Society* 64, part 1 (January 1976): 104–150.

Franke, Joe. "Tiger in the Forest." *Shambhala Sun*, November 1995, 48–53.

Girling, John L. S. *Thailand: Society and Politics*. Ithaca: Cornell University Press, 1981.

Gombrich, Richard. *Theravada Buddhism*. New York: Routledge and Kegan Paul, 1988.

Govinda, Lama Anagarika. *The Way of the White Clouds: A Buddhist Pilgrim in Tibet*. Boston: Shambhala, 1988.

Grabowsky, Volker. "The Isan up to Its Integration into the Siamese State." In *Regions and National Integration in Thailand, 1892–1992,* edited by Volker Grabowsky. Wiesbaden: Harrassowitz, 1995.

———, ed. *Regions and National Integration in Thailand, 1892–1992*. Wiesbaden: Harrassowitz, 1995.

Gray, Christine. "Thailand: The Soteriological State in the 1970s." Ph.D. diss., University of Chicago, 1986.

Gross, Rita. "After Patriarchy: Sacredness in Everyday Life." *Tricycle: The Buddhist Review* 2, no. 2 (Winter 1992): 58–62.

Gunaratana, Henepola. *Mindfulness in Plain English*. Boston: Wisdom, 1991.

———. *The Path of Serenity and Insight*. Delhi: Motilal Banarsidass, 1985.

Harvey, Peter. *An Introduction to Buddhism: Teachings, History and Practices*. New York: Cambridge University Press, 1990.

"Human Rights in Siam: The Case of Phra Phrachak and Prof. Sulak Sivaraksa." *Seeds of Peace* 8, no. 1: 27–32.

Jackson, Peter. *Buddhism, Legitimation, and Conflict: The Political Functions of Urban Thai Buddhism*. Singapore: Institute of Southeast Asian Studies, 1989.

Jan Sirijantho. "Attano prawat" [My Life]. Reprinted in *Si Ubonrattanaram*. Bangkok: Rongphim Mitthai, 1968.

Jiraporn Witayasakpan. "Nationalism and the Transformation of Aesthetic Concepts: Theatre in Thailand during the Phibun Period," Ph.D. diss., Cornell University, 1992.

Joemsak Pinthaung, ed. *Wiwatthanakan khaung kanbukboek thidin thamkin* [Study of conservation forest area demarcation, protection, and occupancy in Thailand]. Bangkok: Institute of Rural Community Development, 1991.

Juan Kulachettho. "Attano prawat" [My life]. In *Phra Ajan Juan: chiwa prawat patipatha lae thammathetsana* [Autobiography and conduct of Phra Ajan Juan], edited by Suriphan Maniwat. Bangkok: Crem. vol. Thauk Mountain Monastery, 1981.

Keyes, Charles F. "Buddhism and National Integration in Thailand." *Journal of Asian Studies* 30, no. 3 (1971): 551–568.

————. "Hegemony and Resistance in Northeastern Thailand." In *Regions and National Integration in Thailand, 1892–1992*, edited by Volker Grabowsky. Wiesbaden: Harrassowitz, 1995.

————. *Thailand: Buddhist Kingdom as Modern Nation-State*. Boulder: Westview Press, 1987.

Khaneungnit Janthabutra. *Kankhleuanwai khaung yuwa song thai run raek, 2477–2484* [The first movement of Thai Young Monks, 1934–1941]. Bangkok: Thammasat University Press, 1985.

————, ed. *Khon di meuang Ubon* [Good people in Ubon]. Ubon: Ubon Cultural Center, 1984.

Kheu Luang Phau Prajak rak pa dong yai [Interview, life and conservation work of Ven. Father Prajak]. Bangkok: Wanaphithak, n.d.

Khomsan Matukham [pseud.]. *Dong Phra Jao, daen morana* [Lord Buddha Forest, a deadly region]. Bangkok: Phithakpracha, 1977.

————. *Khraung Jandawong khao kheu khrai* [Khraung Jandawong, who is he?]. Bangkok: Phithakpracha, 1978.

"Khwamkhatyaeng rawang Phra Siwichai kap khana song" [Conflict between Phra Siwichai and the sangha]. S.R. 0202.10/61. National Archives, Bangkok, 1935–1936.

Ki [Kee] Nanayon, Ubasika. *An Untangled Knowing: The Teachings of a Thai Buddhist Lay Woman*. Translated by Thanissaro Bhikkhu, Barre, Mass.: Dhamma Dana Publications, 1995.

Kirsch, A. Thomas. "Modernizing Implications of the Nineteenth Century Reforms in the Thai Sangha." In *Religion and the Legitimation of Power in Thailand, Laos, and Burma*, edited by Bardwell L. Smith. Chambersburg, Pa: Anima Books, 1978.

————. "Phu Thai Religious Syncretism: A Case Study of Thai Religion." Ph.D. diss., Harvard University, 1967.

————. "Text and Context: Buddhist Sex Roles/Culture of Gender Revisited." *American Ethnologist* 12 (May 1985): 302–320.

Kitirat Sihaban. "Kan ruam khana song isan khao kap khana song thai" [Integrating the Isan sangha into the Thai sangha]. Master's thesis, Thammasat University, 1990.

Klausner, William. "Peter Jackson's *Buddhism, Legitimation, and Conflict.*" *Journal of Siam Society* 77, 2 (1989): 83.

Klein, Anne Carolyn. *Meeting the Great Bliss Queen: Buddhists, Feminists, and the Art of the Self.* Boston: Beacon Press, 1995.

Kohler, Nicholas P., ed. *Radical Conservatism: Buddhism in the Contemporary World.* Bangkok: Sathirakoses-Nagapradipa Foundation, 1990.

Kornfield, Jack. *Living Buddhist Masters.* Kandy: Buddhist Publication Society, 1977.

Kornfield, Jack, and Paul Breiter, eds. *A Still Forest Pool: The Insight Meditation of Achaan Chah.* Wheaton, Ill.: Theosophical Publishing House, 1985.

Kowit Siriwanno, Phra Maha, et al. *Moradok Isan* [Heritage of Isan]. Bangkok: Mahachula Buddhist University, 1990.

La Khempatato, Phra. *Chiwa prawat Luang Pu La Khempatato* [Memoirs of Ven. Grandfather La Khempatato]. Bangkok: Sinlapa Sayam, 1989.

Lee Dhammadaro [Li Thammatharo]. *The Autobiography of Phra Ajaan Lee.* Translated by Thanissaro Bhikkhu. Nonthaburi: Thepphrathan, 1992.

———. *Frames of Reference.* Translated by Thanissaro Bhikkhu. Bangkok: P. Samphanphanit, 1987.

———. *Keeping the Breath in Mind.* Samutprakan, Thailand: C. Sangngam Printing, 1992.

Li Thammatharo. *Chiwa prawat khaung Phra Sutthithamrangsi (Than Phau Li)* [Memoirs of Ven. Father Li]. Bangkok: Kathin ceremony vol. Wat Asokaram (Samut Prakan), 1962.

"Luang Phau Khian Thammarakhito: Wat Samnak Khunnen, tambon Wang-ngiew, amphoe Bangkhunnak, Phijit." *Phra Aphinya*, no. 1 (n.d).

"Luang Phau Noi, Wat Thammasala, *tambon* Thammasala, Nakhon Pathom." *Phra Aphinya*, no. 5 (n.d).

MacNab, Joan. "The Thai Media and Environment Issues." *Friends of Thailand News* (Vancouver) 4, nos. 4–5 (May 1992): 3–4, 9.

Magness, T. *The Life and Teaching of the Ven. Chao Khun Mongkolthepmuni (Late Abbot of Wat Paknam Bhasichareon).* Bangkok: Croake, n.d.

Mani Phayomyong. *Prapheni sipsaung deun lan na thai* [Twelve festivals in Lan Na Thai]. Chiang Mai: S. Sapkanphim, 1990.

Mardon, Mark. "Tropical Forests: Maneuvers in the Teak Wars." *Sierra,* May/June 1991, 30–36.

McCarthy, James. *Surveying and Exploring in Siam.* London: William Clowes and Sons, 1900.

McKibben, Bill. "Bio Essay: Tuned-in but out of Touch." *Wildlife Conservation,* September/October 1992, 67.

McKinnon, John, and Bernard Vienne, eds. *Hill Tribes Today: Problems in Change.* Bangkok: White Lotus-Orstom, 1989.

McNeely, Jeffrey A., and Paul Spenser Wachtel. *Soul of the Tiger: Searching for Nature's Answers in Southeast Asia.* New York: Paragon House, 1990.

Mendelson, Michael E., *Sangha and State in Burma: A Study of Monastic Sectarianism and Leadership,* edited by John P. Ferguson. Ithaca: Cornell University Press, 1975.

Mongkhon Danthanin. *Pa chumchon isan kap kau jau kau* [Forest communities in Isan and the KJK]. Bangkok: Local Development Institute, 1991.

Morell, David, and Chai-anan Samudavanija. *Political Conflict in Thailand: Reform, Reaction, Revolution.* Cambridge, Mass.: Oelgeschlager, Gunn and Hain, 1981.

Muttothai: Thammathetsana Phra Ajan Man [Liberation: Teachings of Phra Ajan Man and his disciples]. Bangkok: Chuanphim, 1972.

Nae naew thang kan patibat vipassana [Guide to vipassana meditation]. Bangkok: Mahachulalongkorn University Press, 1988.

Nanthapanyaphon, Phra. *Chiwa prawat thammanuson khaung Phra Ratwutthajan (Luang Pu Dun)* [Biography of Ven. Grandfather Dun]. Surin: Crem. vol. Luang Pu Dun, Wat Burapharam, 1985.

————. *Luang Pu fak wai: bantheuk khati tham* [A collection of Luang Pu Dun's dhamma]. Bangkok: Kledthai, 1990.

Neal, Donald G. *Statistical Description of the Forests of Thailand.* Bangkok: Military Research and Development Center, 1967.

Nyanatiloka. *Buddhist Dictionary.* Kandy: Buddhist Publication Society, 1980.

O'Connor, Richard A. "Cultural Notes on Trade and the Tai." In *Ritual, Power and Economy,* edited by Susan D. Russell. De Kalb: Center for Southeast Asian Studies, Northern Illinois University, 1989.

————. "Interpreting Thai Religious Change: Temples, Sangha Reform and Social Change." *Journal of Southeast Asian Studies* 24, no. 2 (September 1993): 330–339.

————. "Siamese Tai in Tai Context: The Impact of a Ruling Order." *Crossroads* 3, no. 1 (1990): 1–21.

————. "Urbanism and Religion: Community, Hierarchy, and Sanctity in Urban Thai Buddhist Temples." Ph.D. diss., Cornell University, 1978.

Paitoon Mikusol, "Administrative Reforms and National Integration: The Case of the Northeast." In *Regions and National Integration in Thailand, 1892–1992,* edited by Volker Grabowsky. Wiesbaden: Harrassowitz, 1995.

Paitoon Pongsabutra, ed. *Illustrated Landforms of Thailand.* Bangkok: Chulalongkorn University Press, 1991.

Panyanantha, Phra. *Chiwit khaung khapphajao* [My life]. Bangkok: Commemoration of sixtieth birthday, 1972.

———. "Khwam yu raut khaung phra phutthasatsana [Survival of Buddhism]." *Dhammapadip* 20 (May–June 1995): 12–13.

Phaisan Visalo, Phra. "The Forest Monastery and Its Relevance to Modern Thai Society." In *Radical Conservatism: Buddhism in the Contemporary World*, edited by Nicholas P. Kohler. Bangkok: Sathirakoses-Nagapradipa Foundation, 1990.

Phimontham, Phra. *Phajon Mara: Bantheuk ha pi nai haungkhang* [Confronting Mara: Diary of five years in jail]. Bangkok: Bandit Kanphim, 1987.

Phirot Yumonthian. *Phra Fipak Kla: Chiwit lae kan tausu khaung Phra Phayom* [A bold preacher-monk: Life and struggle of Phra Phayom]. Bangkok: Amnuaiwep Printing, 1990.

Pho Samlamjiak. *Tamnan Thai Phuan* [Stories of the Thai Phuan]. Bangkok: Samakkhisan, 1994.

"Phra Ajan Cha taun tamha Phra Ajan Man" [Phra Ajan Cha in search of Ajan Man]. In *Muttothai: Thammathetsana Phra Ajan Man*. Bangkok: Chuanphim, 1972.

Phra niphon lae niphon somdet [Somdet's writings]. Bangkok: Crem. vol. Somdet Phra Phutthajan, Wat Mahathat, 1990.

Piyasilo. *Buddhist Currents: A Brief Social Analysis of Buddhism in Sri Lanka and Siam*. Petaling Jaya, Malaysia: Community of Dharmafarers, 1992.

Placzek, James. "The Thai Forest Tradition." In *Southeast Asia: Women, Changing Structure and Cultural Continuity*, edited by Geoffrey B. Hainsworth. Ottawa: University of Ottawa Press, 1981.

Pokati: Luang Phau Thian Jittasupho lae sing thi fak wai [Ven. Father Thian: Biography and teachings]. Bangkok: Thian Sawangtham, 1989.

Pracha Pasannathammo, Phra. *Lao wai meua wai sonthaya: atta chiwa prawat khaung than Buddhadasa* [Memoir of Buddhadasa's early years]. Bangkok: Komon Khimthaung Foundation, 1986.

———, ed. *Phap chiwit 80 pi Buddhadasa* [Photographs from Buddhadasa's eighty years]. Bangkok: Phonphan Kanphim, 1986.

Prachuap Sanklang. "Botbat khaung phra song fai vipassana thura thi mi tau sangkhom Isan neua: seuksa korani sai Phra Ajan Man Phurithatto." [Role of vipassana monks in upper Isan: Ajan Man's lineage]. Master's thesis, Srinakkharinwirot University, 1988.

Prajiat Khongsatra. *Luang Pu Waen Sujinno* [Ven. Grandfather Waen Sujinno]. Bangkok: Namo special issue, 1985.

Pramuan hetkan nai yuk mai khaung thai [Events of the new era in Thailand]. Bangkok: Crem. vol. Hoksui Sapsunthon, 1942.

Pranee Wongthes. "Phitikam-khabot pheua phaunkhlai khwamteungkhriat" [Rebellion rituals serving to release stress]. *Sinlapa Watthana-tham* 5, no. 7 (May 1984): 6–21.

Prani Bancheun. *Khwammai lae prawat tambon muban jangwat Loei* [Meanings and history of communes and villages in Loei Province]. Bangkok: O. S. Printing House, 1984.

Prayong Nettarak and Banthon Aundam. "Wiwatthanakan khaung kan-bukbeuk thidin thamkin nai khet pa phak thawanauk chiang neua" [Growth of forest clearance for subsistence in the forests of the north-east region]. In *Wiwatthanakan khaung kanbukbeuk thidin thamkin nai khet pa,* edited by Joemsak Pinthaung. Bangkok: Local Development Institute, 1991.

Pricha Phinthong. *Saranukrom phasa: Isan Thai–English dictionary.* Ubon: Siritham Press, 1989.

Pun Punyasiri (Somdet Phra Wannarat). *Phra Mongkhonthepmuni.* Bangkok: One-hundredth anniversary of Luang Phau Sot, Wat Pak-nam, 1984.

Rabinowitz, Alan. *Chasing the Dragon's Tail: The Struggle to Save Thai-land's Wild Cats.* New York: Doubleday, 1991.

———. "Eye of the Tiger." *Wildlife Conservation,* November/December 1991, 48–55.

———. "In Memory of a Warrior: Seub Nakhasathian (1949–1990)." *Wildlife Conservation,* January/February 1991, 31.

Rajavoramuni, Phra. *Dictionary of Buddhism.* Bangkok: Mahachula Buddhist University, 1985.

Ratchakijjanubeksa [Royal Thai government gazette] (Bangkok) 16–18 (1899–1901).

Ray, Reginald A. *Buddhist Saints in India: A Study in Buddhist Values and Orientations.* Oxford: Oxford University Press, 1994.

Reynolds, Craig J. "The Buddhist Monkhood in Nineteenth Century Thailand," Ph.D. diss., Cornell University, 1972.

———. *Thai Radical Discourse: The Real Face of Thai Feudalism Today.* Ithaca: Southeast Asia Program, 1987.

Ruam phap chut lae prawat yau 80 phra kammathan [Brief biographies of eighty kammathan monks]. Bangkok: Sisayam Kanphim, n.d.

Rujaya Abhakorn. "Change in the Administrative System of Northern Siam, 1884–1933." In *Changes in Northern Thailand and the Shan States,* edited by Prakai Nontawasee. Singapore: Southeast Asian Studies Program, 1988.

Rujaya Abhakorn and David Wyatt. "Administrative Reforms and National Integration in Northern Thailand." In *Regions and National Integration in Thailand, 1892–1992,* edited by Volker Grabowsky. Wiesbaden: Harrassowitz, 1995.

Sam somdet [Three somdets]. Bangkok: Kledthai, 1980.

Samphan Kaungsamut. *Prawat chiwit lae phon ngan khaung Phra Thep-wisuthimethi* [Life and work of Buddhadasa]. Bangkok: Odian Printing, 1987.

Samsip pi kan anurak satpa thai [Thirty years of wildlife conservation in Thailand]. Bangkok: Seub Nakhasathian Foundation, 1990.

Samuel, Geoffrey. *Civilized Shamans: Buddhism in Tibetan Societies.* Washington, D.C.: Smithsonian Institution Press, 1993.

Sangha Wanasai. *Khruba Siwichai,* Chiang Mai: Chiang Mai University, 1979.

Sangharakshita. *A Survey of Buddhism.* Glasgow: Windhorse, 1993.

Sanit Samuckarn and Kennon Breazeale. *A Culture in Search of Survival: The Phuan of Thailand and Laos.* New Haven: Yale University Southeast Asia Studies, 1988.

Sanitsuda Ekachai. *Behind the Smile: Voices of Thailand.* Bangkok: Thai Development Support Committee, 1991.

Sathianphong Wannapok. "Khanchaung song phra pi phae" [Mirror of the sangha in the year of the goat]. *Thai Rat,* 31 December 1991.

Saun Si-ek, Phra Maha. *Prawat kankaukoet Thammayut nikai, prawat Wat Supat, prawat Wat Si Ubon* [History of the Thammayut Order, Wat Supat and Wat Si Ubon]. Ubon: Saphasan, 1979.

Sawaeng Udomsi. *Kan pokkhraung khana song thai* [Administration of the Thai sangha]. Bangkok: Mahachula University Press, 1991.

———. "Pa mai kap phra song" [Forests and monks]. *Phutthajak* 45, no. 5 (May 1991): 29–35.

———. *Seuk somdet* [Battle between somdets]. Bangkok: Amon Kanphim, 1985.

Schelling, Andrew. "Jataka Mind: Cross-Species Compassion." *Tricycle* 1, no. 1 (fall 1991): 10–19.

Seeing the Way: Buddhist Reflections on the Spiritual Life. Great Gaddesden, Hertfordshire, England: Amaravati Publications, 1989.

Seri Phongphit. *Religion in a Changing Society: Buddhism, Reform and the Role of Monks in Community Development in Thailand.* Hong Kong: Arena Press, 1988.

Seri Phongphit and Kevin Hewison. *Thai Village Life: Culture and Transition in the Northeast.* Bangkok: Mooban Press, 1990.

Si Ubonrattanaram [Wat Sithaung, Ubon]. Bangkok: Rongphim Mitthai, 1968.

Sippanondha Ketudat. *The Middle Path for the Future of Thailand.* Honolulu: East-West Center, 1990.

Sitha Chetawan. "Phra Ajan Suthi Thityanno." *Lokthip* 10, no. 196 (March 1991): 15–41.

Smalley, William A. *Linguistic Diversity and National Unity: Language Ecology in Thailand.* Chicago: University of Chicago Press, 1994.

Somboon Suksamran. *Buddhism and Politics in Thailand: A Study of Socio-Political Change and Political Activism of the Thai Sangha.* Singapore: Institute of Southeast Asian Studies, 1982.

———. *Political Buddhism in Southeast Asia* New York: St. Martin's Press, 1976.

Somdet Phra Maha Samanajao Krom Phraya Wachirayanwororot. Bangkok: Department of Religious Affairs, 1967.

Somdet upatcha [Somdet the preceptor]. Bangkok: Mahamakut University Press, 1988.

Sommai Premchit. *A List of Old Temples and Religious Sects in Chiang Mai.* Chiang Mai: Department of Sociology and Anthropology, Chiang Mai University, 1975.

Sommai Premchit and Amphay Dore. *The Lan Na Twelve-Month Traditions.* Chiang Mai: So Sap Kan Pim, 1992.

Spiro, Melford E. *Buddhism and Society: A Great Tradition and Its Burmese Vicissitudes.* Berkeley: University of California Press, 1982.

———. *Burmese Supernaturalism.* Philadelphia: Prentice-Hall, 1978.

Srisak Wallipodom. "An neuang duai watthanatham thaungthin [A matter of local culture]. In *Pheunthin Pheunthan* [Roots], edited by Wannee W. Anderson. Bangkok: Sinlapa Watthanatham, 1988.

Sudara Sujachara, ed. *Sat pa meuang thai khaun ja leua phiang khwamsongjam* [Wild animals in Thailand before they became just a memory]. Bangkok: Thira Kanphim, 1988.

Sujit Wongthes. "Samoson sinlapa watthanatham: bantheuk kan samruat khaung James McCarthy" [Art and culture club: Record of James McCarthy's surveys]. *Sinlapa Watthanatham* 5, no. 1 (November 1983).

Sulak Sivaraksa. "Khamnam" [Introduction]. In *Sam somdet* [Three somdets]. Bangkok: Kledthai, 1980.

———. *Lauk khrap sangkhom song* [Unmasking the sangha]. Bangkok: Yuwawitthaya, 1967.

Suphatthanuson chut Phothiyan Thera [Biography of Phra Ajan Cha]. Ubon Ratchathani: Volume commemorating construction of ordination hall, Phong Forest Wat, 1976.

Suphon Nachom. *Chiwa prawat lae patipatha Phra Ajan Fan Ajaro* [Biography of Phra Ajan Fan Ajaro]. Bangkok: Kanphim Phranakhon, 1977.

Suriphan Maniwat. *Chiwa prawat Phra Khun Jao Luang Pu Chaup Thansamo* [Biography of Ven. Grandfather Chaup]. Bangkok: Commemoration of Chaup's eighty-eighth birthday, 1990.

———. *Chiwa prawat Phra Khun Jao Luang Pu Lui Janthansaro* [Biography of Ven. Grandfather Lui]. Bangkok: P. Samphanphanit, 1990.

———. *Phra Ajan Juan Kulachettho: Chiwa prawat patipatha lae thammathetsana* [Memoirs of Phra Ajan Juan]. Bangkok: Crem. vol. Thauk Mountain Wat, 1981.

Tambiah, Stanley J. *Buddhism and the Spirit Cults in Northeast Thailand.* Cambridge: Cambridge University Press, 1970.

———. *The Buddhist Saints of the Forest and the Cult of Amulets.* New York: Cambridge University Press, 1984.

———. *World Conqueror and World Renouncer: A Study of Buddhism and Polity in Thailand against a Historical Background.* Cambridge: Cambridge University Press, 1976.

Tanabe, Shigeharu. *Nung leuang, nung dam* [Wearing yellow, wearing black]. Bangkok: Sangsan, 1986.

Tate [Thet], Ajahn. *The Autobiography of a Forest Monk.* Edited by Ariyesako Bhikkhu. Bangkok: Amarin Printing, 1993.

Taylor, J. L. *Forest Monks and the Nation-State: An Anthropological and Historical Study in Northeastern Thailand.* Singapore: Institute of Southeast Asian Studies, 1993.

———. "From Wandering to Monastic Domestication." *Journal of the Siam Society* 76 (1988): 64–88.

———. "Living on the Rim: Ecology and Forest Monks in Northeastern Thailand." *Sojourn* 6, no. 1 (February 1991): 106–125.

Tej Bunnag. *Kabot R.S. 121* [Uprisings of 1902]. Bangkok: Thai Watthanaphanit, 1987.

———. *The Provincial Administration of Siam 1892–1915.* Kuala Lumpur: Oxford University Press, 1977.

Thai Book of Genesis: Herbal Medicine in Paediatrics. Translated by Jean Mulholland. Canberra: Australian National University, 1989.

Thalaengkan khana song [Bulletin of sangha affairs], nos. 20, 23, 24 (1932, 1935, 1936).

Thamwarodom, Phra. *Prawat Jao Khun Phra Mongkhon Thepmuni* [Life of Jao Khun Mongkhon Thepmuni]. Bangkok: Rung Reuangtham, 1959.

Thanet Chareonmuang. "When the Young Cannot Speak Their Own Mother Tongue: Explaining a Legacy of Cultural Domination in Lan Na." In *Regions and National Integration in Thailand, 1892–1992,* edited by Volker Grabowsky. Wiesbaden: Harrassowitz, 1995.

Thate Desaransi [Thet Thetrangsi], Phra Ajaan. "Buddho." Berkeley: DharmaNet International, 1994. DharmaNet electronic document, available from DharmaNet Electronic Files Archive (DEFA) at sunsite.unc.edu.

———. "Steps along the Path." Berkeley: DharmaNet International, 1994. DharmaNet electronic document, available from DharmaNet Electronic Files Archive (DEFA) at sunsite.unc.edu.

Thepsumethi, Phra. "Hok kheun nai Pakthongchai" [Six nights in Pakthongchai]. In *Prachum krawi* [Collection of poems]. Bangkok: Crem. vol. Wat Simahathat, 1979.

Thera prawat Phra Suphrom Yannathera (Khruba Phromma Phromjakako) [Biography of Khruba Phromma]. Lamphun: Wat Phra Phuthabat Takpha, 1980.

Thet Thetrangsi, Phra Ajan. *Attano prawat lae thammathetsana* [My life and dhamma teachings]. Bangkok: Amarin Kanphim, 1981.

Thi rareuk ngan phraratchathan phloengsop wiraburut thi sia chiwit naikan paungkan lae prappram phu kaukanrai communit [Cremation volume in memory of the heroes who were killed by communists]. Bangkok: Wat Phra Simahathat, 1969.

Thittila, U. "The Fundamental Principles of Theravada Buddhism." In *The Path of the Buddha,* edited by K. W. Morgan. New York: Ronald Press, 1956.

Thongchai Winichakul. *Siam Mapped: A History of the Geo-Body of a Nation.* Honolulu: University of Hawai'i Press, 1994.

Toem Wiphakphotjanakit. *Prawatsat Isan* [History of Isan]. Bangkok: Thammasat University Press, 1987.

Tossa Wajuppa, ed. *Phadaeng Nang Ai: A Translation of a Thai-Isan Folk Epic in Verse.* London: Associated University Press, 1990.

Uan Tisso. *Niphon bang reuang* [Somdet's writings]. Bangkok: Crem. vol. Phra Maha Wirawong, 1956.

———. *Prawat patipatha lae ngan khaung phra maha thera paet rup* [Biography of eight senior monks]. Reprinted from the 1936 edition. Bangkok: Mahamakut University Press, 1990.

Ubon mani [Jewel of Ubon]. Bangkok: Khurusapha, 1992.

Ubon Ratchathani 200 pi [Ubon Ratchathani, two hundred years]. Bangkok: Chuan Phim, 1992.

Van Esterik, John, "Women Meditation Teachers in Thailand." In *Women of Southeast Asia,* edited by Penny Van Esterik. De Kalb: Center for Southeast Asian Studies, Northern Illinois University, 1982.

Vitoon Panyakul, ed. *People Centered Development.* Bangkok: Local Development Institute, 1992.

Wachirayan, Prince. *Somdet Phra Maha Samanajao Krom Phraya Wachirayanwororot.* 2 vols. Bangkok: Department of Religious Affairs, 1967.

Wachirayan, Prince, and sangha head of monthon Ubon Ratchathani. Correspondence, 1907–1918. Wat Supat, Ubon Ratchathani.

Walker, Anthony R. "The Lahu People: An Introduction." In *Highlanders of Thailand,* edited by John McKinnon and Wanat Bhruksasri. Kuala Lumpur: Oxford University Press, 1983.

Wan Uttamo. "Atta chiwa prawat" [My life]. In *Phra Udomsangwonwisut Thera (Phra Ajan Wan Uttamo).* Bangkok: Crem. vol. Aphaidamrong Cave Wat, 1981.

Wanna Wanno, Phra. *Prawat Thammayut lae Mahanikai* [A history of Thammayut and Mahanikai]. Bangkok: Rungreuangsan, 1985.

Wilson, Constance M. *Thailand: A Handbook of Historical Statistics.* Boston: G. K. Hall, 1983.

Winaikoson, Phra Khru. *Reuang arai di* [Stories worth telling]. Chiang Mai: Wat Jediluang, 1954.

Wiriyang Sirintharo [Yanwiriyajan], Phra. "Prawat Phra Ajan Man." In *Prawat Phra Ajan Man chabap sombun* [Complete biography of Phra Ajan Man]. Bangkok: Crem. vol. Khunya Man Bunthrikun, 1978.

———. "Tai saman samneuk" [With common sense]. In *Prawat Phra Ajan Man chabap sombun* [Complete biography of Phra Ajan Man]. Bangkok: Crem. vol. Khunya Man Bunthrikun, 1978.

Wirot Sisuro. *That Isan* [Stupas in Isan]. Bangkok: Makha Press, 1990.

Wisuthiyansunthon, Phra Khru. "Lao thi Wat Pathum Wanaram" [The Lao at Wat Pathum Wannaram]. *Sinlapa Watthanatham* 12, no. 9 (July 1991): 52–58.

Withaya Chuphan. *Khamsaun Luang Pu La* [Ven. Grandfather La's teachings]. Chiang Mai: Thai News, 1989.

Wolters, O. W. *History, Culture, and Region in Southeast Asian Perspectives.* Singapore: Institute of Southeast Asian Studies, 1982.

Wyatt, David K. "The Beginnings of Modern Education in Thailand, 1868–1910." Ph.D. diss., Cornell University, 1966.

———. "Presidential Address: Five Voices From Southeast Asia's Past." *Journal of Asian Studies* 53, no. 4 (November 1994): 1076–1091.

———. *Thailand: A Short History.* New Haven: Yale University Press, 1982.

Xu-Yun. *Empty Cloud: The Autobiography of the Chinese Zen Master.* Shaftesbury, Dorset: Element Books, 1988.

Zack, Steven J. "Buddhist Education under Prince Wachirayan Warorot." Ph.D. diss., Cornell University, 1977.

Index